Imagining Rabelais in Renaissance England

ANNE LAKE PRESCOTT

Imagining Rabelais in Renaissance England

Yale University Press
New Haven &
London

Published with assistance from the Elizabethan Club, Yale University.

Printed in the United States of America.

Library of Congress Cataloging-in-Publication Data
Prescott, Anne Lake, 1936–
    Imagining Rabelais in Renaissance England / Anne Lake Prescott.
      p. cm.
    Includes bibliographical references and index.
    ISBN 0-300-07122-1 (alk. paper)
    1. Rabelais, François, ca. 1490-1553? — Appreciation — England.
2. English literature — Early modern, 1500-1700 — France influences.
3. England — Intellectual life — 16th century.   4. England —
Intellectual life — 17th century.   I. Title.
PQ1694.P74   1998
843'.3 — dc21   97-31016
                CIP

A catalogue record for this book is available from the British Library.

The paper in this book meets the guidelines for permanence and durability of the Committee on Production Guidelines for Book Longevity of the Council on Library Resources.

10 9 8 7 6 5 4 3 2 1

Contents

Introduction

This book examines how early modern English writers read, cited, judged, enjoyed, reviled, imagined, and appropriated François Rabelais — or, often, the *name* Rabelais — before Thomas Urquhart's obstreperous 1653 translation made him part of English literature. My study is thus in large part an essay in reception history that I hope will also interest those intrigued by reader response theory or by the more specific behaviors and thoughts of Renaissance readers. I have conceived of it as a "sounding" in the nautical or oceanographic sense: What does early modern England look like if we examine how its writers reacted to and reconfigured one famous Frenchman, François Rabelais? But who was "Rabelais"? The following chapters are not an essay on authorship, but they do demonstrate how reception studies are complicated by an awareness that concepts of authorship, author, authority, and authenticity are historically mobile and culturally pressured.

I assume that the historical man Rabelais in fact wrote or did not write certain words and that, with better technology than is at present available to literary historians, some invisible time traveler could watch him writing or not writing and then return to give us a report. But the *va-et-vient* among works undoubtedly by Rabelais and those that "borrowed" episodes or characters from him or from which he "borrowed," together with the willingness of printers to fake their title pages, to attach his name to texts he could not have written, and to publish works by others in volumes that declared themselves to be his *Oeuvres,* makes his a compelling example of authorship's shiftiness.[1] Even a brief look at bibliographies of Rabelais's early editions or at Renaissance titles bearing his name shows how far his age was from the days of copyright, the Authors League, and now-fading editorial fantasies of a determinable and final authorial intention on the part of dead writers. Of Rabelais's most famous characters, furthermore, Gargantua and Pantagruel are probably folkloric and the third, Panurge, is a jumped-up Greek noun often found in dictionaries and Christian or classical writings.

The instability of the name Rabelais only increases the difficulty of tracing what the English made of it and its purported owner. He had, after all, begun his writing career as both Dr. Rabelais the medical authority and Alcofribas Nasier — an anagram, of course — the recorder of deeds and words by his master, Pantagruel. Eventually, Alcofribas became Rabelais, royally licensed protégé of a learned and powerful cardinal, Jean Du Bellay, and of Marguerite de Navarre, sister of François I. But what the English thought this "Rabelais" wrote is not entirely clear, and for me, it is not essential here. They certainly knew him as the author of *Gargantua et Pantagruel,* and no Englishman expresses doubt concerning the *Cinquième livre.* Many would have read such minor works as the *Pantagrueline Prognostication* or *Sciomachie,* although I can find no trace of their impact before my cut-off date.

Some writers seem to have thought that Rabelais wrote at least one of the early sixteenth-century chapbooks recording the life of Gargantua, and they were not wholly wrong: the one they knew best includes several chapters from *Pantagruel.* Robert Hayman, for one, believed the publishers who called two satires by François Habert the work of Rabelais, and a few may have accepted the claim on the title page of *Les Songes drolatiques de Pantagruel* that the pictures in the volume were by that same writer. Were such readers mistaken? Historically, yes. But not in every sense, for these texts came to England as part of a Rabelaisian energy field, so to speak, and they helped create a temporary grid of expectation through which the English read what we would call the real Rabelais, the Rabelais my imagined time traveler could see writing with his own hand and his own — or his patron's — pen and ink.

It would be wrong, though, to overstate the degree to which Renaissance notions of authorship (its "construction," some would call it) differed from our own. However anonymous or multi-authored many texts appear to us as we read centuries later, ignorant of who blushed, who joked, who desired precisely what or exactly whom, who was sad that day or slandering whom, it is hard to think that the writers were unaffected by the smiles or compliments of those to whom they showed their work. Chaucer, for example, was by no means indifferent to mistranscription (as he wrote his scrivener), and Rabelais's pursuit of a royal license for his books may well have been more than a matter of protecting himself against prosecution. The reaction of the poetaster Oronte to the criticisms of Alceste in Molière's *Misanthrope* is a delicious demonstration of authorial egoism, an egoism that must have been shared by many a better poet in the early modern period. Richard Brathwait, if not one of those better poets, spent much youthful energy not on the law his parents had told him to study but on trying to be an author — not a writer, a signature, a socially constructed author-function, but an author, able to impress others as such. In *The Good Wife* (1618) he distinguishes writers from such authors: "Never Age had more writers, and fewer Authors: those onely being admitted of as Authors, whose workes merit approbation and authoritie in themselves"; nowadays, he laments, "experience" is "reduced to ignorance, and a desire of knowledge to a fruitlesse desire of writing: Littora . . . arant, et arena semina mandant" (sig. E5v).[2]

Young Brathwait's hankerings after authorship and celebrity as he recalls them with pious shame in *A Spiritual Spicerie* (1638) had included more than hope for approbation: during his London years "I was proud in bearing the title of a *Writer;* which, I must confesse, together with the instancie of such as either truly applauded mee, or deluded mee, made me ambitious after the name of an *Author*." For he held it

> an incomperable grace to be styled one of the Wits. Where, if at any time invited to a publique feast, or some other meeting of the Muses, wee hated nothing more than losing time; reserving ever some Select houres of that Solemnity, to make proofe of our conceits in a present provision of Epigrams, Anagrams, or other expressive (and many times offensive) fancies. . . . By this time I had got an *eye* in the world; and a *finger* in the street. *There goes an Author! One of the Wits!* Which could not chuse, but make mee looke bigge, as if I had been casten in a new mold. O how in privacie, when nothing but the close Evening, and darke walls accompany mee, doth the remembrance of these lightest vanities perplex mee! How gladly would I shun the memory of them.

(Brathwait is, however, repeating his memory for the world to read.) Being a wit or author increases one's size: thus Alcofribas Nasier grew closer to Pantagruel's size, becoming a giant of French literature, when he rearranged himself back into François Rabelais and made it clear to those outside his circle who had first come out of whose mouth. Whatever we want to call the roles that Brathwait remembered playing or the personae that his many verses and prose pamphlets adopt, and however much his roles and masks differ from those of a typical romantic poet, Victorian novelist, or postmodern experimentalist, his ambition does not feel unfamiliar. In writing this book I have tried to remember such early modern aspirations as well as the differences between our two cultures.

Many English writers, of course, allude to or otherwise give evidence of having read Rabelais himself, whatever their confusion or indifference concerning the actual authorship of texts associated with him. In the pages that follow, I have found it hard to describe the buzz of English references to, comments on, and denunciations of Rabelais and para-Rabelais without distortion. Proceeding chronologically would inflate the narrative element in Rabelais's reception, while moving writer by writer would ignore current criticism's salutary skepticism toward individual self-expressive "authors." In spite of my best efforts, the work of some important and a few unimportant English writers is scattered throughout different chapters. I urge my reader to use the index as a way of reassembling my subjects' disjecta membra. The topical approach I adopt can be arbitrary, but it seems a good compromise. I shall distinguish three cultural sites in which Rabelais's work and name were useful: language, the body, and fantasy; in none was English response or appropriation collectively comfortable, although some readers evidently took a robust pleasure in Rabelais's work. There are, inevitably, overlaps among my categories. Adoption or notice of Rabelais's language can accompany an interest in relating to the private or social body and its desires, while the same concern for language permits entry to the fantastic: new words and newly arranged words make new realities.

Is there a pattern to the allusions and echoes I shall be exploring? I can find the outlines of one. It seems clear that Rabelais was more often appreciated, or more openly appreciated, in the interconnected social worlds occupied by courtiers, lawyers, and scholars. But that does not include everybody. Spenser and his imitators were less likely to mention Rabelais than were Ben Jonson and his tribe (although Spenser's friend Gabriel Harvey read him closely). John Donne mentioned and imitated him, but George Herbert and Henry Vaughan did not, or not in writings that survive. Clergymen, when writing as men of the cloth rather than as playwrights or satirists, were more likely to denounce than welcome him. English reaction to and re-creation of Rabelais is thus difficult but not quite impossible to categorize: he was more likely to find explicit notice among the swaggering young, the self-consciously masculine, the cosmopolitan elite, and people with a touch of what was to be called a "libertin" mentality. But it would be an error to think that he appealed exclusively to those hoping to seem disreputable: those who cited him more or less amicably include the learned John Selden, the meditative Thomas Browne, Francis Bacon in his declining years, and James I himself.

I urge my reader to consider several other matters. First is the virtually universal human practice of shaping language to suit what literature professors would call the rhetoric of a situation. The Englishmen I quote are not, for the most part, expressing an unmediated personal opinion of Rabelais, Gargantua, or much of anything else. Early modern culture was perhaps more self-conscious concerning the rhetorical nature of speech and writing than the ages that came before and after, which — together with reading and composition practices that encouraged imitation and the fragmentation of discourse — makes it all the more impossible to take any given comment on Rabelais as a deeply held personal judgment emanating from a coherently conceived inner self.[3]

I do not wish to deny the existence of an early modern sense of private and individual interiority, for I suspect — although I cannot prove — that such a sense, whatever its later variety and degrees of intensity, arose some time in the Upper Paleolithic. At the moment, indeed, there is a healthy trend away from feeling forced to choose between granting early modern subjects an individual sense of inwardness or even isolation and seeing them as too socially constituted and embedded to have a sense of privacy or selfhood (illusory in any case, according to many cultural materialists and poststructuralists).[4] The issue, however one handles it, is relevant to tracing early modern literary or cultural response of almost any kind. As this book will show, English reactions to and appropriations of Rabelais demonstrate a tense synergy between a set of negative stereotypes — Rabelais the atheist scoffer, Rabelais the dirty-minded drunk, Rabelais the maker of silly stories — that were in some sense public property and a smaller set of more thoughtful (and often more appreciative) reactions that suggest more personal knowledge, memory, and inward pondering.

It is perhaps no coincidence that the more stereotyped reactions are often found in sermons or polemics and the more individual ones in letters, annotations, satires, and texts with stylistic flair. Members of the first group need not be hypocrites, and their remarks can appear in intelligently written texts; nor do those who actually read Rabelais always demonstrate greater capacity for inward and original meditation. Most of us, after all, sincerely hold views derived from those around us. Still, Rabelais's more knowledgeable readers were more likely to be those with an interest in a private if not quite solitary space: James I attacking those who tried to penetrate royal or divine *arcana,* Gabriel Harvey in his study filling the margins of his books with opinionated scribble, John Harington praising the merits of the watercloset, or Ben Jonson drinking with his friends in a tavern room closed to the uninitiated.

It is worth stressing, moreover, how many of the comments and reactions I shall examine indicate a high degree of ambivalence, even confusion. They are precisely for that reason useful as litmus paper, cultural CAT scans. Or, to try yet another metaphor, it is when a major writer elicits such a *variety* of reactions that we know we have a cultural barometer — or set of barometers — to help gauge an age's weather and what pressures it. Few English writers denounced Homer; few (openly or in print) praised Aretino or Machiavelli. But on Rabelais they were collectively and sometimes individually uncertain. As a literary historian of sorts, I take this as good news, for it is through the cracks, the fissures, in a culture's responses that we can perceive the lay of that culture's land. English culture's land was too varied in its configurations (more igneous than sedimentary) to be divided for our intellectual convenience into a hegemonic officialdom on the one hand and a subtly oppositional or abjectly interpellated body of socially constructed subjects on the other. Although Gargantua was as big as Hobbes's Leviathan, the Englishmen who mention him add up to no easily envisioned body but rather to an anamorphic and noisy crowd that was vigorously self-opposed on such matters as the value of novelty, the legitimacy of enjoying old romances and new satire, the role in human affairs of verbal pugnacity, trickiness, or excess, the flesh's distempers and pleasures, and the wilder reaches of the imagination.

It has become customary for scholars to announce their critical or methodological affiliations.[5] I have few. The following pages, written over a span of many years with pauses for such enterprises as editing Spenser and learning more about early modern women, have certainly been influenced by the recent revolution in literary studies. Thanks to that revolution I am more convinced than ever of the futility of setting up a canon of texts on which the respectable should concentrate, a concept better suited to ecclesiastical councils needing to decide which texts are sacred and which ancillary or suspect. That is why I devote as much space to William Vaughan, say, as to John Donne. And thanks to that same revolution I am more aware than ever of the slipperiness of terms and signifiers, of the impact on language and texts, of political agendas and fears, of the existence below a text's surface of the unspoken or unspeakable, and of gender and its complexities.

My reader will not, however, find much explicit comment on the sins of Rabelais and his readers against those peoples and values our own age now cherishes. I am more intrigued by tracing demeanors than by locating misdemeanors, and even while trying to maintain my moral compass in working order I confess to reading these old writers, as I read Rabelais, not with the hermeneutics of suspicion but with the hermeneutics of pleasure. For this hedonism I make no apology. I wish, to be sure, that some Englishwomen had published their thoughts on Rabelais, but they did not. And because they and the men in their lives are now well out of earshot, complaints about the patriarchy that so often limited and silenced their sex would fall only on modern ears, ears already well attuned to Renaissance misogyny and cruelty. I hope, nevertheless, that my grab bag of a study, intended more as a set of meditations on textual or cultural moments than as a linear argument or narrative, will provide materials that can be used even by those committed to methods and theories I do not adopt myself.

Assuming that my readers have at least some acquaintance with Rabelais, I have not described, except in passing and as a reminder, the contents of his four "authentic" books nor those of the more debatable fifth. Needless to say, in looking at Renaissance England's Rabelais, my sight has been affected/deflected by my own culture and situation. I have tried to keep my assumptions about "Rabelais" as flexible as possible. Terence Cave must be right that Rabelais's very complexity of significance depends on a reader's willingness to make precise discriminations that preclude our "saying that *any* reading is possible." "A permissive reading of Rabelais," he argues, "is simply not interesting."[6] Exactly, but there is a further issue here: reception studies often entail some estimate of the texts and writers being "received." That many in the Renaissance called Rabelais a scoffing atheist is a puzzle only if we assume, as most scholars now do, that he was not in fact a scoffing atheist. But what if he really was such an atheist? In that case, those who called him one were admirably perceptive, not squeamish, solemn, or bigoted. To imagine how the English imagined Rabelais, in other words, entails making judgments that are both necessary and nonetheless pressured by the times in which they are made and the mind that makes them. In this book, although I am unable to give the reader the final truth about Rabelais, I have provided a sampling of recent critical views and tried to minimize the impact of my own understanding of his work on how I read the English as they read this difficult and ambiguous French writer.

Inevitably, I do have such an understanding. My Rabelais has been affected by the varied but not quite incompatible views of (to name the chief influences on this book) Michael Screech and Edwin Duval; Barbara Bowen, Florence Weinberg, and Raymond La Charité; Guy Demerson, François Rigolot, Alice Berry, Neil Rhodes, and Gérard Defaux. Nor am I blind to the insights of those with a more avidly deconstructive bent, and my primarily evangelical Rabelais can also live, if a bit uneasily, with the carnival Rabelais of Mikhail Bakhtin, the "vulgar" Rabelais of Carol Clark, and the more radically elusive Rabelais of Terence Cave or even Michel Beaujour.[7] He cannot, though, readily coexist with Abel Lefranc's freethinker or even, I think, with the serene and largely secular humanist others have found. Some of the Englishmen studied in this book would not be surprised by Lefranc's freethinking Rabelais, although what pleased the Third Republic secularist shocked them. To my surprise, however, I have found little English interest in Rabelais the humanist. Some passages that intrigued or amused his English readers have classical sources, but the noble and much-anthologized letter from Gargantua to his son Pantagruel and the Abbey of Thélème seem to have left the English, so far as the written record is concerned, cold. Nor did they much warm to the carnival Rabelais — if, indeed, they noticed him in such terms — although some found Rabelais's world a generous and comic one.

In gathering material on Rabelais and early modern England I have made use of work by two earlier scholars: Huntington Brown and Marcel de Grève.[8] Having gathered more than twice as much primary evidence as they, I am less skeptical than Grève about how early and how much the English read and understood Rabelais. Because my aims are so different from those of my predecessors, and because my focus is less on the degree to which the English read Rabelais and more on the cultural work that references to him could accomplish, I do not usually mention who first noticed a given allusion.

This book has one gap I should mention: there is, alas, little evidence to show just how the English acquired or saw copies of Rabelais's works or other books linked with him, although I have been able to determine when a chapbook on Gargantua was probably published in England. Rabelais seldom turns up in the catalogues of privately owned books. As this book will demonstrate, however, many did read him, and yet others might have enjoyed him had they been able to decode his learned, playful, punning, sprawling, allusive, and demanding French. Perhaps some with less than optimal French heard about an episode from a friend, made out a few jokes, read a chapter or two with a tutor, or even took a look at some now lost partial translation being passed from hand to hand in London's sophisticated circles.

Finally, a word on formal conclusions. This book provides none, although I shall offer speculations to supplement and support the overview offered in this introduction. A traditional rhetorician would, I like to think, find my decision to end with Rabelais's own brief imperative rather than with a terminal summation decorous. The Rabelaisian body and book are notoriously grotesque and open, not classical and closed, just as Menippean satire and its mirror genre, romance, are uneasy with endings. So I present this book to you in hopes that you will find pleasure, profit, and matter out of which to fashion whatever ending seems most fitting or true. "Fay ce que vouldras," and I am well paid.

Like everyone who has worked for many years on a project, I have acquired too many debts to acknowledge without creating a nearly Rabelaisian or even

Gargantuan list. My chief obligation is to Jackson Boswell, who one wonderful day sent me a list of English Renaissance books in which he had seen allusions to Rabelais or Gargantua, some of them entirely new to me. My thanks also to Judith Anderson, Barbara Bowen, Heidi Brayman, Heather Dubrow, Kent Hieatt, Arthur Kinney, Roger Kuin, Stephen Orgel, and Peter Platt for commenting on sections of this book in one version or other or for answering questions. And for their friendship, encouragement, information, and suggestions — if not for providing enticing distractions from this project — I thank Chris Baswell, Patrick Cheney, Bill Engel, Bob Evans, Bert Hamilton, Margaret Hannay, Jim Hirsh, Ray La Charité, Carol Kaske, David Kastan, John King, Paula Loscocco, Hugh Maclean, Germain Marc'hadour, Steve May, Carla Mazzio, Bill Oram, Bob Patten, Richard Peterson, Jerry Rubio, Lauren Silberman, Paul J. Smith, Ted Tayler, Marcel Tetel, Betty Travitsky, Florence Weinberg, and, of course, my chief friend and distraction: Peter Prescott. Finally, this book has been lucky enough to fall into the hands of Yale University Press's Susan Laity, a rigorous, empathetic, and perceptive editor with an uncommon wit and a fine ear.

This book is dedicated to the wittiest woman I know, my daughter Antonia Courthope Prescott. I know Rabelais would have liked her. Certainly, his patroness, Marguerite de Navarre, would have appreciated her observant humor and flexible irony. May her ship always carry a full cargo of Pantagruelion and may she reach every joy toward which she sets her sail.

Abbreviations

BHR	*Bibliothèque d'humanisme et Renaissance*
CA	*Croniques admirables*
CL	*Cinquième livre* (1564)
CLS	*Comparative Literature Studies*
DNB	*Dictionary of National Biography*
G	*Gargantua* (1534 or 1535)
ELR	*English Literary Renaissance*
ER	*Etudes rabelaisiennes*
HLQ	*Huntington Library Quarterly*
JEGP	*Journal of English and German Philology*
JMRS	*Journal of Medieval and Renaissance Studies*
Jourda	François Rabelais, *Oeuvres complètes,* ed. Pierra Jourda (Paris: Garnier, 1962)
MLR	*Modern Language Review*
MP	*Modern Philology*
MRTS	Medieval and Renaissance Texts and Studies
NRB	Stephen Rawles and M. A. Screech, *A New Rabelais Bibliography: Editions of Rabelais Before 1626* (Geneva: Droz, 1987; *ER* 20)
P	*Pantagruel* (1532)
Plan	Pierre-Paul Plan, *Les Editions de Rabelais de 1532 à 1711* (Paris: Imprimerie nationale, 1904).

PQ	*Philological Quarterly*
QL	*Quart livre* (1552)
R&R	*Renaissance and Reformation*
RenQ	*Renaissance Quarterly*
RER	*Revue des études rabelaisiennes*
RES	*Review of English Studies*
RHR	*Réforme, humanisme, renaissance*
SCJ	*Sixteenth Century Journal*
SEL	*Studies in English Literature*
SP	*Studies in Philology*
TL	*Tiers livre* (1546)

Imagining Rabelais in Renaissance England

Para-Rabelaisian Complications

An effort to calculate Rabelais's English image from how English writers alluded to him would gain clarity from knowing what texts by him sustained or shaped such allusions. Yet the ambiguities of early modern authorship and the complexities of readership in any age inevitably cloud the picture. That picture, whatever the mists occluding it, remains significant. Rabelais's fame and the uses to which it was put offer a compelling example, almost a Renaissance emblem, of how reputation can work in an age less concerned than our own with originality of voice, textual authenticity, sincerity of expression, and individually derived convictions. English writers who named Rabelais must often have thought him the author of texts that now languish unread largely because the historical Rabelais — *our* Rabelais — did not, in fact, write them. To see Rabelais's *Oeuvres* in a Renaissance edition, or a number of other works linked to his name, was to learn more about him than was strictly true. On the other hand, many writers could (and still can) cite famous authors without ever reading a word by them, authentic or not: it is in the nature of notoriety to be so cited. That fact, too, both clouds the story of how the English imagined Rabelais and reveals something important about literary fame and the uses to which it can be put by others.

Apocrypha

Considering how unstable notions of authorship, self-expression, and literary property were and are, it may be impossible fully to recapture the responses that the name Rabelais once elicited in England. Indeed, that name was, if anything, even less attached to a settled and authorized body of texts than was, say, the name Lucian or Chaucer. Rabelais eventually acted to protect his writings, publishing under his own name, obtaining the patronage of Marguerite de Navarre and Jean, Cardinal Du Bellay, and acquiring the all-too-thin shield of a royal license. Even then, however, and presumably with his passive permission, texts by other authors were often printed with his own; unwary readers might well think them his. In some sense they were. After all, *Pantagruel* was at first ascribed only to an anagram, "Alcofribas Nasier," and hence in a way was pre- if not quite para-Rabelaisian.[1]

With the exception of one of the many chapbooks starring Gargantua, to which I shall return, in only two cases did English writers leave written evidence of their interest in these texts: *Les Songes drolatiques de Pantagruel* (1565), whose grotesque images were credited to Rabelais, and two satires by François Habert that were sometimes printed with Rabelais's *Oeuvres*. I shall discuss them later. Yet it is unlikely that the other apocrypha surrounding the Rabelaisian corpus like a strong aura — getting or giving energy and at times hard to tell from the body itself — had no impact on readers' imaginations. It seems wise to note some texts to which the name Rabelais was attached, whether through mendacious implication, textual propinquity, or allusion. I omit the *Cinquième livre,* for the English seldom if ever doubted that it was by Rabelais himself.

One playful imitation appeared in 1538 or earlier, probably in Paris; the title page and its verso read: "Panurge disciple de Pentagruel. Avec les prouesses du merveilleux geant Bringuenarilles. etc." and "Le Voyage et navigation que fist Panurge / disciple de Pentagruel / aux Isles incongneues et estranges / de plusieurs choses merveilleuses & difficiles à croyre / quil dict avoir veues: dont il faict narration en ce present volume. Et plusieurs austres joyeusetez pour inciter les lecteurs et auditeurs à rire."[2] In 1542 Etienne Dolet printed this imitation in a book that also contained Rabelais's *Pantagruel* and *Pantagrueline Prognostication* (*NRB* 13, Lyons). There were many sixteenth-century editions of this rambling yet amusing text, sometimes published separately, sometimes with Rabelais's work, and sometimes with a Gargantua chapbook (see *NRB* 128–129, 1544, 1546). An astute parasite, the text mutated. After 1545 a giant named Bringuenarilles often takes over Panurge's role, while in the Lyons 1556 edition Gallimassue (from the chapbooks) becomes Bringuenarilles (*NRB*

140). Soon the "Disciple" ingested bits of the master: *NRB* 138 and 139 lift chapters 22 and 23 of the 1542 *Pantagruel,* title pages sometimes reprint the grinning Pantagruel from *NRB* 10, and a 1576 edition borrows the *Cinquième livre*'s bottle poem (*NRB* 143). Titles also vary: *Le Disciple de Pantagruel, Les Navigations de Panurge, Bringuenarilles,* or *La Navigation du compaignon à la bouteille* (*NRB* 139; backdated by the Rouen printer Dugort to 1545 so as to protect his plagiarisms from *Pantagruel* against Rabelais's newly published privilege).

The *Navigation*'s account of an island-hopping voyage weds archaic motifs to recent excitement at geographical discoveries. Some episodes or species that Panurge and his companions meet reappear, changed for the wittier, in the *Quart livre;* some the anonymous authors took, like Rabelais, from folklore or Lucian's *True History;* and some resemble characters or moments in the chapbooks. Bringuenarilles eats half a million men, swallows boats and windmills, relieves himself, and drives off enemy ships with farts. Like Pantagruel, he needs internal cleansing, and like the chapbook Gargantua he uses his penis as a bridge: when a carter with a four-horse team drives into the urethra, the giant, thinking he has a bladder stone, pisses him out. Three days after he ingests fifty thousand raw eggs, a flock of chicks emerges from his rear end, all hatched and, says the author blandly, ready to eat. Other touches are Lucianic by way of Cockaigne: little windmills that sprout into big ones, a land of lanterns, an island of "farouches" and "andouilles" that Rabelais was to combine into a species of hairy hotdog, hills of butter, rivers of milk or wine, sausage-trees and bottle-trees, literal egg-plants, flocks of roasted birds, pomegranates with coins for seeds. On one island, the elderly are rejuvenated by being drowned in malmsey, simmered, remolded, and revived by air blown up their colons with a bellows. The race has no women, so men are not beaten by angry wives for hanging out at the tavern.

The *Navigation* is fanciful, eventful, and scatological: a dirty Oz book. Its tired misogyny, like its dream of an edible world, deserves mainly anthropological study. It can be amusing, though, and Rabelais read it carefully. How well the English knew it I cannot tell; readers who assumed that Rabelais had something to do with it (or who simply allowed it to mix chemically in their minds with memory of his work) would associate him yet further with wild Lucianic fantasy and open-bottomed, gullet-yawning crudity. They would not have found wordplay, erudite joking, anti-clerical satire, evangelical piety, or humanist affirmation.

Much less popular, but adding a mite to the *Tiers livre,* was *Le Songe de Pantagruel* (1542), a dream vision by François Habert that was written in his evangelical phase.[3] Habert's Gargantua appears twice to his son, exhorting him to be a good pastor and praising clerical marriage. In between these visits comes Panurge, offering contrast and comedy. He is from Babylon, he says, and tells of a tournament in which Hercules, Arthur, Lancelot, Roland, and Huon of Bordeaux took part, all these heroes being revived for the occasion by Mercury. Panurge has escaped from the sultan (cf. *P* 14) thanks to Mélusine, whom he taught to speak French. English readers would have noted Gargantua's reverence for Scripture, Panurge's acquaintance with the trickster Hermes, and Pantagruel's vatic dreaming.

In 1551, someone — probably the critic and poet Thomas Sébillet — published a blithely spiteful *Louenge des femmes: Invention extraite du Commentaire de Pantagruel, sus l'Androgyne de Platon.* The introduction, which cites "Alcofribas" and claims to summarize a book by Pantagruel on Aristophanes' androgyne in Plato's *Symposium* (cf. *G* 8), paraphrases Panurge's consultation with Dr. Rondibilis in *TL* 32.[4] But there is little that is Rabelaisian about the verses that follow. One long poem by "André Misogyne" addresses "Seigneur Pamphile [All-lover]," who, like Panurge, wishes to know whether he should marry. Any reader can guess the reply. More psychologically freighted is a riddle: What is so deep that a man may never find its bottom, eats flesh without chewing, is never satisfied, lacks nose, ears, and eyes but has a mouth ready to devour anything and then vomit it back, is small but capable of such violent combat that the strongest become pitiable and fall dead, gives pleasure yet is hard to see, is well loved but has a dirty neighbor, is base ("vilain") but makes gentlemen, is worshiped by many on their knees, can make those who love it die, and lives in a wood where flourishes a rose? Right.[5] Not a subtle enigma, but the disquiet within its obscenity is worth noticing; and it would have reinforced one image Rabelais was to project in England — that of a filthy scoffer and heartless jester.

The Lyons 1565 edition of Rabelais's *Oeuvres* introduced two works of unknown authorship; many readers would have thought that they were by Rabelais, and a number of the English must have seen them. One is a verse epistle by the same Limousin student at the University of Paris — that "alme, inclite, et célèbre académie que l'on vocite Lutèce" — whom an irritated Pantagruel seizes by the throat and makes gabble in his native dialect (*P* 6; now he speaks "naturally," the gratified giant tells him, thus raising uncomfortable linguistic issues). In some editions the epistle is signed "Debride Gousier" (Unbridled Gullet) and the author identified as the "Limousin de Pantagruel, grand excoriateur de la lingue latiale"; it addresses "ung sien amicissime resident en l'inclyte et famosissime urbe de Lugdune."[6] Now a hanger-on at court, presently at Fontainebleau, Gousier writes to a friend in Lyons, informing him that the weather is terrible and that he should come for a visit in the spring when the nymphs are out. Forgetting Pantagruel's lesson, he praises Lyons's culture for its "eloquentes verbocinations" and hopes that his friend's pen will blacken paper with answering rhymes: "Si obsecrons que ta calame vale / Attramenter charte papyracée; / Pour correspondre en forme rimassée." He concludes with a dizain:

> Pour indaguer en vocable authenticque
> La purité de la langue gallicque,
> Jadis immerse en calligine obscure:
> Et profliger la barbarie anticque,
> La renovant en sa candeur atticque,
> Chascun y prend sollicitude et cure.
> Mais tel si fort les intestines cure,
> Voulant saper plus que l'anime vale
> Qu'il se contrainct transgredir la tonture,
> Et degluber la lingue latiale.[7]

This means, sort of:

> To exhumize in lexical authenticity
> The purity of the Gallic tongue
> Formerly immersed in caliginate obscurity
> (And to expel antique barbaricity),
> Renovating it in its Attic candicity,
> Each one takes solicitude and concern;
> But so anxious is each one's intestinicity,
> That striving to sapientate beyond psychic validity
> He constrains himself to surpass depilitation
> And thus excoriates the linguage of Latiality.

Because this joke is so dependent on *Pantagruel* it is hard to know what it added to the name Rabelais, but it might have intensified a tendency I shall note to link bombast with Gargantua.

The same edition included "La Chresme philosophale des questions encyclopedicques de Pantagruel, Lesquelles seront disputees sorbonicolificabilitudinissement es escholes de Decret, pres Sainct Denis de la Chartre à Paris."[8] This "philosophical cream" (or "chrism") lists *quaestiones* of the sort with which Renaissance humanists liked to suppose scholastics troubled their wits while ignoring philology and rhetoric. "*Utrum,*" asks one, "une idée platonicque voltigeant dextrement sous l'orifice du chaos pourroyt chasser les escadrons des atomes democriticques." Or "*Utrum,* tant seullement par le long poil donné à l'ourse metamorphosee, ayant le derriere tondu à la bougresque pour faire une barbute à Triton, pourroyt estre gardienne du pole articque."[9] If omniform Proteus turns himself into a cicada and musically exercises his voice during the dog days, could he make a third concoction of a morning rose, carefully wrapped up in the month of May, before the completion of one zodiacal turn? The humor is academic, but so is much of that in *Pantagruel;* those who like Rabelais's library of imaginary books might like the *Chresme* too. The questions' wit relies on juxtaposing scholastic nonsense with such fashionable topics as Platonism, mythology, and astronomy. And, like much nonsense (Lewis Carroll's *Jabberwocky* and Edward Lear's flowers, for example), they structure a meaningless or impossible content with coherent syntax or form. The questions raised — How much "meaning" lies in structure and how much in vocabulary? — matter, and these quaestiones might have added to Rabelais's image in some quarters as a maker of sharp fancies and significant nothings.

Rejecting Rabelais's thought while exploiting his name is the anonymous *Nouveau Panurge avec sa navigation en l'isle Imaginaire, son rajeunissement en icelle, & le voyage que fit son esprit en l'autre monde pendant le rajeunissement de son corps* (La Rochelle, ca. 1612).[10] Here Panurge, who in his narrator's preface says he knows how to "rabeliser," recounts underworld sights that parallel those Rabelais had given Epistemon in *Pantagruel* 30. The text's satirical vision of famous sinners smoldering and talkative in Hades, however, conjures up memories of *Pantagruel,* as well as of the *Tiers livre,* only to exorcize or neutralize them. The author revives Rabelaisian characters (Thaumaste, Epistemon, Her Trippa), adopts elements of *Les Navigations de Panurge* (notably the malmsey-bellows geriatrics), ventures some indecencies, imagines a book called *Elysian Chronicles,* and invents a genealogy for his narrator: Panurge was found floating on water, like Moses, with a note identifying his father as Pan and his mother as the princess Orgeo. Visiting Hades while his body soaks in malmsey, Panurge encounters, for example, the haughty Parisienne who had spurned his advances (see *P* 22) and now lives in Vaingloryland. He sees a Protestant university with Hus, Luther, Calvin, and Beza, the last living with his friend Audebert and his floozie Candida in Lustberg's "logis de Sodome."[11] Although locating Gargantua and Pantagruel in the Elysian Fields, the author probably shared the assumption, not mistaken from a papist point of view, that Rabelais had aimed his barbs at the Catholic church; this alone must have made such appropriations satisfying. Within a short time, English Protestants could compare the result with Père Garasse's angrier *Rabelais réformé;* they could not, though, have confused it with Rabelais's own work.

Had an English enthusiast, perhaps already familiar with a translated chapbook on Gargantua, sought out these paratexts, what might he (or that not impossible she) have gathered about "Rabelais"? Perhaps that Rabelais is associated with sex, food, and excrement, with absurdity, fantasy, and laughter at pretension. The Rabelais who was moved by humanist or evangelical faith and hope is missing, although thanks to the *Chresme* and pompous Limousin, there is a trace of the Rabelais whose works are, I was once told, "a network of intersecting semantic fields."

Is There a Reader in This Response?
The Case of Robert Burton

For us to grasp fully how readers responded to "Rabelais," we would need to know what we cannot know: how anyone reacts to anything involves processes hard to deduce in the living and impossible to trace in the dead, especially when the dead had a different sense of the mind's relation to words. Recent decades have seen valiant efforts to descry the dynamics of literary response, but the study of readers reading remains in its infancy.[12] Concepts like Hans Robert Jauss's "horizon of expectation" can seem remote from experience, and the topography and distance of those horizons vary from person to person.[13] Those who follow the mental processes of living readers know the evasions, the omissions, the wild associations, the impact of class, race, age, gender, or nationality, the illnesses, the moods, the dyslexia or inattention that generate readings that would startle even a deconstructionist. So we simplify evidence just to keep control of it.[14] Observing past readers at work, moreover, takes a skepticism that is tiring to sustain. This is particularly true when their culture was more tolerant than we are of plagiarism and of judging texts without looking at them. References to Rabelais, like Petrarchan conceits or classical allusions, circulated like coins: the opinions became worn but still bought rhetorical effect and could be produced out of what passed for personal pockets. Renaissance pedagogy, moreover, encouraged the accumulation and redeployment of discursive fragments without much reference to context.[15]

Robert Burton's allusions to Rabelais show how hard it can be, in tracing the "reception" of a writer/name/persona, to know who read what. At first sight, Burton seems to show familiarity with *Gargantua et Pantagruel*.[16] By the fourth edition of *The Anatomy of Melancholy* (1632) he had referred five times to Rabelais, twice citing specific passages. The first edition, printed in 1621, devotes some pages (Part 3, Section 3, Member 4, Subsection 2) to the sexual jealousy that generates "melancholy" (what we call neurosis, but with an even stronger somatic base). Burton rejects having "wives and children, all common," the Anabaptists' willingness "to consort with other mens' wives, as the spirit moved them" (1621 ed., sig. Xx5), and the brothels that mere "pol-licy" would allow. Ensure fidelity, he urges, rather by setting virtue and educa-tion above birth, fortune, and beauty. Remember that "Coquage God of Cuckolds, as one merrily said, accompanies the goddesse jealousie, and both follow the fairest by Jupiters appointment, and they sacrifice to both together: beautie and honestie seldome agree" (sigs. Xx7–7v). A marginal note reads, "Rablais hist Pontaraguel.lib.3.cap 33 [that is, *TL* 33]."[17]

This seems plain: Burton has read the monitory fable that Dr. Rondibilis recounts to Pantagruel's anxious friend, Panurge. Trying to persuade the would-be husband that cuckolds bring their fate upon themselves, he recalls that when Jupiter granted Cocuage a "day" in the crowded Olympian "calen-dar," the only available spot already belonged to Jealousy; both deities are now happy to take up residence with any devotee. The learned Burton must have spotted the mischievous revision of an Aesopian story that Plutarch adopts twice in his *Moralia*.[18] Indeed, Panurge's luxurious motive for marriage and his dread of being beaten, robbed, and horned so suit Burton's chapter that one might expect further traces of the *Tiers livre*. Burton himself would "rather marry a faire one & put it to the hazard, . . . but doe thou as thou wilt, I speake onely for my selfe" (1621 ed., sig. Xx8), a remark that seems to merge the Abbey of Thélème's "fays ce que vouldras" with a Pantagruelist scorn of fortune. But why conclude that "beautie and honestie seldome agree"? Ron-dibilis himself aims not to decry good looks but to show how fear generates the very thing feared.

Making sense of the reference is easier if one turns to a book Burton some-times cites, Robert Tofte's translation of Benedetto Varchi's *Blazon of Jealousie* (1615). Introducing this buoyantly literate work are lines by one "Incognito" that paraphrase Rondibilis's fable; the margin calls Coquage "God of Cuck-olds" and cites "Rablais in Hist. Pantagruel, lib.3.chap.33." Incognito writes of those "Which blest were with the Fayrest." He explains that the god is "com-panion" to the jealous, adding that by Jove's decree Coquage graces "such as sacrific'd to him." Burton's similar diction, his fondness for Tofte, the infre-quency of his references to untranslated French books, the virtual absence of such books from his library, and the marginal reference Incognito furnishes, show that it was here he found Coquage.[19] Burton drops the point that Co-quage visits those who sacrifice to him, implying rather that men who marry beauty will soon meet Cuckoldry and Jealousy. He does not intend this thought very seriously, crediting it to one who spoke "merrily," but modifies the joke by moving the focus from the foolish husbands to the dishonest wives and chang-ing Jupiter's decree from a plan for Coquage's cult to an assurance that fair women bring horns. This is a trifle old hat. Perhaps Burton felt, as his own prose flowed through his usual heaps and fragments of quotation and allusion, that he could not pause for the fable's complexity; or perhaps he heard a trite misogyny that Rabelais's reputation for scurrility had led him to expect.

The next edition of the *Anatomy* adds nothing about Rabelais. In the third (1628), however, Rabelais is not only "merry" but a doctor. In a Lucianic preface, "Democritus Junior to the Reader," Burton reports that he has consulted what medical texts he could find at Oxford, so maybe he had now seen Rabelais associated with Galen or Hippocrates. In any case, he now imagines Rablais doctoring the globe, for our whole race is "of Gotam parish." Nothing remains but to carry everybody "to Bedlam," says the first edition, and now Burton adds: "and set Rablais to be their Physitian" (1628 ed., sig. k1v). The world could in fact do worse, but since Rabelais is human and thus as crazy as his patients, putting him in charge of a lunatic planet is no vote of confidence. Rabelais will govern Bedlam not because he can help the patients (who are beyond aid) but because he completes Burton's picture of an inverted world with nobody sane left to run it. What distinguishes Burton from Lucian, however, and what aligns him with Dr. Rabelais — whether he knew it or not — is his willingness to implicate himself: "I am as foolish, as mad as any one."

Some pages later, Burton might seem finally to have read *Gargantua*. The chapter "Quantity of Diet" (1.2.2.2) describes those who "tosse pots, and boles, as so many bals, invent new tricks, as Sausages, Anchoves, Tobacco, Caveare, pickled Oysters, Herrings, Fumados, &c innumerable salt meats to increase their appetite. . . . They make lawes *insanas leges, contra bibendi fallicias* [insane laws against failures in drinking], and bragge of it when they have done." And now Burton adds (I incorporate some marginal information): "Crowning that man that is soonest gone, as their drunken predecessours have done, — *quid ego video?* Ps: *Cum coronâ Pseudolum ebrium tuum* ["What do I see?" Ps: "Thy drunken (slave) Pseudolus with a wreath," from Plautus]. — And when they are dead, will have a Can of wine with *Marons* old woman to bee engraven on their tombes. So they triumph in villany, and justifie their wickednesse, with Rablais that French Lucian, drunkennesse is better for the body then physicke, because there bee more old drunkards then old Phisitians. Many such frothy arguments they have" (1628 ed., sig. 13).[20] The chapter is itself frothy, as though the argument against riot had a head on it, and it is paradoxically constructed: a torrent of words and examples dissolves the counsel of restraint in verbal overflow. Brown ends it with a brief, almost anorexic, reminder that much fasting is even worse than surfeit: some "are in the other extreame, and drawe [melancholy] on their heads by too ceremonious and strict diet, being overprecise." Rabelais is linked to a "frothy" impertinence that defends riot, yet his attitudes are healthier than those of the "precise."

This time the margin gives no source, and in fact Burton is quoting Robert Dallington's *View of France* (1604), which recalls a Frenchman who argued that French forces are superior to the English, "Because (sayth he) wee have more old Captaynes in France, then you in England. Much like the reason of Rablais, who would needes prove, that drunkennesse was better for the body then Phisike, because there were more old drunkards, then old Phisicians" (sigs. M3–M3v). Dallington later terms Rabelais "the true Lucian of France" (sig. Q3), perhaps giving Burton his epithet. The information on comparative life expectancies is proffered by Frère Jean to a skeptical Gargantua just before the Picrocholine War. Awaking from a sleep induced by reading psalms, the thirsty monk is advised against taking in more alcohol until his system has cleansed itself. "Cent diables me saultent au corps," says the monk, "s'il n'y a plus de vieux hyvrognes qu'il n'y a de vieulx medicins."[21] Even sophisticated readers could ascribe a character's words to an author, yet Burton himself says at the end of his preface that we have read the words of Democritus Junior, not Robert Burton. Even if we were sure that he had read Rabelais, it would be hard to tell whether Burton thought him a blamable promoter of frothy arguments, a retailer of his monk's froth, or a fellow connoisseur of froth.

A third new reference is in a chapter on how "Scoffs, Calumnies, bitter Jests" (1.2.4.4) inflict pain (1628 ed., sigs. S4–S4v). Socrates rightly warned those concerned for reputation to fear writers, "for they are terrible fellowes, can praise and dispraise as they see cause." Rulers "fear a rayling Aretine, more then an enimy in the field: which made most Princes of his time (as some relate) allow him a liberall pension, that he should not taxe them in his Satyres: the Gods had their Momus, Homer his Zoilus, Achilles his Thirsites, Philip his Demades. The Caesars themselves in Rome were commonly taunted. There was never wanting a Petronius, a Lucian in those times, nor will be a Rablais, an Euphormio, a Boccalius in ours."[22] Burton recalls that when Pope Adrian VI wanted the statue of Pasquil burned and the ashes thrown in the Tiber, a "facete companion" warned that they "would turne into frogs in the bottome of the river, and croake worse and lowder then before," a witty comment on the effect of repression: dismembering a political satirist only spreads him around, like a nastier Osiris or Orpheus. Himself a Menippean writer, Burton was perhaps not wholly dismayed by thoughts of Pasquil's croaks and Aretino's terrorism: if his notion of Rabelais was mixed, so were his feelings toward his own laughter.[23]

If Burton never read Rabelais, this passage represents not a response to

Gargantua and Pantagruel but the reproduction of a common opinion linking the "French Lucian" to libelous mocks. Is Burton's reaction second hand? Yes and no. Whatever he heard or read had a storage place in his mind awaiting it that was both socially fabricated and privately imagined or pressured. Yet that place is affected, in part shaped, by its immediate rhetorical surroundings. For example, although Burton can quote Lucian with little discomfort, he can also condemn him as an atheist who "scoffes at all" (1628 ed., 3.4.2.1). When he calls Rabelais a French "Lucian," is he thinking of the clever satirist or the jesting unbeliever? Both? In different contexts "Lucian" has different tones, just as readers of the 1628 *Anatomy* would find Rabelais writing "merrily" in one section, frothily in another, and here scoffingly . . . about what? The context encourages us to think of Rabelais as a Momus, Thersites and Aretino, as a Petronius and Lucian. All these, Burton implies, badmouthed authorities. Why does Burton assume Rabelais did so? The latter mocked the ecclesiastical and academic establishment, but there is little in his books to offend his kings or patrons themselves.

The fourth edition (1632) finds a last use for "Rabelais," although there is still no evidence that Burton had actually read him. The tone is darker. Having described superstitious folk, Burton turns to "Epicures, Atheists, Hypocrites, worldly secure, Carnalists, Impenitent sinners, &c." (1621 ed., 3.4.2.1). These are "Giants, that warre with the gods, as the Poet fained, that scoffe at all Religion, at God himselfe" (1632 ed., sigs. 3B6–3B6v). Epicures worship their belly, while "Cosin Germanes" are the "peevish" sort who "attribute all to naturall causes." Misled by philosophy, the devil, and their own blindness, they "denie God as much as the rest" and—the 1632 edition now adds— "Hold all religion a fiction, opposite to reason and philosophy though for feare of magistrates . . . they durst not publikely professe it. Aske one of them of what religion he is, hee scoffingly replies, a philosopher, a Galenist, an Averroist, and with Rablais a phisitian, a Peripateticke, an Epicure" (sig. 4R2). Burton's allusions to Rabelais have progressed from a cheerful fable to a frothy amorality or scoffing subversion to a cynical atheism. When he jovially put Rabelais in charge of Bedlam he had implied that he too would be there. Now Rabelais is the stereotypical materialist M.D., a learned fool who says in his heart that there is no God.

Burton had a response to Rabelais, but was he a reader? That he relied on others is understandable, granted the plethora of books: "Our eyes ake with reading, our fingers with turning." Even his admission that what he has "is stolne from others" steals from Martial: "Dicitque mihi mea pagina fur es" [And my page says to me, you are a robber]. Is he ashamed? No, for he has in truth merely borrowed, and can say with Macrobius " 'tis all mine and none mine."[24] Exactly. Yet Burton, who claims to give his "authors" their due by identifying them, forgets to mention that at times he found what he quotes not in the writers cited but in those who had read them. A magpie, he steals from other magpies: if not a circulation of cultural energy, this is at least cultural recycling. Or one might say that in passing down the reception line, some — perhaps most — otherwise honorable guests have forged their invitation cards.

2

Reshaping Gargantua
The Chapbook Giant in England

Aside from his "authentic" works, for England's Rabelais there are no
more important texts than the chapbook histories of a giant named Gargantua. Years ago, Huntington Brown showed — and I have further evidence —
that at least one of these texts reached England.[1] There its hero found fame
and rhetorical employment, if dwindling into a run-of-the-mill giant. Although Rabelais eventually dropped his pseudonymous anagram Alcofribas
Nasier to become a legally privileged and well-patronized author, it is likely
that some readers in England thought that both Gargantuas were made by one
man. And yet the ease with which the two can sometimes be distinguished
shows that notions of authorship were robust enough to help others tell one
giant from another, especially as one lived in a chapbook and the other between the covers of Rabelais's *Oeuvres*.

The chapbooks began appearing in the late 1520s or early 1530s, editions of
them continuing into the next century. Who wrote them and for whom is
unclear; and it has been argued that Rabelais himself contributed to their
production, whatever the irony with which he praises *Les Grandes et inestimables Cronicques: Du grant & enorme geant Gargantua* (1532) in the prologue to *Pantagruel*. From them he took his own giant, adopting for *Gargantua* the hero's trip to Paris on a great mare, and in turn chapters 2–4
of *Pantagruel* became chapters 19–21 of another chapbook, *Les Croniques*

admirables du puissant Roy Gargantua, ensemble comme il eut à femme la fille du Roy de Utopie nommee Badebec, de laquelle il eut ung filz nommé Pantagruel lequel fut roy des dipsodes et des Ama[u]rottes, Et comment il mist à fin ung grant gean nommé Gallimassue. This was printed after 1532 and, if we may trust an inscription in one copy, before 1535. The compiler may have been François Girault, whose surname appears as a concluding verse acrostic, but as his whole acrosticized name is found in the *Grande et merveilleuse vie* (1527–1531?), this may not mean much.[2]

Some English allusions to Gargantua must refer to a now lost chapbook, perhaps called *The History of Gar[a]gantua,* based on *Croniques admirables.* The many references to its giant show that the book was familiar, at least by name, to the educated. Nor, if it faithfully translated its model, were the English wrong to enjoy it. *Admirables* is funny, even if modern critics condemn its flat style and ramshackle structure (in classier texts, this is called the romance form). I offer here a summary:

Merlin goes to the tallest mountain in the East, where, out of two whales' bones, some of Lancelot's blood, twelve pounds of Guenevere's nail clippings, and moss wet with sperm from the god Genius, he forges the giants Grangosier and Gallemelle, his hammer going like lightning. As the two descend the mountain, still naked, Grangosier turns to see his wife behind him on the slope. Spying a wound between her legs, he asks who hurt her; she replies that her condition is natural. Her husband offers to probe the hurt, for looking down at himself he discovers a suddenly usable probe as big as a barrel of herring. From this experience of difference is born Gargantua, conceived during a sexual initiation that is understood as loving first aid. (The abyss in which Grangosier can find "ne fons ne rive," neither bottom nor side, anticipates the empty old woman in *P* 15 whose "wound" a lion and fox staunch with moss.)[3]

Merlin sends the giants to Arthur, Gallemelle giving birth en route with the help of mountain fauns and satyrs. The baby is baptized by a nearby hermit: Morgan le Fay is his godmother, and the fairies report that the gods want him named Gargantua, Greek for "You have a handsome son." The family passes through Beauce, where their huge mare, stung by insects, levels a forest with her tail. Reaching the Channel, Gargantua kills a whale with a single punch, and the family eats it. Alas, the parents soon die for lack of suppositories; today they lie under the rocks they had carried—Mont-Saint-Michel and Tombelaine.[4]

After visiting Paris and playing with the bells of Notre Dame, Gargantua asks Merlin for help. Gargantua, first quelling a ship-eating giant that is afflicting Angers, is then transported by the magician to the court of King Arthur, where he battles the king's enemies, the "Gotz" and "Magotz" (who recall the both the enemy tribes in Revelation and Britain's aboriginal giant, Goemagot [Gogmagog]). Merlin makes the giant an iron club 107 feet long with an end as big as the throat of Notre Dame's bells. When he spies a picture of the old giants piling up hills to reach heaven, Gargantua heaps up seventeen hills so Arthur can see all the way to Paris. After feeding him a huge meal, the king dresses Gargantua as befits a giant who was already 367 cubits high at three years old: his purse belt, for example, is made from 1,780 bull penises.

Dressed in the colors of the rainbow, the natty giant exchanges rondeaux with a local girl, who rejects him because she fears his size, being herself only 300 cubits high. He then woos the king of Utopia's daughter, whom, in pages lifted from Rabelais, he marries and by whom he has Pantagruel. With Merlin's help, he conquers the Irish and Dutch, killing one prisoner with a fart (his farts can knock over three loads of hay or run four windmills) and using his penis as a bridge for Arthur's army. During the campaign he inadvertently swallows a gunboat, so Merlin sends in doctors for a looksee. Gargantua is then positioned with his rear toward an enemy city; matches are put in his mouth, a torch is applied, and the anal explosion burns the town. Soon he sets off to see the chief giant, who lives on Black Mountain in the land of Prester John. At Rome, refused entrance despite his offer of affection, he destroys its walls (recalling the recent sack or the old ruins). Passing through Sinai, he reaches a distant peak where seventeen giants drink the clouds lest the mountains drown, but Merlin fetches him to fight the giant Gallimassue, a friend of Oberon, whom Gargantua defeats with rocks that can still be seen in France.[5] At last our giant joins Arthur, Morgan le Fay, and Huon of Bordeaux in Avalon.

It takes little erudition and no solemnity to enjoy *Admirables*. Yet its compiler was not ignorant or naive; nor, probably, did he write exclusively or even primarily for the humble folk of Paris and Lyons, where most of these booklets were printed.[6]

Traces of archaic material may survive in and deepen this tale of hugeness hammered from fragments of nobler stories. The giant is older than the chapbooks, as witness the legends that Paul Sébillot gathered in the nineteenth century and that are still being found.[7] Nobody can prove their age, but their ubiquity and nature suggest a nonliterary origin. Gargantua acts as one would expect, swallowing boats or people and reshaping the land by relieving himself, vomiting, farting, cleaning his boots, unloading his backpack, and bowling. Many call him "bon," some say "chrétien," and a few think him demonic.

He is always open-orificed, heaping, outsized. And real, as a woman who had claimed to know no legends about him asserted: "Gargantua isn't a tale, he's history; I thought you only wanted tales."[8]

Some scholars have sensed remnants of an even older Gallic — and pre-Gallic — oral myth.[9] Walter Stephens rejects all this in part because traditional giants are evil and Gargantua means well.[10] But those who think Gargantua archaic see ambiguity, not goodness. The giant for them is popular but dark and perhaps (like Greek giants) serpentine, linked by name and topography to throats, gorges, mountains, and rocks — Earth's greedy apertures and menacing outcroppings. If in some places he precedes the Saint Michael who took over heights like Mount Gargan, he is also the chthonic dragon-monster that the angel overcame.[11] Folkloric theories also strengthen Gargantua's kinship with both fertility and terror, for he is profoundly double in nature. If he gets on with Christians, his first well-wishers were pagan, and his mentor a demon-sired magus. He visits Paris, but also the remote East, and although King Arthur uses him as heavy artillery, it is just as well for most of us that he is now in Avalon.

Some English allusions to Gargantua can only be to the chapbook giant. A clown in the anonymous *Tryall of Chevalry* (1605) mentions "Gargantua, that stuft every button of his coate with a load of hay," as in CA 15.[12] Similarly, John Favour's *Antiquitie Triumphing over Noveltie* (1619) claims that Jesuits use numerology to make their lies plausible, just as "the bottle of hay giveth credit to the tale of Gargantuas buttons."[13] Gabriel Harvey rightly recalls in *Pierces Supererogation* (1593, sig. Bb3v) that the giant's gown was "furred with two thousand, and five hundred Fox-skinnes," and John Taylor writes that Gargantua "tooke an Irish bogge."[14]

Three notices of Gargantua's mare, though, show how such allusions vary as solid evidence of English reading, especially as Rabelais took his own horse from the *Grandes cronicques*. A 1594 sequel to the English Faust book has a courser so "nimbly joynted, tall and large" it "might have beene the son of Gargantuas m[a]re."[15] It is the chapbook mare who gallops off to Flanders to bear colts and fillies (CA 12). She reappears, regendered, in Gerard de Malynes' *Saint George for England* (1601), a dream vision that tells how George's victory represents "her Majesties most happy governement." The knight is royal authority, the virgin is treasure, and the dragon is ambition, avarice, devaluation, extortion, greed, monetary instability, prodigality, unfavorable trade balances, and vagabonds: "The horse of Gargantua had not so much strength in his taile as he hath, for the same being pricked of flies, did beate down with his taile, all the trees of a great wood" (sigs. A2–A4, D5). It is hard to say what Malynes has read. Third is a mare in *The Schoole of Potentates*

(1648), by Thomas Nashe—not the pamphleteer but a moralist, to whom I shall return. Saying that "Rablais hath a tale of a mare" whose devastations figure the effects of selfishness, he quotes some French so close to *Gargantua*'s that we may safely call this a Rabelaisian horse.[16]

The chapbook Gargantua, then, was known in England. When was a translation printed? A canceled entry in the Stationers' Register for June 6, 1592, reads: "A booke entytuled, Gargantua." And on December 4, 1594, John Danter entered "A booke entituled the historie of Gargantua. Etc. Provided that if this Copie doo belonge to anie other, Then this Entrance to be voide."[17] I believe we can more precisely date a translation and explain Danter's hesitation. He was wise to be cautious, for there is evidence that *Admirables* was already available in English. In the fall of 1571, Abraham Veale, retired since 1565 as a printer but still active in London's book trade, sued Robert Scott, a bookseller in the bustling port of Norwich, who had owed Veale money since July 1568.[18] Scott had ordered works of piety, school editions of the classics, ballads, almanacs, information on the Inquisition, Scoggin's jests, the cynical *Seven Sorrows of Women,* interludes, pictures of monstrous fish, *The Arbor of Amitie,* four dozen ballads on the heresy hunter Edmund Bonner, "six pictures of Nobody," and "six books of Gargantua." Nobody and Gargantua rightly appear together, for Nobody—Niemand—is on the title page of several Gargantuan chapbooks as a peddler toting the world on his back (*NRB* 119 and 125).

Because most of these items were printed or reprinted in the mid- to late 1560s, a 1567 or early 1568 date for "Gargantua" is probable; packaged with schoolbooks, jokes, ballads, and monsters, it is unlikely to have been Rabelais's difficult text. Furthermore, except for a fleeting reference added to a 1547 translation of Antoine Marcourt's *Livre des marchants* and a passing allusion to "Garganteo" in Thomas Wilson's *Arte of Rhetorique* (1553), I find no mention of Gargantua before 1568. Marcourt's translator could have thought that the audience for his anti-Catholic satire would know the giant's name, while Wilson's coy reference to one who "did phantasy, to praise a gose" might mean he had read G 13.[19] Neither allusion is good evidence for an English Gargantua. When Thomas Greenwood, a fellow of Clare Hall at Cambridge who had studied in Paris, died in 1546/7, he left, along with four beds, learned books, works by Clément Marot, a Hebrew psalter, some shabby clothes, and a lute, a 1537 "Gargantua gallice" valued at twopence. This must be Rabelais's *Gargantua.* It cannot be the 1537 Antwerp quarto of *Les Cronicques du Roy Gargantua* (*NRB* 125), for Greenwood's volume was in 16°. But it could be one of the 1537 Lyons editions of *Gargantua,* both in 16°. Denis de Harsy's (*NRB* 21) is my choice, for the title page says "Gargantua" in big letters above a sweet image of a giant family in which the baby is standing on his father's toes, whereas from François Juste's cluttered title page (*NRB* 22) it is hard to extract the simple name Gargantua. Neither title page names Rabelais, which might explain the item's anonymity in the 1546/47 list.[20]

The chapbook went on selling. In 1585 a Scottish bookseller, Robert Gourlaw, had two copies of "Gargantua."[21] The Stationers' Register for August 4, 1626, lists twenty-eight shillings' worth of stock turned over to Edward Brewster and Robert Birde by the widow of Thomas Pavier; it includes the *History of Gargantua,* catechisms, Henry Smith on atheism, Scoggin's jests and the tale of Long Meg, ballads, a work on equine disease, Shakespeare's *Titus Andronicus,* Jonson's *The Case Is Altered,* and plays by Kyd and Dekker. By June 13, 1642, Birde was dead and the stock went to John Wright.[22] To judge from the list in the Register, it had changed little, although there are fewer plays; a *History of Garagantua* is still there, evidence of continuing readership—or long storage. Since Wright evidently thought that customers would like the vulgarity of Scoggin as well as the Plautine wit or Senecan eloquence of Jonson and Shakespeare, the chapbook's social "place" is again hard to specify. Did anyone think it was by Rabelais? Yes, for John Taylor, who denied he knew French, says in *A Dog of War* (1628?) that "Old Homer wrot of / Froggs and Mice, / And Rablaies wrot of / Nitts and Lice" (sig. A7v), which sounds like the chapter in which Gargantua pulls lice from his codpiece and throws one, bigger than the Bastille, into the sea, where it swallows up and then farts out ships and men (*CA* 15).

More significant than the fact of the chronicle's presence in English imagination is the atmosphere in which Gargantua's name emerges in the discourse of the age. In this chapter I limit myself to moments when the giant seems closer to the chapbook hero than to Rabelais' Utopian king (saving a few especially relevant allusions for later in this book), but the two could be confused, which would affect Rabelais's English image.

Whatever his provenance, "Gargantua" often joined the group of mostly wicked giants in Europe's collective memory.[23] These included the aboriginal Canaanites whom Yaweh told his people to eliminate, Goliath, Titans and giants (the first belonging to that older generation of gods whom Zeus overthrew, the second a newer earthborn race sometimes read as the chaotic material elements that assault the ordered patriarchal world of spirit). Giants war on ancient and new hierarchies, being both archaic—the past that refuses to go away—and novel, threatening violence and terror. Civilization requires their suppression, so the Trojan founders of Britain defeated some indigenous cannibal giants: Corineus wrestled their leader, Gogmagog, off a cliff on the coast of Devonshire. Civic ritual remembered such foundational conquests by exhibiting huge figures of giants. Giants often guarded portals and arches, for they are liminal, obstacles to and yet patrons of transition, the stuff out of which to make a new world. No wonder a lost Stuart masque made Gargantua a giant porter.[24]

Were there ever giants? Many said yes, and some credited legends like those treated — or created — by Annius of Viterbo, in which Noah's sons, known to pagans under such names as Dionysus and Jupiter, were giants. Travelers mentioned giants, the bigger ones being found far from England. But doubts grew.[25] In 1627 George Hakewill wrote that most "giants" were really tyrants, a common theory. Yes, Magellan saw nine-foot Brazilians and there may be fifteen-foot porters in Beijing, but most giants are allegorical. People fancy otherwise because poets' fictions have "infected the vulgar, as those of Guy of Warwick, Bevis of Hampton, Corineus and Gog-Magog, Robin Hood and little John, Amadis of Gaule, Pontagruel, Gargantua, and the like."[26] That Hakewill names "Pontagruel" does not prove familiarity with Rabelais, for the borrowed chapters in *Admirables* mention him. In any case, Gargantua lives among romances and legends that "infect" the populace, as though a taste for giants were a social disease.

Champion and Jester

Linking Gargantua to romances was common, although *Admirables* itself treats such works lightly, opening with a comic paging of heroes. Occasionally the affiliation is less with romance than with jests.[27] The generic issue is knotty. Those who think Gargantua a jestbook hero see the chronicle's humor but also note its disjointed account of absurd exploits and ingenuity; had Tyll Eulenspiegel been big enough, perhaps he too would have shaken bell towers in the faces of a flustered citizenry. Romances are episodic and value cleverness, to be sure, yet if it was truly faithful to its source, *Gar[a]gantua* had gross humor, not politic urbanity, and English readers were rightly undecided whether it was a silly romance or a silly jestbook.

Renaissance comments on romances and jestbooks are legion, some of them close to hysterical, as though to cleanse society's garbage mounds of sin required an Ossa upon Pelion of vehemence and scorn. Gargantua thus fell afoul of a widespread irritation with the romances and jest biographies that many writers — not all of them semi-educated — in fact enjoyed. Not that Gargantua was alone in joining the very figures whom his chroniclers had satirized, for mad Orlando and Don Quixote were sometimes confused with the legendary heroes that Ariosto and Cervantes took so lightly. In *A Discoursive Probleme Concerning Prophesies*, for example, John Harvey rejects tales of Arthur,

Bevis, Guy, "Orlando furioso," and Amadis (1588, sig. K2v), and writing in his *History of Great Britaine* that modern poets should sing of modern heroes, William Slayter says he does not mean "Amadis, Don Quixot, and such like" (1621, sig. ¶4v). *Don Quixote* touches elbows with the texts that drove its hero crazy.[28]

Gargantua's name, then, is among those that signify a pleasure accompanying multiple vices, some festering in those inward parts that authority cannot find. Especially in a postrevolutionary society like the Elizabethan, one with beliefs and practices that were officially sustained but threatened from within and without, many will note unhappily that enjoyment, perversity, betrayal — God knows what — can sprout secretly in some mental or bodily corner that any parent, spouse, trading partner, priest, or ruler might wish to see. Fantasy, that is, allows passage to places where even kindly thought police cannot track prey hidden in forests of desire and enjoying what feels like freedom. Attacks on Gargantua as a romance hero show such deep misgivings about the private, the sexual, and the fantastic because the imagination so easily turns from them to matters of greater public moment. If many in the Renaissance distrusted fiction, this was not just because they accepted a psychology that privileged reason over will and appetite, held didactic views of literary value, or harbored a humanist preference for applicable truths.[29]

Some link Gargantua less to romance than to jesting tales of antisocial or gross behavior. Probably the same motives are at work that led many to read him as a romance figure: soliciting applause for those who frustrate or outwit the sober, Scoggin and his like might well dismay anyone distressed by the potential dangers to public order of ingenuity and the imagination.

Exemplifying this dynamic is a tantrum by the learned "Puritan" divine, Edward Dering. His *Brief and Necessary Instruction* (1572) laments his time's taste for idle, wanton, and childish works, a taste even more degraded than that for such earlier "enchauntmentes" as Bevis, Guy of Warwick, Arthur, Huon. Worse yet are "the witles devices of Gargantua, Howleglas, Esop, Robyn Hoode, Adam Bel, Frier Rushe, the Fooles of Gotham, and a thousand such other." Worst of all are saints' lives (sig. A2v). The progression is from medieval romances with dangerous but lovely fantasy, to supposedly funny tales with japes and escapades ("devices"), to papist fictions that distract readers from the worship they owe God. It is odd to see Aesop here, but Dering may have felt that tales about talking animals constitute a jestbook, whatever their lessons in worldly prudence. Lumping Gargantua with "Howleglas," moreover, may hint at what the lost *Gar[a]gantua* looked like, for *Admirables* ends with a picture of that trickster as a trumpeter taken from a woodcut made by Hans Baldung Grien for the 1515 *Tyll Ulenspiegel* (see *NRB* 127). Gargantua is no Panurge, yet he has some Tyll in him.

Gargantua's unreality had already served Dering's sarcasm. In *A Sparing Restraint of Many Lavishe Untruthes, Which M. Doctor Harding Dothe Chalenge* (1568), he accuses Catholics of inciting the laity to read about Robin Hood, Guy, Bevis, Tristram, Lancelot, and Merlin so that they might forget about Paul, Peter, James, and John (sig. B3v).[30] Perhaps because Gargantua had recently appeared in English, Dering singles him out when correcting Harding's understanding of fiction. John Jewell had written: "It is reported" that Pope Hildebrand was a sorcerer and that "Henry the Emperour, and Pope Victor" were "poisoned in the Communion." In objecting to this, says Dering, Harding assumes that calling something "reported" is the same as calling it true. The point, he explains, is not the stories' truth but rather the undeniable existence of counterfactual narratives as reportable untruths: "What if no man defendeth Papistrie, but enimies of Gods worde, and true religion, yet we may say, that Papistrie is defended? We may say of Gargantua, that it is reported. Of the Legend of lyes that they are written . . . and yet is there no controversie, but these are all lyes" (sig. R4). Philip Sidney might object that Gargantua is no lie but poetry. To Dering, Gargantua is real (and ominous) enough to be a "lie."

Dering is calmer than N. Baxter, who opens a 1580 translation of Calvin's sermons on Jonah by denouncing evil books. God's ministers are scorned, he says, in prose owing more to recent court fashion than to Gospel simplicity; and he notes with outrage what Rabelais had put satirically: romances outsell Bibles. We have

> tennis in steede of the Testament, the cardes in steede of the Catechisme, the boules in steede of the Bible: yea and that more is, men thinke they have made a very good change. We see some men bestowe their time in writyng, some in printyng, and moe men in readyng of vile and blasphemous, or at least of prophane and frivolus bookes, suche as are that infamous legend of K. Arthur (whiche with shame enough I heare to bee newly imprinted) with the horrible actes of those whoremasters, Launcelot du Lake, Tristram de Liones, Gareth of Orkney, Merlin, the lady of the Lake, with the vile and stinking story of the Sangreall, of K. Peleus, etc. some again studye the lives of Huon of Burdeaux, and king Oberon, the king of the Fairies, of Valentine and Orson, . . . some are expert . . . in the court of Venus, some in the Jests of Scoggen the kinges dizzard: some in the subtleties of Howleglas, and Gargantua: some again (and to many) in the pestilent pollicies of that Mahounde Matchiavile: in the puddle of pleasure, and Forist of histories [that is, *Painters Palace of Pleasure* and Belleforest]. (Sigs. A3–A3v)[31]

Baxter's useful list, though, might brighten Hell's sales brochure. Like Dering, he wants to show that sin is multiple, a dappled Wood of Error, but he cannot escape the old dilemma: naming foulness extends its life.

Other Lenten spirits repeated such charges, varying names and titles but hostile to "imaginings" and sometimes to "novelty" and "policy" as well. It is unlikely that all such imprecations derive from personal knowledge: these are Virtue's attack commercials in her campaign against Vice. Introducing his translation of Eusebius (1584), Meredith Hanmer frets that although the queen has liberated the Gospel, courtiers prefer Arthur, "monstrous fables of Garagantua," Bevis, jestbooks, the *Palace of Pleasure* ("though there follow never so much displeasure after"), Reynard the Fox, and "amorous toyes" (1607 ed., sig. ¶3).[32] Francis Meres makes an analogous point in his *Palladis Tamia* (1598), a point derived, as he says, from the French moralist François de La Noue's *Politicke and Militarie Discourses*. Agreeing that books like *Amadis* hurt youths as much as Machiavelli hurts their elders, Meres notes helpfully that "these bookes are accordingly to be censured of, whose names follow: Bevis of Hampton, Guy of Warwicke, Arthur of the round table, Huon of Burdeaux, Oliver of the castle, the foure sonnes of Aymon, Gargantua, Gireleon, the Honour of Chivalrie, Primaleon of Greece, Palmerin de Oliva, the 7. Champions, the Myrror of Knighthood, Blancherdine, Mervin, How-leglasse, the stories of Palladyne, and Palmendos, the blacke Knight, the Maiden Knight, the history of Caelestina, the Castle of Fame, Gallian of France, Ornatus and Artesia, etc." (sigs. Mm4–4v). The usual suspects have been rounded up, and if we are not invited to interrogate them at least we know who they are.[33]

Some allusions are friendlier. In a well-known letter to a city friend on Leicester's 1575 party for Elizabeth at Kenilworth, Robert Langham gives an account of a Captain Cox's library.[34] Cox is a mason, "hardy az Gawyn" (ll. 645–46), who struts about in a borrowed cap and leads a company in mock battle. Playing an antimasque role in the festivity, he provokes mock excitement: "But aware, keep bak, make room noow, heer they cum. And fyrst captin Cox, an od man I promiz yoo." An authority "in matters of story," Cox owns

> king Arthurz book, Huon of Burdeaus, The foour suns of Aymon, Beavys of hampton, The squyre of lo degree, The knight of curteyzy, and the Lady Faguell, Frederik of Gene, Syr Eglamoour, Syr Tryamoour, Syr Lamwell, Syr Isembras, Syr Gawyn, Olyver of the Castl, Lucres and Eurialus, Virgyls lyfe, The castl of Ladyez, The wydo Edith [a verse jestbook by Thomas More's servant Walter Smith], The king and the tanner, Fryar Rous, Howleglas, Gargantua, Robin hood, Adambell Clym of the clough and Wylliam a clooudsley, The churl and the Burd, The seaven wyse Masters, The wyfe lapt in a Morrels skyn, The sak full of nuez, The sargeaunt that becam a Fryar [a comic poem by Thomas More], Skogan, Collyn cloout [by Skelton], The Fryar and the boy, Elynor Rumming [also by Skelton], and the Nutbrooun mayd with many mo then I rehearz heer.

Cox also owns Nostradamus, "The ship of foolz," "The hundred mery talez," "The seaven sororz of wemen," and more than a hundred ballads "wrapt up in Parchment and boound with a whipcord."

The books have been taken as a real library, evidence of what the middling sort was reading in 1575.[35] But "Letter"'s levity makes it suspect as reportage. The author is a man of the court writing humorously to a Londoner about pastimes that do not take themselves or the locals solemnly. The account of a rustic wedding, for example, tells of the middle-aged bride's attendants with "lips so demurely simpring, az it had been a mare cropping of a thistl" (ll. 520–21, 535–36). Langham's affectionately patronizing humor is at work in the section on Cox's books, even if Cox was a real man with real books, and even if Langham liked him. This is a witty court employee's conglomeration, the joke lying in a proliferation of current but not courtly titles and the tone hinting at a shift in taste—somewhat delayed in England—that was to push popular and elite cultures further apart. The split is not yet a chasm, though, and even sophisticates could enjoy these books.

Years later the mock-heroic note has descended further on the social scale. The compiler of *Dobsons Drie Bobbes* (1607; a "bob" is a jibe) says that the "meriments" of George Dobson, "Sonne and Heire to Skoggin" in the city of Durham, are "worthy to be registred among the famous Recordes of the jeasting Worthies: yea hee hath proceeded farther in degree than Garagantua, Howleglasse, Tiell, Scoggin."[36] As a set, the Nine Worthies had become objects of amusement. Once the theme of tapestry and elite story, they had been translated by Richard Johnson into merchant knights and degraded by the efforts of Costard, Armado, and Holofernes to please the swells of *Love's Labor's Lost* with a show presenting them. Yet ambivalence persisted. Shakespeare invites sympathy for the unworthy performers, and whoever wrote *Drie Bobbes* posits a reader who can enjoy Dobson's crudities and yet know that the real Worthies, as Worthies, are now passé.

Gargantua's most convoluted tie to romance, though, may be a brief allusion in Francis Beaumont's *Knight of the Burning Pestle* (ca. 1607, pub. 1613). This clever grotesque of a comedy, out of which protrudes a merchant's pseudoromance, is haunted by giants. To call it carnivalesque would be oversimple, for the matron who bends the play to her old-fashioned tastes opposes such pleasures as tobacco until at last, softened, she offers the company hospitality and pipes. Nor does her husband approve young love or his wife's urgency ("contain thyself," he says). Still, Beaumont exploits transgression: a lover aims too high; a heroine says, "I dare be better than a woman"; playgoers seize the stage; citizens revise Jacobean taste into something more Elizabethan; new money blusters in a hybrid dialect of old ideals and new mobility. There are even generic turnarounds. It is the older suitor who draws metaphors from

Carnival's fat food and the paternal Mr. Merrythought who answers his critics with ballad snatches, praises laughter as medicine, ignores tomorrow, makes scatological insults, and lets his family back over the threshold only when they sing.

In the play, it will be recalled, a London grocer and his wife force the comedy into a romance. Like Captain Cox, their apprentice, Rafe, is a reader. Marginal because young and living in two worlds, he is urged to "Speak a huffing part" (Induction, l. 75). Offstage Londoners were also finding a "part" that was as yet without its own language and dependent on that of chivalry.[37] The disparity between Rafe's reading and his status thus parallels the play's clash of discourses, and in that clash Mrs. Merrythought hears giants. When George, the boy playing Rafe's squire, says: "Mirror of knighthood, this is, as I take it, the perilous Waltham Down, in whose bottom stands the enchanted valley," Mrs. Merrythought cries to her own son: "O, Michael, we are betrayed. Here be giants. Fly, boy; fly, boy; fly!" (II.105–08). Rafe, too, knows enough to fear giants, having already remarked that "They do much hurt to wand'ring damsels that go in quest of their knights" (I.230–31), and his mistress thinks that Portugal's king cannot eat without them snatching his food. Is she thinking of harpies?

This collision of worlds and the presence of "giants" dominate the central act. Visiting an inn that he thinks a castle, Rafe hears from the host that "there is twelve shillings to pay" (III.149). Rafe's boss pays the debt for the sake of the show, but the question remains: How do old values relate to modern money? Mammon himself asks this of an evasive Sir Guyon in *The Faerie Queene*. Spenser's knight has no good reply to Money's reminder that chivalry now demands cash: "Thou that doest live in later times, must wage / Thy workes for wealth" (II.vii.18). The play's tug between knightly fantasy and "twelve shillings to pay" is enacted as a Gigantomachia when Rafe hears of a local giant, "Barbarossa." The name plays on his "true" identity as a barber-surgeon while connoting hairy redness, a giant's primitive wrath—and evoking King Barbarossa, who sleeps in his cave until, like Arthur, he will awaken and resume power. His is not the only significant name: Rafe's "squire" George and Mrs. Merrythought's son Michael recall greater heroes.

The barber shop has become a cave "in which an ugly giant now doth won, / Ycleped Barbarossa." Calling on Saint George, Rafe sets forth. The battle is joined, and once again Rafe cries, "Saint George for me," answered by the "giant"'s "Gargantua for me!" Gargantua is the violent force that captures and imprisons, patron of a being that Rafe calls a "presumptuous" rebel against the "just gods." This is funny, but Beaumont has also intriguingly opposed this giant force to England's dragon-killing patron, just as the folklore Gargantua seems to have yielded some hills to shining Saint Michael. Also suggestive of

deeper energies at work is the procession of liberated "victims" like Sir Pock-
hole, who even while complaining of the tyrant's "loathsome den" indicates
through more than one double entendre ("my bones did ache," for example)
that Barbarossa has been treating his pox. This protégé of Gargantua's has the
same pocky company that Rabelais's prologues had welcomed as readers. The
"giant" is not killed, only made to kiss Rafe's pestle (a scene, and maybe a pun,
to ponder), but Mrs. Citizen is right that "a giant is not so soon converted as
one of us ordinary people." The chronicles had attempted such a conversion in
making Gargantua Arthur's servant, but in England the conversion did not
always hold.

A generation later Gargantua remained a companion to jesters and knights.
Henry Glapthorne's *Wit in a Constable,* acted in 1639, opens as a servant sorts
his master's books, having already spent two days, he reports, separating
"Poets from Historians." When a friend advises the master that beyond reading Aretino and Ovid, what a gentleman really needs is good clothes, the latter
sells off his library, including his dictionary and prayerbook, and pretends to
the lady he is wooing that "I ne're read book in all my life, except / The
Counter scuffle, or the merry Gossips, / Raynard the Foxe, Tom Thumbe, or
Gargantua, / And those I've quite forgotten: I a schollar! / He lyes in's throat
that told you so." The miser's daughter to whom he gives this (unwelcome)
assurance is unimpressed: she herself has recently laughed at a vulgar youth
who courts her with terms picked up, she says, from "the learned Legends of
Knights Errants" and — such was the hunger of this topos to ingest new titles
— "The Knight o' the Burning Pestle."[38]

If Gargantua's name can figure in parodic romance, in the works of John
Taylor it contributes to the persona of a jesting worthy; even a compliment to a
fellow jester, Tom Coryat, cites the latter's "wits Gargantua Colume."[39]

It is hard to know what to make of the "Water Poet" (Taylor was a water-
man, rowing passengers along the Thames). The *DNB* calls his books "brutal,"
which seems harsh for so unassuming a writer. Even his royalist politics bark
harder than they bite, despite jokes like an anagram in his 1643 *Mercurius
Aquaticus* that turns "A New Assembly" into "Many Blew As[s]es" (sig. B3v).
More recently, he has been called "inventive, witty, passionate, often a shrewd
observer and endlessly curious about his world."[40] The persona he constructs
is loquacious, loyal, possessing a good eye for folly, lowbrow compared to
egghead professors ("all my Schollership is Schullership"), and, although ignorant of foreign tongues, able to admire the by-now translated Du Bartas and
Cervantes, paraphrase Montaigne, and mention Rabelais on nits.[41]

Taylor may have thought Rabelais wrote *Gar[a]gantua,* but even though he
claimed not to know French his work has parallels with that of the "real"
Rabelais. He likes scatology and indecency (a whore, "though she seeme

unmeasur'd in her pleasure, / 'Tis otherwayes, a Yard's her onely measure"); carnival (see *Jacke a Lent . . . with the Mad Prankes of His Gentleman-Usher Shrove-Tuesday*); made-up tongues and made-up books.[42] Panurge himself would envy Sir Gregory Nonsense's polyglot throat-clearing: "After three sighs, smilingly uttered in the Hebrew Character, two grones from the Chaldean Dialect, five sobs from the Arabian Sinquapace, six dumps from the Germane Idiome, nine Moods of Melancholly from the Italian tongue, with one hub hub from the Hibernian outcry . . . he laughed in the Cambrian tongue, and began to declare in the Utopian speech, what I have here with most diligent negligence Translated into the English Language."[43] In *The Praise of Hemp-Seed* (1620) the claim that hemp and flax are the male and female of one species makes Taylor's tribute even closer to Rabelais's digression in *TL* 49–52 on the hempen/flaxen herb Pantagruelion. Like that plant, Taylor's hemp helps sailors link countries, rings bells, encourages mercers, discourages crooks, raises questions about naming, makes paper and drapery, sustains lawyers, and (more explicitly than in Rabelais) spreads the Gospel. Taylor cites many paradoxical encomiasts, but not Rabelais.

Taylor occasionally includes "Gargantua" in his hyperkinetic jostle of names. Sometimes "Gargantua" means "big," as when Taylor exclaims at the size of some "Gogmagog Gargantua Geese."[44] More often, the giant fools around in whimsical verses such as those hailing a stalwart captain: "Thou never fear'dst to combate with Garganto, / Thy fam's beyond the battaile of Lepanto."[45] Taylor's method is to mix names, frames of reference, and levels of diction without slowing his lines' forward quickstep march. A brief sonnet sequence on Tom Coryat begins: "Conglomerating Ajax, in a fogge / Constulted [played the fool together] with Ixion for a tripe, / At which Gargantua tooke an Irish bogge, / And with the same gave Sisiphus a stripe."[46] *Sir Gregory Nonsence* (1622), with its liminary alphabet of such authorities as Amadis, "Garagantua," Long Meg, Nobody, Tom Thumb, and "Yard of Ale," says that "three salt Ennigmates well appli'd / With fourscore Pipers and Arions Harpe, / Might catch Garagantua through an augor-hole."[47] In 1653 lines still fall from the same mold: "We have both eight and eighteen parts of speech, / Whereby I learn Ash burns as well as Beech, / Gargantua's scull is made a frying pan / To fry or follow the Leviathan."[48] The whale's grandson meets Hobbes's 1651 title page.

Sizing up the Giant

Because Gargantua is bigger than other giants, many allusions play on his size. To some, it is risible; to others, it represents much that is wrong with the world: pride, misused speech, and opposition to the good. In this latter regard Gargantua resembles Gogmagog and Goliath, but references to him tend to be jocular or sarcastic, and he remains more literary than the former (nobody wrote a life of Gogmagog) and more secular than the latter. One matter often elicited memories of his name: the relation of the immense to the nugatory, of excess to defect, an issue with philosophical, psychological, and political implications and one that encouraged thoughts on perspective. Such thoughts precede the Renaissance. In the thirteenth century Jacques de Vitry observed that "just as we consider Pygmies to be dwarfs, so they consider us giants. . . . And in the land of the Giants, who are larger than we are, we would be considered dwarfs by them."[49] Similarly, the thirteenth-century *Image du monde* imagines that "the geaunts that ben in som place have right grete mervaylle of this that we be so lytil ayenst them; lyke as we mervaylle of them that ben half lasse than we be. . . . And they ben the Pygmans whiche ben but iii foot longe. And in lyke wise mervaylle they of us of that we ben so grete, & repute us also for geaunts."[50]

Fascination with big and little suits an age of renewed optical discovery as well of *curiosa* collections and exploration, for giants and pygmies had long been linked as geographically marginal peoples, a process that raised questions about size's relation to status. Indeed, one of the earliest English allusions to Gargantua is an unfriendly size joke. In an epistle prefaced to his handsome 1569 treatise on prodigies, *Certaine Secrete Wonders of Nature,* Edward Fenton grumbles that although God has inscribed Creation with legible marvels, "the unlearned sorte runne over the fruitlesse Historie of king Arthur and his round table Knights, and what pleasure they take in the trifeling tales of Gawin and Gargantua: the which bisides that they passe all likelihode of truth, are utterly without either grave precept or good example" (sigs. A3–A3v). The book that follows offers an amazing array of portents and wonders: the Gargantua chronicles are only slightly less credible, although, as Fenton says, not as edifying. Since Gawain was sometimes called a giant, this reference to "trifling" tales about him and Gargantua is an acerbic oxymoron.

Fenton's dismissal of romance marvels on behalf of his own monsters raises a question: Was Gargantua a monster? Giants are what most people mean by monsters, more monstrous than the whales and giraffes in Ambrose Paré's book on teratology, for example. But, like those whales and giraffes in the view of other authorities, a giant might be a *lusus naturae,* a sport or joke of nature.[51] Whether as sports or monstrous races, giants and pygmies have a connection with illusion and ingenuity, which is why the name Gargantua figures in comments on fantasy and stratagem. Jokingly or scoffingly, therefore, Gargantua was sometimes grotesquely juxtaposed to his opposite, whether dwarf, generic pygmy, or one famous creature who had, perhaps, his own ancient genealogy in folklore, even if printed English references to him do not start until the late 1570s.

It was probably Richard Johnson who first introduced Tom Thumb to Gargantua. Indeed, he claims that Tom is "of more antiquity" than "that monster of men," "Garragantua."[52] His *History of Tom Thumb* (1621) centralizes the mini-pygmy by displacing the maxi-giant. I assume that this intertextual — intermonstrous — foolery was deliberate: Johnson was not thick-witted. Tom is a champion of King Arthur in that golden time when plowmen could "come uncontroled to a Royal Princes presence" and a farmer could be "of the Kings Counsell." Johnson was no revolutionary, but his joking nostalgia and his replacement of the big by the little would have had resonance for his implied audience of city tradesmen and apprentices. Outfitted as smartly for his size as the chronicle Gargantua had been for his, Tom sets out on adventures that, like the giant's, involve considerable scatology: here, too, the pygmy has tried to overtake Gargantua, although, in another reversal, he is the victim of farts and swallowings, not their perpetrator. Perhaps because the book's perspective arises from so near the ground, its giants are the boasters and eaters of legend. One sits alone in his moated castle, "boyling, broyling and roasting the joynts and quarters of men, devouring them all one after another" (p. 15). In spite of his taste for cooked meat and his upscale residence, he carries an oak branch, lacks candles, and roars out in the darkness, "Now fi, fee, fau, fan."

Vomited up by this giant, swallowed and disgorged by a fish (analogue of the whale that figures in Rabelais and the chapbooks), and now "a Courtier" with a coach, Tom encounters Gargantua one day as the giant is out riding "to solace himselfe, his horse being of that great bignesse, as is described in the booke of his honourable deedes, and himselfe being in height not inferiour to any steeple" (p. 24). But Gargantua has changed. No royal champion, he is the old enemy of civilization. Unlike the giant in his castle, though, he takes the air, and although he calls himself "the terror of the people," he does not view Tom as food. Rather, perhaps dimly recognizing a folklore sibling who has ousted him as Arthur's pet, he carries on like any giant windbag. When he laughs so that "the whole earth where he stood shooke," he does so scornfully. This, too, is a departure: once, he had laughed "graciously" from such delighted love of Arthur that the noise resounded for seven leagues (*CA* 18). Although Johnson's *History* is cheerful, its festivity is more thinly layered than that of *Admirables,* and the difference between the two laughs parallels shifts in the cultural weather. Stuart England was hardly joyless, and carnival is still with us, but the changes some have sensed — Peter Burke's "triumph of Lent" — are just audible here.

Now comes a contest between big and little. Gargantua asks, "Who was the better man, and could doe the most wonders"? and then brags: "I can blow downe a Steeple with my breath, I can drowne a whole towne with my pisse, I can eate more then a hundred, I carry more then a hundred, I can kill more then a hundred: all this can I do, now tell what thou canst doe?" (p. 25). Such boasts recall Gargantua's old prowess with piss and mouth, as well as the connection giants have with wind and steeples, but the bullying arrogance is unlike his old self. Tom subverts such excess through cunning, diminuendo, and abstention — even sexual knowledge is displaced from Gargantua to the tiny voyeur who operates through lack and absence and whose capacities as a spy must be handy at court:

> I can doe more then this, saide Tom Thumbe, for I can creepe into a keyhole, and see what any man or woman doe in their private chambers, there I see things that thou art not worthy to know. I can saile in an egge-shel, which thou canst not: I can eate lesse then a Wren, and so save victuals: I can drinke lesse then a Sparrow, and therefore I am no drunkard: I cannot kill a Rat with my strength, and therefore am no murtherer: these qualities of mine are better then thine in all mens judgements, and therefore great monster I am thy better.
> (P. 25)

Baffled by logic working by negation and "lesse" — a puzzle to one defined by "more" — Gargantua is furious, and "would with his foote have kicked downe the whole wood, and so have buried Tom Thumbe." But Tom immobilizes him with a spell and then, leaving him poised on one foot (half-detached from the natural matrix of giants), returns to court to recount his adventure to an "amazed" Arthur. And so the book ends. From the flaccid verse version of 1630, which eliminates Gargantua, we know that Tom will die and be taken to Fairyland. Again, he follows in giant footsteps, for the chapbook Gargantua rests in Avalon.[53]

Johnson follows a common tendency to make famous figures fit a generic norm or familiar type. This process began almost at once with Gargantua after he reached England, yet it is unlikely that everyone who considered him another Goliath or Ascapart had read *Gar[a]gantua*. Johnson had, which is why he could undo it so intelligently. Others, too, linked Gargantua with some minuscule figure, but none is more provocative in playing with the paradoxical virtues of defect.

For the most part it is the indecorum of juxtaposing big and little that troubles or amuses these writers. Robert Farley simply rejects monsters of either extreme: his Neo-Latin poem *Neanica* (Edinburgh, 1628) urges schoolteachers to avoid sterile and witless *nugae*, whether tiny *figmenta* like *Polliculus*

(Thumbkin) or big ones like Gargantua (sig. B2v). Despite the pallid wit of calling Gargantua nugatory and finding the Latin for "Tom Thumb," Farley's elegant lines are sober stuff and his rejection of fripperies a predictable sign of wider cultural and pedagogical prejudices. His advice, though, may hint that flexible or desperate schoolmasters and schoolmistresses were giving *Tom Thumb* and *Gar[a]gantua* to young pupils.

Farley would have dismissed as figmenta the chapbooks of Martin Parker, but to a relaxed eye they have raffish charm. *Harry White His Humor* (1637) reports White's earthy yet playful opinions, one-liners that read as though some sturdy yeoman had hired Henny Youngman ("Item. He cares not much for a dancing-schoole, because if need be [rather than fast] he can eat Mutton without capers" or "Item. He is loath to marry a Widow because he will not taste of that which another man dyed after"; sigs. A6–A7).[54] White has read the chapbooks, whether ironically or naively: "Item. He is of this opinian, that if the histories of Garragantua and Tom Thumbe be true, by consequence Bevis of Hampton, and Scoggins Jests must needes bee Authenticall" (sig. A8). Whatever Parker's own views (he also wrote pamphlets about Arthur, Guy of Warwick, and Robin Hood), his giant and pygmy are, again, company for both knights and tricksters and, like them, both objects and means of thought on fiction.

Less insipid is Parker's nonsense *Legend of Sir Leonard Lack-wit,* printed in 12,000 ("Or else," says the title page, "1633") and "Translated out of all Christian Languages into the Kentish tongue." Parker knew that effective nonsense requires correct form, so he provides liminary poems; dedications; an "Alphantasticall (Alphabeticall, I should have said)" list of authorities, including Cock Robin, Elinor Rumming, Ignatius Loyola, Ogier the Dane, Robin Goodfellow, Xantippe, and Zoroaster; and such errata as "for merchant read a meere cheater ... for Poetry read poverty." Like Gargantua's biographers, he is precise ("Asculapius gave a glister to Aristippus, and made him vomit as much hors-bread as served to feed Bucephalus eight hundred yeeres and fifty foure moneths," sig. A8). He also likes mixing categories ("The Turkish Sultan led an army into Plutarches Morals," sig. A8v); reversals like making Gogmagog a pygmy (sig. C1v); hudibrastic rhymes ("I that lived like a Lord among thy Laquies, / Now know not at what rate a pint of Sacke is," sig. B5v); and irreverence toward celebrity ("An invincible navy of Gnats . . . landed at Rotterdam; which so amazed Erasmus, that he turned over twelve leaves of his Booke," sig. B2).[55] Let doubters, Parker says, read the "incredible true Histories of Garagantua, Tom Thumbe, Bevis of Southampton, with a thousand more, and they shall finde that unlesse there bee lyes in them, this must needs bee true. Yet the Authors who published those, thought they had wit enough:

but I in my Title confesse lacke of wit; and therefore I hope I am the more excusable" (sig. C2). Gargantua and Tom — the odd couple — once more sustain the problematic world of unreality. Perhaps in 1633 Parker was not yet fussed by England's growing political divisions, but his later royalist writings suggest that he found burlesques, nonsense, and romances pleasantly unpuritanical — "popular" in the way bells, bonfires, football, and May games were popular: subversive not of kings and bishops but of their glum opponents.

Paired opposites can indicate disquietude or desire. Again, giants are double-natured, for although it would seem from their size and antiquity that they should represent parents (as babies we have all been Toms or Thumbelinas to adult Gargantuas and Badebecs), they are allied to the infantile. Guarding, blocking, or marking the threshold, they terrify because the future is as yet unreal — and will swallow us up. This may further explain why Gargantua appears in attacks on romances (like monsters and the future, romances are structures of the imaginary) and why the Renaissance, witness to so many transitions, had such an interest in giants. Sometimes the threshold is political. Spenser might reject the leveling giant in Book V of *The Faerie Queene* (although it was he who invented him), but to John Hare, writing in 1642, giants are in the right: Enceladus, "eternal monument of dejected greatness" who sighs "sulphureous blasts of indignation" from underneath Aetna, is a model to Englishmen who lie so abjectly beneath Norman oppression's "mountain of dishonour."[56] Renaissance giants were erected by a culture that was aghast at excess even as it incubated excesses to come.

Several appearances by Gargantua show this ambiguity. When talk turns to the topic of hierarchy in Thomas Nashe the Younger's *Quaternio* (1633), a dialogue on various walks of life, a lawyer argues that just as laws "binde Subjects in loyall obedience to their Soveraignes," servants must obey their masters, pupils their tutors, and children their parents (1639 ed., sigs. S1–S1v). We should not "place age where youth should fit, nor yet youth where age should fit; Mars where Mercurie should fit, nor yet Mercurie where Mars should fit, for that were to put the Gyants habit upon the little Pigmee, and the Pigmees habit upon the great Gargantua." Nashe doubtless agreed that giants should remain giants, and pygmies (that is, most of us) pygmies. Yet his analogy has problems: if Gargantua is a joke, and if nobody has seen an actual pygmy, the analogy needs rethinking. Nor is it wise to compare authority to Gargantua, considering giants' habit of drowning and swallowing us. Opposing Gargantua to a pygmy opens a gulf between governor and governed that leaves no room for hierarchy and intermediaries, for parliaments, mothers, and teaching assistants. In sum, Monstrosity supports Nashe's humor but betrays his argument: Gargantua is a father figure to give any pygmy pause.

Another unsteady perspective on big and little enlivens a moment in Thomas Randolph's *Hey for Honesty,* a modernization of Aristophanes' *Plutus* that was composed in the late 1620s. The comedy's relevance grew as Britain's constitutional crisis worsened, so in the late 1640s one "F.J." updated it and the new version saw print in 1651.[57] In one scene, three bumpkins, a rich parson, and Poverty debate curing the blindness of Plutus, the god of wealth who distributes his favor with so little insight. Because a sharp-eyed Plutus might revise the economy, talk turns to equality. According to Poverty, "Plutus makes men with puffed faces, dropsy bodies, bellies as big as the great tub at Heidelberg; . . . I keep men spare and lean, slender and nimble; mine are all diminutives, Tom Thumbs; not one Colossus, not one Garagantua amongst them; fitter to encounter the enemy by reason of their agility, in less danger of shot for their tenuity, and most expert in running away, such is their celerity."[58] Poverty's boast had bite in the 1640s, but it raises questions. If it is best to be poor, should we not change Gargantuas into Toms? Although "F.J." prefers the old order, even a new one would wrestle with such issues: Can one fatten the little without making it big? Must old priest be writ large as new presbyter? Will parliamentary Toms swell into executive Gargantuas?[59]

The younger Nashe had imagined inverted hierarchy as a pygmy and giant swapping clothes; others fancied a giant outfit dwarfing its wearer, forcing him to play Tom Thumb to his costume's Gargantua. Samuel Purchas's *Purchas His Pilgrim* (1619) sets big against little to explore other and same. Indians in Virginia, he says, have taught some to wear the "sinister Love-Locke" that Tomocomo, a native, told Purchas that his tribe had learned from its devil. But because Purchas knows that to foreigners the English are the aliens, and because he has a semi-satirical agenda, he asks what might a "Traveller thinke of [a European's] Gargantuan bellyed-Doublet with huge huge sleeves, now with a contrarie smalnesse imprisoning his body? and the then Ghost-like, skin-close Breeches, since volumniously swolne into Rolles, Slops, Barratashes, Bumbasted Plaits, and Sailers knee-sacks, (as if we minded to . . . keep the Taylor a continuall Novice, in getting his Trade as well as his Money)" (sigs. S5–S6).[60] Purchas is no Montaigne defending cannibals, but his shift of perspective is refreshing.

Richard Brathwait, too, was disturbed by modern dress. His *English Gentlewoman* (1631) defends gender difference against a riot of ruffs, hoods, and fancy cloth. He does not warn his lady against male clothing, but his plea that she be plain and moderate — ungigantic — is meant to keep her feminine. The book gives itself more liberty: indulging in his own cross-dressing, Brathwait imagines his tract as a lady "adorned" with "divers ornaments" and "many choice endowments," but without the "Phantasticke habits or forraine fashions" that might "disfigure" her. This idealized lady (the book and the woman it fashions) has "a covenant with her eyes never to wander," is unambitious, and shows her lineage through gracious self-government. The lady/text, adds Brathwait, will walk with the lady/reader and tell her "time-beguiling Tales." One of these comes in a section advising against "Phantastike" dress. A good woman will "wear" Christ, not soft silks, for "Delicacy in the habit begets an effeminacy in the heart" (sigs. C1v–3v). Since Brathwait means to fashion a lady, not a gentleman, this seems needless counsel. By *effeminate,* though, he may mean sexually undefined. A lady should have female modesty and — although Brathwait does not put it like this — manly self-control. Inward masculine rectitude will prevent the rest of her from relaxing into a sensuality that blurs the outline of gender.

"Superfluity of Apparell," continues Brathwait, is selfish and proud, as witness those many who, ignoring the naked and needy, "will have long garments, purposely to seeme greater" (sig. C4). Such a one was the "diminutive Gentleman" who asks his tailor how many "yards of Sattin would make him a Suite." Hearing a number smaller than he expected, he "with great indignation replied, 'Such an one of the Guard to my knowledge had thrice as much for a Suite, and I will second him.' " Hoping to profit further by keeping the leftover cloth, the tailor agrees to make "a Gargantua's Suite for this Ounce of mans flesh, reserving to himselfe a large portion of shreads, purposely to forme a fitter proportion for his [the short gentleman's] Ganimede shape" (sig. C3v). "Gargantua" connotes "big," but what of "Ganimede"? His abduction by Zeus was sometimes allegorized as contemplative rapture, but the name more often indicated, pejoratively, the young male object of male desire.[61] What is the name doing here? "Ganimede" means "too little for such big cloth," but Brathwait's analogy hints that gender is unstable under outlandish dress: monstrous costume turns a woman into a catamite who thinks (s)he is Gargantua.

In Henry Glapthorne's *The Hollander* (1635, printed 1640), Gargantua's name appears, less directly, in a more comic confusion over gender. The "Hollander" is Sconce, a deep drinker and overweight "naturalized Dutchman" who boasts an ancestry going back almost sixty years to "Duke Alvas time." (Why he swears in French — "A mon Dieu," "Foutra!" — is unexplained; bad company, maybe.) A Captain Pirke, on the other hand, is a short, angry, and vainglorious "Tom Thumbe." At one point, as part of a scheme to rob Sconce, he agrees to pretend to knight him. His co-conspirators find the disparity in size funny, asking what the little captain will dub the big Hollander. Pirke replies, "Gargantua."[62] Of course: Sconce is large, noisy, and a boozer. The comedy eventually maneuvers this Gargantua into an amazing shuffle of sexual identities. Sconce has, for convoluted reasons, been married in female disguise to a woman dressed as a man. Bewildered, he says to his new spouse, "But let me see and feele you better, it is no periwigge this but are you my husband, a woman, wife?" Dismayed to find her indeed female, he asks for an unguent to "eat off the wen of manhood, make all whole before . . . I would faine be a Hermaphrodite, or a woman to escape this match, I do not like it." Poor "Gargantua," though, cannot find a female w/holeness and must keep his male "wen."[63]

Bigmouth

Gar[a]gantua featured a giant of huge appetite, evacuations, and laughter.[64] Nor was he sexless: his French original writes love verse and makes his penis a bridge for soldiers. Yet there are few English allusions to this. As a giant he is phallic, but not like Spenser's *gigas erectus* Orgoglio (incarnation of the hero's own tumescent desire).[65] It was his mouth that drew the most notice: laughter or disgust at the chronicles' indecency being displaced upward, at least in print. Even a mention of soiled Gargantuan breeches in Jonson's *Every Man in His Humor* (1598, I.iv.123–30) has a context of belligerent speech, as though the loose anus represented the angry mouth. Was this stress on the mouth prudery? Or awareness that although men rape and murder, giants (like dragons and whales) swallow people?[66] Gargantua never does so on purpose, preferring a human diet, supplemented with boats and windmills. Traditionally, though, into a giant go people and structures and out come challenges and scoffs. So, although Gargantua is not in fact given to sneers or bragging, the English used his name to figure oral danger or excess.

In his 1593 *Pierces Supererogation*, Gabriel Harvey called Tom Nashe a "huge Gargantua of prose, and more then the heaven-surmounting Babell of Rhyme" (sig. Z2). Nashe returned the compliment. *Have with You to Saffron-Walden* (1596) tells how just one of Harvey's *Four Letters* outweighed a barrel of herring and three Holland cheeses; his door had to be removed merely to get this "Gogmagog Jewish Thalmud of absurdities" inside. Yet when he comes "to unrip and unbumbast this Gargantuan bag-pudding," he finds only "dogstripes, swines livers, oxe galls, and sheepes gutts."[67] The letters make "an unconscionable vast gorbellied Volume . . . more boystrous and cumbersome than a payre of Swissers omnipotent galeaze breeches." Nashe's style is so "popular" in its jigs and leaps that it is easy to forget the hostility with which the author viewed rebellion and change. Novel in manner, Nashe was conservative in much of his spirit, even when not paid to be; perhaps it was his dislike of the new (Puritans), the old (Catholicism, romances), and the other (Spain, Italy, Jews) that led him to mention giants so often. Martin Marprelate is a "whelpe" of their race; a Spaniard "talks like one of the Giants that made warre against Heaven"; false nobles are "buckram giants" [hollow effigies], while real aristocrats have "titles of their Gogmagognes"; the devil mingled with men "when Corineus and Gogmagog were little boyes"; and the Armada's ships were "Gargantuan boysterous gulliguts."[68] No wonder Harvey's letters say "Fy, fa, fum" (p. 37). Yet the letters are also food. This "pudding," bigger than the giants Magellan found, is bad carnival sausage. It is "Jewish," so its "absurdities" recall dietary legalism; and crammed with gall and dogmeat, it sounds inedible.[69] Worse, it is also "bumbast," stuffing for breeches. Harvey's corpulent letters, then, are idiot brothers of Nashe's own texts, pseudo-Menippean satires. Gargantua is once more in bad company: a creature of the old dispensation, he is linked with the Talmud and Gogmagog.

Harvey and Nashe were not alone in associating Gargantua with bombasted emptiness. Rabelais's eloquent Utopian kings do not talk fustian; the chapbook Gargantua is plain spoken; and folklore giants are unlikely to exchange "Ho Ho Ho" and "Fee Fi Fo Fum" for the inkhorn. Yet the notion is not illogical, granted giants' tendency to stomp their big feet and shout. Even the metaphor "stilted language" recalls how some "giants" walked in parades. This myth of giant-verse underpins tributes printed with James Shirley's *Grateful Servant* in 1630. (Shirley himself can laugh at swollen words; his Gorgon, an usher at "the Complement school" in *Love Tricks,* says things like "I will not implicate you with ambages.")[70] Philip Massinger, for instance, refuses to "raise / Giant hyperboles," while one John Fox observes that Shirley does not "swell with mighty rhymes." More cleverly, Thomas Randolph writes a parodic *recusatio:*

> I cannot fulminate or tonitruate words
> To puzzle intellects, my ninth lasse affords
> No Lycophronian buskins, nor can straine
> Gargantuan lines to gigantize thy veine.
> Nor make a jusjurand, that thy great plaies
> Are terr'd el fo-gos, or incognitaes;
> Thy Pegasus in his admir'd careere,
> Curvets no Capreols of nonsense here.[71]

Tierra del Fuego is named here because giants were said to inhabit it, as well as to suggest hitherto unknown words or the false fire of overblown inspiration. Thunder-words, I assume, stun the mind with syllabic mass: placed near the adjective *Gargantuan* they recall the old affinity of giants with storms.

Other English remarks accent Gargantua's mouth itself. It did not vex everyone. In *As You Like It* (1599), Shakespeare's Rosalind begs her cousin Celia to report to her about Orlando's appearance, speech, whereabouts, and behavior: "Answer me in one word." Celia replies, "You must borrow me Gargantua's mouth first; 'tis a word too great for any mouth of this age's size" (III.ii.214–21). Editors usually assume that Shakespeare evokes the chapbook giant. I am less sure. Gargantua is not of "this age," a term that makes sense if Celia is thinking of Arthur's servant, and her phrasing may show that she is taking sides in the debate over what time has done to human size: we are smaller now, and the giants are gone. Yet the playful notion of a physically enormous megaword containing lots of little normal words (linguistic precedent for the giant made of tiny men that dominates the title page of Hobbes's *Leviathan*) is the same sort of humor that led Rabelais to imagine frozen words, lists, and nonsense. Reading this satirical/satyrical pastoral comedy with Rabelais's Menippean world in mind gives it even more depth and texture.[72]

Nor is Gargantua the play's only giant, for Rosalind's words to Orlando as he faces the wrestler Charles, "Now Hercules be thy speed, young man" (I.ii.205), imply a contest with Antaeus. Hercules was himself a giant, or so many believed, but whereas liberators were praised as heroes, monsters such as Antaeus or Geryon were more explicitly "giants." That Shakespeare was alert to such matters explains why he transferred the association with Hercules to Orlando from Charles, where his model, Thomas Lodge's *Rosalind,* had ineptly put it. Which sort of giant is Celia's Gargantua? To meld many words into a single, giant one, not so much reversing Babel's curse as infoliating Adam's multiple sign-system back into a unitary signifier, might be monologic tyranny or parodic blasphemy. Celia's teasing tone is so sunny, however, that one may take this Gargantuan mouth as more Herculean than Antaean, a communicative hugeness that might speak, if "this age" could only borrow it, for the openness that the play tests and values.[73]

Sometimes Gargantua's mouth is simply thirsty or hungry, poignantly so in a time of chronic famine and Cockaigne dreams of limitless food. The negative version of such dreams is the fear of a deforming and selfish gluttony that, like a modern astronomer's black hole, absorbs and distorts matter and thereby denies it to others. The picture can be cheerfully sketched in, moral repugnance softened into social satire at once didactic and seductively easygoing. "W.M."'s *Man in the Moone . . . or, The English Fortune-teller* (1609) alternates black-letter descriptions of the sinners and lowlifes anxious to have their fortunes read with roman-letter forecasts of their painful futures. The result is fairly funny as well as improving, suiting a pamphlet that might as well, despite passages of mannered elegance and Latin, be called popular.

One visitor is a glutton. The well-read page Mockso calls him "Monstrum horrendum informe ingens,"[74] a "Grecian horse" of a man who must squeeze indoors "sideling, like a Gentlewoman with an huge Farthingall: how he puffeth and bloweth like a shortwinded Hackney: now he approacheth wallowing like a woman with childe: he might be an Oxe for his soule, a Bull for his necke, a Cow for his belly, and a Calfe for his wit." And, adds Mr. Opinion, "Phago ["eater"] might be his grandfather, for his full feeding, and Garagantua his Sire, for his gormandizing." Gargantua has fathered a grotesque: swollen, bestial — and sexually ambiguous, for this monster, like a man cross-dressed for carnival, resembles a pregnant woman. A hungry one, too: "A Rabbit is but a bitte with him, and he will cranch capons as fast as a begger wil cracke Lice." One day the gorging will stop, and the "gorbelly Glutton" will himself "be food for the wormes" (sigs. E2–E3).

The Gargantua of Thomas Dekker's *Shoemaker's Holiday* (acted in 1599) is harder to place. An aristocrat disguised as a Dutch cobbler finds a welcome at a London shoemaker's — but only if he is friendly: "Thou shalt be fought with, were thou bigger than a giant," says one, or "drunk with, wert thou Gargantua," adds another (I.iii.96–97). Here is a rare glance at Gargantua's drinking, inspired by the young lord's Dutch disguise. Perhaps because he is thought foreign and hence suspect, the invitation has a faintly bullying tone, an enforced conviviality with a hint of contest. The good cheer of London's "gentle craft" can, if need be, combat a reluctant giant.[75] The festivity of John Cooke's *Greene's Tu Quoque, or The Cittie Gallant* (1614) is more brittle, although Gargantua still has a good appetite. As prisoners gather to receive alms from the "Bread and Meat-man," one jailbird demands priority: "I have a stomacke like Aqua fortis, it will eate anything." He must be starving, for he is told not to drool into the basket, and when given a morsel he objects that "Heer's a bit indeed: whats this to a Gargantua stomack?" (sig. I2v). A man's body, in a hungry age, can seem to contain a giant digestive tract. In *Epigrames Served out in 52 Severall Dishes* (1604), though, Cooke thinks of Gargantua's mouth in terms of deceit. His tenth "dish" presents one Varius, a traveler who says he has caroused from "Solymans owne pot" and danced with Prester John's daughter. His "lies are monstrous great, and yet but young, / Gargantua sure was father of his Tounge" (sig. A7). Again, the image is grotesque: Gargantua achieves paternity by begetting a speaking part, if a phallic-shaped one. The giant who may seem to represent the material world becomes a comment on language.

So does the giant in "A Whetstone for Liars" (ca. 1630), a ballad on how the narrator can run to Scotland in a morning, walk on the Thames, swim naked to Greenland, and

> The victuals that would
> Gargantua sustaine
> The space of a yeere,
>   I doe hold but a bit:
> For bring me ten thousands
> Of Waynes strongly laden,
> And I in a day
>   will devoure every whit
> . . . .
> And blow thorow my nostrils
> Such a blusterous gale,
> 'Twill make thirty thousand
>   tall Ships for to sayle.[76]

The narrator adds that he hates liars. But what if lies endanger others? Polemicists found giants useful as proud scoffers, rebels, or tyrants, so Gargantua sometimes became a heretic or rebel, not least when the topic included the body — ours and Christ's — or threats to the body ecclesiastic and politic.

It would be hard to overstate how often writers used giants as a metaphor for evil. There is nothing like this in later polemic. A capitalist might be a running dog, a union leader a commie rat, a leering whistler, or a sexist pig, but rarely a giant. Liminal, phallic yet infantile, alien yet earthy like us, once real but perhaps no longer so, giants were valuable to a stressed age. Often they stood for Catholics.[77] Thomas Brice expects in 1559 "That great Golia shall be put to death, / By our good Queene Elizabeth"; Edward Campion is a Philistine champion, says Meredith Hanmer in 1581; and James I was warned against "the Popes Giants."[78] Jesuits march forth "like joly champions to encounter with the Saintes of God, bearing upon their shoulders like Atlases, the pynacles of the Romish Babylon"; Catholicism is a "Cacus fatted and pampered with the bloud of innocentes." Is the Pope a pastor? So was Ulysses' one-eyed enemy; and Jesuits, rekindling the Gigantomachia by teaching regicide, feed victims to "ille pastor Polyphemus."[79]

Arthur Golding adds Gargantua to this thuggish gang in his 1571 translation of Calvin's psalm commentary. When Ps. 73 frowns on those who speak "from aloft," a note explains: "Theis Gyantes, or one eyed Gargantuas, of whom David speaketh, not only surmyse themselves too bee lawelesse, but also beeing unmyndfull of their owne weakenesse, spit out their fome unmeasurably, as if there were no difference between right and wrong" (sigs. Mm3–Mm3v). In in his 1567 translation of Calvin's *De scandalis*, Golding had inserted the phrase "Giauntes with one eye in theyr forehead" into a reproof of the spiritually blind (*A Little Booke Concernynge Offences*, sig.

G7); now he has a name for them. He knows about Rabelais, for the same passage in *De scandalis* calls Rabelais a profane mocker, but his 1571 Gargantua may owe more to the recently printed chapbook. In any case, Golding merges a biblical mighty man, a pagan cannibal of myopic impiety, and a chapbook hero: outdoing David, he fells three species of giant with one lapidary piece of sarcasm.

So, too, William Fulke thinks of Gargantua when writing on bodies and space. His *D. Heskins, D. Sanders and M. Rastell Overthrowne* (1579) asks whether Christ can be in two places at once and whether two bodies can inhabit one place, questions that are relevant to the Mass. Heskins, says Fulke, argues that the risen Christ, a single body, can occupy many places. This is unscientific and irrational: "Heskins in this Chapter like a monstrous Gyant, cryeth open battell against naturall Philosophie and reason," thinking it enough to cite God's power. "Now riseth up this Gargantua, and will prove by scripture, that one bodie may be in another, and two bodies in one place" (sig. L2v).[80] Gargantua symbolizes a corpulent if imaginary multiplication of Christ's physical being on altars throughout Europe and beyond. He also "riseth": it is giants, not pygmies, who strain upward, and the pope is, of course, one of them. George Goodwin's *Melissa religionis pontificiae* (1620) calls the pope "Sacerdotum Gargantua," the inciter of Guy Fawkes in this novelty-loving "powder-Age."[81] Rome's "Monsters mouth and throate is large and hollow: / And, at one draught, can many thousands swallow" (sig. N8v). An "Amphibious Gorgon," the pope is a cannibal "Christ-eater" and "blood-bibbing Bishop" (sigs. K8v–L1) And just how many heads does the Church's body need?:

> But tell me this, Ghostly [spiritual] Gargantua:
> Is Christ thy Head? He is (no doubt) thou'lt say:
> Suffice thee, this Head? Yes: Well, why then,
> As well as thee, not Mee and other Men? (Sig. D3)

Is it not monstrous for the body of the faithful to have two heads? Does Rome aim to eat the globe even while trying to explode it?

Catholics likewise call their opponents giants. Protestants contend that the pope is Antichrist, complains William Rainolds's *Refutation of Sundry Reprehensions, Cavils, and False Sleightes* (Paris, 1583). Only a fool would try to refute as "palpable a lie, as any of Lucians *True Histories*." Yet Rainolds will reluctantly drop his serious studies to deal with such fantasies (sigs. a2v–a3). One is the denial of Christ's substantive presence in the bread and wine of the Mass, a denial based on mere "Aristotle and Euclide," on the "natural and mathematical conditions of a bodie" (sigs. L8v–M1). Because the issue is the relation of Christ's words ("This is my body") to flesh, space, and language, it is not surprising that giants appear in the rhetoric as Rainolds becomes heated. Protestants, he complains, call Catholics "Pigmees" whom their "Capitayne" Beza can sew "in a bagge, and knocke out their braynes, as Polyphemus did to Ulysses companions." But these "Pigmees" have "so put out the eye and diminished the estimation of your Poliphemus, that of the Catholikes he is knowen to have bene but a wicked sicophant, of detestable maners, a feared conscience, and meane learning" and no "Hercules or Atlas." When others interpret Scripture, this "Giaunt cometh and shouldereth them all out" with mistranslations. What can Beza reply? Let him be "as great as Gargantua, or the great divel of hell, if he bear away that with which we charge him withal" (sigs. P4–P5v). Gargantua's grossness again helps figure a body's relation to space and words. And he again shares rhetorical turf with Polyphemus, enemy of the wily hero who called himself Nobody and invented devices better than any the not-really-Gargantuan Beza can dream up.[82]

Protestants could also call each other giants. Aging but unmellowed, the Presbyterian John Vicars denounced John Goodwin, founder of a Congregational church on Coleman Street. Goodwin's *Conclave,* says the title page of *Coleman-Street Conclave Visited* (1648), comprises the "Heresies, Errours, Malice, Pride, and Hypocrisie of this most huge Garagantua." Bewitching others by "Swaggering Writings, full-fraught with Six-footed Terms, and flashie Rhetoricall Phrases," Goodwin's book, jeers Vicars, is in fact a "paultrey pamphlet" (sig. D3).[83] That Gargantua was a chapbook hero fits the argument's shifting perspectives: Goodwin is a "formidable white-Devill," but as a writer he is puny. He is "great Goliah," for "50, or 100 at once, are nothing for this Garagantua to encounter and scuffle with" (sig. D3v), but Vicars is David: a "poore, mean, and despicable younger brother," he will fight "this great Goliah, this huge Garagantua" who defies "the Presbyterian Army royall of the living God" (sig. G3). What makes one work a "pamphlet" and the other a "plain Display"? Nothing, except that Goliath-Gargantua speaks for Israel's enemies, while the weakling Vicars replies with authority for the Lord of Hosts.

Renaissance England made the chronicle Gargantua a conventional giant who knew his generic or symbolic place, and this treatment of him as another Ascapart, another Gogmagog, another Goliath or Polyphemus, eventually had to affect England's Rabelais. It was easy to conflate the latter's giant with this now less appealing if still rhetorically useful Gargantua, and also easy then to invest the author with his giant's presumed inanity or excess. Alarm at slander, ambivalence toward fantasy, rumors of Rabelais's atheism, and a tradition of giants as windy cannibals often coalesced into an image that left scant room for Pantagruelism. This did not mean, however, that "Rabelais" — name, work, and life — was any less valuable in giving English writers another way to convey what they felt and thought.

3

Copia Verborum *and the Seat of the Scorner*
Rabelais and the World of Words

Many Englishmen and doubtless a few Englishwomen knew the "real" *Gargantua et Pantagruel.* Even when what they say is derivative, their allusions demonstrate what cultural work "Rabelais" — name and texts — could do. Some readers delighted in his verbal overflow. Others found him, or liked to be seen to find him, a running sore.

Borrowed Babble: John Eliot's Rabelais

Ortho-epia Gallica, John Eliot's 1593 user-friendly guide to French, comprises "merrie" dialogues with "stories no lesse authenticall" than Lucian's "devises" (sig. B1v). Eliot allows that in concocting these "phantasticall plaisanteries" he has taken "a few pleasant conceits out of Francis Rabelais that merrie Grig" but insists that "put all together that I have bought, begd or borrowed, it will not all amount to make two sheets of printed paper," the rest being "of mine owne invention and disposition" (sig. B3). No it isn't. As David Thomas puts it, Eliot "skips and prances in and out of all five books of Rabelais, unfolding . . . an exquisitely contrived patchwork of colour and animation."[1] Eliot may have meant his borrowings to slip unnoticed into his crowd of speakers. Those familiar with Rabelais, though, might smile to find phrases once used for the sweatless, unorthodox Abbey of Thélème now applied to the workaholic Philip II's Escorial (sigs. I2v–I3v). The bone-gnawing dog that had allegorized the reading of allegory in *Gargantua*'s prologue reappears in a dialogue on animals (sig. v3), while the same prologue's grotesque boxes with precious drugs are now for sale in an apothecary's shop (sig. l4). Language describing Panurge is applied to a thief and a debtor, and Pantagruel's giant genealogy adorns the braggart Captain Crocodile (sig. s1).

Thomas thinks that Eliot preferred Rabelais's "comic" episodes, literalizing them to serve his realism. Perhaps so. But Eliot also enjoys verbal inventiveness and fancy. His dialogues do evoke physicality: a tailor tells a customer to stand still, a pregnant woman stops friends from jostling her, a girl shows a guest his bed and chamber pot (pertly rejecting his advances). Often, though, dialogues modulate into fantasticality and logophilia. One shop sells some exotic millinery:

> Lacke you a good hat or a cap?
> I seeke for a Bever.
> There is one which will fit you just, with the feather.
> I weare no plume.
> It becometh you very well.
> It is too large and too great for me.
> It is after the Babilonian fashion, and the feather after the Polonian slant.
> It is all the fashion now a daies. (sig. d4v)

Nor is there much realism in a shop selling pictures of "the Idees of Plato" and "the Atomes of Epicurus," a portrait of Echo, and a tapestry with seventy-eight panels depicting Achilles (sig. l1; measuring four by three fathoms, the tapestry costs ten thousand crowns). Such items are imported from *QL* 2, in which Pantagruel's crew, visiting the Isle of Medamothi (Greek for "no place"), buys these and several others just as unlikely, including unicorns and a color-changing reindeer. When a ship arrives with a message from Gargantua, Pantagruel sends his father the tapestry and animals. Alice Berry finds in this a comment on imitation, origins, and paternity, on the venture into waters that lead to exile and to freedom from the dispensation of the father. Pantagruel's gift to Gargantua is one reply to the anxieties of sonship, influence, and memory. I would add a geographical poignancy: Pantagruel reaches Medamothi — Nowhere — only to receive a message from the king of Utopia: Nowhere. Can one never leave home? And what of the future? The "transfer across generations will not stop with him," says Berry, and Pantagruel's book "must now pass into the hands of readers, who possess . . . the ability to misread and revise *him*."[2]

Eliot does just that by transporting the goods from a market in Nowhere to a shop in London. Gone is any link with fathers, exodus, origin. The issue of imitation remains, linked here to questions of identity and genre. The painter has been working on a portrait of the notoriously ugly Aesop. Pointing to it, he asks the customer's opinion. "I say that if it be Venus, she hath not her face well painted." No, says the artist, that's not Venus, and it is, "beleeve me, verie well counterfeited for a foole." But not, retorts the customer, "verie well shadowed for a wise man." And is that a picture of Christ? No, that's Tiberius. (The buyer is not the first to confuse God and Caesar.) The customer wants the pictures of atoms and so forth for his countinghouse walls, but when he offers to pay in "Jack-an-apes pence," the painter says angrily: "You mocke me. . . . Have you not prated and tatled inough yet?" (sigs. k2–l2). The dialogue evaporates into Eliot's chief interest: words. The *Quart livre*'s "monnaie de singe" that invites us to think of imitations, by sons as well as by painters, is mockery's small change. Yet the prattling customer makes a good bargain: he may never hang pictures of atoms and Ideas, but he joins a satisfying exchange system of snappy urban backtalk.

Eliot's London, then, is not as solid as it seems, whatever the stuff it imports from the newly discovered edges of its world. Undermining its physicality, if adding to its decibel level, is a fascination with language, whether different tongues or words at play. Eliot relishes puns and, like Alcofribas, slips into his text as an anagram: Master "Noe-Jonas & Ely" rearranges "Joannes Elyote." He also admires strange tongues: Mexican ones are "so flowing, full of grace and eloquence" that Greek, Latin, Italian, Spanish, and French seem "effeminate notes or barbarous prittle-prattle in comparison of their loftinesse, profoundnesse, and sweet phrase of speech." As for the Japanese, their speech is "princely, thundering, proud, glorious, and marvellous loftie." Indeed "Antarticke tongues of the East or West Indians and those of the other parts of the world, have farre greater lustre, magnificence and generousnesse in them than those that we speake in this other moitie of the Earth" (sigs. H2–H3v). What was Eden's language? In Flanders they claim to speak it, but "these are Flemish flamflues," and their tongue is in fact a "barbarous hibber-Jybber, corrupted, effeminat and variable" compared to Hebrew, in which the best writer, affirms Eliot, is God (sigs. F2–F2v).

No wonder Eliot enjoyed Rabelais's logorrhea. An account of a storm turns Panurge's terror in QL 18–21 into the sounds of sea and sky: "Dish, dash, plash, crack, rick-rack, thwack, bounce, flounce, rounce, hizze, pizze, whizze, sowze. O God helpe us and the Virgine Marie. Paish, flish, flash, rowze, rittle, rattle, battle, rish, rash, clash, swish, swash, robble, hobble, bobble" (sigs. o2–o4). Panurge's panicky nonsense disregards the reason and charity that can, with faith and sensible effort, endure the storms of fortune; Eliot is more concerned to reproduce a tempest's sizzle and splash. The opening letter to London's "gentle doctors of Gaule" is an even more impressive example of Rabelaisian overflow. Imitating the prologue to the *Tiers livre,* Eliot is Diogenes, rolling his barrel to

> turn it, overturne it, spurne it, bind it, wind it, twind it, throw it, overthrow it, tumble it, rumble it, jumble it, did ring it, swing it, fling it, ding it, made it leape, skip, hip, trip, thumpe, jumpe, shake, crake, quake, washt it, swasht it, dasht it, slasht it, naild it, traild it, tipt it, tapt it, rapt it, temperd it, tamperd it, hammerd it, hoopt it, knockt it, rockt it, rubd it, tugd it, lugd it, stopt it, unstopt it, tied it fast, then losed it againe, rusht it, crusht it, brusht it, pusht it, charmd it, armd it, farmd it, set it on end, laid it along, harnest it, varnest it, burnisht it, furnisht it, stickte it full of feathers, caparrassond it, and rold it amaine from the steepe rocke to the low bottome, overtakes it, takes it on his shoulder, mounts the hill, and turles it downe agayne with violence, staies it, plaies with it, and fetcheth it a mile from him. (Sigs. A3v–A4)

Diogenes travestied his fellow citizens' lunacy, but Eliot, like Rabelais, affects to think that the Cynic hoped to avoid seeming unpatriotically lazy: so he has "dezinkhornifistibulated a fantasticall Rapsody of dialogisme, to the end that I would not be found an idle drone among so many famous teachers and professors." "I have," he says, "labourd, sweat, dropt, studied, devised, sought, bought, borrowed, turnd, translated, mined, fined, refined, enterlined, glosed, composed, and taken intollerable toile to shew an easie entrance and introduction to my deare countrimen, in your curious and courtesan French tongue" (sig. A4).[3]

In Eliot's dialogues words do not swell or obfuscate (no Limousin scholars, no Sorbonnists) or perform ambiguous tricks (no frozen words).[4] His world inscribes cuckolds, crooks, and con artists with more humor than consternation, offering a bustle of shops, churches, schools, bookstalls, the exchange, partying, gambling, and cheating; of travelers, traders, talkers, topers, tennis (complete with soft shoes, the score, and a smash — "O divell! w[h]at a firking stroke is that. You have an arme of yron," sigs. h2–h3). Language and commodities from all over the globe pour into this marketplace of words and matter, of "Fine Venice Glasses, French garters, Spanish gloves, sweet, Flanders knives, fine Silke stockes of Italie" (sig. d4). By mentioning cheats and scoundrels, cuckolds and robbers, Eliot acknowledges the dark side of this circulating verbal energy and vendable or edible material, even if (whatever his friendly words on the now-conquered Mexico City) he ignores at what human cost the exotic tongues, pearls, silks, and gold have made their way to London. His stress is on motion, choices, places to go, things to see or sell, opinions, food and drink to consume, and — above all — words. This is a book about

Babel by one who would have liked to have been there transcribing what he heard, and who now dwells among "prattlers," as he calls them in his subtitle, "The Parlement of Pratlers." Even the gestures to something beyond this urban scene, such as a parody of Petrarchan lovechat (sigs. v4–x1), a nightingale's song (sig. t2), and encomia to Queen Elizabeth and France (sigs. L2, y4) are designed primarily to show what the French language can do when it tries.

Was Eliot a Pantagruelist? He knew *Gargantua et Pantagruel* well. One might call his method "recombinant imitation," but he projects no "image" of Rabelais beyond the allusion to him as "merry." For most readers, "Rabelais" does no work, even if the words he wrote help Eliot's dialogues seem even more comic, festive, fantastic, and verbally inventive — although not learnedly humanist, seriously obscene, blasphemous, philosophical, obscure, or scatological.[5] What gets lost, paradoxically, is both Rabelais's persistent hint that there is some meaning to his clowning, some spiritual wine in Diogenes' barrel, and on the other hand his disturbing slipperiness, the sense he gives some readers that there is a void below his highwire verbal gymnastics.[6]

Authorship by Definition: Lexicography and Glossing Rabelais

Although it is unclear whether Eliot counted on our familiarity with *Gargantua et Pantagruel* or on our ignorance, by the early 1590s he could drop the name Rabelais and expect it to mean something. Before Thomas Urquhart's translation, however, anyone wanting to read this "merry Grig" would need more French than Eliot can teach. Rabelais's prose, with its enormous vocabulary, wordplay, and idiosyncratic Frenchifying of Greek and Hebrew, is daunting.[7] One can sympathize with anyone who read the following:

> —Voulez-vous (dist Her Trippa) en sçavoir plus amplement la verité par pyromantie, par aëromantie, celebrée par Aristophanes en ses *Nuées,* par hydromantie, par lecanomantie, tant jadis celebrée entre les Assyriens et ex-provée par Hermolaus Barbarus? Dedans un bassin plein d'eaue je te monstreray ta femme future brimballant avecques deux rustres.
> —Quand (dist Panurge) tu mettras ton nez en mon cul, sois recors de deschausser tes lunettes. (*TL* 25)[8]

Even readers whose Greek and expertise in ancient augury enable them to identify Her Trippa's methods of reading Panurge's destiny can see how difficult this is. Nor did the difficulty go unremarked. In a prefatory poem for J. Mabbe's translation of Mateo Aleman's *Rogue* (1623), Leonard Digges mentions Rabelais when explaining why it has taken so long to English this Spaniard:

As, few, French Rablais understand; and none
Dare in our vulgar Tongue once make him known,
No more; our Plodding Linguists could attaine
(By turning Minshewe) to this Rogue of Spaine,[9]
So crabbed Canting was the Authors Pen
And phrase, ev'n darke to his own Country-men;
Till, thankes and praise to this Translators paine,
His Margent, now makes him speake English plaine.

It was to be a generation before anyone could say the same of Rabelais (not that Urquhart's English is "plaine"). Rabelais's French continued to seem difficult: Thomas Browne's essay "Of Languages," published in 1683, warns that without "some knowledge" of Breton, a language he equates with Provençal, "you cannot exactly understand the Works of Rablais."[10]

True, the English had French-English dictionaries.[11] One of the most popular mentions Rabelais. Claudius Holyband (as the Huguenot Claude de Sainliens called himself after immigrating in the 1560s) published guides to French that amuse as they instruct. It is uncertain what the 1580 *Treasurie of the French Tong,* expanding an anonymous *Dictionarie French and English* (1570), owes to Rabelais. Some phrases that Holyband's biographer, Lucy Ferrer, cites were not uncommon.[12] Holyband knew Rabelais, though, citing him here and in the enlarged 1593 *Dictionary French and English.* It says something about the "image" now forming of Rabelais that one allusion is mildly scatological and the other echoes a scene of sexual banter. Both relate to evangelical moments that Holyband remembered with pleasure, if vaguely.

One appears in a set of entries derived from *trespas* (death). As though to cheer up those consulting the dictionary, Holyband includes an atypically long definition: "*Il pisse pour les Tres-passez, Rabelais,* doubtfully spoken, for it may be taken, as it is pronounced, he pisseth for the dead, alluding to the custome of the Papistes, sprinkling the graves of the dead with holy water to cleanse their soules, or in deede it should be written, *Il pisse pour les traicts passez,* that is, he pisseth for, or bycause of the draughtes [*traicts*] of wyne or drinke which he hath swalowed downe." Holyband writes from memory, acknowledging the author but casual about the wording. His source must be an anti-papist jibe in *QL* 49, sharpened by economic conflicts in the early 1550s between the papacy and the French monarchy.[13] Pantagruel's crew is visiting the Papimanes (Pope-maniacs), who accord papal decretals an awe they should save for Scripture. Panurge and Frère Jean, ravenous after their trip, do not welcome the thought of a Mass and further fasting. Make it quick, says the monk, although if he had had a good breakfast and it were a requiem mass, he could have brought "pain et vin par les traicts passez" (bread and wine made by/destined for the swallowings/dead). The sally refers to the custom of bringing an offering of wine and bread to a funeral, but the pun hints that in this case the gifts would have been transmuted inside the monk into something few would deposit by hand. Frère Jean's little carnival of hungry scatology opposes the abstract text obsession of the Papimanes even as the implied excrement parodies the gold they so fervently seek to attract and retain.

Holyband cleans up the humor a bit and changes the wine to water. But he does not undo the satire: papist superstition — as he saw it — can be fought by earthy jokes that ridicule false claims concerning words and the transmutation of matter. Some find these chapters, concerned with language and significance, subversive of Christian meaning.[14] But Holyband seems easy with both the irreverence and the piss: whatever his Protestantism, he had remnants of an older style of humor. Or he may have believed — as some said of Lucian — that wit directed against false religion should hold no terror for the faithful. So he pressed Rabelais into the fight against popery, unconcerned that Calvin had thought the satirist no ally of the godly.

Defining *Poupon* for his 1593 *Dictionary*, Holyband writes: "as, elle tenoit son petit poupon, parlan[t] de Pentagruël" (She held her little babe, speaking of Pantagruel). The joke assumes a reader who can affix the name Pantagruel to a giant, for this "poupon" is hardly "petit." Holyband must be remembering G 6, which has Rabelais's only *poupon*.[15] In this agreeable scene Grandgousier exhorts his wife to be brave during the birth of her "poupon": happiness will soon make her forget her travail. "Ha!" replies Gargamelle, with remarkable spirit for a woman in labor, "That's how you talk while at your ease, you men. Very well, by God, I'll force myself, since it pleases you, but by God I wish you had cut it off." Amused, sympathetic, alarmed, her husband offers to take a knife to the offending part; but, although still blaming with — I think — friendly humor the "membre" that had given itself such "ease" and herself (now) such pangs, Gargamelle says she hadn't meant it. No wonder Holyband was impressed. If he read the first edition, he would have seen a remark, later prudently dropped, that labor pains are better assuaged by the Gospel than by saints' lives. He has reworked the scene, though, granting poor Badebec, who dies bearing Pantagruel, a maternal joy that belonged to Gargamelle. And by explicitly nestling the baby in the mother's arms, he makes the moment more comfortable, with no marital joshing about sex and castration. This would have no place in so brief a definition, to be sure: it is the image Holyband fleetingly creates that suggests some erasure in the back of his mind where Memory, they say, does her editorial work.

To anyone baffled by Rabelais's French, Randle Cotgrave's *Dictionarie of the French and English Tongues* (1611) would have come as even more welcome relief, not least because this marvelous book is one of the funniest works in the history of lexicography. Without narrative or characters, it gives an impression of having elements of fiction, largely because Cotgrave creates a voice that can loosely be called Rabelaisian. It is true that most of the definitions are straightforward, true that many derive from such dictionaries as Jean Nicot's, and perhaps true that Cotgrave used assistants. And he could make mistakes.[16] To browse through the book, however, is to enjoy a particular tonality, one due in part to the approximately five hundred words taken from Rabelais, most of them flagged by a noticeable "¶Rab" after the entry and many defined in ways suiting their provenance (fig. 1). Cotgrave mentions Chaucer and Du Bartas, but Rabelais is the only writer regularly cited as a source. He is more than a source, however: through frequency of citation and through the nature of the citations he becomes an author and authority. On occasion, moreover, allusions to him are quite precise, as in the definition of *commenial:* "(¶Rabelais l.4.chap.44.) A barbarous jeasting repetition of the word comme going some two lines before, and used by Frier John."[17]

This definition suggests another reason for the sense that an English cousin of Rabelais's persona presides over the dictionary, a figure as opinionated as Samuel Johnson and as ebullient as Urquhart. Some words from Rabelais, moreover, have scant utility unless one wishes to complain in Graeco-French of a "goutie leg" [see *Oedipodique*], learnedly call someone an "excrement-eater" [*Scatophage*], or see the future by looking at "a falling on the ground of bread given unto chickens" [*solistisme*].[18] Entries like these are helpful chiefly for reading Rabelais. Why else would one need to know that for "¶Rab" *cope gorgée* is "in stead of, Gorge coupée"?

The personality Cotgrave projects is of a man energetic, friendly, a touch eccentric, amused, unsqueamish, and captivated by words. He will editorialize. Saying that "apres compter il faut boire" means "the reckoning ended we must drink together," he calls this "a Dutch conclusion." A *villon* is a "wittie rogue," for "such a one was Francois Villon, whose death a halter suited to his life." Under *greal* (with a "¶Rab") he sends us to *sangreal:* "Part of Christs most pretious bloud wandering about the world invisible (to all but chast eyes) and working many wonders, and wonderfull cures; if we may credit the most foolish, and fabulous Historie of King Arthur." At times he attempts to reproduce a flavor. "Apres tout dueil boit on bien" becomes "So tipling succeedeth teene," while "Celuy de bon sens ne jouit, qui boit et ne s'en rejouit" still rhymes as "He that in drinking feels no pleasure, his wits be surely out of measure." The chief impression is of language flowing from a lexicographical horn of plenty. If there are many French words to list, there are even more

La bonne Lune. *The later end of September, and beginning of October; the beſt time to ſow Winter-corne in, and therefore ſo tearmed by good husbands.*

Abbayer contre la lune. *Seeke* Abbayer.

Auoir vn quartier de la lune en la teſte. *To bee halfe franticke, or haue a ſpice of Lunacie; The like is;*

Il y a de la lune. *He is a foolish, humorous, harebraind, giddie-headed fellow.*

Coucher à l'enſeigne de la lune. *To lie without doores all night.*

Garder la lune des loups. *To waſt indeuors vpon ſubiects that need them not; or ſpend time in watching of that which of it ſelfe is ſafe ynough.*

Dieu gard la lune des loups. *An ironicall anſwer vnto a bragging foole, that threatens to kill them whom he cannot hurt.*

Le fourrier de la lune a marqué le logis. *Said of a woman that hath her flowers.*

Prendre la lune aux dents. *To doe impoſſible matters.*

Tenir de la lune. *To be inconſtant, fickle, mutable, giddie, vnſetled, wauering.*

Les biens de fortune paſſent comme la lune: Pro. *what fortune giues vs for a boone, is quickly waſted like the Moone.*

Luné: m. ée: f. *Round, compaſſe, rounded, or bowed like a halfe-Moone.*

Luner. *To round, bow, compaſſe; and hence;*

Luner vn arc. *To bend a bow.*

Lunette: f. *The merrie-thought; the forked craw-bone of a bird, which we vſe, in ſport, to put on our noſes.*

Lunettes: f. *Spectacles.*

Il n'y a pas bien aſsis ſes lunettes. *He hath not obſerued the matter ſo neerely, he hath not looked into it ſo narrowly, as he might, or ſhould, haue done.*

Lupaſſon. *as* Loupaſſon.

Lupege: f. *The whoope, or dung-hill Cocke.*

Lupin: m. *The pulſe Lupines; alſo, the Baſe, or Sea-Wolfe.*

Lupoge. *as* Lupege.

Lurré: m. ée: f. *Lured; inticed, allured.*

Lus: m. *A Pike (fiſh.)*

Lus marin. *A Cod, or Cod-fiſh; ſome alſo, call the Haddocke ſo.*

Luſerne: f. *A Gloe-worme; alſo, as* Luzerne.

Luſtre: m. *A luſter, or gloſſe; a ſhining, or gliſtening; a gracefull bright colour; alſo, a terme of foure yeares, or fiftie moneths; alſo, a Cenſorian onerſight ouer Citizens eſtates, and behauiour.*

Donner luſtre à. *To grace, beautifie, illuſtrate, adorne; ſleeke, burniſh, brighten; ſet a gloſſe on, giue a luſter vnto.*

Luſtrer. *To looke round about, view, or ſuruey on each ſide, behold euerie way; to weigh diligently, examine throughly, ſeriouſly conſider of, prie narrowly into; alſo, to purge, or cleanſe by ſacrifice; alſo, as* Donner luſtre.

Luſtreux: m. euſe: f. *Luſterous, radiant, ſhining, gliſtening, gliſtering, glittering.*

Luſtruetx. *as* Luſtreux.

Lut: m. *A Lute; alſo, clay, mould, loame, durt; alſo, a kind of barke, or boat.*

Luté: m. ée: f. *Dawbed, cloſed, or done ouer, with clay; alſo, bemired, berayed, beſmeared.*

Luter. *To dawbe, or clay; to cloſe, or doe ouer with loame, or clay; alſo, to bedawb, defile, bemire, beſmeare, beray.*

Luth: m. *A Lute.*

Lutin: m. *A Goblin, Robin-good-fellow, Hob-thruſh; a ſpirit which playes reakes in mens houſes anights.*

Lutiner. *To play the Goblin, or night-ſpirit; to keepe a foule rumbling, or terrible racket vp and down a houſe in the night.*

Lutiz: m. *Clay, loame; durt.*

Lutre. *as* Loutre.

Lutrin: m. *A deske in a Church.*

Luxation: f. *A luxation, looſeneſſe, or looſſening; a being out of ioynt.*

Luxe: m. *Exceſſe, riot, ſuperfluitie.*

Luxer. *To looſſe, or put out of ioynt; alſo, to be out of ioynt, or out of due place.*

Luxure: f. *Luxurie, ſenſualitie, concupiſcence, fleſhlineſſe; any ſuperfluitie, or exceſſe in carnall delights.*

Luxurieux: m. euſe: f. *Luxurious, voluptuous, fleſhlie, luſtfull, ſenſuall; exceſſiue, riotous.*

Luy. *He, him, the ſame man.*

Luyton. *as* Luiton, *or* Lutin.

Luz: m. Lus.

Luzerne: f. *as* Luſerne.; *Alſo,* Medicke fodder, Spaniſh Treſoyle, horned Clauer, ſnaile Clauer.

Luzerner. *To glow, gliſten, or glimmer. (v.m.)*

Luzerniere: f. *A cloſe, field, or plot ſowed with Medicke fodder.*

Ly. *as* Le: ¶ Gaſcon.

Lyarre: m. *Iuie;* Seeke Lierre.

Lyaſſe. *as* Liaſſe.

Lycanthropie: f. *A frenzie, or melancholie, which cauſeth the patient (who thinkes he is turned Wolfe) to flie all companie, and hide himſelfe in dennes, and corners.*

Lyce: f. *A bitch, &c; as in* Lice.

Vne fauſſe lyce. *A lewd queane, falſe trull, vngracious whoore, wicked harlot.*

Lychnobien: m. *The weeke of a candle; or one who in ſtead of the day vſeth the night, doing all his buſineſſe by candle-light:* ¶Rab.

Lychnocoſomité. *The chiefe ſlight, or lanterne of the world.*

Lychnon: m. *A light, candle, or linke; alſo, the wieke of a candle, or match of a lampe; alſo, a lanterne:* ¶Rab.

Lycopſe. *A kind of the (red-rooted) hearbe Orchanet.*

Lycopthalmie: f. *A pretious ſtone of foure ſundrie colours:* ¶Rab.

Lye. *as* Lie.

Lyerre. *Iuie;* Seeke Lierre.

Lymitrophe: com. *Bordering vpon, adioyning, or lying next or vnto.*

Lymon. *as* Limon.

Lymphatique: com. *Allayed, or mixed with water; alſo, madde, furious, beſtraught; giddie, fantaſticall.*

Lyncée: f. *A Linx; a Wolfe-reſembling beaſt that is full of ſpots.*

Yeux de Lincée. *Sharpe, quicke, piercing eyes.*

Lyncurie: f. *A pretious ſtone bred of the congealed vrine of a Linx, and preſeruing the eyes from charmes.*

Lynges. *as* Liens; *Bands, &c:* ¶Rab.

Lyon. Seeke Lion.

Lyonceau: m. *A Lyons whelpe, or young Lyon.*

Lype. *as* Lippe; *A lip.*

Faire la lype. *To powt, lowt, lowre, hang the lip, as a child that is ſullen, or about to crie.*

Lypothomie: f. *A kind of deadlie ſwooning.*

Lyre: f. *A Lyra, or Harpe.*

Ly-

Figure 1 A typical page from Randle Cotgrave's 1611 *Dictionarie of the French and English Tongues*, showing words associated with "¶Rab" (Courtesy Beinecke Rare Book and Manuscript Library, Yale University)

English words available to define them. Thus *foriboles* ("¶Rab") are "trifles, nifles, flim-flams, why-whawes, idle discourses, fond tatling, tales of a tub, or of a roasted horse." Or take *tirer:*

> To draw, drag, trayle; tow, hale; pull, plucke, lug, tug, twitch; bring, lead along or towards; also, to stretch, retch, dilate, extend, wiredraw; also, to dart, shoot, sling, fling, hurle, cast, throw, pitch fromwards; also, to shoot one with a Pistoll, etc; also, to take, extract, wrest, or force from; also, to yerke, winse, fling, or flye out with the heeles; also, to wend, goe, travell, make along or towards; also, to draw, delineate, or pourtray; also, to resemble, or draw neere unto.

Tirer can indeed unfold legitimately into a paragraph of synonyms, but Cotgrave goes beyond duty into holiday pleasure, implying something about the capacities of his own language. The *Dictionarie* offers two plenitudes: a huge alphabetical array of often lively French on the one hand and on the other a tumult of English unpacking and commenting on it.

In Cotgrave's definitions the body itself seems more open than closed. *Chiche-face* is a "chichiface, micher, sneake-bill, wretched fellow; one out of whose nose hunger drops." "Faire jambes de vin" means "to take in store of liquor before the undertaking of a journey; to supple his legs, by soaking his head, in wine." As for *chier,* this is "to shite, cacke, scummer, untrusse the points, goe to the stoole, doe that which no bodie can doe for him." Although avoiding obscenity, Cotgrave is never queasy; his very euphemisms (like Rabelais's) suggest hang-loose humor, not shamefast reticence: *con* is "A womans etc." and *nuc* is "con, turned backward (as our Tnuc) to be the less offensive to chast eares."

What "Rabelais" emerges from the five hundred or so entries associated with him? He appreciates the body. A few words like *Nephrocartaticon* ("physicke that purgeth the reines") imply an authority on medicine and anatomy.[19] Words for the genitals are often his. Thus under *comment* ("how, in what sort") we also find "Le comment a nom de sa femme": "his wives how-should-I-call-it." In this category, however, Cotgrave makes less effort to outdo French copia. If *verretre* is "a mans yard," so is *mentule; niphleset* is "membre viril," as are *balletrou* (also a "sweepe-hole") and *caiche. Brisgoter* is merely "to swive," while *fredinfredailler, jouer du serrecropiere* and *lanfrelucher* all mean "to leacher" and *coignaufond* is a "knocking, leacherie, venerie." Some entries have more color: *Cuscoamy* is "well hanged, well stoned"; "Je luy appresteray un clystere barbarin" means "I will provide for her bellie a plaister of warme guts"; and *desmorché* is "without powder in his touch-hole." Still, the indecency for which Rabelais remains famous is here fairly subdued.[20] So is the scatology. True, we find *habeliné*, meaning "distempered; or . . . all-to-bepissed"; *peder* as a variant of "petter, To fart"; *scybale*, a "hard or hardened, turd"; *syparathe* as "the dung of a Goat, or Sheepe"; *tyrepet* ("a great farter"); the *scatophages* noted above, and a few others. Granted the wealth of material that Cotgrave had to work with, however, the "image" he gives of Rabelais in this regard is unexpectedly decorous. Under *merde* (shit) he alludes to Rabelais, but not scatologically: "Robbe d'argent brodee de merde" is "an excellent Text ill expounded, or commented on; (for which cause Rabelais calls so Justinians Institutes)."

More frequent in the *Dictionarie* are words associating Rabelais with food and drink: from *alloyandier* ("a roster of short ribbes of beefe") to *utagues* ("olive plants or suckers"), from *babuc* ("a bottle") to *ventripotent* ("bigpaunch, bellie-able, huge-guts"), a sizable proportion of "¶Rab" entries suggests a world of laden tables and of brimming cups for anyone with the *Mort Roland* ("thirst") who wants to be a *mouille-vent* ("a tipler, quaffer, bibber; one that often wets his windpipe"). Here nature is rich in edibles like *condignac* ("marmalade of Quinces") and *porcausou* ("sowsed Hogs flesh"), and *risses chevreaux* ("fat Kids"). The effect is not carnival reversal so much as imaginative generosity with material comforts and pleasures, with partying and pigging out (*morpiaille*: "greedie eating; ill favoured or hastie devouring").[21]

Other entries project a "¶Rab" who might suit some modern readers, if not those chiefly concerned with his religion (the evangelical anti-papist is largely missing) or his epistemology ("¶Rab" is not a protodeconstructionist, either). Many entries suggest learnedly skeptical wit. For example, Cotgrave creates a running gag by defining means of prognostication. They come from Panurge's search in the *Tiers livre* to read his marital destiny.[22] If only because of their cumulative effect, no one could take such words very seriously, whatever their source in ancient practice; each gets a "¶Rab." So those consulting Cotgrave with some sober purpose will find, if they browse, *axionomantie* ("divination by a hatchet"), *cephaleonomanie* ("divination by an asses head broyled on coles"), *conscinomantie* ("divination by a sive, and a paire of sheeres"), *ichthyomantie* ("divination by fish"), *tephramantie* ("divination by ashes blowne, or cast, up into the aire"), and others, including the chicken method mentioned above.

Even more indicative of Cotgrave's understanding of Rabelais is his interest in language as language, for entries marked "¶Rab" can attend to the nature, as well as the meaning, of a word. Some indicate tone. For a word like *magistronostralement* ("dunsically"), there can be no doubt (one addressed a professor as "magister noster"), but sometimes Cotgrave needs to clue us in. When he translates "c'est matiere de breviaire" as "tis holy stuff, I tell you," he adds the word *ironically;* so too, "faire trembler le lard au charnier" means "to swagger extremely, to threaten horribly, to use big, or bugs words; (Ironically)," while *Mordienne* ("Gogsdeathlings") is a "foolish oath in Rab." Is a word new? *Cababezancé,* or "loaden with bags, and wallets; also, commented on" is "coyned by Rab."; *carimari carimara* are "fained words expressing a great coyle, stirre, hurlyburly, or the confused muttering of a rude companie"; and *hen heu hasch* are "fained words, wherewith Rabelais expresseth a coughing" (see G 19). Such entries recognize a fellow logophiliac.

Cotgrave's Rabelais is an appealing, scholarly, and inventive writer. He is also an author and authority, able to pass on his culture's language and to "fain" new words, phrases, puns, sounds (impersonating even babies — see *mies mies*). Unlike many English images of Rabelais, furthermore, this one shows a happy respect: Cotgrave comes as close as a lexicographer can to true Pantagruelism. Perhaps the moral, if we may attach a moral to a dictionary, is that no stereotyped view of another writer can survive a truly thoughtful curiosity about and examination of his (or her) vocabulary.

The margins of two copies of Rabelais's works show that some in England found Cotgrave helpful. One was the reader, perhaps an Oxford scholar resting from his labor, who copied a few definitions into a 1599 *Oeuvres.*[23] He notes, for example, that *rataconiculer* means "to reiterate lecherie," that a *douzil* is a spigot, that *debragueter* has to do with a codpiece, that *gaudebillaux coiraux* are the "fat tripes" of "stal[l]fed oxen," and that "mettez tout par escuelles" means "to through [throw] the house out at the windowes" — to waste everything. He seems particularly interested in words having to do with food and the body: this is the festive Rabelais and not, for instance, the laughing retailer of Greekish neologisms, satirist of prognostications, medical authority, or imitator of mewling babies.

The other copy belonged to Ben Jonson. It is well known that Jonson alludes to Rabelais; it is less widely known that he glossed some pages of his copy of the 1599 Lyons *Oeuvres.* Now in the British Library, the volume is inscribed "The Gift of Beniamin Johnson the Poet to Tho Skynner. 1628."[24] The margins of *Gargantua*'s opening chapters are heavy with Latin and English translations of underlined words; to judge from the hand and some markings, these are by Jonson.[25] The gift's significance is uncertain: was Jonson tired of Rabelais? Bedridden by his recent stroke, did he seek to simplify his library? Had he bought a newer edition? Was he short of shelf space? Did Skynner or a mutual friend beg persuasively? The pattern of glosses is of little help here, for their presence in the margins of *Gargantua* alone suggests several possibilities: that Jonson was working on his French and found Rabelais's novel too tiring to practice on, that he switched his glossing to some now lost copy, that he got bored or irritated with what he read (hard to believe, but possible), that he mislaid the volume for a while, or that he wanted to give Skynner a book that would be easier to read. Another puzzle is that although Jonson glosses chapters in *Gargantua,* the allusions in his plays and masques are to the later books.

I cannot tell when Jonson made these glosses. He must have done so at different times: no one could have done it at a sitting. Nor can we know what help he got from friends. He seems to have consulted Cotgrave, though, which would mean that some or all the English glosses date from 1611 or later. Jonson's method seems to have been to read Cotgrave — perhaps (but not certainly) together with other dictionaries — and then to select or devise a definition he liked. His translations are on occasion the same as the first definition in Cotgrave, but they are just as likely to parallel a word or phrase near the end of an entry in the *Dictionarie.* In a few cases the gloss shows that, more than the anonymous owner/reader of the Oxford copy, Jonson pondered which English word or phrase might do best. It is the picking and choosing that make his marginal translations seem so thoughtful.

This evidence for Jonson's use of Cotgrave is sparse but compelling. Several words or phrases glossed in English are in Cotgrave but not in Holyband. The former says *monochordisant* is "to quaver with the fingers, to wag or play with them, as if he touched a Manicordion"; Jonson's margin has "playing." Jonson writes "whippers (or whip pots)" next to *fessepinte,* which Cotgrave defines as "a tipler, bibber, quaffer, can-killer, pot-whipper, faithfull drunkard." Jonson's definition, in fact, better captures the order of the word's elements, and, because Cotgrave gives "whipper" for *fesseur,* Jonson would have had no doubt as to which syllable meant what. A *pinte* is a "pint," but Jonson sticks with Cotgrave's "pot." Another example: Holyband defines *poulain* only as "a colt," which would not have helped Jonson understand the answer to a question in Chapter 5, "What is a synonym for ham?" Ham is "un compulsoire de beuveurs [a goad for drinkers]: c'est un poulain." Cotgrave helps us understand: "A fole, or coult; also, the rope wherewith wine is let downe into a seller; a pullie rope; also, a botch in the groine, a Winchester Goose" (London slang for "whore"). Jonson underlines *poulain* and calls it a device with which "they let wine downe into ye cellar." Next to *huchant,* part of the phrase "huchant en paume," Jonson writes "whistle." Holyband defines *hucher* as "to call" and Cotgrave as "To whoope, or hallow for; to call unto." But under *huchant* the latter adds "huchant en paume. Whistling for, or calling unto by whistling in the fist." And only in Cotgrave, under *frimas,* would Jonson have found "avalleurs de frimats." His gloss reads "swallowers of mists," a brief version of Cotgrave's "cousening knaves, idle companions, loytering rogues; also, a nickname for Judges; who using to rise, and goe abroad early, swallow a great deal of mist in their dayes."

Jonson could pick and choose among Cotgrave's synonyms ("vigilant" for *veillant* is Cotgrave's fourth definition, and "covertly" for *en tapinois* is his seventh); he could also deduce a more precise English word. For *trongne* ("a face or countenance," says Holyband), Cotgrave gives "the face, aspect, looke, visage, countenance." Jonson has "chappes," specifying the area that includes the mouth. He does so, I suspect, because Cotgrave's subsidiary phrases concern drinking: "à la trongne cognoist on l'yvrongne" means "two things a drunkard doe disclose, a fierie face, and crimson nose," and "bonne bouche bonne trongne" signifies that "a temperate mouth breedeth a fresh complexion; or, a well-shap'd mouth makes all the face shew faire; or, a silent mouth settles the countenance." To consider all the aspects of *trongne* is to think not just of the face in general but of that consuming and talking part so relevant to *Gargantua* — and to Jonson.

Jonson's glosses are too localized and clustered to show much about what in Rabelais interested him; he is, after all, beginning at the beginning. It may be significant, however, that most of them are in Latin, as if Jonson tended to think in that language when considering words as words, or as if whatever his conscious understanding of the social nature of language, Latin had such gravitas and breadth that only on its weighty ground could other languages meet and communicate. That he devoted much thought to the nature of words is clear from his writings, including his tract on English grammar and *Discoveries,* and because he apparently believed that how words are used indicates the user's inner reality, they were for him intimately if indistinctly connected with the self that so concerned him and the authorship he claimed.[26] His margins, heavy with Latin, suggest a mind imagining a similar heft within itself. Perhaps Jonson recognized in "¶Rab" a fellow spirit — even a fellow author. And he was well equipped by interests and habits to catch Cotgrave's affectionate joke on Rabelais and authorship: next to *Alcofribas* (with no "¶Rab") we read "A greedie glutton; a great devourer."

Lists and Latinisms

It can be tempting to misread samples of English wordplay as owing something to Rabelais when they are in fact just as likely to derive independently from a culture-wide fascination with copia. But English awareness of *Gargantua et Pantagruel* may have given further impetus to verbal accumulations that are comic thanks to arbitrary excess (the "effet plaisant créé par un langage gratuit," says Marcel Tetel) and to mock-learned language that satirizes pomposity by lobbing heavy words back at it.[27] Unreliable as evidence of Rabelais's English readership, lists and Latinisms are elements in the atmosphere that surrounds his reception.

Lists turn up in many places, not least in controversy. Post-Reformation polemic is a nasty business, but a number of its practitioners seem to have enjoyed its perversities. Even respectable writers, not just impudent nose-thumbers like that scourge of bishops Martin Marprelate, can be rambunctious, playing with alliteration and rhyme, taking up words so as to "writhe them and tosse them to and fro nimbly," as Tom Nashe put it when taunting Gabriel Harvey for being unable to do so.[28] The conscious hope must often have been to make such silliness illustrate the folly under attack, to suggest mimetically the frivolity of those preposterous others.

Lists take an explicitly anti-theatrical turn in Bishop John Jewell's *Replie unto M. Hardinges Answeare* (1566), which calls his opponent's taste for epithet the stuff of stageplays, of *"vetus comoedia"*: Harding has called his opponents

> Goliath, Thersites, rash, presumptuous, wicked, unleavened, ignorant, peevish, Lucians, scoffers, coggers, Foisters, pert, insolent, vaunters, braggers, sectaries, schismatics, heretics, sacramentaries, new masters, new fangles, false reporters, slanderers of the church, terrible seducers, enemies of the sacrifice, enemies of the church, ministers of the devil, sitters in the chair of Pestilence, Monsters, Heathens, Publicans, Turks, Infidels, Antichrists, and forrunners of Antichrist. (Sigs. ¶4, ¶7)[29]

These insults are comic only if heaped up, and it is Jewell who makes the pile. But Catholics, too, made lists. Robert Parsons's spirited *Discoverie of J. Nicols* (1581), which calls Nicols's recantation mere disinformation, claims that the supposed Jesuit had termed Rome's supporters

> Cainites, Gyantes, Sodomites, Egiptians, Scribes, Pharasies, Herodians, Monkes, Friers, Cardinals, Adulterers, Idolatours, Parasites, Poyseners, Pardoners, Bawdes, Flatterers, Traytours, Rebels, Murderers, Theeves, Canibals, Varlets, Shavelings, Eategods, Makegods, Hypocrits, Illuders, Conjurers, Wiches, Knaves, Enchanters, Exorsistes, Monsters, Worshippers of wheaten cake, horrible, abhominable and detestable Blasphemers, and chosen children of the Divil him selfe. (Sig. M8)

Such are Nicols's "modest, sober, and charitable wordes," scoffs Parsons, but the effect of rhetorical overkill is his own doing.

The Harvey-Nashe flyting has lists that more precisely recall Rabelais; both writers knew *Gargantua et Pantagruel* and both name its author. My point is not Rabelais's "influence" but how Harvey and Nashe have observed his particular verbal play: excess (and puns) combined with repeated words or syntactic units on the model of the prepositional *à/au* in G 22 or the multi-adjectived *couillons* and *fols* in TL 26, 28, and 38. According to Harvey's *Pierces Supererogation* (1593), Nashe is:

the *Bawewawe* of Schollars, the *Tutt* of Gentlemen, the *Tee-heegh* of Gentlewomen, the *Phy* of Citizens, the *Blurt* of Courtiers, the *Poogh* of good Letters, the *Faph* of good manners, & the *whoop-hooe* of good boyes in London streetes. Nash, Nash, Nash, (quoth a lover of truth, and honesty) vaine Nash, railing Nash, craking Nash, bibbing Nash, baggage Nash, swaddish Nash, rogish Nash, Nash the bellweather of the scribling floke, the swishswash of the presse, the bumm of Impudency, the shambles of beastlines, the poulkat of Pouls-churchyard . . . (Sig. Z2v)

Nashe's *Have with You to Saffron-Walden* (1596) gives Gabriel's brother Richard the list treatment:

This is that Dick of whom Kit Marloe was wont to say that he was an asse, good for nothing but to preach of the Iron Age: Dialoguizing *Dick, Io Paean Dicke, Synesian* and *Pierian Dick, Dick* the true *Brute* or noble *Troian,* or *Dick* that hath vowd to live and die in defence of *Brute,* and this our Iles first offspring from the *Troians, Dick* against baldnes, *Dick* against *Buchanan,* little and little witted *Dicke, Aquinas Dicke, Lipsian Dick,* heigh light a love a *Dick,* that lost his Benefice & his Wench both at once, his Benefice for want of sufficencie, and his wench for want of a Benefice or sufficient living to maintaine her, *Dilemma Dick,* dissentious *Dick* . . . (*Works* III 85)

Nashe and Harvey fling name-calling beyond insult into Tetel's "language gratuit." More than Rabelais's, though, their lists seem staged: words jig past communication, gesticulating rudely as they go, which is not quite the same as undoing significance by proliferating signifiers down the page.

Latinisms likewise slow discourse, if for nanoseconds, by demanding attention. Professional verbiage, an older fashion for aureate poetry, and a recent influx of neologisms combined to create a surge of long words that made ridicule inevitable. Old scholastic jargon and new humanist word-forging could even mingle. Rabelais did not invent such comedy: Lucian's *Lexiphanes* anticipates both Rabelais and the word vomiting in Jonson's *Poetaster.* But he was among the first to give it its Renaissance shape, and I have shown how the English could call thundering polysyllables Gargantuan. Parody of them persisted, directed at boasters, lawyers, and social climbers stepping up to the middle class on sesquipedelia. Readers would have found such terms displayed by Janotus de Bragmardo, the theologian secularized into a "sophist" in later editions, who orates at Gargantua in hopes of getting him to return the bells of Notre Dame (*G* 19); by the Limousin scholar whom Pantagruel throttles until he returns, soiling his pants, to his "natural" dialect and stops saying things like "penitissimes recesses des pudendes de ces meritricules amicabilissimes" (the depths of amiable whores' vaginas, *P* 6); and by the para-Rabelaisian "Epistre Limousine."

As with the word lists, it is hard to tell what someone has been reading. The letter from a Lincolnshire man seeking a benefice that Thomas Wilson quotes or invents in his *Arte of Rhetorique* (1553) recalls Rabelais's provincial and aspiring Limousin: "Ponderyng, expendyng, and revolutyng" his friend's "ingent affabilitee," he asks to be "collaude[d]" to the Chancellor, "or rather Archigrammacion." If the "Garganteo" he mentions is not the chapbook giant, and if the writer who praises "a gose" is Rabelais, then Wilson was among those who read *Gargantua* with an eye to the comedy staged by pretension and ignorance.[30]

It is even more likely that Philip Sidney modeled the pedant Rombus in *The Lady of May* (1578?) on Rabelais's Janotus.[31] Pedants were nothing new, but Rombus and Janotus each mix scholastic logic, irrelevant Latin tags, and bombast. Each grabs attention by throat-clearing: "Ehen, hen, hen!" begins the Frenchman; "Heu, Ehem, Hei," says Rombus. Janotus refers to "la complexion elementaire que est intronificquée en la terresterité de leur nature quidditative" (the elementary complexion that is enthroned in the terrestialness of their essentiality). Rombus can do that: "I am gravidated with child, till I have indoctrinated your plumbeous cerebrosities." If Janotus says mysteriously that "Ego occidi unum porcum, et ego habet bon vino" (Me, I have killed one pig and I myself has gut wein), Rombus can say, "et ecce homo blancatus quasi lilium" (and behold the man blanchified like a lily). And in the manuscript version he ends the play with "Plauditamus et valeamus," a Plautine tag recalling Janotus's more grammatical "valete et plaudite."

It is easy to believe, then, that Sidney knew Rabelais's satire of scholastic ineptitude. More than Wilson's petitioner or the Limousin scholar, Rombus and Janotus are schooled in methods Sidney and Rabelais found outdated.[32] Yet the pedant's grammar ("O Tempori, O Moribus!") may owe as much to rustic deficiency as to passé scholarship. In this entertainment for Elizabeth I, Sidney plays the urbane courtier as well as the satirical humanist, whatever the affection he also shows to this country schoolmaster. Rombus is no serious threat to him, whereas Janotus represents forces that could literally be the death of a writer. Having been to France during the civil wars, Sidney would have measured Rabelais's courage; and maybe he knew that Panurge addresses a helmsman by a name Sidney was to adopt when punning in his love poetry on "Phil . . . Sid": "maistre Astrophile" (*QL* 18; the Pantagrueline Prognostication calls stargazers "astrophiles").

Like Sidney, Shakespeare had little to fear from aged scholastics, but he too thought Latinisms preposterous. In *Loves Labor's Lost* Holofernes has been, as the page Moth puts it, "at a great feast of languages, and stol'n the scraps" (V.i.36). In name and obtuseness, if with humanist touches, he resembles Gargantua's slow scholastic tutor, Holoferne (*G* 14), while his belief that "the posterior of the day" is a "liable, congruent, and measurable" way of saying "afternoon" (V.i.91–92) recalls the Limousin scholar.[33] The author of *Tom a Lincoln* (possibly Thomas Heywood) may have noticed Rabelais's scholars. His boaster uses words like *metagrabilized,* which, although it is what he has done to four "ladyes Collosodiums" (l. 2071), is also what Janotus did to his speech ("il y a dix huyt jours que je suis à matagraboliser ceste belle harangue"). Jourda defines this as "méditer," Cotgrave as "to dunce upon, to puzzle, or (too much) beat the braines about," and Jonson as "excogitare."[34] It seems a sorry way to treat collosodiums, whatever they may be.

"Merrie Conceits of Good Words":
Putting Rabelais's Wit to Work

No one before Urquhart approached Rabelais with Cotgrave's lexical expertise and curiosity; nonetheless, a number of writers likewise found him a repository — an author — of telling words and phrases. Like Cotgrave, that is, some enjoyed Rabelais not for (or not only for) gusty talk about the body or satirical fantasy but for self-conscious lexical creativity and disorienting verbal play. Many allusions show readers engaged by energetic vocabulary that might do new service. A few also show interest in how or whether words mean.

Readers would have found a label for Rabelais's eruptive heap of words — together with a definition of the genre or mode in which he heaped them — in an essay that is probably by the scholar Pierre Pithou. Appended to the anti-Ligue (but not anti-Catholic) *Satyre ménippée* (1594) by Pierre Le Roy and other "Politiques," it explains that the adjective *Menippized*

> is not new or unusuall, for it is more then sixteene hundred yeares agoe, that Varro called by Quintillian, and by S. Augustine, the most skilfull amongst the Romanes, made Saytres of this name also, which Macrobius sayth were called Cyniquized, and Menippized: to which he gave that name because of Menippus the Cynicall Philosopher, who also had made the like before him, al ful of salted jestings, & poudred merie conceits of good words, to make men to laugh, and to discover the vicious men of his time. And Varro imitating him, did the like in prose, as since his time there hath done the like, Petronius Arbiter, & Lucian in the Greek tongue, & since his time Apuleius, and in our age that good fellow Rabelaiz, who hath passed all other men in contradicting others, and pleasant conceits, if hee would cut off from them some quodlibetarie speeches in tavernes, and his salt and biting words in alehouses.[35]

(Readers, though, would also have seen Rabelais happily cited as an authority on the flatulent Isle of Ruach [*QL* 43], in a scene worthy of any alehouse.)

English writers could notice Rabelais's "quodlibetarie" moments, but they could also take pieces of his text for such purposes as the micromanagement of tone. Although this hardly means that they took the full measure of Rabelais's interest in how words relate to things, examining the appropriation of his prose, name, or notions can illuminate their texts.

Citing Rabelais was not a neutral or simple matter. Welcoming him into one's pages, if sometimes with a distancing smile because of the air of notoriety or levity hovering about his name, implies several things about oneself. Not readily shocked, naively rustic, or "Puritan"—indeed, graced with a latitudinarian and urbane temper—one knows the secular world and its follies and can take obscenity and scatology in stride; one is cosmopolitan enough to know French literature beyond the faded delicacies of Desportes, for example, or other writers associated with female audiences (despite the patronage of Marguerite de Navarre, Rabelais's implied readership is less feminine than that of Marot or Ronsard); one probably has a tough-minded, masculine, and disabused taste for satire rather than—or as well as—romance or love toys; one can catch jokes that require an erudition beyond that of most gentlemen and virtually all ladies; finally, one is skeptical toward pretty legends, airy idealism, and pretension. Although no one who cited or quoted Rabelais as the witty author of adoptable anecdotes or comments claims all these characteristics, the nuggets borrowed from him seem designed to give this impression.

On September 17, 1598, John Chamberlain, tireless author of gossipy letters, wrote his friend Dudley Carleton, who was then "attending on the Lord Governor of Ostend," that happily a cold has kept him from accompanying Rowland Lytton in escorting a lady home to her father, Lord St. John: "for how so ever they use me, yet me thincks still I am out of my element when I am among Lords, and I am of Rabelais minde that they looke big *comme un millord d'Angleterre*."[36] Chamberlain was the son of a Lord Mayor, a worldly man who knew France well, had such friends as William Camden, Thomas Bodley, and William Gilbert (in whose London house he was living during these years), and kept in touch with the court. To his eye, however, aristocrats look large, the very redundancy of saying that English lords appear big like English lords indicating some momentary frazzlement.

Chamberlain's allusion suits his faintly self-mocking urbanity, as he plays not so much the naive country mouse as—implicitly—the amused city mouse with digs near St. Paul's buzz and bookstalls. Lords may be "big," but Chamberlain has the large world of books and news at hand and can quote a French writer who might not suit all ears. For it is possible to hear, I think, a hint that although Carleton and Chamberlain can enjoy Rabelais, the "big" lord would not appreciate him. The rueful allusion, relaxing the tone even while admitting anxiety about rank, sets up what one might call a homosocial claim to shared taste. Carleton would remember that Rabelais's giants are bigger than any "millord d'Angleterre." Yet the words quoted are not in Rabelais's extant works. *Pantagruel*'s Thaumaste is an English blowhard, not a lord; indeed, Rabelais's only specifically English "millords" are the Lord Deputy of Calais, the subject in *TL* 47 of complex and indecent puns on *debts*, lighthouses, and *fellows* but not called big, and the duke of Clarence — more famous for drowning in malmsey than for size (*QL* 33). This "Rabelais" is less an author than the memory or illusion of one.

Chamberlain's citation adds cosmopolitan texture to his prose. The politically naive do not read Rabelais. The same dynamic is at work decades later in a book by the ardently royalist Thomas Nashe "Philonomon," as he signed his edition of Acatius Evenkellius' *Schoole of Potentates* (1648). A monitory study of the falls of magnates, the translation announces itself as showing "The Mutability of Worldly Honour," but Nashe's appended "Illustrations and Observations" are hardly solemn, several times quoting Rabelais to quicken the argument. If one may judge from three examples, he was drawn to moments of heightened descriptive or rhetorical energy.

Annotating a quotation from Sallust that calls avarice a "Beast insufferable," Nashe says that some beasts prey upon "harmlesse creatures, and are unprofitable both in life and death"; others, "milde" and "sociable," live on what "the earth naturally brings forth, and are profitable both in life and death." A covetous man is the former, who "spoyles and depopulates"; thus

> Rablais hath a tale of a Mare, which Phaio King of Numidia sent out of Africa, who comming into a Wood neare Orleans, containing in length 35 miles, and in breadth 37, with her very taile in a moment hewed it down, *parmi par-là comme un faucher fait d'herbes*, as the Authour saith, as a mower would doe a handfull of grasse with the sythe. I cannot compare our Beast here to any thing more aptly then to this Mare, who by an Art which hee [the covetous man] hath, is able to throw downe Townes and Steeples, and like another Circe turne the Inhabitants into stones, having eaten them up. (Sigs. X2v–X3, more or less from G 16)

There is something odd here, for although Gargantua's mare does level a forest, provoked by insects into swishing her big tail, she is no carnivore and has the narrator's amused sympathy. In Nashe's train of thought she expresses an early capitalist greed that is also a Circe combining Medusa (she turns people to stone) with traditional giants (she eats people and is associated with steeples).

Nashe's epilogue, reiterating his disdain of the many-tongued multitude and stressing statesmen's need for wise guidance through the world's wilderness of voices, starts with a quotation from *TL* 28 that tells how when Panurge "consulted with the multitude concerning his marriage, Friar John utterly diswaded him from it, and why? because the bels sounded forth nothing els, but *marie point, marie point, point, point, point, point, si tu te marie, tu t'en repentiras, tiras, iras, coqu seras*, marry not, marry not, not not, not not, if you doe, you will repent, pent pent, for you will be a Cuckhold; which put Panurge into such an agony that hee never durst adventure upon a wife by reason of the sound of the Bels" (sig. Ee6v). Again, Nashe has certainly read Rabelais; again, his understanding seems insecure, for Panurge in fact continues to seek advice on marriage. A Greek word in Nashe's margin identifies him as *Panurgos*, returning the man to his lexical origin and showing—as does this passage's proto-Urquhartian English—that some readers were alert to Rabelais's verbal inventiveness.

Later, arguing that mortals are pilgrims lodged in an inn run by Delilah, Nashe urges us to treat spiritual enemies with contempt: for, "*Oingnes vilain il vous poindra poindrez vilain, il vous oindra* (saith Rab.) annoint a villaine, and he will annoy and sting thee; but sting and annoy him, and hee will annoint thee; the way to make a knave know himselfe, is to neglect him; and the way to have honour in the world, is to trample upon the world, and to neglect it; especially that frothy windy honour which consists in popular applause" (sig. Ff5–Ff5v; cf. *G* 32). Shrewd counsel, if hardly Christian, and phrased with pleasantly chiastic assonance and rhyme. It was originally proffered, however, not by Rabelais but by an adviser to Grandgousier's boastfully choleric enemy, Picrochole. Since Picrochole loses the ensuing war, the advice may not be very sage after all. Is Nashe imperceptive? Perhaps what he says shows again the detachable nature of quotations in a culture that encouraged the collection and manipulation of decontextualized fragments of discourse. "Saith Rab." need not mean "thinks Rab." In any case, "Rabelais" and his words, misread or not, help political observations seem penetratingly worldly and hence credible. All to no avail, of course, and Nashe, it was said, died of a broken heart after the execution of Charles I the following year.

The great antiquary John Selden likewise found Rabelais funny and serviceable. I will describe later how he excerpted passages to promote skepticism toward legend even while evoking alternatives to the very historicism he helped beget. Shortly after performing this double feat in the interstices of Drayton's *Poly-Olbion*, Selden published his learned *Titles of Honor* (1614, but written, he says, some time earlier). Perhaps because here he must think more about words than about stories, his allusions to Rabelais show his interest in vocabulary. With an eye out for lexical evidence that a document is what it claims to be, Selden is concerned with etymology and linguistic transmission, with words as referential units that have histories of their own, just like institutions, practices, and public roles or positions indicated by honorific titles. No wonder he treated the misuse or misprision of language with disdain, applying his most trenchant humor to older scholars like those Rabelais, too, found ridiculous. In their impatience with much medieval learning and legend, if not always with medieval literature, the two were kindred spirits.

Honor explains why Selden relies so little on older legal authorities. Lacking good history and philology, they are not as useful as the "learned Budé, Alciat, Hotoman, Cujas, . . . before whom the Bodie of that Profession was not amisse compared to a faire Robe, of Cloth of Gold, or of Richest Stuff and Fashion, *Qui fust* (saving all mannerly respect to you, Reader) *brodée de Merde*" (sigs. d3v–d4). The margin sends us to "Rablais livre 2. chap.5," where we find Pantagruel, having recently studied law, remarking that lawbooks remind him of "une belle robbe d'or, triumphante et precieuse à merveilles, qui feust brodée de merde." For "au monde n'y a livres tant beaulx, tant aornées, tant elegans, comme sont les textes des *Pandectes,* mais la brodure d'iceulx, c'est assavoir la Glose de Accurse, est tant salle, tant infame et punaise, que ce n'est que ordure et villenie."[37]

Selden's Rabelais is here, for once, the humanist satirist, burster of margins that deform through pride, laziness, or ignorance whatever is good in the texts that their constricting edges surround. Stupid or vain glossators give texts constipation, so to speak, binding them up so as to prevent the flow of words, knowledge, ideas. To Pantagruel, however, the margins *are* shit. True, if dirt is just matter out of place, then the problem with scholars like Accursius is simply that they don't know where to put the stuff or from which orifice to void it. After Selden adopts the sarcasm, detaching it from a book full of such humor and thus turning it to mere insult, he apologizes. The words are crude, but he has the delicacy to keep them in French, the civility to beg our pardon in mid-quotation, and the scholarly precision to send us to the right place in the author cited. The joke is, after all, not his own, and the marginal identification of its origin protects Selden against blame even as he slides it into his own sentence. Selden was not much of a stylist, but this maneuver has elegance.

A little later Selden again complains of older commentators who, writing "on the Digests or Code" before "the cleerer light of Learning began mongst our Fathers, talk for the most part like Rablais his Bridoye." There is no marginal citation, perhaps because nothing is quoted, and this time Rabelais is clean enough to enter the main text with his name announced. Bridoye is the judge in *TL* 39–44 whom Panurge consults. Although well-meaning, he has a laughably awful way of talking. For example, he explains why he reviews the legal evidence even when he will decide a case by tossing the dice:

> Premierement pour la forme, en omission de laquelle ce qu'on a faict n'estre valable prouve très bien *Spec, tit. de instr. edit et tit. de rescript. praesent;* d'adventaige, vous sçavez trop mieulx que souvent, en procedures judiciaires, les formalitez destruisent les materialitez et substances; car, *forma mutata mutatur substantia, ff. ad exhib. l. Julianus ; ff. ad. leg. falcid. l. Si is qui quadringenta, et extra., de deci., c. ad audientiam, et de celebrat. miss c. in quandam.* (*TL* 40)[38]

What pleases Selden is humanist satire not just of older attitudes but of an older jargon so clogged with citations that no human ear could follow the argument, and persuasion is impossible. Justly or not, those affected by Renaissance humanism associated failure to get at the heart of things with older, less rhetorical views of language. Selden himself cared little for eloquence and fancy tropes, but he did agree with Rabelais that ignorant late-medieval scribbling impeded understanding and that it would take informed excavation to retrieve past texts and learning. Some, although by no means everybody, would take Bridoye's dice throwing as holy folly; Bridoye trusts in Providence (and his cases are never overruled). Selden is not concerned with the dice, however, but with the judge's multiplication of authorities that do him no good.

   Since Selden stuffs his own prose with names and titles, he may have harbored some fellow-feeling for Judge Bridlegoose (as Urquhart calls him). His magisterial and controversial *Historie of Tithes* (1618) refers to Bridoye again, saying of scholars who wrongly think tithing to be required by ancient law that such opinions "are so frequently obvious, that to cite Authorities for them, were but to imitate Rablais his Bridoye." Yet, says Selden, "we may specially remember . . . ," and cites more authorities. In *Honor,* recollecting poor Bridoye's language had reinforced the dismissal of past incompetence. Now the same allusion admits a touch of self-mocking humor and permits Selden to sidestep gracefully around the fact that he too is a piler-up of citations that demand inclusion even while impeding the prose. Rabelais makes only three appearances in these two long books, yet they show sage care for what might give sarcasms the right mixture of skeptical urbanity and earthy humor, rendering more attractive the arguments' weighty learning and risky implications.[39]

   Selden's *De Diis Syris,* a study that approaches what we would call comparative religion through language and etymology, again notices Rabelais the philologist, if with a somewhat sidelong glance. Chapter 5 of Part II explores various words for the erect male member; the heading reads: "Priapus. Miph-letzeth. Maachae, Asae regis matris, idolum. Unde, apud Ebraeos, deductum. Graecorum & Latinorum Phallus. Francisci Rablesii Nephleseth Numen." Speculating on the possible Hebrew origin of the word *phallus,* Selden ex-ecutes a characteristic dance of approach and reversal, admitting a possibility and then shrugging it off. Rabelais helps him shrug: "sed conjecturis huius-modi fidem prodigere, moris nostri non est. Numen hoc, nisi me fallat memo-ria, Nephleseth pro Miphlezeth nuncupatur in Satyricis lepidissimi doctissimi-que Francisci Rablesii facetiis."[40] It is heartening to see Rabelais recognized for learning and witty grace — *lepidus* suggests charm and irony. Yet he is here "remembered," not consulted; the books now open on Selden's table do not, we are probably to gather, include these "most learned jests," whatever their relevance to Priapus and phallus. The tone of pleased recollection and slight distancing, the evocation of someone both learned and facetious, is probably just what Selden wants for this typical moment of skeptical inclusion, of re-cording opinions without according belief.

Selden was not the only one to adopt Rabelais's excremental vocabulary while making a complex gesture of summoning up and brushing aside. Sir William Moore's verse satire *A Counter-Buff to Lysimachus Nicanor [John Corbet]: Calling Himself a Jesuite* (Edinburgh, 1640), takes on "Popish hyrel-ings" who threaten both the Scottish Covenant and Charles I. All the Cove-nantors really want, argues Moore, is true religion, ancient liberty, the sup-pression of gamesters and sycophants, and the arrest of libelers and sowers of sedition. Having spent time at the English court, Moore wishes he could tell Charles how to recapture his people's love and stop peering through "gommie spectacles." It is Jesuits who hate kings, says Moore, which is why Corbet secretly hopes to make readers think that kings derive their rights from the "peoples suffrage." Priests use an analogous method in the confessional, teaching sin by offering absolution:

> Those mang-merd priests, drunk with the dregs of sin,
> When they a novice to confesse begin,
> They make him first bread-band his guiltinesse;
> And all his sinfull thoughts, words, deeds, expresse. (Sigs. B1–B1v)[41]

A marginal note to *mang-merd* correctly says that "Rabelais cals them so," crediting an author while giving us someone to blame for a repellent notion.

The *Quart livre*'s "Briefve declaration" gives *masche-merdes* as a synonym for *scatophages,* meaning excrement-eaters. But Cotgrave defines *mangemerde* as "a fish thats otherwise called, Saupe." A *saupe* is in turn "a small-headed, little-mouthed, blunt-nosed, large-scaled, unsavorie, and unwholesome sea-fish, having many golden lines all along from her gills to her taile; and thence, likened by some to the Gilthead; by others mistaken for the fish whereof Stockefish is made." Cotgrave gives neither word a "¶Rab," evidence that Moore had actually read G 40, in which the giant explains why monks are retired from the world: "Ils mangent la merde du monde, c'est à dire les pechez, et comme mache-merdes, l'on les rejecte en leurs retraictz."[42] If Cotgrave is right in thinking that a *mang-merd* is also a fish, this seems — as a recollection of Lenten rules — an appropriate epithet for monks. Snatched from its surrounding atmosphere of friendly dialogue, though, this is an ugly taunt: Moore finds in others the failures of charity that his genre requires of himself. So he insists that Corbet is a pig, a Cerberus, a scurrilous "pasquiller" who spits in the face of his mother, Scotland. The irony could not have been lost on Moore, for he understood the paradox of writing sneeringly while claiming moral authority, and he smoothly performs the requisite preliminary moves, explaining that he must speak out and . . . it *is* hard not to write satire.

Francis Bacon noticed Rabelais's thinking on language and interpretation, as one might expect from his ties to those two readers of *Gargantua et Pantagruel,* John Selden and James I. His acquaintances at court and in town made up precisely the political and professional milieu in which "Rabelais" might find appreciation. Amused by *Pantagruel*'s parodic library (see below), he also knew the prologue to *Gargantua,* recycling a few sentences for *The Advancement of Learning* (1605). Because he does not credit his original, this "borrowing" (the term seems apt) matters less for what it contributes to Rabelais's English image than for demonstrating how Bacon read with attention to texts' thoughts on signs and authorial intention. These issues were important to him: in work after work, his project of "advancing" learning necessitated identifying, clarifying, and reforming the relation of words to things, in enterprises ranging from scientific discovery to the elucidation of myths.

Understandably, Bacon was struck by a passage that provocatively touches on questions that consumed him. A politician, he poignantly applies to statesmen the conceit he adopts. In a discussion of how learned but indiscreet men can bring learning into disrepute, Bacon reflects:

> Many may be well seen in the passages of government and policy, which are to seek in little and punctual [minuscule] occasions. I refer them [the observers] also to that which Plato said of his master Socrates, whom he compared to the gallipots of apothecaries, which on the outside had apes and owls and antiques [antics: grotesques] but contained within sovereign and precious liquors and confections; acknowledging that to external report he was not without superficial levities and deformities, but was inwardly replenished with excellent virtues and powers.[43]

Bacon is not paraphrasing the *Symposium,* which compares the ugly and seemingly inane Socrates to statuettes of Silenus that open up to reveal handsome gods, nor Erasmus' *Folly* or his adage on the Silenus of Alcibiades, but Rabelais's medicalized revision in the prologue to *Gargantua.* To show how one important mind recalled it (for Bacon's summary suggests memory, not recent rereading), I quote at length. After noting Plato's comparison, Rabelais says that

> Silenes estoient jadis petites boites, telles que voyons de present es bouticques des apothecaires, pinctes au dessus de figures joyeuses et frivoles, comme de harpies, satyres, oysons bridez, lievres cornuz, canes bastées, boucqs volans, cerfz limonniers et aultres telles pinctures contrefaictes à plaisir pour exciter le monde à rire (quel fut Silene, maistre du bon Bacchus); mais au dedans l'on reservoit les fines drogues comme baulme, ambre gris, amomon, musc, zivette, pierreries et aultres choses precieuses. Tel disoit estre Socrates, parce que, le voyans au dehors et l'estimans par l'exterieure apparence, n'en eussiez donné un coupeau d'oignon, tant laid il estoit de corps et ridicule en son maintien, le nez pointu, le reguard d'un toreau, le visaige d'un fol, simple en meurs, rustiq en vestimens, pauvre de fortune, infortuné en femmes, inepte à tous offices de la republique, tousjours riant, toujours beuvant d'autant à un chascun, tousjours se guabelant, tousjours dissimulant son divin sçavoir; mais, ouvrans ceste boyte, eussiez au dedans trouvé une celeste et impreciable drogue: entendement plus que humain, vertus merveilleuse, couraige invincible, sobresse non pareille, contentement certain, asseurance parfaicte, deprisement incroyable de tout ce pourquoy les humains tant veiglent, courent, travaillent, navigent et bataillent.[44]

The boozy and pocky readers whom Rabelais summons are given a lesson in reading, advised a few lines later to gnaw for meaning like a dog seeking a bone's "sustantificque" marrow.

Whether Bacon fully gauged Rabelais's caginess, he certainly changes his tone, arguing for a merely reversed perception: some politicians who are deficient in minor points are nonetheless wise. Rabelais is more Erasmian: the "wise" may not know what ugliness and beauty truly are. Bacon asks us to look beyond important men's surface faults to the energies and powers within. Rabelais asks us to relocate value and ironize our perspective on what is inside and what out, on what matters and what does not. Bacon's project was to clarify mankind's vision, whereas Rabelais created paradoxes that were inexpressible by reasonable language. And it is he who recalls that the wise Socrates had no talent for public service; Bacon's gauche magnates are by contrast valuable to the state.

One paradox of Bacon's mentality, as of Plato's, was that although his project demanded a distrust of the imagination, he himself was a brilliant imaginer, as witness his utopian *New Atlantis,* and he was drawn to mythical imaginings by others, as witness his *Wisdome of the Ancients.* In the *Advancement*'s section on poetry, Bacon again remembers *Gargantua*'s prologue, converting into a statement its skeptical question concerning allegory: "Croiez vous en vostre foy qu'oncques Homere, escrivent l'*Iliade* et *Odyssée,* pensast es allegories lesquelles de luy ont calfreté Plutarche, Heraclides Ponticq, Eustatie, Phornute, et ce que d'iceulx Politian a desrobé?"[45] Rabelais gives a complex instruction: find the marrow but do not impose meanings (especially, he may hint, those inviting prosecution). Bacon could vacillate about what ancient poets intended their stories to mean. Sharing Rabelais's impatience with arbitrary allegorizing, he still felt capable of decoding ancient myths to find meanings their creators had hidden. Here he plays the skeptic: "Surely," he says, "of those poets which are now extant, even Homer himself (notwithstanding he was made a kind of scripture by the later schools of the Grecians), yet I should without any difficulty pronounce that his fables had no such inwardness in his own meaning." True, he adds that "what they might have upon a more original tradition, is not easy to affirm; for he was not the inventor of many of them."[46] Rabelais asks for interpretive tact; Bacon suspects that import and intention lie in the earliest authorship or invention.

The prologue to *Gargantua* indicates, ambiguously, something of Rabelais's hermeneutics and linguistics. Such concerns become narrative when Pantagruel's crew, sailing the northern waters, finds some once-frozen but now thawing noises and words, newly audible echoes of a recent wintry battle (*QL* 55–56). Some are solid enough to be picked up and warmed in the hands. Rabelais did not invent the notion of quick-frozen sound that later liquefies into significance, although his gellid noises now sport heraldic colors and, whatever they sound like when melted, look to the eye like puns. In this ironically chivalric context, for example, "Motz de gueule" are both "gueules" (which Cotgrave defines as "gules; red, or sanguine, in Blazon [heraldry]") and come from the "gueule" (throat), which makes these red remnants of bloodshed appear as jokes (a "mot de gueule," says Cotgrave, is "a jeast, or merrie word").

In his "Progress in Virtue," Plutarch recalls how Antiphanes had wittily compared Plato's conversation with young men to words that in a certain city froze when spoken in winter and became audible only when thawed by summer; so too, only in old age, if then, would his auditors take Plato's meaning.[47] Castiglione adapts the fancy for Book II of *The Courtier:* Il Magnifico laughingly cites, as an example of outrageous lying, the tale of a Tuscan merchant in Poland who despite a Russo-Polish war bargains with some Moscovites across the frozen Dnieper; when Russian words freeze in mid-air, the Poles build a fire on the ice that melts them into sound. Rabelais's episode may also evoke reports on the icy reaches of the North Atlantic and islands resounding with strange voices.[48]

The episode has multiple associations: with theories on the materiality of words, with pedagogy, with travelers' not-always-credible accounts of their adventures, with recent arctic exploration, with courtiership, with mercantile discourse, with words' relation to time, and perhaps with the Word's release after centuries of frost and the need, nevertheless, for endangered evangelical Christians to keep silent.[49] In Rabelais's version, delayed noises become recognizable as cries, trumpet blasts, and canon shots, while words, because in a barbarous tongue, remain uncommunicative. The phenomenon is epistemologically fascinating, as are the biblical and classical analogues that Pantagruel cites. It is the practical pilot, though, who recognizes the words as aural relics of a fight between the Arismapiens and Nephelibates, evidence (although he does not say so) of how far language and humanity have declined since Adamic naming in a peaceful Eden.[50]

How the English read the episode's philosophical or religious implications is hard to tell, but it did inspire several writers to amused allusion. If they seem to have found the notion of frozen words more entertaining than philosophically threatening, it should be recalled that both Plutarch and Castiglione likewise treat it as a jest, a "mot de gueule," albeit in Plutarch's case a pointed one. Some palimpsestic mixture of Plutarch, Castiglione, and Rabelais (it is hard to be sure of the proportions, but I see no reason to exclude any of the three) lies behind a less-than-jesting but determinedly suave passage in a letter that John Donne wrote in about 1600 to Sir Henry Wotton. Along with affection, the writer sends "seald up" words that will thaw when read by designated recipients (I expand the contractions):

> Sir That love which went with you followes & overtakes & meetes you. if words seald up in letters be like words spoken in those frosty places where they are not heard till the next thaw they have yet this advantage that where they are heard they are herd only by one or such as in his judgment they are fitt for. I am no Courtier for without having lived there desirously I cannot have sin'd enough to have deserv'd that reprobate name: I may sometymes come thither & bee no courtier as well as they may sometymes go to chapell & yet are no christians. I am there now where because I must do some evill I envy your being in the country not that it is a vice will make any great shew here for they live at a far greter rate & expence of wickednes. but because I will not be utterly out of fashion & unsociable. I gleane such vices as the greater men

(whose barnes are full) scatter yet I learne that the learnedst in vice suffer some misery for when they have reapd flattery or any other fault long there comes some other new vice in request wherein they are unpracticed. only the women are free from this charg.[51]

After more satirical reflections on court life, the letter concludes with a report on the disgraced Essex and his followers, "no more mist here then the Aungells which were cast downe from heaven nor (for anything I see) likelyer to re-tourne."

This sounds like Donne: adept at witty analogy, self-conscious, adroit at seeming to disdain in an offhand way the very court society, so desired by others and so transparent to himself, that he has admittedly sought. Castiglione would admire the self-protective and casually sophisticated tone; indeed, by mentioning frozen words Donne may gesture self-mockingly at *The Courtier* even while playing the anti-court card that is so useful to experienced courtiers. Since Plutarch's *Moralia* was easily read by the educated, the gesture may also recall not just Il Magnifico's joke about Muscovite bargaining but the notion of words that melt at some appropriate time. If so, the focus shifts from *oral* pedagogy (the hearer, now older, can finally comprehend what a philosopher once said) to aiming *written* and "seald" words at the right reader in a world of conspiracy and censorship.

At some point, though (a topic to which I shall return), Donne read Rabelais. He too is relevant here; even the vague "frosty places" seem closer to what Pantagruel finds somewhere up north than to the more specific Dnieper or city in Castiglione and Plutarch, and both writers had an interest in voyages and newfound lands ("The Storme" describes to Christopher Brooke a tempest Donne saw on Essex's 1597 expedition to the Azores). Also significant is the hint some have heard in Rabelais's episode that forbidden words — perhaps Gospel words — can survive to be heard when the times allow. Together with his self-portrait of a (non)courtier, Donne sends news of Essex that must be so prudently worded it will melt only when warmed in the right fingers; the relation of language to time and time-serving cannot have escaped his ironic mind. The frozen words he is likely to have known about, then, make a set of associations fitting his circumstance. The allusion helps him sound worldly but undeluded, well-read but unpedantic, engagingly humorous but with meanings that unwanted readers can see without understanding and wanted ones can "melt" and hear.

Several years later Thomas Coryat published his *Coryates Crudities* (1611), a fairly straightforward, cheerful account of a walking tour on the Continent preceded by a carnival of amicably teasing verses by a crowd of well-known writers that included some celebrities.[52] A well-read and clever gentleman, Coryat annotates these, taking their joshing in good part and, when he can, interpreting them as praise — much as Panurge in the *Tiers livre* twists bad news about cuckoldry into marital encouragement. According to the "character" of him by Ben Jonson, Coryat was "a great and bold Carpenter of words, or (to expresse him in one word like his owne) a Logodaedale." The humor of this "Tongue-Major of the company," says Jonson in a compliment that sounds a lot like Alcofribas touting *Pantagruel,* can cure abscesses, remove the stone, and relieve gout, effective even when "Physick hath turned her back, and Nature hung downe her head for shame." *Crudities* is travel literature, but Jonson and others are just as interested in Coryat as a macaronic cornucopia of language; he is, says Henry Neville, a "Great Merlin Cockay [the writer Folengo] in recounting marveiles." The liminary verses, too, show their authors' fascination with words and how to invent, read, or play with them: the poems include shaped poetry, anagrams, pseudoclassical meters ("encomiological antispastics"), outrageous rhymes like "hop it"/"poppet," Utopian verses, such neologisms as *itinerosissimus,* and parody ("I sing the man, I sing the woful case, / The shirt, the shoes, the shanks").

One poem on Coryat the "Sesqui-superlative" is by "Joannes Donne"; another, which alludes to Rabelais, is by "Joannes Dones." I cannot identify "Dones." He may well be Donne with a typo, although the poems are separated by many pages. Whoever he was, he knows Rabelais's later books, for he links them to travelers' "marveiles." What might Coryat have written about even vaster travels, wonders Dones, since in Europe, "almost for every step he tooke a word":

> What had he done had he ere hug'd th'Ocean
> With swimming Drake or famous Magelan?
> . . . .
> It's not that French which made his Gyant see
> Those uncouth Ilands where words frozen bee,
> Till by the thaw next yeare they'r voic't againe;
> Whose Papagauts, Andoûilets, and that traine
> Should be such matter for a Pope to curse
> As he would make; make! makes ten times worse,
> And yet so pleasing as shall laughter move:
> And be his vaine, his gaine, his praise, his love.
> Sit not still then, keeping fames trump unblowne:
> But get thee Coryate to some land unknowne. (P. 71)

Coryat glosses *French* as "Rablais," and *Gyant* as "Pantagruel." *Papagauts* are the greedy "popehawks" who inhabit *CL*'s Ringing Island, and the *Andoûilets* are the ferocious female but phallic sausages with "Mardigras" as their watch-word against whom Pantagruel's crew fights in *QL* 3 5–43. Several points need stressing: Dones imagines further travel by Coryat as cause for further laughing discourse, not as a source of real news; this discourse is associated with Rabelaisian voyages into linguistic fantasy and with satire that is easily read as anti-Catholic; and the anger of orthodox Catholicism at Rabelais is well known (and something Coryat could likewise provoke).[53]

Although it does not refer to frozen words, Lawrence Whitaker's poem on Coryat mentions both the sausages and the library of Hugh of St. Victor. Again the focus is on words: linguistic difference and the frustration it causes; language as invention and inflation; language as cloth and food (Coryat's work is costumed as mincemeat stew). As a contribution to *Crudities*'s macaronic jumble, Whitaker writes quasi-French, starting with a preface that tells us where to shelve this book:

> Sonnet composé en rime à la Marotte, accomodé au style de l'Autheur du livre; faict en loüange de cet Heroique Geant Odcombien, nommé non Pantagruel, mais Pantagrue, c'est à dire, ne Oye, ny Oison, ains tout Grue, accoustré icy en Hochepot, Hachis, ou Cabirotade, pour tenir son rang en la Librairie de l'Abbaye St. Victor à Paris, entre le livre de Marmoretus de baboinis & cingis, & celuy de Tirepetanus de optimitate triparum; & pour porter le nom de la Cabirotade de Coryat, ou, de l'Apodemistichopezologie de l'Odcombeuili Somerseti (Soti) en, &c.
>
> Tay toy Rablais, rabbaissé soit l'orgeuil
> De tes Endouilles, qui d'un bel accueil
> Recevrent ton Geant en la Farouche,
> A ce Geant d'Odcombe pierre & souche
> Parla, fournit des comptes, l'entretint
> Le muguetta, voire & son sens maintint
> En ce travail: Mais scais-tu bien pour quoy?
> Son Chef Cresté luy donna ceste loy,
>   Que des hommes du lieu ne scachant le language,
>   Parmy troncs & cailloux il passeroit sa rage. (Pp. 42–43)[54]

Coryat's notes, also in French, deliberately misidentify "à la Marotte" (a *marotte* was a fool's scepter) as "selo[n] le style de Clément Marot, vieil Poete François" and, more straightforwardly, the *Geant* as "Pantagruel" and *Farouche* as "Une Isle ainsi appellee par Rablais." *Crudities* is in truth only intermittently Rabelaisian, for the real satirical medley is found here, in the liminary antics by city and university wits. Finding shelf space for Coryat in the Renaissance's most famous imaginary library is no compliment to his veracity, yet the insult is affably offered, and the comparison to a hodgepodge defines the work as a prose *lanx satura,* as Menippean satire.

There is one more printed notice of Rabelais's frozen words. Thomas Tomkis' *Lingua* (1607) is an academic comedy about language, fiction, women, the body, and more. "Lingua" herself — the play's sole woman — is the tongue.[55] She has, say the Five Senses, "made Rhetorique wanton" and reduced "Logicke to bable"; "a Woman in every respect," she should not have the "dignitie" of being "a Sense" (sig. F3). By the play's end she has been remanded to the care of Gustus and his guardian teeth. These have their work cut out for them, for Lingua is a rowdy with a taste for paradox: although she calls Truth a "Una" who "cannot be divided," when accused of dishonesty she replies with swift duplicity, "I say so too, therefore I do not lye" (sigs. A3–A3v). *Lingua* is also an anthology of discourses that in Tomkis's view begged for parody or comment. His Phantastes satirizes "puling" Petrarchans (sig. D3), for example; when summoned to court, Lingua talks jargon similar to that of Rabelais's lawyers; and Appetite adopts with puns the language of Carnival's war with Lent, vowing to fight with spears of spareribs, discharge "Hartichock pies," and use "boyled pickrills" for pikes (sig. C4, a fish joke). Even Olfactus's friend Tobacco, king of Trinidad, has a strange tongue that Memory recalls as Arcadian but Phantastes imagines to be Antipodean. Perhaps Phantastes learned Antipodean from Panurge, who speaks it.[56]

Common Sense, of course, dislikes such idiosyncratic language, condemning the macaronic "Gallemaufry" of words that Lingua speaks at her trial: "I am perswaded these same language makers have the very quality of cold in their wit, that freezeth all Heterogeneall languages together, congealing English Tynne, Graecian Gold, Romaine Latine [a pun on *Latin* and *latten*] all in a lumpe" (III.5). Because this play elsewhere echoes Rabelais, and because its lying Mendaccio boasts that he dictated *Gargantua et Pantagruel,* it is likely that *Lingua* alludes to Pantagruel's adventure with colorfully material language.[57] The tone, however, has shifted. Rabelais mixes pathos and comedy, blood-red sounds with sanguine jests. His travelers warm ice into the cries of those who are now past speech; they do not freeze common words into portentous legalese. Both authors comment on the linguistic rubble near Babel, but whereas Rabelais acknowledges loss and distance, Tomkis satirizes conglomeration and anachronism, a monstrous verbal promiscuity that this play calls female.

The writers I have quoted all assume that Rabelais is an inventively comic writer and that his comedy is acceptable to their readers. Citing him helps exclude as readers the rustic, the solemn, and the dull. No wonder Nashe called him merry. Nashe dedicates *An Almond for a Parrat* (1590), an attack on Martin Marprelate that a modern scholar with mild exaggeration calls "one of the most scurrilous and venomous accounts ever written," to the famous clown "Monsieur du Kempe, Jestmonger and Vice-regent generall to the Ghost of Dicke Tarlton."[58] If Kemp rejects it, "Ile preferre it to the soule of Dick Tarlton, who, I know, will entertaine it with thankes, imitating herein that merry man Rablays, who dedicated most of his workes to the soule of the old Queene of Navarre, many yeares after her death, for that she was a maintainer of mirth in her life. Marry, God send us more of her making, and then some of us should not live so discontented as we do; for, now a dayes, a man can not have a bout with a Balletter, or write *Midas habet aures asininas* in great Romaine letters, but hee shall bee in daunger of a further displeasure."

Nashe's authorship of this scruffily entertaining pamphlet in support of episcopacy has been doubted; so has his knowledge of Rabelais, who dedicates only the *Tiers livre* to Marguerite, before her death. Yet the error is not the sort one makes without some knowledge; nor is it astonishing that Nashe would not know when the queen had died, especially since Rabelais claims that she has left her body on earth and asks her to look down from her "divine mansion" on the "joyous deeds of good Pantagruel."[59] It seems highly probable that Nashe knew a writer whose style and self-presentation his own can resemble, at least superficially.[60] He never names Rabelais elsewhere, however, and the evidence that he read further in *Gargantua et Pantagruel* is not certain.

Nashe's Rabelais retails mirth, and his Marguerite seems more the writer of the lively *Heptaméron* than the devout poet of the *Miroir de l'âme pécheresse* (England knew both Marguerites). Yet Rabelais's dedication in 1546 has serious implications: the queen's spirit is lifted by Pantagruelism, not weighed down by Sorbonnical anxiety. If Marguerite patronized the "merry," she also gave her only sometimes successful protection to those, like Marot and Rabelais, whose humor was read as heresy and who remained "in daunger." And that is what Nashe — from ignorance or calculation — omits, his anonymous dedication reducing this drama to the encouragement of merriment. The irony is that Marprelate offered a more strenuous version of the unorthodoxy that upset the *bien pensants* of Marguerite's day. Yet the need for congenial patrons and the risk of pamphleteering in a world where merely noting Midas's ass's ears could cost a writer his own were matters about which Nashe cared. So "merriment" is tied, through denial (and a pun on "merry/Marry"?) to political meanings — hidden or advertised by typographical play — and to the risk of misreading by authority. Secret meanings are denied, just as *Gargantua*'s prologue denies them, in words that can double as an invitation. That Nashe already has a queen able to patronize writers, that he writes on behalf of that

queen's government, that the same queen had translated Marguerite's un-
merry *Miroir,* and that his wish is nevertheless for more Marguerites, further
confuses this enigmatic moment.[61]

"To Sit Downe in the Chair of the Scorners": Rabelais's Atheist Mockery

Thus there he stood, whylest high over his head
There written was the purport of his sin,
In cyphers strange, that few could rightly read,
BONFONT: but *bon* that once had written bin,
Was raced out, and *Mal* was now put in.
So now Malfont was plainely to be red;
Eyther for th'evill, which he did therein
Or that he likened was to a welhed
Of evill words, and wicked sclaunders by him shed.
— Edmund Spenser, *The Faerie Queene* V.ix.26

Poor Malfont: Has he in truth been slandering others? Spenser's knight of
justice sees him as he enters Queen Mercilla's royal court of equity, but outside
Fairyland, and sometimes even there, whether a writer's words are a fount of
"bon" or "mal" depends to a disturbing extent on who is listening. Perhaps it
was not Bonfont who took to calumniating others but those (sometimes powerful) others who took his satire as slander. Rabelais was clearly a wellhead of
wit for the sophisticated, especially those in the university, court, and legal
worlds who from youth or conviction had what the French called a libertin
attitude. Dropping his name could signal impatience with moralistic solemnity, Platonic airiness, mental rigidity, or provincialism. One person's fine jest,
however, is another's cruel sneer: the goodness or badness of verbal founts is in
the mouth of the taster.

It is not simply that Rabelais was misjudged by those relying on hearsay:
humor was itself subject to doubt.[62] Although the God of Israel, says David in
the second Psalm, "shal laugh: the lord shal have [his enemies] in derision," the
Psalter opens by condemning those who "sit in the seat of the scorner" (Ps. 1).
Paul disallows "foolish talking" and "jesting [*eutrapelia*], which are things not
comelie" (Eph. 5:4), yet a note in the 1560 Geneva Bible explains that this
forbids only what is "vaine" or "may hurt your neighbour; for otherwise there
be divers examples in the Scriptures of pleasant talke, which is also godlie."
Indeed, secular theories of the risible stress ambivalence, noting its effect on
the body, particularly the heart. As we react to a speech or spectacle that gives
pleasure and pain (neither pure joy nor pure sorrow is comic), our hearts swell

and contract; the fluttering pericardium then pulls on the diaphragm, causing air in the lungs to be expelled as "Ha, ha, ha."[63] Laughter is ambiguous, its element of pain admitted even by those who asserted its therapeutic powers and told of patients cured by monkeys' capers or fools' jests.[64] This medicinal quality seems to have been particularly associated with purgation and hence the colon. "Jestes, and scabbes are much alike," wrote Sir William Cornwallis in his *Essayes:* because both result from "superflous humours," jesting "is only tollerable in them whose natures must of force have that vent, which use it as some bodies do breaking of winde" (1600, sig. I3).

Wit, however, can bruise others in body and spirit. Thomas Wilson's *Arte of Rhetorique* remarks — not wholly in sorrow — that a "nippynge taunte" can "abashe a righte worthy man, and make hym at his wittes ende, . . . I have knowen some so hit of the thumbes, that thei could not tell in the world whether it were beste to fighte, chide, or to go their waie" (p. 275). Wit has a verbal start but somatic finish. Its frequent alliance with eating affirms this physicality: jests promote merriment and appetite, but only if you are invited to the feast, not excluded like, say, the nippingly taunted Malvolio in *Twelfth Night.* As a social climber, though, Malvolio is not a "righte worthy man," for Renaissance joke theory is class conscious. Rabelais's humor has struck readers as laudably or unpleasantly vulgar, but often it only strengthens elements already present in learned discussions and Neo-Latin jestbooks that were not read by the multitude. The theory behind such collections, as behind the section on jests in Castiglione's *Courtier,* was that being *facetus* — having wit, *sal, eutrapelia* — characterizes the well bred and the mentally agile.[65] Those hostile to humor must be socially inadequate: the preface to Poggio Bracciolini's 1470 jestbook admits ironically that he cannot please "rustics."

One need not be *rusticus* to read wit as malice. Was Rabelais the French Lucian? Hardly a recommendation! Did not Lucian mock religion, spurn Christianity, and die torn apart by dogs?[66] Rather than adopt Rabelais's words and anecdotes to leaven or energize discourse, one could exploit the power of "Rabelais" as a bad example: still a citable author, he is an evil well of scornful blasphemy.

Francis Bacon's Rabelais is in this regard a medial figure. Yes, Bacon found *Gargantua*'s Prologue worth paraphrasing for *The Advancement of Learning,* but in the 1625 essay "Of Unity in Religion," Rabelais is "a Master of Scoffing," a scoffing made all the more problematic by Bacon's nearby condemnation of atheists and "prophane Persons" whom Christian disunity encourages "to sit downe in the chaire of the Scorners." Similarly, "Of Atheisme" speaks severely of "contemplative" atheists like Lucian; it blames disbelief in part on modern "Profane Scoffing in Holy Matters."[67] One of the "mucrones verborum," or "pointed speeches," that Bacon collected, published in 1624 as *Apothegms New and Old,* might well seem a "scoff" against "holy matters": "When Rabelais lay on his death-bed, and they gave him the extreme unction, a familiar friend of his came to him afterwards, and asked him; *How he did?* Rabelais answered; *Even going my journey, they have greased my boots already.*"[68]

Did Bacon take this as mockery of religion? Protestants do not accept extreme unction as a sacrament, so Rabelais's jest might seem one of those apothegms that Bacon says Cicero "prettily" defines as "*salinas, saltpits;* that you may extract salt out of, and sprinkle it where you will." Yet expressed in a Catholic country, and, in this anecdote, by one submitting to its customs, the wisecrack might seem as troublesome as Lucian's disrespect toward Zeus. It was, moreover, just one of the deathbed jokes circulating about Rabelais: it was said that he compared the priest who brought him the communion Host to the donkey that carried Christ into Jerusalem; that he died dressed in a Benedictine frock or "domino" because "Beati sunt qui in domino moriuntur" (Rev. 14:13); that he said "Je vais quérir un grand peut-être" and "Tirez le rideau, la farce est jouée."[69] Needless to say, the Rabelais of legend was also gluttonous, fat, and drunk — the historical author is remodeled to fit his persona. A self-indulgent man who ridiculed his own false religion, many must have thought, would have mocked the true one had he lived in a land possessing it.

Rabelais could seem a mocking atheist in part because, condemned by Catholics, he was also excoriated in Geneva. Some of the English gave notice to Rome's opinion, if one may judge by a note John Morris wrote in his Rabelais: "Monsieur Rabelais was for these workes by the holy father in the Councell of Trent condemned for an atheist."[70] A decade or two into the seventeenth century, says Marcel de Grève, French libertins came to consider Rabelais the same sort of free-thinking deist many of them considred themselves.[71] In England, however, Catholic and Genevan accusations of outright "atheism" convinced some that his jesting did not derive from older Franciscan humor, newer humanist disdain of obscurantism, or evangelical opposition to rigidity and superstition but from disbelief in anything beyond the body and its laughter. This view of Rabelais as an impious Epicurean was almost certainly further enabled by religious war and by shifts in mentality and manners that made earthier forms of humor seem offensive and joviality concerning religion seem frightening.[72]

The English would have found the atheist Rabelais in many texts, some printed or known in England, although *atheist* was still a loose word and could impute heresy rather than disbelief in any deity. Whatever *atheism* meant to the scholar-printer Robert Estienne, when he calls Rabelais "sceleratus impiusque

...ac plane atheus" and condemns his work as replete with sacrilegious trifling, he expels the writer beyond the Christian pale.[73] And Jean Chassanion, a Protestant expert on giants, writes in *Histoires memorables des grans et merveilleux jugemens et punitions de Dieu* that Rabelais, having drunk the poison of Epicurism, "wished to scoff at all religion like the profane villain he was. God removed his reason, so that having lived as a pig he died just as brutally, utterly drunk and mocking those who spoke to him of God and His mercy" (1586 ed., sig. L5v).[74] Such stories were circulated with little concern for fact or, one imagines, for Rabelais's own words. An author becomes an exemplum, a signifying pig in a cautionary fable.

The tale reappears in England. The popular *French Academy*, translated by "T.B." [Bowes?] from the French of Pierre de la Primaudaye, is an omnium gatherum of thoughts on just about everything. "T.B."'s preface to the second part has a section on atheists (1594, sig. b2). Their obduracy is surprising, he explains, for God has punished such people in spectacular ways: Epicurus died of bladder stones as he sat in a hot tub; Lucian, "currishly" barking "against the gods of the Heathen, and against Christ," was eaten by dogs; Pliny was felled by volcanic smoke; a maddened Lucretius killed himself; Pope John XIII was stabbed by a cuckolded husband; Pope Leo X died of laughter upon hearing of a French defeat. And, says "T.B.," "French histories" mention "one Frances Rabelais, who having sucked in the poison of Atheisme made a mock at al religion, as Lucretius his forerunner had done before him: but the selfesame author and defender of true religion, that tooke from Lucretius al use of reason, did so deprive this beast of all sense, that as he led a brutish life, so he died like a swine in the midst of his drunkennes, deriding those that spake unto him of God and of his mercy" (sig. b2v).

Thomas Beard adopted such stories for his *Theatre of Gods Judgements* (1597), translated from the French, says the title page, and "augmented by more than three hundred examples." Some examples might well give the impious pause. Take the governor of Masçon, a magician: Satan snatched him up and flew him three times around the town while the terrified man cried, "Helpe, helpe," and this despite the store of "holy bread" he kept by him as a precaution against mishaps (sig. H3). Writing on "Epicures and Atheists," Beard, too, reports that Leo X died of wicked laughter, that Jodelle starved, and that "Francis Rabelais, having suckt up also this poison, used like a prophane villaine, to make all Religion a matter to laugh and mocke at: but God deprived him of his sences, that as he had led a brutish life, so he might die a brutish death; for he died mocking all those that talked of God, or made any mention of mercie in his eares" (sig. L1). Some years later Edmund Rudierd published a condensation of Beard's smugly sadistic work; perhaps busy sinners found it handy. The section on Rabelais in *The Thunderbolt of Gods Wrath, or An Abridgement of Gods Fearefull Judgements* (1618) now read: "Frauncis Rabelais is a certaine Atheist, would mocke and laugh at true Religion. But as he lived brutishly, so God deprived him of his sences, and hee died as hee lived like a bruite beast" (sig. E2v). Gone is the deathbed rejection of mercy, but *Atheist* says it all.

With such slanders in the air, no wonder the witty could mock Rabelais. In *Epigrammaton . . . centuriae sex* (1616), John Dunbar feigns puzzlement:

> In Franciscum Rablaeum
> Neve Anabaptista est, neve est Papista, Rablaeus,
>   Neve reformatae relligionis homo:
> Ergo quam sequitur sectam, si forte requiris:
>   Nullius aut sectae est, aut Atheista fuit. (Sig. K5v)[75]

One of the "reformatae relligionis," Dunbar was also a skilled maker of taut lines in the Roman style. One way to be both clever and Reformed is to attack Rome, so Dunbar offers such barbs as the suggestion that Cardinal Bellarmine might better be named "Malarmine" (sig. B5). Catholic slanders irritate him (he laments the lies told about Beza), but the irony of making a pot-calling-the-kettle-godless jab at Rabelais escapes him.

Because anger at Rabelais ranged across the religious map, many found it easy to believe in his malice and atheism. An English reader who looked at the monk Gabriel Dupuyherbault's *Theotimus, sive De tollendis et expungendiss malis libris* (Paris, 1549) would have found a corrosive passage that may have been taken from Nicolas Le Picart, a zealous critic of heretics. Here Rabelais is a buffoon (*scurra*) condemned even by Geneva for impiety, lacking both fear of God and respect for men, treading upon and deriding everything divine and human, spewing poison and slanders (sigs. m2v–m3v).[76] He is a "glossogastor" (word-monger) and a "gelotopoios" (joke-maker), a man of pernicious morals and harmful to the commonweal; it is appalling to see such a writer protected by a cardinal of the Church (that is, Jean Du Bellay). Indeed, Du Bellay and the Gallican views he represented may be the real target.[77]

The most rhetorically inventive reprimand of Rabelais may be François Garasse's *Rabelais reformé* (Brussels, 1619), in the Bodleian Library by 1635.[78] The title refers to the "Reformed" pastor Pierre du Moulin, whom the Jesuit accuses of borrowing buffooneries from *Gargantua et Pantagruel*. Garasse starts by quoting Psalm 1:1 ("Beatus vir qui . . . in CATHEDRA IRRISORUM non sedet"), although he himself can retail such gibes as the anagram revealing "CALVIN" as another "LVCIAN" (sig. A3v). Lucian assaulted religion with scoffs, and now Rabelais has "ravagé les esprits" (sig. A4). Garasse even creates for

Rabelais a verse autobiography complete with career changes, boozing, over-sleeping, gathering material for the *Cinquième livre* when he was in Rome, and hanging out in Paris with pus-vomiting vipers like Calvin (sigs. A5–A7). But if Moulin is "bien versé en Rabelais" (sig. E3v), Garasse is similarly versed, recognizing in Moulin's work traces of Grandgousier, Frère Jean, Panurge, Judge Bridoye, Thélème, Popehawks, and furred cats. When Moulin envisions an owl alighting on a pope, Garasse identifies this as a jest in Rabelais (sigs. E3v, L5, Q3v). He confuses *QL* 9 with *CL* 8 but quotes accurately. The bits of Rabelais, the nasty verve, a mock almanac, and snatches of poetry make *Rabelais reformé* fair Menippean satire: readers in the Bodleian would have made haste to pull down the library's copy of Rabelais and read more.

Echoes of these charges sound in a Catholic text translated into English and dedicated to Queen Henrietta Maria: Nicholas Caussin's *Holy Court* (St. Omer? 1626). Here, too, "scoffing" is "a harbinger of Atheisme":

> Aaron striking the dust with his rod, made flies to spring up, the greatest scourge of Ægypt: I cannot tell who it is that hath receyved the ashes of Rabelais, nor who hath beene versed in this putrifaction, but by a manifest vengeance from heaven, we dayly behold new vermine to arise, which endeavour to gnaw, and dissipate all that which hath any piety, or feare of God in Christianity.
>
> Blind Creatures, . . . you have thornes in the middest of your feastes, and recreations, which will pierce you even to the drawing of bloud. Take away the sollaces of a Pagan, & present to God the alacrity of Christians; know you not, that the grashoppers of the Apocalyps, have the visage of a Virgin, and the tayle of a Scorpion, all these taunts, and scoffes have the seeming apparence of generosity, but the poyson is in the Tayle. (Sig. Bb2)

The complaint is of *seeming* wit, of poison disguised with jollity. Mockers claim to promote festivity (*generosity* is a good word for Rabelais's humor), but the "recreations" are terminally stinging: feminine to look at but phallic in the end. Merging images from Exodus and Revelation, Caussin may also allude to the slanders of which David complains in Psalms 12 and 35, among others, which were often read as referring to parties at Saul's court. Also arresting is the image of Rabelaisian mockers as a plague of insects. God is one; his fork-tongued enemy is Lord of the Flies.

English Protestants could take with a grain of salt denunciations by Catholic writers. Those by Huguenots carried more weight, and there was no one weightier than John Calvin. Calvin was too perceptive not to have seen early that he and Rabelais had basic differences. Thélème's "Do what thou wilt" is not Genevan thinking. Yet Calvin was himself said by his enemies to be morally lax (quaffing wine from silver flagons and cursing on his deathbed as worms gnawed his overused genitals).[79] If a modern myth reads Calvinism as repression, an older one called it antinomian libertinism. Calvin's anger at Rabelais, I suspect, was more than distaste for obscene or skeptical humor or disillusion with one who had at first seemed an ally. Calvin would also have found Rabelais dangerous precisely because some people thought that the "Rabelais" of growing legend was exactly what Calvinism encouraged.

Calvin's *De scandalis* (1550), translated by Arthur Golding as *A Little Booke Concernynge Offences* (1567), tells how God punishes those who taste the Gospel but then cast it away and, "like Lucian, scoffe and jest at the whole Religion of Christe." They "laugh smoothely at the foolish toyes of the Papistes: but themselves are unwoorthie that ever they shoulde returne to the papistrie," and because they voluntarily "jest away or drive away their Phisicion," they "procure themselves any death." See, for example, the deaths of Agrippa and Dolet, who "like Giauntes with one eye in theyr forehead [Golding's Cyclopean addition] fearyng neither God nor manne," fell into "suche madnesse and outrage, that they not onely spewed out moste abhominable blasphemies against the sonne of God, but (as much as perteineth to the life of the soule,) did thinke themselves to differ nothinge from Dogges and Hogges. Othersome, (as Rabelayse, Deper [Des Périers], and Govean [Degovean, a jurisconsult]) after they had tasted of the Gospell, were striken with the same blindnesse. And why happened this, but bicause they had by their wicked malapertnesse of jestynge and scoffynge, heretofore profaned that holy pledge of eternall life?" Such men "playe the scoffers," laughing when at the table, and through "overthwart nippes, or covert conceytes," insinuate that religion is a human invention and doomsday "a bug to feare children with" (sigs. G5–G8).

This godlessness, says Calvin, is found near kings, lawyers, and the rich. And near princes of the Catholic church, he elsewhere protests: witness Jean Du Bellay's patronage of Rabelais. This is the import of a few lines in Calvin's *Sermons upon Deuteronomie,* translated by Arthur Golding in 1583. The third sermon, preached in 1555, explicates Deuteronomy 13:6–11 (on executing those promoting idolatry) and mentions a "Royster" who

> casteth forth lewd scoffes against the holy Scripture, as doeth that divelish fellowe which is called Pantagruell, and all his filthie and ribauldly writings: and this sort of men pretende not to set up any newe Religion, as though they were deluded by their owne foolish imaginations: but like madde dogges they belke out their filthinesse against the majestie of God, and their meaning is to overthrowe all religion: and should such be spared? Why not? for they have the Cardinalles for their upholders, they be favoured and maintained by them:

> in so much that the names of these Lord Cardinalles are blazed in those goodly bookes, which serve to mocke God as well as Mahomet. (Sig. Zz3)

Calvin objects not to a cardinal protecting a mocker but to mockers being aided by men whose position is illegitimate to begin with. Rabelais's own sin is derision masquerading as good humor.

Other Protestants agreed, or said they did. The often Menippean *World of Wonders* (1607), a version of Henri Estienne's *Apologie pour Herodote* (1566), claims that everyone knows "that this age hath revived Lucian againe, in the person of Francis Rabelais, making a mock of all religion in his devilish discourses." Such "varlets" hope "outwardly indeed to make as though they would but drive away the melancholike dumps, and passe away the time with pleasant discourse," but under the guise of jesting at old abuses they "gird even at Christian religion it selfe" (1608 Edinburgh ed., sig. H1v). The allegation is a grave one in a culture anxious about the relation of cleverness to slander and interpretation, a culture with an urgent desire to figure out, despite opaque hearts and shifting fashions, who really thought what.

Many in England, then, would have read that Rabelais's jests were not anodyne pastimes or therapeutic satire but threats to civilized and godly discourse. To the easily shocked the charge might seem credible (and in later centuries the conviction that Rabelais ridicules religion was sometimes part of his appeal). True, some might have found him wicked but enjoyable; others doubtless thought that the likes of Calvin had overreacted. A few (Jonson? Donne?) might even have sensed in Pantagruelion a Christian ballast or medicine. Still, "Rabelais" the venomous mocker was useful, especially in contexts that tempted a writer to find in others the sins besmirching his own tongue. Allusions to Rabelais serve self-defense: I may chide and scoff, but while others sit in the scorner's seat, mouthing off like Rabelais, I have no choice.

It is the politics of mockery that worries Simon Paterick in his 1577 preface to a translation of Innocent Gentillet's *Discourse . . . against N. Machiavell* (1602). Is this evidence that Rabelais was being read in England in the 1570s? Perhaps not, for this Rabelais is more name than author. That Paterick has a section on atheists who were struck down by God (Jodelle, for example, starves after "having like an Epicurean eaten and drunken his patrimonie," sig. I6v) sets "Rabelais" in the land of shameful and monitory labels. In this case, "Rabelais" supports a narrative of how Europe's political discourse collapsed into cynicism. To Patericke, laughing at vice merely smooths its path. Witness France:

> For when the cleare light of the Gospell began first to spring and appeare, Sathan (to occupie and busie mens minds with toyish playes and trifles, that

they might give no attendance unto true wisedome) devised this policie, to raise up jeasters and fooles in Courts, which creeping in, by quipping and prettie conceits, first in words, and after by bookes, uttering their pleasant jeasts in the Courts and banquets of kings and princes laboured to root up all the true principles of Religion and Policie. And some there were whom the resemblance of nature, or vanitie of wit had so deceived, that they derided the everlasting veritie of the true God, as if it were but a fable. Rabelaysus amongst the French, and Agrippa amongst the Germanes, were the standerd-bearers of that traine: which with their skoffing taunts, inveighed not only against the Gospell, but all good arts whatsoever. Those mockers did not as yet openly undermine the ground work of humane societie, but onely they derided it: But such Cyclopian laughters, in the end prooved to be onely signes and tokens of future evils. For little by little, that which was taken in the beginning for jestes, turned to earnest, and words into deedes. (Sigs. ¶3–¶3v)

Then came foolish poets, corruption, and Machiavelli. Which of Rabelais's taunts does Paterick mean? Perhaps his jokes on law, medicine, poetry, cooking, navigation, and other "arts"; or Paterick may assume that Rabelais was a mocker and that sneering at human effort is what mockers do. Had not Calvin — whose opinions are audible here — said Rabelais ridiculed everything divine and human?

Several English texts make similar charges but without Patericke's story of cultural decay. What is striking about some of them is less how banal they are than how quick they are to imagine a world filled with amorality and atheism. Eventually, as the names of the wicked pile up, the mountain of blasphemy and disbelief threatens not so much God's throne as the *consensus gentium* that comforts faith. If one impulse in the Renaissance was toward religious syncretism, another was to distinguish one's own saving remnant from the evil majority. "Rabelais," that is, more often served those whom anthropologists call splitters, not lumpers. When analyzing the sneers that encourage atheism, for example, John Hull's *St. Peters Prophesie of These Last Days* (1610) seems almost to relish their frequency. Here is the usual scornful crew: the Assyrian messenger Rabshakeh (2 Kings 18), Julian the Apostate, dog-eaten Lucian, Machiavelli, Aretino, and "Francis Rabelais," who "made religion a matter of mocking" (sigs. Hh4, Vv3v, Tt1, 4D1).[80] Such comments explain Rabelais's presence in these objections to railing, although few objectors were themselves innocent.

Gabriel Harvey's brother Richard lacked true polemical ingenuity, but his *Theologicall Discourse of the Lamb of God* (1590) shares Gabriel's shoot-from-the-lip verve; its reproof of Tom Nashe sparked the Harvey-Nashe quarrel. Opposing both Martin Marprelate and his enemies, Harvey chides the chiders. The Lamb of God is "no scoffer," he says: the world has folly enough without pamphlets fostering presumption, public disorder, and "universall confusion." "Fantasticall" Martin is a "spitefull rayler an odious jester," one of "the most pernicious and intollerable writers" in English. Harvey himself is not railing, for "it becommeth me not." Rather, he easily yields "to Martin in that veyne; Lucian is his, Rabelays is his." Yes, he has "peradventure read them," but no, he will not imitate them: "The Lamb of God needeth no such Autors." He has heard the slurs against these writers: "Lucian himselfe, and Rabelays himselfe have felt the common saying true, *Qui moccat moccabitur,* so doe, so suffer." So let Martin remember that "he is like to taste of the same sauce, though I hould my peace, as unfit by nature, but more unmeete by profession [Harvey was ordained], to deale that way." "Rabelays," in sum, "is no good reformer of Churches and States" (sigs. a1–a1v).

We have it on high authority that many can see a mote in another's eye while ignoring the beam in their own; Harvey's is an extreme case. He growls his preference for lambs, condemns authors he half-admits to reading, holds his peace while writing, and makes a macaronic joke about the pangs of jokers. God's lambs must do more than bleat, Harvey apparently felt, if they are to affect a fallen world. Rabelais may be a bad reformer, but scoffing gets attention, and Harvey knows that.

John Cecil, a Catholic priest who is defending himself in *A Discoverye of the Errors* (Paris, 1599) against the slurs of William Crichton, S.J., likewise denounces in another the techniques he himself uses. He is, he says, sending Crichton some new glasses; at first the Jesuit's "sore eyes" may hurt from "the violent reverberation off the beames of veritye, which must necessaryly accompany the purity and cleernes off this transparent instrument," but he can minimize the pain by reading with sight no longer "obfuscate with the vapors and exhalations" of passion (sigs. A2–A2v). Not bad. But Cecil then lectures us on the necessity of arguing with decency. All "diologues, discourses, and pamphlettes, destitute of this essentiall decencye and formalitye that have not trueth for theyre center, and temperance, urbanitye and civilitye for their circumference, are rather to be baptised by the names of Satyres, Epigrammes, lybels, and pasquinados farre fytter for slaves, Sycophantes, poetes, and parasites" (sigs. A3–A4v). Sure, but what about those eyeglasses? Or saying that the "juvenilitye, scurrilitye, and prophanitye of your worthye volume savoreth rather of . . . Rabells, Lucian, Aretine, Howleglas, and scoggine, then of the gravitye and modestye of a cath[olic] pryest" (sig. G1v)? Cecil faces an old dilemma: How does one moderately respond to excess? The soft answer and turned cheek were not often tried, although some made a show of proffering them by distancing themselves from Lucian and Rabelais.[81]

Thomas Carew's Rabelais is more entertaining, figuring briefly in *Coelum Britannicum*, the dazzling masque he and Inigo Jones created for Shrove Tuesday 1634. The masque begins with Mercury greeting Momus, patron of detraction and the gods' resident naysayer.[82] Momus's robe has poinards, serpent tongues, eyes and ears—tools of his trade as calumniating satirist and prying court busybody—and he sports a porcupine as a hat. He has a genealogy, being "Momus-ap-Somnus-ap-Erebus-ap-Chaos-ap-Demogorgon-ap-Eternity," as well as some impressive titles: "Supreme Theomastix, Hypercrittique of manners, Protonotarie of abuses, Arch-Informer, Dilator [snitch] Generall, Universall Calumniator, Eternall Plaintiffe, and perpetuall Foreman of the Grand Inquest." He gets around: "My privileges are an ubiquitary, circumambulatory, speculatory, interrogatory, redargutory immunitiy over all the privy lodgings behind hangings, dores, curtaines, through keyholes, chinkes, windowes, about all Veneriall Lobbies, Sconces or Redoubts." He can do hermeneutics: "I have yet a Praerogative of wresting the old to any whatsoever interpretation, whether it be to the behoofe, or prejudice, of Jupiter his Crowne and Dignity, for, or against the Rights of either house of Patrician or Plebian gods" [that is, the Throne, Lords, and Commons]. His "Parallel" is Aretino (a "Bird of mine owne feather") and "Frank Rablais suck'd much of my milke."

The allusion is brief but resonant, for according to Renaissance medical theories, Carew's Rabelais must have swallowed with his milk the traits Momus describes to Mercury. This matters: although Mercury calls Momus an "impertinent Trifeler" given to "scurrilous chat," it will be the latter's job to describe Zeus's reform of Olympus. Riches and Poverty are corrected or sent packing, Fortune is dethroned, spouses embrace fidelity, and pretty young Ganymede will stick to serving nectar. To symbolize this change, Momus presides over the replacement of monstrous constellations by stellar British and Saxon heroes, even if he soon leaves the stage to less problematic figures. Richard Harvey calls Rabelais "no good reformer of Churches and States," but Carew credits his wetnurse with a creative negativity that makes room for a new dispensation.

Momus expresses his relation to Rabelais as the transfer of physical fluid. Others, too, linked Rabelais to bodily needs and behavior, so I shall return to this topic after a look at Panurge, a trickster born of words but interested in flesh.

Quicksilver Interlude
Panurge and *Panourgia* in England

Rabelais's words are nowhere more disconcertingly located than in Panurge. It can be hard to distinguish English allusions to Pantagruel's friend from derivatives of the Greek words that begot him, yet English *panurge* and its lexical cousins add up to something like Rabelais's trickster. He began as a noun: a *panourgos* has *panourgia*, the capacity to be cunning and to do (*ourg*) anything (*pan*).[1] Pagans had used the word to describe the fox, the rhetor, the deceitful gods. In the Septuagint, *panourgia* is astuteness, but Paul uses it for injurious craftiness (Eph. 4:14), subtlety (2 Cor. 11:3), cunning (1 Cor. 3:19; the margin of the Geneva Bible adds, "When they them selves are entangled in the same snares, which thei laid for others"). This *panourgia* is diabolical, and although Rabelais's figure calls "Panurge" his "nom de baptesme" (*P* 9), sacramental water has not quite washed off his demonic birthmarks.[2] *Panourgia* is a medical term, too: Galen uses it for adulterated or false drugs.[3] Yet Panurge is a healer, able to cure decapitation (*P* 30). Indeed, medical prowess is another capacity he shares with Hermes: the latter's caduceus parallels the former's codpiece, even as memories of the god's psychopomp augment Panurge's uncanny quality.[4]

Looking up *panurgus* was easy. Cooper's *Thesaurus* (1565) calls it a "craftie, deceitfull, or wily person: an old beaten foxe" (1584 ed.). Jean Vernon's *Dictionary* (1575; 1584 ed.) says much the same. The word *beaten* carries the now-lost sense of "experienced," but the other meaning is also apt for tricksters, so often outfoxed and — especially if they are comic servants — beaten. Holyband's 1593 dictionary defines *panurge* as "cault, astut, fin, afféte, rusé, a craftie one, also one that medleth to doe all things"; Cotgrave gives "A slye, craftie, deceitfull companion; an old beaten fox; one that hath experience, or hath been tampering, in most things; also, one that will meddle with, or have a flirt at, anything." Francis Holyoke's *Dictionarium* (1640) cites Plautus under *Panurgia,* and learned readers would recall that Aristophanes' *Knights* (424 B.C.) subjects the dictator Cleon to multiple panurgic epithets.[5] Demos (People) has a slave named Paphlagon (Cleon), a great rogue and devil (*panourgotaton kai diabolutaton*).[6] He is a rascally (*panourgotata,* l. 56) cheater who plays tricks (*panourgia,* l. 331). Outfoxed by a bigger rascality (*poly panourgiais,* ll. 683–84), he claims to be the victim of knavery (*panourge,* l. 902). As he is beaten with sausages and tripe, a chorus of knights cries: "Smite the panurge, smite the panurge" (ll. 247–50). Panurge's fear of the rod is not misplaced.

Many would remember another Panurge. The Roman actor Roscius had agreed to train one Panurgus, slave to Fannius. Panurgus would go on the stage, and tutor and owner would share the profits. The poor slave was murdered, but Roscius had invested his takings and, sued by Fannius for half his earnings, he hired Cicero to plead his case.[7] This Panurge is an older cousin of Rabelais's: socially marginal, theatrical, and with a name hinting at a fate that is hard on him but comic for us. Compare Michel Coignet's warning in *Politique Discourses upon Trueth and Lying,* translated by Edward Hoby in 1585: "Wisedom and eloquence, without truth and justice, are a Panurgie, that is to say a guyle or sleight, such as we reade the slaves to use in Comedies, which still turneth to their owne domage and confusion" (sigs. N2v–N3). This comes in a chapter advising us to avoid lawsuits "because of the lyinge and cautell [craft] of the practisers," and indeed Rabelais' Panurge has a taste for litigation (*P* 17).

If Coignet remembers stage panurgists, Thomas Heywood remembers the devilish ones. In *The Hierarchie of the Blessed Angells* (1635), after discussing marvels, magic, and witchcraft, he says he will "conclude with that Pannurgist Sathan, . . . to whom not unproperly may be given these following characters:

> Fontem nosco boni bonus ipse creatus
> Factus at inde malus fons vocor ipse malus.
> Of Goodnesse I the Fountaine am,
>   Bee'ng good at first created;
> But since made Evill, I the Well
>   Of Ill am nominated. (Sig. 3D5v)

Such evil is *clever:* Heywood also tells how Satan, disguised as a servant in a noble house, persuaded his master to send the local monks gourmet delicacies, turning their minds from books to bellies. "Against these subtile temptations of this crafty and deceitfull Pannurgust," there "are no such profitable and wholesome preventions as fasting and prayer" (sigs. 3E4–3E5). With part of his mind, though, Heywood liked *panourgia,* just as he recognizes Lucian's impiety but often cites his dialogues. Did he know Rabelais? His *Philocothonista* (1635), a likably scatological book on drink and drunkards, ignores him.

Panurge or Panurgus, emerging from its lexical chrysalis as a proper name, appears in several English texts. Sometimes it relates problematically to money, recalling *panourgia*'s tie to Hermes, thieving god of merchants and, before that, of liminal places for barter.[8] Here talk, travel, mental agility, deception, and trade intersect. Even those with no French could have read, in a 1587 translation of François de la Noue's *Politicke and Militarie Discourses,* how "Rabelais reporteth that Panurge in his voiages into Italy learned above 78. inventions to colme by money: but after he had a while haunted the Spanish and French nations, he was perfect in above 100. gallant waies to spend it, which made him continually to eate his corne in the blade, which good custome is yet in practise among us."[9]

Panurge's paean in *TL* 3–4 to debt — like trickery and dickering, vital to capitalism — provoked attention.[10] Fascinated by how money flows around or piles up, Jonson must have liked the paradox when he read it, although Carlo Buffone's defense of debt in *Every Man out of His Humor* (1600; I.ii.110–18) probably derives from Rabelais's own model, Erasmus' *Ementita nobilitas* (it is amusing to see Renaissance writers borrowing their defenses of debt rather than reaching into their own mental pockets). And at some point Jonson would have seen the "Encomium debiti" adapted from Rabelais by an English priest, Robert Turner; it was printed in Dornavius' *Amphitheatrum* (1619; II, sigs. P4–P4v), which Jonson owned.[11] Jonson's satire is darker than Rabelais's, as one might anticipate from a preface that calls Buffone a "prophane" slave whose "religion is rayling, and his discourse ribaldry." Panurge, but without the ambiguous allure.

Also indebted is Thomas Tomkis's clever *Albumazar,* which was played in Cambridge before James I in 1614. This Panurge-haunted work satirizes the ease with which the mind receives the false impressions projected by con artists; again, Rabelais helps an English writer represent social issues, although Panurge himself is split between Pandolfo, an old suitor headed for cuckoldom, and Albumazar, an astrologer with something of Herr Trippa.[12] As the play opens, Albumazar summons his "mercurial" cronies "sublim'd in cheating." When he mentions that Mercury fails to smile on learning, his colleague Harpax objects that the learned nevertheless steal, "one author from another. / This poet is that poet's plagiary. / And he a third's, till they end all in Homer." Yes, agrees Albumazar, and "Homer filch'd all from an Egyptian priestess" (I.i). Robbery, he says, typifies the cosmos and the human body, his argument and terms (*meseraics*, for example) being themselves heisted from Panurge. He revises a bit: a tendency to steal will not make one's creditors friendly or servants obedient, so it is best kept secret. For Panurge, the world requires a circulating indebtedness visible to and enjoyable by all; nor does he shrink from applying his theory to the matter that moves through the body's ureters and colon. Albumazar skips this account of matter flowing back out of the flesh and into the world; rather, he imagines it safely stashed like thief's booty:

> Guts from the stomach steal, and what they spare,
> The meseraics filch, and lay't i' the liver:
> Where, lest it should be found, turn'd to red nectar,
> 'Tis by a thousand thievish veins convey'd,
> And hid in flesh, nerves, bones, muscles, and sinews:
> In tendons, skin, and hair; so that, the property
> Thus alter'd, the theft can never be discover'd.
> Now all these pilf'ries, couch'd and compos'd in order,
> Frame thee and me. Man's a quick mass of thievery. (I.i)

Tomkis may want us to recall Rabelais (his audience would include some — like the king — who had read him), for Harpax replies, "I thought these parts had lent and borrowd mutual." Exactly.

But Tomkis has spotted a flaw in Panurge's analogies, one he perhaps consciously worsens by not mentioning the evacuation of waste: whatever is true of the cosmos, a live human body takes in more than it gives back. Hence Albumazar replies, "Say they do so: 'tis done with full intention / Ne'er to restore." The moon can shine the sun's light back, but a pheasant pasty, once eaten, cannot be returned in any palatable form; to do good, most of what we eat must be consumed and transformed, not recirculated. Consuming, in fact, is just what Panurge, as his patient but skeptical master knows, has done with his estate. Tomkis thus opens his play with a panurgic joke of some consequence, one improved by reference to the French text that his astrologer distorts but whose deeper comedy the author perceives. Before the play ends, Albumazar has been robbed and then taunted with reminders of his earlier theories. He should have known better than to be a *panourgos* in a comedy.

The first panurge named as such to emerge publicly in England outside a translation is, so far as I know, a miserly thief in Jonson's *The Case Is Altered* (1597). Rabelais's Panurge is a better spendthrift than skinflint, but when in the *Tiers livre* he trades in his doublet and sword for a plain robe and slippers he is dressing like an old miser and hence, to anyone brought up on farces and fabliaux, like a cuckold; even his codpiece vanishes behind his countinghouse costume as though retracted in a sort of sexual hoarding.[13] Panurge thus undergoes a shift of character: the Mercurial, uncanny figure of *Pantagruel* is not quite the would-be husband of the later books, whatever his continued mischief-making. But tricksters and misers inhabit overlapping worlds of plot and discourse: both tend to cheat, conceal, misuse money, and be outwitted or discovered.

Panurge's counterpart in *Case* is Jaques, a miser who years ago stole off with his master's child and gold. Jonson found him in Plautus' *Aulularia* but gives him a touch of the Bible's out-foxed Laban by naming the stolen daughter Rachel (Gen. 30). Jaques is a sour *panourgos* with a liking for walls and an obsession with gold. Bearing a name sounding like "jakes" (privy), he buries his treasure in his "back side" (back yard) beneath manure. The love with which he addresses this gold, thinking it smells good in its dungy hiding place, gives his lines proto-Volponean energy. No mere miser, he is a fox (the title puns on *case* as legal term and pelt) who will lament that "my gold's gone, Rachel's gone, / Al's gone!" and that "I have no starting hols! . . . I plaid the thiefe, and now am robd my selfe."[14] The culprits are the cobbler Juniper and Onion, a rich man's servant who has observed Jaques checking on his gold. When the miser goes offstage, Juniper asks, "What's the old panurgo gone? departed? cosmografied, he?" (IV.ix.3–4). Juniper probably means "trans-mographied," but why a "panurgo"? Jonson's editors C. H. Herford and Percy Simpson cite the lost chapbook on Gargantua, but its French models have no Panurge. Perhaps we have here an instance of parallel evolution: *panurgo* may derive not from Pantagruel's friend but from the same dramatic and lexical material on which Rabelais drew.

The prolific Richard Brathwait, too, considers Panurge an appropriate name for the miserly. Despite a story about sheep that has parallels to Panurge's encounter with Dindenault, to which I shall turn shortly, it is not certain whether Brathwait read Rabelais. The figure of whom he complains, however, is part of what "Panurge" means in Renaissance England. His brief miscellany, *A New Spring Shadowed in Sundry Pithie Poems* (1619), comprises epigrams, moral reflections, pastoral, and a poem on hospitality that has the tone and agitated rhythms of late Elizabethan satire. This last, a kind of anti-"Penshurst," laments the decline of hospitality in country houses: as gentlemen flock to court, their deserted mansions decay; even worse is the parsimony of those remaining behind.

> Alasse poore Country, thou hast nothing then
> But vast penurious houses without Men;
> A row of smoake-lesse Chimneyes which agrees,
> With barme-lesse Hogsheds, empty Butteries,
> Worme-eaten Rafters, Windores Spider-woven,
> Walls Snaile-belimed, a Loome-mudded Oven
> Estrang'd from Bake-meats, nasty Dayeries,
> Halls hung with Caules and forlorne Nurseries.
> And yet Panurgus thou art more to blame
> Then Court house-keepers, for thou thinks no shame
> When foot-bet Travellers that's like to burst
> With heat, come to thy house to quench their thirst,
> To boult thy Buttry-dore and bid them goe
> To th'Alehouse, where th'ave nothing to bestow:
> Wherefore to save their money, thou dost bring,
> These wearied Travellers to some wholsome Spring,
> Where they may drink their fill; whenc't may appeare
> Thou'lt rather wast thy water then thy Beere.

This Panurge is churlish enough to tell hot travelers to try the local pub and cunning enough to remark, in further hopes of saving his own cellar, that his ale-seeking guests will find his springwater "wholsome."

Rabelais's Panurge is distinctly himself in John Day's meditation on the Psalter. Although Panurge's trickiness is most evident in *Pantagruel*, one later episode (*QL* 5–8) shows that this aspect of his identity has not been erased by his roles as narcissist, would-be husband, and ship's coward. Meeting with one Dindenault, a merchant taking a flock of sheep to market by boat, Panurge is enraged by the man's sexual insults. Alerting Frère Jean and Epistemon (but not Pantagruel) that he will stage a little farce in revenge, Panurge bargains for and buys the bellwether. Suddenly heaving it overboard, he watches as the rest of the flock, baa-ing all the way, jumps over the side after its leader. Grabbing the sheep as they leap by, Dindenault and his assistants follow, and while they struggle in the water Panurge plies an oar to keep them from reboarding and preaches to them *de contemptu mundi* until they all drown. The cruel scene is funny, not least because Panurge, playing against type, sets his own laconic patience against the merchant's malicious loquacity.[15] Rabelais stages yet another linguistic performance, while the issue of authority arises briefly when the narrator refers us to Aristotle in *"lib. 9, de Histo.*

animal," on the dimwittedness of sheep. And there is religious resonance to a semi-devilish figure who punishes an uncharitable merchant who cannot protect his flock.[16] Day calls this a good metaphor for fashion-driven commentators, recounting Panurge's trick in the introduction to his *Day's Descant on Davids Psalmes* (Oxford, 1620).

Day was the son and namesake of a distinguished printer; he had traveled on the continent, and although the *DNB* says the experience fortified his Calvinism, it may also have mellowed him, for he quotes with pleasure More, Ariosto, and Montaigne as well as Calvin and Beza. Yes, he says, he is just one in a long line of commentators, and, no, he will not offer any new readings. He is a follower, he admits with calculated candor, for "in Matters of Divinity, let them single themselves that list, I had rather be last in a Troope of good Interpreters, then be the Leader of a Band to Schisme and Singularitie." His self-defense would not displease Rabelais — or anyone diverted by the role in hermeneutics of sheepish conformity on the one hand and self-inflated innovation on the other:

> Nor am I dismaid with those Flowtes which Lodovicus Rouzeus, a merry Gentleman it seemes, bestowes upon Commentators out of Rablais.[17] Hee questioning in a Booke of his to whom Commentators may be likened: *Such kinde of men,* saith he, *may not unfitly bee likened unto Sheepe, the most simple,* saith he, *(set the Asse aside) of all Beasts whatsoever. For as those Commentators doe follow their first Leader quietly and peaceably without any more adoe, and tread in the self same Steps, even so doe Sheep* saith he, *as* Panurgus *in Rabelais* hath *taught us in* Pantagruells *Navigation.* With that he tels the *Story,* and the *Story* was this: So it was that *Panurgus* having nothing else to drive away the time withall, bargained with a *Sheep-master* that with an whole *Flocke* of *Sheep* was in the selfe same *Ship* with him, for one of his *Weathers,* which when he had separated from the rest, he presently cast it overboord. This when the rest of the *Sheep* beheld, they immediatly after their *Fellow,* and striving with one an other which of them should over next, many of them in conclusion leapt into the *Sea,* insomuch that the *Sheepmaster* himselfe with his *servants* endeavouring to withhold the rest, and holding them by the Hornes, were driven overboord with the violence of the *Sheepe,* and the *Sheep,* and they, duckt togither. (Sig. B2)

Day tells this story against himself: yet he is serious in preferring to follow faithfully rather than lead others to error. His application of the story has problems that charm cannot hide (the sheep do drown), but charm helps him lower the reader's hopes or fears of "singularity," just as the name Rabelais helps him distinguish his treatise from works of bleaker temper.

A marginal note reports that a lawyer told Day of a similar incident that ended in court. Maybe he refers to the case Brathwait retells in *Times Curtaine Drawne* (1621), reporting that it was "argued in our Court, / with much delight." The poem has the sheep, but the staged trickiness is gone. The River Humber, we read,

> In her imperious Surges, keepes a shore
> A Boate to waft way-faring people ore;
> 'Mongst other Passengers were ferried over,
> Chanc'd to resort a Pedler and a Drover,
> Both at one time; the Drover he did bring
> Sheepe to the Faire, which he was carrying,
> Of Ewes good store (right Butcher-ware) there came
> And 'mongst the rest a bonnie butting Ram,
> Whose awfull front the rest securely kept,
> And all this while the Cup-shot Pedler slept.
> With many a nod drawne from his drowsie braine,
> Which th'Ram observes, and butts at him againe;
> The Pedler now, feeling belike some smart,
> With such like words as these began to thwart
> The careless Ram, *Sir I am at a word,*
> *Butt you at mee, I'le butt you over-boord.*
> And not one word the Pedler could speake more,
> Till he began to nod just as before;
> Wherewith th'incensed Ram thinking he ment
> To push at him, so fierce a stroake him lent
> As his distemper'd Noddle seem'd dismaid,
> With violent assault his hornes had made:
> Yet part through grief and anguish which he felt,
> He now resolv'd to wash the Rams white pelt,
> Which he perform'd, his fury to discover,
> And roundly takes the Ram and throwes him over;
> The loving Ewes seeing their Sweet-hart swim,
> Resolv'd with one consent to follow him;
> Which th'Lawyer in his pleadings noting than,
> *"Brother* (quoth he) *this was a lustie Ram,*
> *For much I doubt whether our wives or no,*
> *If we should be thus us'de would follow so.*
> But to be briefe, not any one was found,
> Of all the Drovers flocke, which was not drown'd,
> So as a Suite's commenc'd betwixt these twaine,
> Wherein the Plaintiffe seemeth to complaine,
> And by petition humblie doth crave
> That for his losse he some reliefe may have. (Sigs. D4–D5)

After briefly debating the roles here of fate, intent, and alcohol, Brathwait moves to the impossibility of preventing adultery: "Hornes can we not prevent, though we foresee" (sig. D5v). His story has no trickster punishing a merchant, yet a ghost of that conflict appears in the opposition of peddler and drover, wanderer and salesman. Panurge might envy the ram: its horns signify only its gender, and its mates are suicidally loyal.

That this is a real "accident" is quite possible. Yet it also sounds like a case for "mooting" at the Inns of Court, particularly as we do not hear the verdict.[18] The son of a barrister, Brathwait had been sent to study law at Cambridge and then in London. Although he preferred the muses and soon returned north, his time in London would have introduced him to the culture of the Inns. Perhaps he had read or heard about Panurge's sheep during his stay; in any event, he gives this anecdote a legal and mock-philosophical context similar to the city-court world of Donne, Selden, Bacon, and Robert Dallington. Writing in the Lake Country, he treats his rustic story with *urbanitas*.

Another panurgic type is less openly tricky, more devious. He is the "curieux" with whom some have associated Panurge.[19] A prying courtier — Jonson's Sir Politick, but smarter — he is also the judgmental narcissist that Edwin Duval locates in a paradox of unwitting self-reference lying at the center of the *Tiers livre*.[20] Alexander Craig rebukes him in *Poeticall Recreations* (Aberdeen, 1623), a collection of moral verses with a satirical edge. Slandered by "murthering Mouthes," Craig defies the "Critik, Scratch-pate, and Find-faulte" and asks us to "judge with Love." Panurge is the reader he does not desire:

> Panurgus pryes in high and low Effaires;
> Hee talkes of Foraine, and our Civill State:
> But for his owne hee neyther countes nor cares;
> That hee refers to Fortune, and his Fate.
>> His Neighbours faultes, straight in his Face hee'll finde,
>> But in a Bag hee hangs his owne behinde. (Sig. C1v)

Carping self-love does not figure in Panurge's lexical matrix, although it may motivate Satan, foxy Nick-of-all-trades and calumniator. This "curieux," though, shares much with Rabelais's own. Missing is the sexual fear and show-off rhetoric, but Craig's Panurge is a meddler and a spy, knows foreign countries, neglects his own "state" — his goods and circumstances — and sees his own faults in others. As for the bag, during an exchange in *TL* 15 an exasperated Epistemon tells Panurge:

> "It is a very usual and common matter among humans to understand, foresee, know, and predict the shortcomings of others. But how rare it is to foresee, know, predict, and understand one's own! Thus wisely did Aesop represent it

in his *Apology,* saying that everybody in this world is born with a pair of bags on his shoulder, one hanging in front with the faults of others always exposed to our view and notice, one hanging behind for our own faults and shortcomings; and never are the latter seen and understood except by those on whom the Heavens look kindly."[21]

As for leaving one's "state" up to fate and fortune, I take Craig's "his own" as "his own state," the referent sliding from res publica to private estate or goods and, maybe, spiritual condition. If he has read Rabelais—and the Aesopian bags make that likely—Craig has reversed Pantagruel's counsel to Panurge: first determine what you want and leave the rest to fate and fortune. As Pantagruel has it: "Are you not certain of your own will? The chief point lies there: everything else is chance and hangs on Heaven's fateful decrees. . . . One must chance it with eyes bound and lowered head, kissing the earth [like Swiss soldiers before battle], and for the rest commend oneself to God, once one has wanted to put oneself to it. Any other assurance I do not know how to give you" (*TL* 10).[22] Craig may think that fortune and fate are pagan notions, whatever Pantagruel's ascription of "fatales" decrees to God. He reads intelligently but a shade conventionally, morally alert but without the subtler Pantagruelism that brings scorn of happenstance and a willingness to let fate take its course.

It is possible that at some point in the 1590s John Donne contemplated Panurge's marital dilemma, together with his neglect of his state and his selfishly timorous inability to know and act upon his will (it is no accident that *Gargantua,* written after Rabelais had already invented Panurge, concludes with an abbey named Thélème, Greek for "will"). It would not be surprising that an alert young man in London's smarter circles knew Rabelais. His Satire IV, though, explicitly calls Panurge a linguist. Donne alludes to Pantagruel's initial encounter with his shabby friend-to-be during a stroll with his entourage on the outskirts of Paris—a suitably liminal place for such a meeting (*P* 9). Donne's satirist, in contrast, has gone to court, a "Purgatorie, such as fear'd hell is / A recreation to."[23] Like Pantagruel, he encounters a walking piece of *panourgia:* a loquacious braggart, seedily got up despite his francophile taste, a seducer of widows, a gossip and sponger. Worse, he is probably an informer on the lookout for Catholics.

This motley *panourgos* is a squalid cousin of Panurge's, another down-on-his-luck boaster, traveler, busybody, borrower, sexual predator, and courtier. Politically, the creature's demonic overtones derive less from wit and mobility than from his role as a government spy who seeks to "make men speake treason" and thus have them ingested by an intolerant state's "Giant Statutes" that "ope" their jaws "to sucke me in" (like a crueler Pantagruel, perhaps, or the pilgrim-swallowing Gargantua). Rabelais's Panurge retains only a devilish tinge, but Donne's *panourgos*, while descended from the bore that Horace cannot shake off in Satire I.9, uncomfortably resembles the Father of Lies (also a wanderer up and down the earth). Generically, he is what Rabelais's trickster becomes when he leaves Menippean prose for the shaggy bravado of Elizabethan verse satire. Thematically, he serves Donne's insistence that the abuse of language corrupts society.[24]

The man that Donne's satirist describes is too strange for even Adam to name, more monstrous than "Guianaes rarities." Although he claims to know "what to all States belongs" and to speak "all tongues," his macaronic language is scrappy, deceptive, and (unlike Panurge's) flattering. Attaching himself to the unwilling narrator and unctuously praising his judgment, he asks "Whom doe you prefer, / For the best linguist?" When the satirist replies dryly, "Calepines Dictionarie," he presses the matter: "Nay, but of men, most sweet Sir?" Beza, he is told (perhaps because that Genevan leader, so learned in Latin, Greek, and Hebrew, had in 1588 published a congratulatory poem on the Armada in eight different languages). Or maybe a couple of Jesuits and one or two professors. " 'There / He stopt mee,' and said, 'Nay, your Apostles were / Good pretty linguists, and so Panurge [variants are "Panirge" or "Panurgus"] was; / Yet a poore gentleman, all these may passe / By travaile [travel, probably, rather than travail]' " (ll. 20–61). The comedy lies partly in the suspect assumption that Apostolic glossolalia (Acts 2) is obtainable by wandering or work, and in the belief that Panurge, the promoted substantive, is substantial enough for an Englishman to admire. But nobody can emulate Panurge, for in addition to the major European languages, Panurge speaks Utopian, Lanternish, and Antipodean, tongues that Satan himself would be hard pressed to learn through travel.

Panurge's show leaves his hearers entranced, frustrated, and obscurely collaborative as they act the straight men in an elaborate joke, listening to one alien tongue after another, until the hungry talker resorts to what he calls his native French and asks for food in words the friends must admit they understand.[25] Donne would have grasped the comedy — a Greek noun claiming to be native-born French, a naturalized and jabbering French *substantif* asking for sustenance. He would also have noticed that even as Pantagruel's friends *hear* Panurge's incomprehensible requests for help, they do not act upon what they must *see* as signs of distress, delaying the aid that charity requires.[26] Donne may have recalled the episode precisely because he, too, examines how language and its misuse relate to love, whether the love that is so lacking in this *panourgos* or the love that the narrator owes even this wretch. To be sure, his companion is less ambiguous than Panurge, whose verbal prowess, it has been said, "can be viewed either *in malo* as an allusion to Old Testament Babelism ... or *in bono,* to the New Testament gift of tongues."[27] The satirist's scorn, however appropriate generically, contrasts with Pantagruel's rush of love for his disreputable other self.

In the *Tiers livre* Panurge is still a *panourgos,* but as a trickster in need of a wife yet fearing to marry he cuts a different figure from the one he does in *Pantagruel.* Afraid of domestic treason, he wants to foreshorten time by knowing at once what only an unfolding life can reveal at its own pace, to risk himself and his goods only if assured from the start that they will be safe. Perhaps this is another reason Donne found Panurge noteworthy, for the latter's perplexity concerning marriage profoundly resembles the religious uncertainties of Satire III. Panurge and Donne's speaker share a difficulty: how to commit themselves to a woman (a bride or the Church as Christ's spouse) who may be false. Panurge's fear of being cuckolded, beaten, and robbed may seem silly, but when one remembers how often marriage has represented other sorts of commitment, not least the religious, his anxieties take on further resonance. The *Tiers livre* is not an allegory, yet Panurge's dilemma is interesting in part because it suggests other paralyses of the will, other self-loving refusals to submit to the process of time and generation.

If the pestilent courtier in Satire IV is a *panourgos* who has read Rabelais, Satire III has a Panurge among its butts: "Carelesse Phrygius doth abhorre / All, because all cannot be good, as one / Knowing some women whores, dares marry none" (ll. 62–64). Panurge's problem exactly, and attended by a similar cynical misogyny and what Joshua Scodel calls Phrygius's "Epicurean avoidance of pain."[28] Why Phrygius? For Thomas Hester, the name suggests the Barrowists, who revived the Phrygian Montanists' disbelief in marriage ceremonies.[29] But the name also recalls the Phrygian Cybele and her priestly eunuchs. Indeed, commenting on Panurge's dilemma (*TL* 48), Gargantua mentions with distaste a group of "moles" — monks — who "abhor" marriage and live like "pontifes de Cybele en Phrygie." In a fine discussion of Satire III, James Baumlin says that comparing each sect's adherents to a wooer of some wench reduces "the differences between contemporary forms of religion to domestic comedy."[30] But this domestic comedy has geopolitical range and eternal consequences.

Donne hardly needed Rabelais to tell him that an inability to identify true religion can be figured as a failure to locate Christ's spouse. Religious eros and symbolic weddings are old stories, and allusions to sex and adultery run throughout Donne's satires, not least a double entendre: "To will," says Satire III, "implyes delay, therefore now doe" (l. 85)[31] Donne's notice of Panurge, though, gains texture when we juxtapose Satire III's sexual imagery to Rabelais's demonstration of how timorous narcissism can puzzle the will. Donne, too, satirizes a "courage of straw" (l. 27) that leads to mere bravado, a cowardice that pleases the devil (ll. 33–34), a taste for that "worne strumpet," the World (ll. 37–39). With some daring, the satirist condemns those who love a particular sect because a theologian or government tells them to. Whether Donne was at this point a Catholic fideist, and however he read Rabelais's religion, he would have found in the later books a telling example of how those in power need not force consciences. When Panurge cannot decide whether to marry, his master does not compel him. Rather, Pantagruel joins him on his voyage to resolve the dilemma; to paraphrase Donne, the giant, in effect, says that "to sail inquiring right is not to stray." True, in the third and fourth books Panurge gets no answer he will accept—but neither does Donne say *what* Truth stands on the hill we are to climb (relative of the mountain near Gaster's home in the *Quart livre*). The only hint he gives us is the advice that we ask our fathers what their fathers said and so on back, presumably, to the apostles, a process that presupposes, given the poem's metaphors, many past decisions to marry. Had Panurge fully believed the pronuptial urgings of Pantagruel's father, this novel, so interested in the patrilinear, would have taken a different turn. As an incarnate noun, though, Panurge has no real father, and Gargantua himself descends from Nimrod and Goliath — unsafe religious guides.

If Donne reflected on Panurge's sexual anxieties as well as on his polyglottism, he would have had company as the seventeenth century wore on. The *Tiers livre*'s fuss over cuckoldry is inherently interesting, of course. Sex is. But it is not only spouses who can betray us, and cuckold's horns make handy loudspeakers for expressing other doubts, philosophical or political. Panurge himself never finds a wife. His fears, though, give him anticipatory headgear, and it has been said that visible somewhere in the resulting picture are such horned figures as Pan and the Celtic god Cernunnos.[32] Certainly Shakespeare plays with such associations in *The Merry Wives of Windsor* when giving the would-be cuckolder Falstaff horns like those of Acteon or Herne the Hunter (Cernunnos's English equivalent, said to haunt Windsor Forest; the play disperses Panurge: Mr. Ford dreads robbery and a cuckold's horns, Falstaff gets a beating and antlers).

Panurge's probable fate received early notice, although the first printed allusion is in a translation: Henry Wotton's *A Courtlie Controversy of Cupids Cautels* (1578), "Tragicall Histories . . . medled with divers delicate Sonets and Rithmes" based on Jacques Yver's *Printemps d'Yver*. The setting is a gathering at Pentecost during a pause in the civil wars. As the fourth day closes, one speaker says that love looks different in different circumstances, citing "the

arrest pronounced sometyme in a redde robe uppon the doubte of Panerge"
and "daring well say, that Love of it selfe, which willingly ruleth us, hath
hindered us to judge justly aswell you Gentlewomen, as also my cousyns" (sig.
Ii3v). The "arrest" (judgment) he means may be Epistemon's accusation that
self-love distorts Panurge's view. Spenser's friend Gabriel Harvey is blunter: in
the margin of Erasmus's *Parabolae,* which he acquired as a student in 1566
and reread in 1577, he writes: "Panurge, a cuccu."[33] If Harvey wrote this in
1577, let alone 1566, he was one of the first in England to read Rabelais.

The crowd of cuckold jokes in English drama has been linked to early
capitalism and, because jealousy inspires close watching, to troubled thoughts
on spectatorship.[34] Rabelais himself is more concerned with Panurge's dys-
functional will and his attempts to take epistemological shortcuts. In a world
ignorant of DNA, cuckoldry well represents the difficulty of truly knowing
anything and, in an age of debates over marriage, it threatens a patrilinear
descent of names, land, and — implies Donne's Satire III — knowledge of which
church God will marry.

In the last scene of the notorious *Eastward Ho!* (1605), by Jonson, Chapman, and Marston, the satirical Touchstone reassures a worried Master Se-
curity with a brief paradox on cuckoldry taken from Frère Jean's words to
Panurge: "If you be a cuckold, it's an argument you have a beautiful woman to
your wife; then, you shall be much made of; you shall have store of friends;
never want money; you shall be eased of much o'your wedlock pain; others
will take it for you."[35] And, he adds, revising Jean's promise that salvation
follows cuckoldry, "you being a usurer, and likely to go to hell, the devils will
never torment you; they'll take you for one o'their own race." The whole play,
with its taverns, prodigals, and journey (not to a bottle, but downriver to
"Cuckold's Haven") suits Panurge's more squalid moments, and this argument suits the work's risqué, city-slicker tone.

It is likely that Shakespeare was taken by Panurge, if not taken in. Gonzalo's
jesting assurance in *The Tempest*'s opening storm scene that the boatswain is
born to be hanged, not drowned (I.i.28–33), may be proverbial (the implied
commentary on charity, fortitude, and the tempest of fortune going back to
Erasmus or beyond), but it also echoes Frère Jean's words to Panurge during
the *Quart livre*'s tempest. Both writers, moreover, include nautical technobab-
ble, a suggestion that the fearful would do better to lend a hand, an injunction
to pray when all seems lost, and a longing for a patch of even poor dry land.

A more significant analogue is *All's Well That Ends Well*'s Parolles: called
by a name meaning "words," he is as much made of language as is Panurge.[36]
Like him, this "equivocal" liar, coward, "fox," and "manifold linguist," this
"good drum" full of "businesses" and stratagems, is nonetheless loved by his

master and, eventually, told that "though you are a fool and a knave, you shall eat." No wonder the French king says to him, as Pantagruel might have said to Panurge, "Thou art a knave and no knave."[37] Resistance to marriage drives the plot, although panurgic cunning and interest in cuckoldry are removed from the reluctant husband, Bertram, and embodied in a loquacious trickster. Others in the play, moreover, know a panurge when they see one; a French lord tells Parolles: "The devil it is that's thy master . . . Methink'st thou art a general offense, and every man should beat thee . . . you are a vagabond and no true traveller" (II.iii.249–60). This panurge even receives the same sort of comfort given his Rabelaisian predecessor, for the play's clown shares Frère Jean's (and *Eastward Ho!*'s) view of cuckoldry, his "ergo" recalling the logic's origin in *TL* 28 as well as in proverb lore: "He that ears my land spares my team, and gives me leave to inn the crop: if I be his cuckold, he's my drudge. He that comforts my wife is the cherisher of my flesh and blood; he that cherishes my flesh and blood loves my flesh and blood; he that loves my flesh and blood is my friend: *ergo,* he that kisses my wife is my friend" (I.iii.44–55).[38]

One did not have to be a playwright to grasp how allusions to cuckoldry can energize discourse in a society apprehensive about all sorts of infidelity. Annotating Michael Drayton's *Poly-Olbion,* John Selden found Panurge's craving to know the future relevant to his own need to deduce the past. Drayton's title page, after all, shows England as a simpering lady draped in a map and surrounded by four husbands: nationhood in a land that was so often invaded demands serial monogamy, and if politics makes strange bedfellows it also makes erotic metaphors. One note tells of a man who feeds his wife a magic ram's shoulder to trick her into revealing any adulteries of which she might be guilty. Because this method also predicts the future, it might have helped "jealous Panurge in his doubt *de la Coquage*" better than the experts he consulted (Selden names "Rondibilis, Hippothade, Bridoye, Trouillogan") or "the Oracle it self." A jest germane to Selden's research: How *do* we know who did what to whom? Who were England's true spouses, and who begot her ancient law? Will James be faithful to her if he claims new powers? Feeding him magic mutton would be a ready way for England to test the rights of free monarchy and avoid Panurge's fate.[39]

Sometimes, to be sure, a tale of love's anxieties can simply illuminate love's anxieties. As I have noted, Robert Burton paraphrases Rabelais's fable about the god Cocuage, borrowing it from "Incognito"'s prefatory poem to Tofte's translation of Benedetto Varchi's *Blazon of Jealousie* (1615). "Incognito"'s story makes a good introduction to Tofte's performance as a Menippizing translator who stuffs the margins of this already resourceful text with opinion, quotation, anecdote, and jokes (such as: "Veritas Odium parit" means "Verdjuyce and Oate-meale good for a Parrot," sig. G1). "Incognito" credits his source, calling Coquage "The God of Cuckolds" and citing "Rablais in Hist. Pantagruel, lib.3. chap.33." In *TL* 33, it will be remembered, Dr. Rondibilis warns Panurge that obsession with cuckoldry merely encourages infidelity: by giving Coquage and Jealousy the same feast day, Jupiter ensures that any man with a pretty wife who worships Jealousy will receive a visit from Coquage. "Incognito" sharpens the point and adds a complication Rabelais had omitted: marital jealousy spoils male friendships. He addresses "the Jealous Husband":

> Thou that beleev'st no Female Virtue, Thou
> Which so good lookes, and such false love canst show
> (Enough for fashion) but still doubt'st thy friend,
> Least to thy choisest Piece he make his end.
> Unhappy soule! that to what's Good art blind,
> That always seek'st, what thou fearst most to find.
> That runst before thy Faire one in the street,
> So, with foule mouths, that thy sly ears may meet,
> Such as dare black the name of Goodnesse, such
> As n'ere speake true but when they say, 'ts too much,
> Thou shouldst enjoy what Fortune, not thy worth
> Hath giv'n thee in her. . . . .
> . . . .
> Thou that to Coquage sacrificest, when
> The Calender of Gods was made, mongst men
> Coquage was occupi'd, while Jove assign'd
> To all the other Gods what speciall kind
> Of Sacrifices, and what Place, what Day
> Their Tides should be on; none but he away
> No room in Heaven left him; Jove's Decree
> Was that he should with Goddesse Jealousie
> Partake in Tide, but that, on Earth alone,
> (Excluded Heaven) his Dominion
> Should be mongst those whose liberty was lost
> By Female union, but of all, those most
> Which blest were with the Fayrest, yet of them
> Onely o're such as sacrific'd to him
> With feare, suspicion, searching, spyes and doubt.
> None should his Godlike presence Grace without
> Such daily rites; no favour, help, or aid,
> To any from him, while those dues unpaid.
> But, as an Appanage, his Deity
> Should to the Jealous still companion be.
> Thou that unable fram'st thy policy

> Gainst the Braguettes, and with Treachery
> Vainly resists what the sweet sex would doe
> With him they call on, great St. Balletrou.
> Thou that deservst it, nor hadst so long mist
> What thou so seekst for, if a Spagirist
> Could save hir Honors individuall part,
> Yet give the blow, thou knowst, would never smart.
> You that are n'ere at rest but when you wear
> Hans Carvel's Ring. (Sigs. B3–B3v)

Rabelais's fable is now verse satire in the rough Elizabethan manner, with added Rabelaisian touches for the delectation of those able to place them.

Echoing several of Rabelais's seemingly misogynist moments, such details make "Incognito"'s apostrophe to husbands more sardonic. St. Balletrou, added as another calendrical joke, is a penis ("A sweepe-hole; Membre viril: ¶Rab," says Cotgrave); Panurge says his will clean out—"decrottera"—a pack of enemy camp followers (*P* 26; cf. *CL* 15). Hans Carvel dreamed that the devil gave him a ring, telling him that while he wore it his wife would never be faithless; he awoke to find his finger in her "how-should-I-call-it" (*TL* 28; cf. *G* 8). A *braguette* is a codpiece; the margin cites a "shrine" of them, which may recall the fantasy *Dignité des braguettes* mentioned in *Gargantua*'s prologue. In sum, "Incognito" solicits readers who will be charmed by sharing mild indecency and able to deduce that the text to follow is not *Othello* but semi-serious anatomy.

Who was England's Panurge? Seldom quite Rabelais's figure, he moves within a system of nouns and names as a quasi-diabolical bundle of foxiness, quicksilver talk, economic misbehavior, "curiosity," and sexual trepidation. His amoral magnetism and sophistical charm are less in evidence, perhaps because much commentary on what *panourgia* represents is so piously didactic, while intellectually complex allusions like Donne's are so brief. English writers did create compelling *panourgoi,* but they are named Volpone, Mercutio, Falstaff.

Panurge may be a promoted noun, but he can fuss over his body: how to feed it, find it a wife, avoid having it beaten or drowned. Rabelais's own interest in the body, moreover, is just what some English readers found worth remarking upon.

4

Body Matters

Gargantua et Pantagruel's relation to the body is hard to pin down. Alcofribas in Pantagruel's mouth, sampling food as it passes by and relieving himself in his master's throat, or young Gargantua searching for the best *torche-cul* (arse wipe) — such figures seem at ease with the flesh. Even "materialists," though, deal in words, words that may or may not reach the solid shore of things-as-they-are. Enclosed in heads ablaze with firing neurons, we cannot tell matter from its representations, for as Jacques Derrida did not quite say, "Il n'y a pas de hors synapses."

In fact, allusions in England to what seems a Rabelaisian materiality are often concerned more with words than with stuff. No wonder: those who write about Rabelais are . . . writers. How words affect matter is at the heart of Reformation debate, moreover, while Panurge's perplexities are as much epistemological as sexual. There is little actual sex in *Gargantua et Pantagruel*: everybody talks about making the beast with two backs, but nobody does anything about it. Although characters can love their families, friends, and Christ, passion takes place off-page or dwindles to innuendo (in *QL* 9, for example). We never see Pantagruel's Parisienne, and the unexpected sign of her existence is just that — a sign, a fake diamond that forms part of a rebus encoding an accusation of abandonment and falsity (*P* 25: "Dy, amant faulx"). Panurge boasts of conquests; we see failures. His fancy of walling Paris with genitals is no less political and philosophical than sexual, and his story of filling a hag with moss suggests male worry more than male enthusiasm. Nurses dandle their giant's penis, a peasant scares a young devil by lifting her skirt to show her "wound," and Panurge's trip to the Bottle is sexualized at the outset by puns on *lanterne* and *falot* (light and lighthouse, vulva and fellow/ phallus). Mostly, though, Rabelaisian sex is talk — dirty talk, to unclean ears, but talk. Unsurprisingly, Rabelais's sexual lexicon was, as far as written evidence goes, most appreciated by a lexicographer: Cotgrave.

There are exceptions, like Selden on Rabelais's word for penis. And Everard Guilpin, writing satire in the late 1590s when moral posturing was chic in such male circles as the Inns of Court (Guilpin was at Gray's Inn), ostentatiously recoils from Rabelaisian smut. He adopts the requisite persona: disgusted by corruption, impatient of euphemism, playing with angry self-satisfaction the roles of prosecutor, doctor, and corrections officer. A "Satyre Preludium" in his *Skialetheia* (1596) first scorns "whimpring Sonnets, puling Elegies" that "melt" valor by rousing "Cock-sparrow thoughts," and then condemns one who "ransacks every roome" of a brothel and like a gynecologist can "anatomize" each "nook." We English outdo the Continent:

> Let Rablais with his durtie[-]mouth discourse
> No longer blush, for they'le write ten times worse:
> And Aretines great wit be blam'd no more,
> They'le storie forth the errant arrant whore:
> And speaking painters excuse Titian,
> For his Joves loves; and Elephanticke vaine.
>   Thus all our Poets as they had carousde
> A health to Circes, are in hogsties housde,
> Or els transformd to Goates lasciviously,
> Filthing chast eares with theyr pens Gonorrhey.[1]

What vexes this satirist about Rabelais is dirt — dirt like that of Nashe, if it is he who pokes a finger, or something like a finger, into whorehouse nooks (see his *Choise of Valentines*).

Guilpin's editor calls him obsessed with sex, filth, and disease. And why not, in a city filled with sex, filth, and disease? These lines need not be subjective opinion, for the next satire praises Aretino as "the whip of fooles," but Guilpin's persona is indeed quite unlike Rabelais's: he cures with whips and caustics, Rabelais (whatever his Cynic growl, "gzzzzzzzz") with comedy; the satirist pretends to have a centered identity ("My lines are still themselves, and so am I," concludes the final satire), while Rabelais's "Je" slips and slides. Guilpin's assumed personality better suits the Aretino who made vice tremble than the genial Alcofribas who *likes* drunks and syphilitics.

Guilpin is unusual in closely connecting Rabelais with sex. Just what makes a mouth "dirty" is not obvious, for medical theories considered sexual and execretory functions analogous: both were ejaculatory purgations that kept humors healthily balanced, so sexual and scatological jokes were less distinct than they are now.[2] Still, it would have been a very confused reader who could not tell jokes about the privates from jokes about the privy. For some reason the English thought Rabelais's use of the former, except when cuckoldry was the topic, not worth much notice.

Two epigrams in an early seventeenth-century manuscript collection of verse, to be sure, hint that a liking for Rabelais ran more to crude humor — sexual and scatological — than the printed evidence suggests. The first is taken from the prologue to the *Quart livre,* the second is a dixain Panurge claims that he wrote to illustrate the old observation that a little rain calms a high wind (*QL* 44). The verses are headed "Translated out of Rabeleys," although in fact Rabelais found the first, probably by Mellin de Saint-Gelais, in a 1544 *Recueil de vraye poésie françoise.*

ex pag: 572
stout Tybaulte being joyus for to couche
by his new-married yonge & fayre wyves syde
And very willing . . . to avowche
A lustie bridegroome to so sweete a Bryde
    having observ'd a Mallet's driving force
    brought one to bedd to backe him in his course

Sweete love (q[uo]th shee) why is this Mallet tell
To dryve (q[uo]th he) when courage gins to quayle
To dryve (q[uo]th she) then he hath pleased me well
and had no Mallet but his naked tayle.
    Poore Tybaults looking as his powle were shorne
    sayd then my Mallet may knocke downe my hornes[.]

de pag. 710
fayr Quelot w[i]th Jenyn hee wedded I heere
feasting w[i]th qarlicke beefe beware[beer?] & new Ale
felt strange effecte of that their Ill appeare
yea savor conflict soe she toppets[?] the Tayle
    Jenyn frighted slept not & noe wonder
    Sweet Quelot garlicke charge went like Thunder

Turning each waye and smelling noe safe [. . .]
he banisht dread and on his guard now stands
and bravely pist against h[er] garlicke bum
She wakt and Cried good husband hold yor hands
    Oh wife (q[uo]th) he) softe raynes lowde wynd allaye
    she jerc[k]t her Bum and sweetly slept till day[.]
        finis.[3]

In printed texts, though, and with one or two exceptions, the English seem to have felt less easy with Rabelais's earthier humor, mentioning it more obliquely or, like Guilpin, only while holding their noses. I cannot find overt notice of Panurge's genital walls, say, or the "wounded" farmer's wife. Rather, allusions to the Rabelaisian body tend to be dipsodic or scatological. Some writers also recalled that Rabelais was a doctor, and he contributed a little to the period's not always happy sense of the open or reversible body.

Down the Hatch and Beyond

Renaissance Europe regarded the body's netherworld with an easy humor that later generations would find puerile, but Rabelais's own scatology is ambiguous.[4] At times, in his earlier books, excrement is primarily if unpleasantly natural, something that emerges from one end of a human animal because the other end has been eating sensibly. Panurge will even use the stuff, with medical precedent, in recapitating Epistemon. And when toward the end of this same book Pantagruel is constipated, his reaction is to seek medical aid in restoring the progress of matter through the body and out into the nourishing world. Nevertheless, as Rabelais's work evolves, and within the early books individually, scatology tends to diminish the thing it describes or to indicate something nasty. Calling a glossed text similar to a lovely robe edged with excrement (*P* 5) is no compliment.

The most remarkable appropriation of Rabelaisian scatology is by Sir John Harington: courtier, wit, royal godson and royal (with a bar sinister) cousin, translator of the Italian poet he called his friend "Harry-Osto," epigrammatist, affectionate husband, and promoter of the flush toilet. *A New Discourse of a Stale Subject, called The Metamorphosis of Ajax: Written by Misacmos, to His Friend and Cosin Philostilpnos* (1596) is a burlesque reversal of polite society's standards that jests with priorities and posteriors — the body's and logic's fore and aft.[5] "Ajax" is "a jakes" or privy, for this Menippean book, like Apuleius's *Metamorphosis*, degrades Ovidian pathos and Pythagorean philosophy. Any jakes, even when unreformed, serves the end result of change, the transformation of nature's creatures not into trees and birds but into excrement. That excrement will in turn fertilize the ground, so it is with some justice that a modern scholar has seen in Harington's text a satire of "projects" and monopolies that owes as much to the fluid and circulatory economics of Panurge's encomium of debts as to Rabelais's excremental humor.[6]

Harington farces his text with scraps: parodic verses, pedigrees, teasingly anal-retentive postponements, pictures, lists, objections to his own book, a trial of the author, puns, marginal foolery, stories, and much else. Working in a genre that pulls down even the comic mighty from their seats, he does not spare Harry-Osto: having sung "Of Dames, of Knights, of armes, of loves delight," says the prefatory letter from Philostilpnos (quoting the start of *Orlando Furioso*), let Misacmos not disdain "Of vaults, of sinkes, privies & draughts to write" (p. 57). Like Rabelais, Harington devises a self-reflexive fantasy in which author and reader are present to each other in the same space-time continuum, for example, interrupting himself to send for a dictionary, scrambling to find his copy of Martial, or concluding a section of his book by inviting the reader to stretch his (or her?) legs while the writer puts on his boots to "go a peece of the way with you" — after a visit "to the house we talk off" (p. 159).

Like Rabelais, Harington is less arsy-versy than his scatology would suggest. His assertion (p. 174) that the water closet was collectively invented during a "dialogue" of ladies and gentlemen comments dryly on the taste for projections and on nobler but less useful dialogues by his philosophical betters from Plato to Castiglione. Yet his explanation does not turn the world upside down: fine folk and urbanites, Misacmos observes, need the watercloset more than do rustics, who have all outdoors. Moreover, as William Engel has shrewdly remarked, Harington's purpose is less to praise the open body than to devise a means of *making dirt disappear.*[7] Gargantua and Pantagruel seek to wipe off or expel fecal matter, but neither hopes to banish it from sight and knowledge, whereas the flush toilet does just that.

Misacmos makes a show of respecting the reader's presumed sensibilities by executing little bows of "save reverence" when from time to time he remembers his book's topic. His is merely a mock delicacy, of course, but that he adopts it at all is a sign of changing times. The same witty oscillation between bluntness and evasion characterizes his treatment of Gargantua's feathery torche-cul. Assuming that Rabelais plays the rhypographer (writing ingeniously on unworthy matters), Misacmos defends himself by citing *Gargantua* and other precedents. Some, he says, have written of folly, the pox, usury, Nero, "bawderie," or whores, while

> A seventh (whom I would guesse by his writing, to be a groome of the stoole to some Prince of the bloud in Fraunce) writes a beastly treatise onely to examine what is the fittest thing to wype withall, alledging that white paper is too smooth, brown paper too rough, wollen cloth too stiffe, linnen cloth too hollow, satten too slipperie, taffeta too thin, velvet too thick, or perhaps too costly: but he concludes, that a goose necke to be drawne betweene the legs against the fethers, is the most delicate and cleanly thing that may be. (Pp. 63–64)

Harington will "go before this filthy fellow," though, for Aristotle tells us that the broader cause is "Architectonicall" to the lesser, and this present text treats

of the house it self, & he but of part of that is to be done in the house, & that
no essential part of the businesse: for they say "there be three things that if one
neglect to do them, they will do themselves; one is for a man to make even his
recknings, for who so neglects it will be left even just nothing; another is to
mary his daughters for if the parents bestow them not, they will bestow them
selves; the third is that, which the foresaid French man writes of: which they
that omit, their lawndresses shall finde it done in their linnen. (Pp. 64–65)

The margin, less reticent, informs us that "this matter is discoursed by Rables,
in his 13. chap. of his first booke," quoting the French ("Un moyen de me
torcher le cul le plus Seigneurial, le plus excellent, le plus expedient que jamais
fut veu").

Has Rabelais been marginalized or centralized, denigrated or given his due?
Misacmos outdoes him as a sterco-rhypographer, or so he claims in his little
cacamachia, because his own humble topic contains that of Rabelais as a
building contains a privy. Harington himself offers two Rabelais. One, inhabiting the main page, is a nameless "filthy" writer on whose employment
Misacmos can only speculate, a writer whose "beastly treatise" makes this
present text look wholesome. Yet the reference to a "Prince of the bloud"
signifies royal patronage. The other Rabelais lives in the margin as an author
whom Harington — or is it still Misacmos? — can name and quote, one who
helps him present himself as a Menippean satirist conversant with French
writers. The page has the Rabelais of some English legend, its margin a major
European author.

Within a few paragraphs the work of this author, as it had already done
several times in France, inspires supplement — for Harington imagines a bit of
Gargantua that Rabelais left out. His Prologue tells how Ajax, after a quarrel
with Ulysses, becomes a "mal-content" and rages off to the woods (Harry-
Osto might call him a Jakes Furioso). There he dies, his blood generating the
hyacinth, "which is a very notable kind of grasse or flower." Misacmos medi-
tates on this metamorphosis for a while and then "remembers" something that
is worth quoting here as the period's most significant English contribution to
para-Rabelaisiana:

> Further I read that now of late yeares a French Gentleman son to one *Mon-
> sieur Gargasier* [the margin adds, "Rabbles lib.I.cap.13. *Come Gargasier cog-
> noit l'esprit excellent de Gargantua a l'invention d'un torche cul*"], & a yong
> Gentleman of an excellent spirit & towardnesse, as the reverent Rabbles
> (*quem honoris causa nomino,* that is whom I should not name without save-
> reverence) writeth in his first booke 13. Chap. but the storie you shall find
> more at large in the xiiii. book of his tenth Decad [the margin, a little heavily,
> explains, "Lib. Fictitius"]. This young Gentleman having taken some three or

a foure score pills to purge melancholy, every one as big as a Pome Cyttern [a citrus fruit], commanded his man to mowe an halfe acre of grasse, to use at the privy, and notwithstanding that the owners (to save their hay perhaps) sware to him it was of that ancient house of AJAX, & therefore reserved of purpose onely for horses of the race of Bucephalus, or Rabycano [from Ariosto], yet he would not be perswaded: but in further contempt of his name, used a phrase that he had learned at his being in the low Countreys, and bad *Skite upon* AJAX. But suddenly (whether it were the curse of the people, or the nature of the grasse I know not) he was stricken in his Posteriorums with S. Anthonies fier; and dispairing of other helpe, he went on Pilgrimage in hope of remedy hereof to Japana, neare Chyna: where he met a French Surgeon, in the Universitie of [Kyoto] that cured him both of that & the Verol [the French pox], that he had before in his priorums. (P. 70; see also *QL* 52's sore-giving decretals?)

Crossing "both the Tropickes, Cancer, & Capricorne," Gargantua returns "by Magellanes, swearing he founde no straightes there; but came from thence straight home. And so in 24. houres saile, and two or three od years beside, he accomplished his voyage," taking on fresh wine and water at the "Capon" of Good Hope.

Gargantua is now so pious that he vows "of all offices of the house, he should do honour to that house of office, where he had committed that scorne to AJAX: and that there he should never use any more such fine grasse, but rather, tear a leafe out of Holinsheds *Chronicles* . . . then to commit such a sinne against AJAX." So he constructs "a sumptuous privie, and in the most conspicuous place thereof, namely just over the doore; he erected a statue of AJAX, with so grim a countenance, that the aspect of it being full of terrour, was halfe as good as a suppositor: and further, to honour him he chaunged the name of the house, and called it after the name of this noble Captaine of the greasie [dirty] ones (the Grecians I should say) AJAX: though since, by ill pronunciation, and by a figure called *Cacophonia*, the accent is changed and it is called a Jakes" (p. 71). Misacmos now reports the discovery of a "petygrew" showing Ajax's descent from the dung-god Stercutius by way of Jove. Like *Pantagruel*, this text situates its hero in genealogical time: inventions, too, have lineage. After local monks hymn Ajax in Latin lines that all end in "culum" or "cula" (Misacmos prints the music), the prologue concludes, but not before noting how "a mad French man wrote, we did carrie our drinke in our bootes" (p. 77). This sounds like Rabelais, perhaps an echo of "Bennet's Boot/Tun" in *G* 39).

And now Misacmos is ready to reveal his invention, complete with diagrams, in a section walled off from the main text, as though it were itself a privy, by a new title page. The author is ostensibly Harington's servant Thomas Combe, for the practical mechanics of the watercloset are confined to the rear of the book and seated a rung or two down the social scale. Yet the style is (im)pure Harington and, hesitantly disagreeing with his learned editor, I suspect he wrote this, too.

Having appeared in the prologue and vanished in the main body of the text, "Rabelais" re-emerges, if ambiguously, in this practical "Anatomie." Like his master, "T.C." defends his topic and vocabulary against the prissy, touching not only on the common temptation to forget the flesh but also, like many Renaissance writers, on readers' tendency to take texts *in malo:* "But I smyle at some whose manners proove that thear mynds admit all wickednes, and yet forsooth theyr ears cannot brooke a litle scurrilytye. Ys it not pittye that men of so fyne ears should *male audire.* Yf one name a merd they thinke they are mard but a fylthyer thing then that mard them. What doe they with Rabbles and Aretyne in theyr studyes?" (p. 200). A note in the manuscript instructs the printer to drop this passage so as to make room for a picture, but it may also be that Harington felt he had crossed some line.[8] The masturbatory implications shift the tone from good clean scatology to what might sound like obscenity, associating the sexual imagination with solitude.

In this passage Harington's (or "T.C." 's) fancy first allows and then suppresses a glimpse into how one Renaissance reader could imagine other Renaissance readers studying Rabelais with only one hand on the book. And yet, compared to Aretino's rich food for solitary thought, there is surprisingly little in *Gargantua et Pantagruel* to inspire readers alone in their studies to much besides laughter at sexual joking, allusions, or fears. Where are the sexually dirty bits? Did Harington think he had read some? Or is he, too, willing to take "Rabbles" as an all-purpose naughty writer in order to make a rhetorical point? He himself has read Rabelais, even if he mentions him here with hat-doffing euphemism, but he could have deleted "Rabbles" and left the more relevant Aretino. Perhaps he hesitated to move from a health-promoting meta-morphosis of the privy to what one might call an invasion of privacy.[9] The implications for the way sex and reading relate to domestic space and mental interiority are provocative. Harington imagines a private indoor area that in turn requires a degree of wealth, his mind resting for a time on the gap between an outward fastidious moralism and the pleasure of being alone with a certain kind of book.

Some pages later Misacmos offers an "Apologie," now that he has "sufficiently evacuated [his] head of such homely stuffe" (p. 205). He needs one, for he can be thought scurrilous, satirical, and "a writer of fantasticall Pamphlets" (p. 227). He begins by reporting a dream or trance in which "a nimble dapper fellow" told him about a recent dinnertime discussion by Momus, Zoilus (inept critic of Homer), and "three or foure good natured Gentlemen more of the same crew"; unlike Rabbles and Aretino in the passage quoted above, *Ajax* is read in company. The scene is remarkable evidence of how a writer could envision incompetent or malicious reading in the 1590s. We hear one man's inane jest on Lipsius's *De cruce* (all those pages on the cross put no crosses in his purse!) and another's on being bored by Rainolds's refutation of Bellarmine (so much for religion). Spenser? His stanzas' final hexameters, they say, "disordered their mouthes." And

> at last one of them pulled out of his bosome, a booke that was not to be sold in Paules churchyard [because still in manuscript?], but onely that he had borrowed it of his friend, and it was intituled *The metamorphosis of AJAX*, at which they began to make marvellous sport: and because it was a rainie night, they agreed to read over the whole discourse to pass the time with. First they read the authors name, & though they understood it not, yet that it might not passe without a jest, they swore that it signified *Myse in a sack of mosse*. They read the letters, and stumbling once or twice on a figure called *Prolepsis* or prevention [that is, the anticipation of objections], they were angrie their scoffes were so prevented. But when they found Rabbles named, then they were at home, they looked for pure stuffe where he was cited for an author.

The friends examine the pictures, tut-tutting, and then start to read the main text, which they admire as "scurrill, base, shallow, sordidous." All is well until they are so taken aback to discover that Misacmos *hates* dirt — for they confess themselves to be "counted but filthie fellowes among the grave gray-beardes" — that they must restore their spirits with "fiftie pipes of Tabacco between five of them" (pp. 206–08). The scene is itself a "prolepsis": it posits a group of scoffingly scurrilous readers fond of Rabelais's "stuffe" from whom Harington — fond of the same stuff — can distinguish himself by having them reject his own book. He is and is not Rabelaisian.

Other English writers focus on Rabelais's urinary scatology. Joseph Hall associated it with Earth's own lower stratum, Hades, which is where he locates Pantagruel. At the conclusion of *Pantagruel*, in fact, Rabelais promises us a book on how the giant fought devils, burnt five rooms of Hell, sacked its great hall, tossed Persephone on the fire, and broke four of Lucifer's teeth and a horn on his derrière. Since Pantagruel was once a thirst-demon, it seems right to imagine this walking abyss of a giant in that other abyss, the underworld. An unfinished satire in *Virgidemiae* (1597) reports that when the drunkard Gullion's "dry soule" arrived in Hades he had the nerve to ask "the Feryman of hell, / That he might drinke to dead Pantagruel."[10] Charon agrees reluctantly, fearing lest "thirsty Gullion, / Would have drunke dry the river Acheron," and indeed the newcomer drinks so deeply that Hades' black ferry "stands still fast gravel'd on the mud of hell." Shades must now wait to reach the far shore until

"Gullion his bladder would unlode." Pantagruel's admirer will not be joining them, though, as by now Charon wants no part of him. The lines are curiously festive, for Gullion not only thinks of the absent Pantagruel—he is "dead," so presumably somewhere in the underworld neighborhood—but hoists one on his behalf. That what Charon fears he might hoist is the entire flaming Acheron fits Pantagruel's residually demonic nature, his affinity for fire as well as for the rivers that are created when giants urinate.[11] The scene even has a touch of Saturnalia: Charon stops work while a shade carouses with either firewater or, worse, Styx.

Perhaps Hall had read Ronsard's perhaps affectionate epitaph on the "good Rabelais." The singer of Gargantua's mare, of Panurge, of the Pope-maniacs, it says, always drank while he lived. But Death, who does not drink, drew the drinker from this world and now makes him drink from waters that flow into Acheron.[12] Hall's less engaging Rabelais is a drunk in a satire on one Labeo, a dirty and loose poet who imports immorality:

> But who conjur'd this bawdie Poggies ghost,
> From out the stewes of his lewde home-bred coast:
> Or wicked Rablais dronken revellings,
> To grace the mis-rule of our Tavernings?
> Or who put Bayes into blinde Cupids fist,
> That he should crowne what Laureats him list?
> Whose wordes are those, to remedie the deed,
> That cause men stop their noses when they read?
> Both good things ill, and ill things well: all one?
> For shame write cleanly Labeo, or write none. (II.i.55–64)[13]

Did Hall think Rabelais wicked? If satire is a "Porcupine, / That shoots sharpe quils out in each angry line" (III.3.1–2) its job is not to discriminate; that is not how porcupines go to work. A comparison of astrological signs to inns, a phrase or two, and a claim that "now can every Novice speake with ease / The far-fetch'd language of th'Antipodes" (VI.i.137–38) suggest that Hall, like others in his city and academic circles, had read this reveling drunk.[14] Not for the last time, the English response to the risqué shows a writer who is shocked, *shocked,* and a reader who realizes he can appropriate the shocking text. Hall praises Spenser and Du Bartas; praising Rabelais would let his cover slip.

Hall may call Rabelais a drunken reveler, but when he writes about drunks in *Mundus alter et idem* (1605), a satire concerned in part with the body's tendency to guzzle and bulge, he largely ignores him.[15] Sandford M. Salyer noted the parallels between *Gargantua et Pantagruel* and this clever prose dystopia, so Lucianic as a travel guide to the moral Antipodes yet so stay-at-home as social commentary.[16] Hall and Rabelais share a land of thieves, a god of gluttony (All-Paunch, Gaster), and lexical caprices like "argentangina" — a "silver quinsey." Hall's paradoxically carnivorous Lent-bird, RUC, may merge Quaresmeprenant with the Popehawk of *CL,* and there is a quest for holy liquor from a cave with bottles. But Hall works chiefly through easy reversals or literalizations of European follies: his satire's *alter* really is its *idem,* and what makes it less than Rabelaisian (and less than Morean) is not moralism but transparency. It has been said that Hall "fails because there is no clear concept of an ideal state" behind his satire.[17] Yet the ideals behind his laughter at gluttony, theft, gynococracy, and folly are all too legible: reading them requires merely turning the book around so as to see a rectified world of temperance, honesty, patriarchy, prudence. Greater Menippean satire, even when not as amoral as Petronius's or Lucian's, is less categorical.

One passage may show that Hall has taken a look at Panurge's plan for walling Paris. In the capital of gluttonous Pamphagonia ("Eatallia," his translator was to call it, although Hall puns not on Italy but on Patagonia, home of presumably hungry giants), there is a wall built "from the bones of cattle[,] . . . erected in such a manner that the larger support the whole pile like pillars. The smaller ones are then placed on top, and the smallest, finally, fill in the cracks, and the whole is joined together with cement made of egg whites — an artificial wonder."[18] If Hall recalls Rabelais, he has unsexed the joke, converting vulvas into relics of past feasting. The future Protestant bishop has thereby also excised the antimonastic humor of having the walls held firm by interlaced monks' penises.

Another English reference to Rabelais's scatology revises Panurge's practical joke on the highborn Parisian lady who rejects his advances (*P* 21–22). To the distress of some readers but with parallels in carnival humor and possibly with an evangelical point, Panurge smears her with the minced vulva of a bitch in heat — whereupon more than 640,000 city dogs, enticed by the smell, converge to pee on her.[19] That is not the part of the story that John Searle recalls, however, when composing a newsy letter in August 1608. Although the letter from "the family at Spa to the Household at Brussels" is written in the first person singular, two of its signatories are women; and because the letter refers to a "bedfellow" of one recipient as a man, it is likely, if not certain, that Searle also addresses a female reader. In other words, the letter's tone is not man-to-man but family-to-family, with room for women's laughter and for their recognition of Rabelais's name. At Spa,

> Our whole morning exercise is nothing else but drinking *quaeque illud consequentur* [and what follows it] and according to the differences of our sexes, some are cullenders, some lembecks [alembics], some stream it out again,

some distill it, but what residue of metals and minerals it leaves in the body, *ick weets niet* [I don't know]. I am monstrously afraid of an iron mill in my belly. . . . Our gentlewomen thrive well in spitting and spawing by their Spa sipping, but I am half in doubt that if they stay long here they will grow wild. We can never keep them out of the wood, for when we look behind us to see and ask how they fare, we find that we have lost them as Orpheus lost his wife Eurydice by turning back to look on her. . . . I thank God my daughter is like to do wondrous well here; she is able already with one week's practice to piss point-blank through the eye of a pack needle, like the fellow in Quintilian that could throw millet seeds through a needle's eye. It was a laudable pool that Francis and little Billings pissed at the Channoiness' door of Anderley, which running down the hill 17 geometrical paces long, threatened to carry the quondam house of Erasmus of Rotterdam into the Duke of Aumale's pond. Rabelais likewise tells us that the dogs of Paris coming upon occasion to piss all at one place, they caused a new brook which yet is called *Le ruisseau des Gobelins* and is sovereignly good to dye scarlet in. But this is nothing to our *pisseresses* of Spa.[20]

Searle goes on to mention tripe, chitterlings, a lanced boil, energetic horses, and other items that give the prose a sense of slightly ironized jollity and minor domestic adventure.

He ends his self-consciously comic letter, "Thus for want of matter I break off the matter, being well assured that there is no great matter in this discourse of Spa water," and signs himself "Grammatofamilias." Why has he dropped the sexual part of Panurge's prank? To spare the feelings of wives and daughters (perhaps unfamiliar with Rabelais)? Did he find incontinent dogs funnier than humiliated ladies? Because his aim is to laugh at the overflowing bladders of Spa and not at sex? This is, after all, family entertainment. His phrasing, furthermore, seems to allude to an episode complete as described, not to one that misses its major point. Rabelais's brief concluding etiological joke about Paris's dyeing and textile industry, added in the later editions, has become the main jest. That Searle mentions it at all is a useful reminder, however, that such humor was once thought suitable in family correspondence.

Thomas Lodge's response to Rabelais and bodies had been, if not squeamish, then disapproving. Yet *Wits Miserie, and the Worlds Madnesse* (1596) wears its moralism jauntily, wrapping its arm around vice's shoulders even while kicking it in the ankles. *Miserie* portrays London's infestation by the seven deadly sins and their instigatory devils, doing so with a readable mix of personification, jest, classical exempla, character sketches, and a breeziness that can sound like Nashe — or Rabelais. Although it aspires to sober and purify us, its verbal intoxication and cavalier manner might sooner encourage, as they certainly express, a genial laxity. Nor does Lodge deny that he has tasted those poisons he labels as such, for he has actually read Rabelais, or at any rate can quote him. Either the Rabelais legend could survive an encounter with his writings or whatever Lodge's own opinion the atheist French drunk was too handy — reprehensible but comic — to abandon.

Lodge begins with Leviathan (Pride), wagger of wicked tongues, and his progeny, Scandal, Detraction, and Contempt ("there is no Philosophie [saith he] but in my Method"; he sounds like a twentieth-century academic, but he must be a Ramist).[21] Rabelais goes unmentioned. Nor does he serve Belzebub (Envy). Rabelais first appears, rather, when Lodge describes the sons of Baalberith (Ire). One, Blasphemy, will make a "lothsome jeast out of the scripture" and another, Brawling Contention, will swear with dirty irreverence in (bad) French or Italian: "Cancre, vienne la bosie, la peste l'estrangle, la diable, le rage te puisso emporter" (A pox on't, plague take it, may the pestilence strangle him, the devil, rabies take you) and "Pota d'iddio, putana d'iddio" (God's cunt, God's whore). "Hire him to write a comedie," and "he is as arrant an Atheist as Rabelais in his Pantagruel, so that it is wonder that . . . he is not stroken blind, and by devine justice loose his sences" (pp. 69, 71–72).

This is half the Rabelais legend — scoffing atheism — and its impieties stink with disease and sexual nastiness. The equally legendary Rabelais of the fleshpots emerges, together with a glance at Rabelais the fantasy writer, when Lodge comes to Beelphogor, "Prince of belly-cheere," described in scatological detail. He carries a sausage "to drive down drinke" and instead of a book on the Nine Worthies has one on "faithfull drunkards." Cavorting and swilling in the tavern, he "alledgeth you these verses out of Rablais (but with this breathing point, One pottle more of that next the doore Ned)":

> Furiena est de bon sens ne jouist,
> Qui boit bon vin & ne s'en rejouist.
> Mad is the knave and his wits have the collicke,
> That drinkes good wine and is not frollicke.

After more partying, "fill his cup againe of Madera wine, and let him wipe his eies after his fashion, you shall have stories too as true as the voiage of Pantagruel" (p. 86). The lines are spoken by Panurge in *QL* 65 when, in a companionable shipboard scene after the visit to Gaster, "Pantagruel haulse le temps avecques ses domesticques" (a pun on "carouse" and "make a wind rise"). Lodge's mention of a "voiage" is further evidence that he has been reading about the Belly in the chapters relevant to the devil under consideration. He is not just remembering the reputation of "Rabelais," however abjectly he perpetuates it.

Among this devil's brothers are Immoderate Joy, who sings bawdy sonnets and cracks jokes; Multiplicity of Words, who jabbers about travel and wastes time; and Scurilitie, who makes faces and lewd gestures. This last is "perfect" in the "abhominations of Priapisme," enjoying lascivious jests and cruel scoffs. Let those seeking "further insight into the filthy nature of this fiend" consult "Aretine in his mother Nana, Rabelais in his Legend of Ribaudrie, and Bonaventure De Perriers in his Novels," where "he shall be sure to loose his time, and no doubt, corrupt his soule" (pp. 94–95).[22] But what are we to make of Lodge's familiarity with this "Ribaudrie"? He too can quote Rabelais. As a moralist, Lodge did not have his heart in his task: the Menippean satirist in him kept sneaking off to the tavern to join the Rabelais he thought he might find there, if only for good talk.

Jonson, Rabelais, and the Body

A telling demonstration of how attention to the body can merge with or dominate a concern for other topics can be found in Jonson appropriations of Rabelaisian moments. Whatever the origin of *The Case Is Altered*'s "panurgo," by 1616 (and probably earlier) Jonson had read around in *Gargantua et Pantagruel*. For Huntington Brown, who first laid out the evidence for this, Jonson was "a hearty animal, honest, convivial, and frank to the point of bearishness."[23] More recently he has looked less hearty: drawn to the material world, he was also disturbed by it, his own eventually mountainous body an embarrassment to him despite the comic roles he found for it (using his obesity, says one critic, as a personal antimasque).[24] Late twentieth-century criticism has scrutinized the connection between Jonson's bulk and his writings, his claim to authorship, his stance toward his audience and toward an economy based on increased consumption of matter and words.[25] Far from taking materiality for granted, says Katharine Maus, Jonson "struggles with the problem of *whether* material life, however it may be defined, really possesses this priority."[26] Our current Jonson finds holiday misbehavior as much a problem as a delight; his scatology is anally clenched; and the mouth as he perceives it is a hole from which too many words spew and into which too much matter enters. In sum, he is *not* Rabelais: in *Volpone* "Rabelaisian gusto is on the verge of collapsing into an antisocial, indeed repulsive, miserliness of the body," for the "flesh of Jonson's experience" is far from what "Bakhtin discovers in Rabelais."[27]

Work on Rabelais has taken a similar turn.[28] Still, compared to Jonson, he is easier in his skin (or more willing to appear so), happier (in books) to hand around the cakes and ale or relish the grotesque, more indecent, and more interested in disputes over sex and marriage. What the two writers share is fascination with language, notably language halfway to being matter and matter that behaves like words. Allusions to Rabelais that appear scatological or bibulous can suggest, when examined closely, issues of language and faith. These moments, quiet borrowings or intertextual gestures, seem Rabelaisian in the popular sense; when pressed, they become . . . Rabelaisian.

A reference to Gargantua that may in fact recall the chapbook giant shows how Jonson's scatology is as much about speech as about dirt. Bobadilla, the miles gloriosus of *Every Man in His Humor* (1598), sneeringly calls Giulliano, another ill-tempered gentleman, a "scavenger" (a cleaner of privies and streets). Giulliano is furious: "By this good day (God forgive me I should sweare) if I put it up so, say I am the rankest ——— [the 1616 folio has "cow"] that ever pist. S'blood and I swallowe this, Ile neere drawe my sworde in the sight of man againe while I live . . . Scavenger? 'Hart and Ile goe neere to fill that huge tumbrell slop of yours with somewhat and I have good lucke, your Garagantua breech cannot carry it away so."[29] Like the pissing ——— (or cow), this Gargantua conveys Giulliano's choleric "humor," which will later lead him to thrash Bobadilla. He himself is big, for his brother asks tolerantly, "Whats a musition unlesse he play? whats a tall man unlesse he fight?" (IV.iii.11–12), and his speech shows his vulgarity, even if he scorns those who read "Ballads and Rogery, and Trash" (III.iv.172–73).

Something has happened to the scatology, though, for as usual Jonson is fascinated yet repelled by what hides in civilization's breeches. Gargantua and the imagined excrement associated with him express explosive wrath, not comic acceptance or festive reversal. To be sure, it would be unwise to read Rabelais's own scatology only as hearty acceptance of the flesh, for in his works, excrement—like food—can be closely associated both with words and with whatever needs purging.[30] Still, in the chapbooks, colonic looseness shows fluent vitality, just as in *Gargantua*, the giant's early curiosity about his own bottom is humorously indulged. In Jonson's scene the threatened filth is a fecal humiliation projected onto an enemy. The implication is that an angry mouth can move another's bowels, but there is no actual "somewhat" here, only a whiff of it in the invective. This is the discourse, but only the discourse, of the lower body. It has been said that "Jonson's constant ridicule of jargon, cant, affected speech, rhetoric, and swearing of oaths is structurally transformed into food and its byproducts, feces, farts, and vomit."[31] He can also proceed in an opposite way, however, making a body of words pointing to but also veiling a materiality much spoken of but—understandably, in this case— not staged.

Rabelais's scatology is more precisely audible in *Volpone* (printed 1607).

Playing the mountebank, Volpone claims he can cure teeth so loose they dance like virginal jacks (II.ii.246–47), just as Rabelais proffers the pseudomedical advice in his prologue to *Pantagruel* that teeth leaping like virginal keys have been helped by the application of dung and a Gargantua chronicle. And, in *The Alchemist* (printed 1612), the first scene's aborted reference to licking figs from something nasty recalls a story in *QL* 45 about Milanese prisoners forced to remove and replace figs from a mule's rectum with their teeth. More significant is the nature of what struck Jonson. The contexts of both sets of loose teeth also share the "step right up, folks" rhetoric of the marketplace that is as seductively energetic as it is untrustworthy.[32] Even more intriguingly, the figs appear in a chapter telling how a once happy land of Pope-scorners has been laid waste by Pope-worshipers. One would like to know what Jonson thought of this. It was in the year of *Alchemist*'s first performance, 1610, that he rejoined the Church of England, impelled in part, thinks David Riggs, by vexation at Catholic militants.[33]

The Devil Is an Ass (1616) gains resonance from just such topics, its counterfeit diabolical possession an echo of the recent fuss over some exorcisms that the government accused Catholics of faking. Huntington Brown thinks that a mock polyglot fit in act V, scene viii, recalls Panurge's first meeting with Pantagruel, and Jonson clearly remembers Rabelais in scene ii when the young demon Pug begs to go home. Outslicked by London's city slickers, he begs Satan for easier work:

> O, Call me home againe, deare Chiefe, and put me
> To yoaking foxes, milking of Hee-goates,
> Pounding of water in a morter, laving
> The sea dry with a nut-shell, gathering all
> The leaves are falne this Autumne, drawing farts
> Out of dead bodies, making ropes of sand,
> Catching the windes together in a net,
> Mustring of ants, and numbring atomes; all
> That hell, and you thought exquisite torments, rather
> Then stay me here, a thought more: I would sooner
> Keepe fleas within a circle, and be accomptant
> A thousand yeere, which of 'hem and how far
> Out-leap'd the other. (V.ii.1–13)

Pug's plea suits a tangle of issues that the drama of those years explored: projection, fantasy, devils, and Catholic deceit. Of the eleven tasks, six are those at which servants work in the land of Quintessence, where Pantagruel's crew is wined and dined (*CL* 21). Along with enterprises that Jonson ignores, the queen's *abstracteurs* yoke foxes, milk billygoats, pound water in a mortar, measure flealeaps, catch wind in nets, and pull farts from a dead ass.[34] These unlikely jobs may hint at the vanity of works and at what seemed to the author(s) the illusive project of transubstantiation. If so, then once again a Rabelaisian text that Jonson remembers mocks a faith he has renounced.

Pleasure Reconciled to Virtue, performed on Twelfth Night 1618, struck its first audience as insipid, perhaps because what Jonson calls pleasure is what most of us call behaving ourselves. Written for a night of revels, his masque examines misrule with amused scorn. It begins with the entry of the "bouncing belly," named after Bacchus's friend Comus but modeled, as many have noted, on Rabelais's Gaster, whom Pantagruel and his shipmates meet soon after leaving the Pope-worshipers (QL 57–62). Like Comus, Gaster lives near a mountain, identified by Pantagruel as the Hill of Virtue and thus related to the one into which *Pleasure*'s Atlas has mutated. Both giants are "premier" masters of arts; both ride in triumph, fart, teach birds to talk, invent technologies, tell time, lack ears, take Poverty or Hunger as a companion, and are linked to tripe and Carnival (Jonson's "saturnalls"). True, Gaster denies he is a god and sends the unconvinced to see his chamberpot; nor does Pantagruel despise him — Rabelais was too good a doctor to devalue the stomach. But the giant detests the belly-worshiping Gastrolators and the Ventriloques who, by speaking from the "venter," appear to perform divinations. As a satirist of deceptive magic and possession, Jonson must have read about them with heightened attention.

Pantagruel's scorn anticipates that of *Pleasure*'s Hercules, who enters as the first antimasque concludes. But Rabelais *begins* with a giant's noble distaste at the natives' piles of food and worship of a gastric god. Whereas Rabelais juxtaposes hero and fools, *Pleasure* separates folly from reason discursively and temporally. Jonson's aims require this: his Virtue cannot embrace a Pleasure made grotesque by a swollen belly and sodden brain. Rabelais might agree, but he allows his giant to linger for six chapters before getting back on course. As he sails away, Pantagruel leaves behind faked prophecy and technological ingenuity. In focusing on this episode, Jonson's eye has again lit on "projects": Gaster has invented farming — hardly progress, if we may believe the ancient poets — and also war engines, elaborate defense systems, and the gunpowder that Rabelais calls diabolical. Jonson, that is, was drawn to a scene in Rabelais's text that concerns the material world, certainly, but also the dark uses to which our race, driven by deaf appetite, has put its wits.

A decade later Jonson recalled Rabelais in his splendid, unperformed masque *Neptune's Triumph* (1624), meant to put a patriotic spin on Prince Charles's failed effort to woo the Spanish Infanta. In the opening scene a cook argues that "the Art of Poetry was learnd" first in the kitchen, and there discovered "the same day, with the Art of Cookery." When a poet says, "I should have giv'n it rather to the Cellar," the cook replies, "O, you are for the Oracle of the Bottle, I see; Hogshead Trismegistus: He is your Pegasus." A note in the printed text says "Vid. Rabl.lib.5" (*CL* 33–47): Rabelais is author enough to join Lucian, Strabo, Homer, and others in these weighty margins.[35] Drink was so important to Jonson that there must be some self-mockery here. But the connotations go further, and we are invited to ponder them when Jonson identifies the source of his imported bottle. After voyaging past many marvels, it will be remembered, Pantagruel's crew reaches the priestess Bacbuc (Hebrew for bottle) and the Oracle that will resolve Panurge's doubts. Jonson would have noticed several material elements in this conclusion to the quest. The question, as in the geopolitical events lying behind his masque, is whether marrying is worth the risk of being beaten, robbed, and betrayed. After drinking from a book-shaped bottle, Panurge decides that it is. With regard to the Spanish marriage, also the object of a royal trip across the water, the English disagreed; Jonson's allusion carries some irony.

Drink drives Panurge to frenzied rhyme. No wonder, for the oracular bottle appears in *CL* 44 both as a shaped poem and an illustration: in the text the bottle contains wine, but in the picture it holds text (fig. 2). The bottle announces that it contains both mysteries and the liquor of Bacchus, vanquisher of India, but no "tromperie" (no *panourgia*, in effect, although one should mistrust self-referential bottles). If Jonson's poet is "for" this bottle, then he is claiming Bacchic rapture and insights beyond the architectural arts and mimesis of Renaissance haute cuisine—beyond Inigo Jones.[36] The end of Book V, for all its quasi-parody, may make a serious religious point. Bacbuc's bookish liquor has a scriptural as well as hermetic flavor. After the first watery sip, each drinker delightedly tastes a different but familiar wine in the temple's fountain, which is probably a comment on both biblical hermeneutics and communion. Each drinker's mind, unforced, makes of the liquid what it will and according to what it knows.[37] Jonson's (inter)textured allusion thus recalls a scene germane to the joys of wine and the claims of poetry but also to the risks of marriage or of the commitments marriage may symbolize—and to spiritual truth's relation to the self.

Jonson recycled this passage for *The Staple of News* (1626; IV.ii.7–10), this time having his cook call the poet a "heretic" and the oracle "vain." The printed text has no marginal identification, and in its new context the reference has a new tone. *Staple* satirizes gossip and the press, but it is structured by tensions between youth and age, prodigality and stinginess, Carnival and Lent (a battle found also in *QL*).[38] The dispute between cook and poetaster mocks poetry's airier claims, although one would have expected winebottles to be the

Ceste chanſon paracheuée, Bacbuc, ietta ie
ne ſçay quoy dedans la fontaine : & ſoudain
commença l'eau bouillir à force, comme fait

Figure 2 The oracular bottle that inspires Panurge in *Gargantua et Pantagruel*
(*Oeuvres*, 1599), Book V, chapter 44 (Courtesy the Bancroft Library)

kitchen's allies in Feast's war on Fast. Those who recognized the allusion may also have remembered Panurge's ecstatic anticipation of his wedding night — a pleasure denied during Lent — and the opposing verses by Frère Jean resolving *not* to be a husband. It matters politically who will marry the heroine, Lady Pecunia; still, marriage here seems less immediately topical (although the king had recently taken the plunge) and more closely related to the play's interest in containment and release, hoarding and circulation.

Another echo of Rabelais again shows how the festive or scatological passages that Jonson remembers can have political and religious relevance. The cook, wanting news to "strew" at dinner, asks for the latest on Gondomar, the recent Spanish Ambassador who suffered from an anal sore and had been further humiliated by insults in Middleton's *A Game at Chess*. We hear that he has unwisely used leaves from the play's printed text to wipe himself: "A second Fistula, / Or an excoriation (at the least) / For putting the poore English-play, was writ of him, / To such a sordid use, as (is said) he did, / Of cleansing his posterior's." The cook cries "Justice! Justice!" (III.ii.207–12). The joke recalls one that occurs close to the scene from which Jonson probably took *Alchemist*'s anal figs. Visiting the Papimanes, Pantagruel is disgusted by their worship of the pope and his edicts. In a set of anecdotes about the punishments attending profane use of such edicts, each example followed by papimanic exclamations at divine justice, Frère Jean recalls how when he wiped himself with one he developed terrible hemorrhoids (*QL* 52). God's vengeance, he is told. Like the figs and Queen Entelechie's projects, the conversation must have resounded complexly in Jonson's now Protestant ear.[39]

Jonson alludes to Rabelais twice in *The New Inn*, performed in 1629 before an apparently unimpressed audience of sparks and scholars at the Blackfriars Theatre. The inn's host is a gentleman in disguise and its charwoman, a nurse who claims to be Irish, is his unrecognized wife, driven to disguise by "melancholy" over her husband's neglect. When the host asks the whereabouts of her charge, and the nurse replies "Gra chreest!" [For the love of Christ!], she is told "Goe aske th'oracle / O'the bottle, at your girdle, there you lost it: / You are a sober setter of the watch" (IV.iv.343–45). This comment on careless insobriety may have invited the urbane audience to remember Bacbuc's bottle and its encouragement of a worried older man's nuptial plans. Although the insult seems primarily a passing sarcasm, it has psychosexual oddities, not least in Jonson's rhetorical fastening to an injured wife's waist the bottle he so often used himself.

Inn has one other Rabelaisian moment. Lovel, described in the printed play's list of characters as "A compleat Gentleman, a Souldier, and a Scholer," was once page to Lord Beaufort and later "companion of his studies." Beaufort had refined taste:

He had no Arthurs, nor no Rosicleer's,
No Knights o'the Sunne, nor Amadis de Gaule's,
Primalions, and Pantagruel's, publique Nothings;
Abortives of the fabulous, darke cloyster,
Sent out to poison courts, and infest manners. (I.vi.124–28)

Lovel may be thinking of the Gargantua chapbook. But in the 1620s, before this audience, it would have been hard to say "Pantagruel" without evoking "Rabelais," even if he did appear briefly in *The History of Gar[a]gantua*'s model and even if one can find a few allusions to him in similar contexts.[40] Perhaps Jonson wants to make Lovel look a little snobbish and narrow in a play that is itself a romance encouraging hospitality and forgiveness.

Jonson's Rabelais is only in part the "dirty" writer of legend, for his dirt, although enjoyable in itself, serves nonfestive satirical purposes. In Jonson's clearest textual echoes, Rabelais is the creator of sea voyages, of fantastic worlds, and above all of Panurge's search to know his own will and find the bottle of bottles, the one with the answers, the one with potable words full of truth and rapture. This is the bottle Jonson may recall in lines written for the Apollo Room at the Devil's Tavern:

Welcome all, who lead or follow,
To the Oracle of Apollo.
Here he speaks out of his Pottle,
Or the Tripos, his Tower Bottle:
All his Answers are Divine,
Truth itself doth flow in Wine.[41]

The word from Rabelais's Oracle is "Drink," good advice in temple and tavern: *in vino Veritas,* not to say *in vino Verbum.* It is poignant to reflect how often Jonson mentions this bottle, as though his mind kept running on its promise of inspiration, self-knowledge, and freedom from deception. A whole tun of sack, for all the real pleasures to be found there, would not be its equal.

Doctor Rabelais

As a physician, Rabelais had a professional interest in the body: its workings and structure, its diseases, its responses, competing theories concerning it, and the curative effect on it of laughter. The body is laughing matter in several senses, and laughter, as Rabelais points out (following Aristotle and the scholastics), is uniquely the property of our species.[42] His medical career was a source of good-humored notice in England, although those consulting medical texts he edited perhaps took a more sober view of his expertise.[43] He had, after all, attended Cardinal Du Bellay and edited Manardi's *Epistolae medicinales* (1532), as well as works by Hippocrates and Galen (1532). When his name appears in quasi-medical contexts, though, he is not quite cited as an authority, as though his levity somehow outweighed his gravitas. That is why Gabriel Harvey could retail a comic anecdote about Rabelais praying to a statue of Charles VIII in gratitude for the French soldiers who brought back syphilis — and work for doctors — from Italy.[44]

It was not so much that Rabelais's gross humor made his learning and status suspect. Rather, if one may judge from the admittedly few allusions to him in connection with medicine, the juxtaposition of his roles set up a dissonance that led the relaxed to smile and the straitlaced to disapprove yet further. Or, more precisely, it encouraged those striking either pose to wink or frown. As so often, "Rabelais" advances individual agendas and cultural ambivalence. Thus Robert Hayman, whose verse I shall discuss shortly, cites "that excellent witty Doctor, Francis Rabalais." On the other hand, Robert Burton, as I have noted earlier, imagines a godless materialist calling himself "with Rablais a phisitian, a Peripateticke, an Epicure."

One French writer hoped to modify this view in a passage that quickly became available in English. Those who made it all the way to Book VII in Thomas Milles's *Treasurie of Auncient and Moderne Times* (1613–19) would have found a tepid defense of Rabelais buried in this huge compendium of writings by Pedro Mexia, Antoine du Verdier, and others. Rabelais appears on the long prefatory list of sources, along with Lucian, Merlin, Moses, More, Poggio, and Socrates, although I cannot tell why. The thoughtful if finally illiberal comments on him in Book VII, chapter 33, are from Dr. Louis Guyon's *Diverses leçons* (Lyons, 1617).[45] In a section on Saint Luke (a physician) Guyon denies that doctors are impious:

> Some will allege Rabelais unto mee, an excellent Physition, who is thought one while to speake like an Atheist; another while like a Lutheran. [The margin glosses, "Divers opinions, concerning the book of Rabelais."] I an-swere, that it is a difficult matter to judg in such cases, and to comprehend a mans intention: especially, in such people as have no knowledge, neither any solid judgement. But they that looke upon him a little neerer, shall find, that he is a Democritus, laughing at all our humaine actions. Or a Lucian, who maketh a mockery of such abuses, as daily are committed among men: but he medleth not with anything, which toucheth the Apostolicall Church. Nev-erthelesse, I am of opinion, that, for the better orders sake; and in regarde of such obscuritie in conceiving his intention, that he should bee neither read, nor received; for so he was censured by Counsell of Trent. But as for the last Booke that is added among his workes, which is entitled L'Isle Sonnante; and seemeth (indeede) to blame and mocke at men, bearing office in the Church: I

protest, that he never composed it, for it was made a long while after his death. I my selfe [Guyon] was at Paris when it was done, and I knew very well the Author thereof, who was never any Physition. (Sig. Mmm6)

Reasonable enough, granted Guyon's priorities. Identifying authorial intention takes delicacy, and the fear that rash interpretation might harm public order was not misplaced. Yet the words "they that looke upon him a little nearer" could sound like an invitation. Perhaps Guyon wishes to defend a writer he has enjoyed while appearing obedient to the edicts of the Tridentine Church and wary of satire's contagious skepticism. Also notable, in a time when views of authorship were shifting, is his desire to remove a troublesome text from an author's canon: for Guyon, knowing who wrote the *Cinquième livre* affects how one should judge Rabelais — and doctors.

An even sager Dr. Rabelais helps John Healey defend his *Discovery of a New World* (1609), a translation of Hall's *Mundus*. Like Rabelais's prologues, which it resembles, Healey's spirited preface to his 1613–14 edition is a remarkable document in the history of attitudes toward language, authorship, and readers. Pretending to give readers "Instructions for their voiage into this new world," Healey asserts that Hall has been wronged by "over-weening" readers guilty of "grosse misprision."[46] *Mundus* has no "immodest, light, scurrilous, and ridiculous passages"; it is probably not the work of that now dignified bishop anyway, or, if his, was made in his youth; and it does not resemble this translation in "stile, or discourse, but onely in the invention and project," having no more likeness to it "then chalke hath to cheese" except in a "generall kind of essence as they are both corporeall substances." Are there any "scurilous or immodest" passages? Maybe some "carry not that pondrous respect in them which an ancient judgement, or retired gravity may seeme to require," but "they are flashes of youth" and others have written such. "Oh but not in print, saies some severer Critique!" Such a critic forgets Ovid's *Amores* and Seneca's "pumpkinification" of Claudius (by "print" Healey must mean "public"; pp. 146–47).

Healey now attempts more explicitly to fashion a better reader, a daunting task for anyone writing in so dubious and defensive a mode as satire. Flattery helps: "You (right Joviall spirits) and none but you, are they to whom I consecrate these my travels, since none but you can discerne the sence which they include." Such "gentlemen and friends" should remember that any seeming allusions to England carry no "sinister" implications. Good voyagers/readers will avoid the nautical disaster of misunderstanding by reading in company ("for one you know may apprehend more then another can"). Be sure "to go over the country thrice, ere you shalbe able to make any exact platforme [that is, map or outline] of it: Once for Strabo, once for Socrates, and once for Merlin Cocaius; the first for the Geography, the second for the Morality, and the third for the Language, and Etymology." And "a good gale of wit go along with you." First, though, the reader should medicate himself: "And know all you that have not yet seene these Lands, but intend to take a view of the hereafter, that you must first of al take one of that French Doctors pills, *Despouillez vous de tout[e] affection,* and this will enable you to endure the alteration of all ayres in this clime" (p. 148).

Healey assumes we shall have no trouble identifying his French doctor. The "pill" in question is dispensed in the same liminary poem to *Gargantua* that claims laughter as our "propre": "Amis lecteurs, qui ce livre lisez, / Despouillez vous de toute affection" (Friendly readers who read this book, / Strip yourselves of all passion/bias). This book, we read, has no wickedness or infection. Because the prologue that follows addresses readers as infected drunks, however, it seems that there are two distinct authorial voices guiding us into *Gargantua*. Like Healey's directions for travel, each shapes an implied reader, offering advice on how to proceed without the ingenious malice that prefers to take a writer's words *in malo*. For both Healey and Rabelais, if more for the latter, bad readers are a real threat; the fiction is that they read badly, but of course the reality was that the malicious were sometimes reading very well. *Gargantua* can rightly discomfit the rigidly orthodox, and although *Mundus* affirms virtues Milton also valued, Milton's denunciation of it and its conservative author show that it got under some readers' skins.[47]

Healey's Dr. Rabelais is a good physician who comprehends the psychodynamics of readership. James Howell's Dr. Rabelais is the impious reprobate familiar from other contexts. *A German Diet* (1653) imagines a council of German leaders at which speakers by turn describe the virtues and vices of European nations. Praising such French scholars as Vatablus and Beza and such French poets as Du Bartas, one lord says that the French are a "people greedy of wine." Take the "notable wine-bibber, which was Rablais, who though he was very well instructed both in the Greek and Latin toungs, and an excellent Physitian, with other choice parts, yet at last leaving all other serious studies, he did totally inslave himself to Epicurisme, to gluttony and drunkennesse, in which humors he belch'd out that Atheistical kind of book which goes under his name though under pleasant notions able to turn ev'ry Reader therof to a Democritus" (sig. R1v). Is this Howell's opinion or merely one ascribed to a German with an attitude? Howell had recently edited Cotgrave's *Dictionary* (1650), with its many citations of "¶Rab," and in a joking will he had made on March 6, 1643 (when he was in fact seriously ill), which leaves his languages to various legatees, he gave his French "to my most honoured lady the Lady Cor, and it may help her something to understand Rablais."[48] The tone of the mock testament is hard to judge, though, and Howell may have thought Rabelais enough of a greedy drunk to suit his German lord's attack on French moral fecklessness.[49]

Was there no serious praise of Rabelais as a medical authority? I have not found any. Rabelais appears, however, in guides to health by William Vaughan, a Welsh gentleman and failed colonizer of Newfoundland, whose ambivalence toward Rabelais I shall examine later. Overlooking his doubts concerning Rabelais's spiritual health, Vaughan amusedly cites him in his down-to-earth works on diet and cures. His popular *Naturall and Artificial Directions for Health* teaches that, for example, milk is safer for the teeth if you add sugar; ginger sharpens the eyes and "provoketh slothful husbands"; and sex "exhilarateth the heart and wit" (1600, sigs. B7, C5v, D7v). Before publishing his 1617 edition he had read Rabelais, quoting him in a section on garlic. Although it bolsters courage, expels worms, and salves arrow wounds, garlic increases choler; so avoid it in summer except during travel, when our stomachs, like the ostrich's, "can almost digest iron, being as Rabelais writes, as hollow as Saint Bennets boote" (sig. G3v). Vaughan remembers Frère Jean's festive bravado at Gargantua's table: "J'ay un estomac pavé, creux comme la botte sainct Benoist, tousjours overt comme la gibbessiere d'un advocat" (*G* 39: I have a paved stomach, hollow as Saint Benedict's tun, always open like a lawyer's purse). He must be very hungry, for Bennett's Boot—a *botte* is both boot and tun—was a famously large barrel at the Benedictine monastery in Boulogne.

Vaughan knew the medicinal and rhetorical effects of mirth; naming Rabelais in this context signals as much. It is an index of how that name functioned, however, that Vaughan cites the creator of thirsty monks, not the editor of Galen and Hippocrates. Elsewhere in the volume he mentions a doctor from the *Cinquième livre*'s prologue, although he does not add that Rabelais was a doctor himself. English doctors, Vaughan laments, stupidly prescribe potions instead of abstinence and refuse to follow a "sparing diet" themselves: "On the contrary have we not seene them feed themselves with the wings and best parts of the Partridge, carving onely the bones unto the sicke, like unto the Physitian in Rabelais" (sigs. B3–B3v).[50] The French text had compared Pythagoras, who forbad others to eat beans (which, perhaps because they make wind and are thus literally inspiring, symbolize Pantagruelian books), to the incompetent doctor who kept the succulent parts of a fowl for himself, leaving the sick only the little bones to gnaw.

Vaughan wants to say that patients and doctors should eat sensibly and that doctors should not be selfish. But his greedy doctors harm only themselves, not their patients, by wolfing down fancy partridge. In the *Cinquième livre*'s prologue, which invokes readers given to drink and the pox, the issue is less confused and more paradoxical: we are urged to eat beans — hardly fat food — in terms that nevertheless suggest festivity because we are to devour them like cordial opiates, incorporate them into our bodies, and buy the vernacular and joyous books they represent. The reference to Rabelais's doctor, like the evocation of Bennett's Boot, adds to Vaughan's cheerful bedside manner, but his anger at doctors who deny others the unhealthy food they eat themselves appears, with insouciant illogic, in a passage that urges restraint. Rabelais's beans are plain but provoke joy; Vaughan's regimen is more truly sober.

Country Bodies: Robert Dallington's France and Robert Hayman's Newfoundland

Robert Dallington's *View of France* (1604) is a cultural and geographic survey that combines informed appreciation with acerbic impatience.[51] Dallington knew Rabelais well, although he did not always check his quotations. What he remembers seems designed to give his persona gaiety and *energeia* as he plays the sagacious yet morally discriminating observer. We can trust him to know French culture, for he has read and seen much of it, but he is not taken in by its charms, quoting French writers on its flaws and recalling with dismay the civil wars that disgraced it. The image his Rabelais projects is satirical and earthy, more comic and materialist than Erasmian or dryly ironic, and thus not exempt from the flaws of his clever compatriots. Witty enough to quote, he lacks the moral solidity of, say, Du Bartas. Not that Dallington quotes merely to amuse, for most fragments of Rabelais in the *View* allude to the body and its desires or failures, collectively contributing to a sort of running allegory in which France is a sick or wounded nation. Not for the first time, response to Rabelais merges verbal and material concerns.

The French, says Dallington, spend too much on architectural glory. Even the architect La Noue admits this, and "I am for my part, of Frier John of Antomaure his mind, who seeing in a great Palace such stately Halls, such goodly Galleries, such fayre Chambers, such well contrived Offices: on the other side, the Kitchin so leane, the Chimneyes so cold, and the Cellars so dry, Un beau Chasteu dit-il à faire de belle promenades, et me curez mes dens à jeun à la Napolitaine: A faire Castle (said he) to walke faire turnes in, and picke my teeth fasting after the Neapolitane fashion" (sig. D1v). A marginal note says "Rablais." Dallington had translated Francesco Colonna's *Hypnerotomachia Poliphili,* with its erotic architectural fantasies, but here he treats such splendors more skeptically. The passage that best explains his allusion is Frère Jean's recollection of a monk from Amiens who preferred the kitchens and girls of his home town to the fancy buildings and statues of Florence, a city with plenty to look at but no "roustisserie" (*QL* 11).[52] Dallington's monk celebrates the lower body and material needs that the new Italianate styles cannot satisfy; his Rabelais is the creator of such a comic monk. English readers, of course, are free to laugh at both newfangled chateaux and French gourmandise.

Dallington does not find the civil wars funny, but he expresses condemnation through lively analogies, one based on the same passage in the *Cinquième livre* that Vaughan cites in *Directions for Health*. During the civil wars, says Dallington, French statesmen were bad doctors. For example, the duc de Mercueur (a leader of the ultra-papist Ligue) "playd the good Kitchin Doctor, of whome Rablais speaketh, who gave his patient the necke and bones to tyre upon, and kept the wings himselfe: for he left them all France, tyred and tewed, as bare as a birdes bone, and kept Bretaigne, one of the fattest wings of the Countrey, to himselfe" (sig. G2). The margin directs us to "Rabl.l[iber].2" (in fact, book 5). France is now in the care of her Asculapius, Henri IV, but her wars offer lessons to the English: "As Rablaies saith, 'Un fol enseigne bien un sage: A foole may teach a wise man wit'" (sig. G3, quoting Pantagruel's comment to Panurge in *TL* 37). Not that Dallington is impressed by French military might; he compares — in a passage that Robert Burton appropriated — the logic of a Frenchman who boasted that there were more old French captains than English ones to "the reason of Rablais, who would needes prove, that drunkennesse was better for the body then Phisicke, because there were more old drunkards, then old Phisicians" (sig. M3v; from *G* 41, quoting Frère Jean).

Nor does Dallington admire the volatility of the French, who are ready to fight a duel one moment and be friends the next:

> Hereat Rablais scoffingly glanceth, where he telleth a tale of a Gascoigne, that having lost his money, would needs in the heat of his choller fight with any man that bore head: and for want of an enemy fell asleepe. By that time he was waking, comes mee another Rhodomonte, and upon like cause of losse, would have this fellow by the eares: but then the edge of this other was off. In conclusion (sayth Rablais) they went both to the Taverne, and there for want of money which they had lost at Dice, drunke themselves friends upon their swords, without farther mediation, or troubling of others to take up the quarrell. (Sig. X1v; from *TL* 42, in which Judge Bridoye describes a case)

Dallington's Rabelais writes "scoffingly," not just comically. So too, when adopting the word *doriphages* to describe bribe-eating pettifoggers, he says that the "Lucian of France" tells "scoffingly" how the devil had lawyer for breakfast: "Whereupon he was so vexed with the Collicke (saith he) finding a worse devill then himselfe rumbling in his belly, as there was no stirre with the collericke Marchant, till he was bounde" (sigs. Q3–Q3v).[53] Rabelais does "scoff" in these passages, yet he seems less Lucianic there than a maker of facetiae and preposterous arguments. How Dallington characterizes Rabelais does not quite suit the humor he borrows, for what tugged at his memory is social comedy expressed in sharply phrased sentences and smartly told tales that sets the world of food, drink, sleep, and folly against the solemnity of church, medicine, and law.

The past decades have seen much commentary on the treatment of land as a female body. Understanding how we imagine matter/materia/mater is important for our future — Mother Earth will not forever take her ravishment lying down. Rabelais seems not to have been intrigued by gendered landscapes labeled as such, although he was fascinated by voyages to new worlds. One English admirer, however, adapted verses that he thought were by Rabelais on women, doing so in part, I think, because they are relevant to the terrain that surrounded him: Canada. This was Robert Hayman, a belated verse satirist and unofficial governor of Newfoundland. His taste for Rabelais may have been a relic of his youth at Lincoln's Inn when verse satire was becoming fashionable with young men about town, or perhaps he read him when studying at Poitiers. Hayman also admired the now sober Bishop Hall, Donne, Jonson, and George Wither, writing each of them verses that he published in 1628 when, back in England, he saw his collected epigrams, *Quodlibets,* into print.[54] His lines treat topics not unconnected with Rabelais: grotesque and classical bodies, the feminine, and the New World.

After four books of epigrams and translations of Neo-Latin verses by John Owen and others, *Quodlibets* concludes with a pair of poems on two old women. The first, to a decrepit bawd not unlike the hag in Horace's appalling twelfth Epode, is "A rayling Epistle, written in French by that excellently witty Doctor, Francis Rabalais: Wherein though I follow him not verbatim; yet whoso can compare them, shall find I have done him no wrong" (sig. G4v). The other salutes a virtuous elderly lady: "Another Epistle of the same witty Author, Francis Rabelais, in praise of a grave Matrone; translated as the former" (sig. H1v). The translations are faithful enough, the only "wrong" done Rabelais being the belief that he wrote the originals. Hayman should not be blamed, for the poems often appeared in Rabelais's *Oeuvres* after the 1584 Lyons edition, the title pages ascribing these "Epistres à deux Vieilles de differentes moeurs" to him. They are by François Habert, author of the *Songe de Pantagruel,* and were first printed in the 1551 edition of Habert's *Sermons satyriques du sententieux poete Horace.*[55]

In reworking the first epistle, Hayman makes the poem more vivid, exaggerating the hag's sins and ugliness and edging the verse closer toward semi-Spenserian quasi-allegory, mixing concrete and abstract. Habert calls his old bawd, "Vieille qui fais de ton lit un bordeau [that is, bordello]," but Hayman has her sin while "senting each bed with lust, where thou hast l[a]ine": immoral motions of the heart become a physical smell. So too, whereas the Frenchwoman's ugliness is "l'image & le pourtrait / De ce qui est dedans un creux retrait," in the English version she is "crusted in evil," and "Sinne, and want of grace, / Are ditched in the wrinkles of thy face." Her "head hangs down through thy sinnes weightines, / Thy body doubles with thy wickednes." She is "the patterne of all villanie," and, with no warrant in the French, devils fly around her like fallen putti. Hayman ignores her bowel trouble — "Vieille qui fais (je veux bien qu'on le sçache) / D'ordure plus que ne fait une Vache" — and once inserts a modest blank:

> Thou damn'd damn'd Bawd, that do'st procure thy meales,
> By tempting wenches to turne up their ———.[56]

But he is not prissy, writing: "Thou that hast piss'd away thy unknowne shame: / Thou that hast entertain'd each one that came."

The woman practices sorcery — Habert remembers Horace's Canidia.[57] Hayman retains her power to affect the sun and moon and also her devil's teat, adding that she delights "foule Toads to foster; / And alway say'st the Divels Pater noster." Another new touch is what some might call Protestant: the hag "did'st never take delight to worke." Not only a "patterne" of female depravity, she is lazy; no wonder she prefers horizontal labors. The epistle, then, is indeed "rayling":

> Thou bunch-back-bug-beare-fac'd, splay-foot, Cat-hand;
> Thou rough bark'd-stinking Elder, worse then damn'd;
> Thou, about whose scurfe-head the Devils flutter;
> Thou viler vild, then I have words to utter:
> Amend thy lewd life; or I sweare to thee,
> For one ill-favour'd word, I'le give thee three.

Habert had merely offered her two for one.

The good "vieille" is quite another sort of woman. With nothing like the hag's "bunch-back" or splayed foot to disfigure her "grace and forme," no smells (not even perfume) that might cloud her body's perimeters, no ugly parts that mix human and animal, and no intestinal problems, she is seemly, "traitable," and contained: a shapely "paragon," "hansome, proper, neat, and faire," sexually open only "for procreation, / And for thy Husbands recreation." In Bakhtinian terms, the bawd is open and grotesque, not closed and classical, but if the good matron's heart, ears, and hands remain unshut and her feet swift, it is to aid the poor and suffering. She reads much, but not "love-toyes" (the French has "vieux Romans et livres dissolus"). Drinking wine rather than hot aphrodisiacs, setting a wholesome table with no "luxurious cates," this "Christian Palace [Habert has "Pallas": Athena] / Wherein the Holy Ghost doth take his solace" makes all honest men "truly, heartily in love" with her. As the bawd is a "patterne" of evil, so she is an "extract of good women." More domestic than her aristocratic French counterpart, she bustles about, putting plasters on the sick and mixing remedies from kitchen herbs. In sum, she is a gracious gentlewoman, whom the speaker addresses without impertinence as "Sweet-heart."

It is pleasant to reflect that even as he was busy helping to subdue the Canadian wilderness Hayman had Rabelais's *Oeuvres* by him. Why not translate better pages? Because he thought of himself as a verse satirist, presumably, and because there is a subtextual similarity between the two epistles and Hayman's hopes for his colony.[58] "Rabelais'"s epistles have nothing to say about America; yet Hayman's liking for them can be better understood by reading his poems on Newfoundland. Perhaps he knew that Donne, with a complexity of feeling not found here, had called a mistress his "America" and "new-found-land." And Walter Ralegh said that Guiana "hath yet her maidenhead," a comparison with some pathos: if many men come (in)to her, attracted by her innocence, will she turn into Habert's whorish "vieille?"[59] Ralegh and Hayman significantly differ, however: *Quodlibets*'s wilderness is a grotesque body in need of reshaping, not a virgin. Now a nicer version of Habert's hag, if taken in hand she could be the fruitful matron of the second epistle, giving pleasure and babies, and, although closed to despoilment (Hayman denies that colonists seek quick wealth), open with food and succor.

Hayman starts his invitation to support and admire his plantation with an epistle to Charles I, "Father, Favourer, and Furtherer of all his loyall Subjects and right Honourable and worthie Plantations." He also provides a striking picture of an iguana, a "West-Indian Guane," who utters an anagram of "Robert Hayman": "Harm I bare not." An Americanized version of satire's ancient disclaimer (paralleling the identification of "rayling" Rabelais as a doctor), the phrase implies that the New World will not bite, whatever its strangeness and some investors' losses. But if as a picture the iguana is the colonized West Indies, as an anagram it is Robert Hayman the colonizer. To whom does he bear no harm? His readers? The objects of his wit? America?

To encourage the public, Hayman has two contradictory arguments. The first is that Newfoundland is an Eden free of taxes, lawyers, bad news, fear, plague, pox, and the need to dress up (II.117; II.88). Its winters are "short, wholesome, constant, cleare" (II.81). Food? Some say Newfoundlanders rough it with otter, fox, and crow, but in truth they have venison, partridge, and clean fish "neatly drest" (II.103). Nor will colonizers do harm, for unlike courtiers they aim only to make things grow, not to usurp: "Yours is a holy just Plantation," Hayman tells them, "And not a justling supplantation" (II.86a).[60] Like the iguana, harm they bear not.

But Newfoundland needs cultivating and its natives civilizing, just as England was once "unlovely" but is now tidied up. One day Newfoundland, too, will see its bottoms dry, its contours shaved, and its stones rearranged:

> Strange, not to see stones here above the ground,
> Large untrench't bottomes under water drown'd.
> Hills, and Plaines full of trees, both small and great,
> And dryer bottomes deepe of Turfe, and Peate.
> When England was us'd for a Fishing place,
> By Coasters only, 'twas in the same case,
> And so unlovely 't had continued still:
> Had not our Ancestors us'd paines, and skill. (II.100)

Hayman can explicitly figure Newfoundland as a body. Epigram II.94 begins with Alcibiades' praise of Socrates in the *Symposium* (cf. *Gargantua*'s prologue), then claims that Hayman has seen beggars well-endowed under their rags, and concludes that his colony is a slut capable of being ladylike if given good "husbandry":

> 'Tis said, wise Socrates look't like an Asse;
> Yet he with wondrous sapience filled was;
> So though our Newfound-Land look wild, salvage,
> She hath much wealth penn'd in her rustie Cage.
> So have I seene a leane-cheekes, bare, and ragged,
> Who of his private thousands could have bragged.
> Indeed she now lookes rude, untowardly;
> She must be decked with neat husbandry.
> So have I seene a plaine swart, sluttish Jone,
> Looke pretty pert, and neat with good cloathes on.

Such lines indicate one reason Hayman liked the poems he thought were Rabelais's. The smelly hag is a violently imagined version of wilderness, being "rude" — sexually overcooked but culturally raw. The sober matron is, as we say, cultivated: busy but settled, loyal to her cultivator and the cultivator's God.

It is remarkable to find Rabelais, of all people, associated with a longing to see the grotesque body and untended lands made to shape up. Yet it would be wrong to read Hayman as just one more thoughtless colonizer on the make: the energy with which he attacks his hag, together with his affection for Newfoundland even while she still looks like Socrates, hints at a countering fascination with wilderness and misbehavior, with undrained bottomlands and unfelled forests, with the exotic "Guane" that inhabits America but speaks English anagramese. When Hayman was little, he reports, Francis Drake called on his father, and the explorer came upon young Robert "walking up Totnes long Street." Hearing that he belonged to his old friend's house, "The Dragon" [a pun on "Drake"] who on "our Seas did raise his Crest / And brought back heapes of gold unto his nest" gave the boy a kiss, a blessing, and "a faire red Orange." Along with his more practical motives for encouraging colonial investment, Hayman treasured the image of England's Devonshire dragon and an orange that must have glowed in his memory like fruit from the Hesperides. Perhaps he thought Rabelais "witty" not just for sneering at dirty old women in verse but for inventing Panurge and sending him and his friends, likewise impelled by desire and curiosity, on a voyage even stranger than that which Hayman had taken across the North Atlantic.

Carnival in Hades

Ever since Mikhail Bakhtin's *Rabelais and His World* was published in English, many critics have agreed that *Gargantua et Pantagruel* affirms the lower body's holiday claims.[61] And there are indeed passages in Rabelais's work that mock professional and ideological solemnity: much solemn professional and ideological ink has gone into saying so. Carnival itself appears, ambiguously, in QL 29–42, an extended revision of the popular war between fat feast and fishy fast. Yet Rabelais was less subversive of "official" culture than Bakhtin's polarities allow: in real life, as in Menippean satire, there's official and then there's official. Bishops can disagree murderously over "official" ideology (so can peasants), and magnates can fund and control popular revelry. In any case, the English seem largely to have ignored the carnival Rabelais, whether from hostility, indifference, or bafflement at his Lenten "Carnival" (the usual meaning of "Quaresmeprenant") and fierce sausages.[62] Even writers who are called Rabelaisian—Nashe, Harington, Jonson—are usually so named in other than Bakhtinian terms, while many texts on which one would think to find Rabelais's impact show no such trace. Perhaps "popular" contexts discouraged engagement with so erudite a foreign text. The giant Gar[a]gantua is occasionally paraded in carnival (con)texts; Rabelais, on the whole, is not.

One scene in Rabelais, however, turns greatness on its head, making a Saturnalian inverted world that drew English attention. This is the moment in *Pantagruel* when Epistemon sees strange goings-on in the world of the dead.

Perhaps because it is so often imagined as an anticosmos with inverted values and sardonic justice, Hell can serve a humor plausibly called "carnivalesque." In one gratifying tradition, dead magnates earn their bread by the sweat of what is left of their brows, laboring in the world's lower bodily stratum, so to speak. After being decapitated in the battle against Picrochole, Rabelais's Epistemon spends time in Hades while Panurge reassembles his body by holding the head under his codpiece and smearing the neck with excrement (*P* 30).[63] Restored, Epistemon settles down to dinner and describes what he saw. His report recalls a scene in Lucian's *Menippos* in which, after parodic necromancy, Menippos enters Hades and finds a topsy-turvy world where the great sell salt, for instance, or teach the alphabet; King Philip mends sandals, while Xerxes, Darius, and Polycrates beg. Rabelais was probably the first man in France to put together *Menippos* and accounts by those who were resurrected, naming more names, discarding the tortures found in older texts, and turning Lucianic skepticism into apocalyptic reversal.[64] To see how others twisted the result without destroying it is an exercise in intertextual topology: the torsion, distortion, and adaptation of a topos, in this case the physical and social relocation of a once important body within the earth's greater body now that Death has done his work.

A taxonomy of reports on postmortem life would distinguish between those describing torments and those showing the dead at work. In the late medieval *Calendrier des bergers,* Lazarus sees a torture chamber; Menippos and Epistemon see a workhouse. And whereas Lucian reverses earthly lives, others literalize them: in the *Calendrier* gluttons are force-fed venomous frogs, and the anonymous "News from Heaven and Hell" (1588) reveals that "his Robinship" the earl of Leicester now works his way around a cycle of labors that, for example, punish his promiscuity by turning "his pricke of desier into a pillor of fier."[65] Caelius Curio's *Pasquine in a Traunce* (trans. 1566) tells of a man tied between two posts; on his head grow antlers and a heavy purse hangs from his feet as he swings in the wind. This, we hear, is Erasmus: the antlers show his deerlike cowardice, the purse his cupidity, and his rotation a flexible "Neutralitie" (sigs. T2v–T3).[66] He is himself, just more visibly so.

Renaissance England saw a small cluster of allusions to Epistemon's vision. Running through them is an interest in illusory demonism, lying narrative, and, sometimes, that mix of darkness, sulfur, role-playing, and Catholic subversion known as the Gunpowder Plot (1605). The admittedly few notices of Epistemon's trip, then, form a curiously coherent group at a time of fascination with lies, misapplied ingenuity, story, reversal, and earthy depths.[67] True, by 1593 John Eliot had already noted Epistemon's adventure in *Ortho-epia Gallica*, his "phantasticall" guide to French that I described earlier. Claiming to have "diversified" his work with matter "no less authenticall then the devises of Lucians dialogues" (B1v), he summons one of Epistemon's shades, Epictetus. In Eliot's fancy, the Stoic had always enjoyed himself (the verses are some Rabelais had imagined declaimed in Hades):

> I pray the God Aesculapius patron of Phisitions, Mercurie the God of cunning, and Dis the father of French crownes, in santy [that is, "santé," health] long time to conserve your Signiories, that you may have as faire a life in this world, as had the goodly and wise Philosopher Epictetus, who did nothing else all his lifetime but take his eases, and as a renowned poet sayth in your owne language:

> Saulter, dancer, faire les tours,
> Boire vin blanc & vermeil,
> Et ne rien faire tous les jours,
> Que conter escuz au soleil.
>   Id est,
> Skip and dance, trip on toe,
> Drinking White and Claret-wine:
> And naught every day did doe,
> But tell crownes and bags of coyne. (Sig. A4v)

In *Pantagruel* such frolicking must be the envy of hardworking shades, and it is good to know that Hades has wine. The French king's gold has gone home to Plutus, even as the suns on the écus au soleil recall a brighter sky. Eliot retains from the underworld, however, only its doctor, ruler, and psychopomp.

Eliot restores a philosopher to earth and makes him dance. In *King Lear* (1606–08), Shakespeare sends an emperor to Hell, although the playwright's underworld is as problematic as everything else in the tragedy. Disguised as Poor Tom and feigning to believe himself possessed, Edgar tells his distracted king that "Fretereto cals me, and tels me Nero is an angler in the lake of darknes, pray innocent beware the foule fiend."[68] Whatever other functions it has, the report intensifies a vision of familial destruction, and Nero's old association with Antichrist makes him at home in a play whose horrors gesture uncertainly at time's "promised end."[69] The image of a dead emperor fishing in the Styx (often called a "lake") suits the play's terrible carnival of inversion. As Lear's fool tells him, "Thou madest thy daughters thy mother" when "thou gavest them the rod and pullest down thy breeches." While the language parallels popular printed images of the upside-down world, Nero's occupation also recalls the Lucianic tradition of infernal royal labor.[70] Or so I think, although fishing was one of Nero's recreations, and in any case there are worse afterlives than angling, even if one shudders to think what might be biting, and on what bait.

Where did Shakespeare find Nero? Early annotators cited Epistemon's sight of Trajan fishing for frogs and Nero scraping out a living on the hurdygurdy. Fishing in Hell is not in itself a strange notion, and there are several rivers available. But the closest parallel for what Frateretto reports is Epistemon's account of the famous dead. Wanting to use Nero because of his associative relevance, Shakespeare was perhaps also taken by the notion of Trajan angling and combined the two. The frogs were dropped, but they may have encouraged Shakespeare to change Trajan to Nero. Nero had been linked to frogs. One legend tells how, curious about childbirth, he ordered his doctors to make him pregnant. Reluctantly, they gave him a drink that coagulated into a frog in his belly and then an emetic to make him vomit it up. Reassured that his baby was normal for a newborn, he housed it in a palace that came to be called Late*ran* for *rana*, frog.[71] If Shakespeare knew this story, which I offer with more delight than confidence, it would have eased a shift from the frog-catcher Trajan to Nero. Better known was a vision Plutarch recounts in his *Moralia*. A passage in his dialogue on the delays of divine justice tells how, unconscious from a blow to the neck, one Thespesius saw the forms of the wicked being reshaped by demon smiths. Nero was being rewrought as a viper when a voice cried that in recognition of his having freed Greece he was to be turned into a frog instead.[72]

Rabelais's part in all this has been denied. After all, Chaucer's Monk, following Suetonius, tells how Nero would "fisshe in Tybre" with "Nettes of gold threed." Back in 1935 F. E. Budd suggested that when Shakespeare read Samuel Harsnett's *Declaration of Egregious Popish Errors* (1603), source of the play's imaginary demonic names, he liked *Frateretto*, saw the word *fiddler* a bit later, and remembered Nero.[73] Maybe so, but I suspect some memory of *Pantagruel* also intruded. In *Love's Labor's Lost*, Berowne, denouncing hypocrisy after witnessing it from above, claims to have beheld "a scene of fool'ry" not unlike that in *Menippos* or Rabelais: "To see great Hercules whipping a gig, / And profound Salomon to turne a jug, / And Nestor play at pushpin with the boys, / And critic Timon laugh at idle toys!" (IV.3.165–68). True, this folly takes place on earth and concerns adult and child, not high and low. *Lear*'s Nero is closer in situation to Rabelais's dead magnates. Harsnett's fiddler, moreover, recalls Epistemon's "vielleux" Nero sooner than Chaucer's, who plays no music, and Edgar's Nero is not on the Tiber but in Hell, angling. His technique matters, for even if he were fly casting, his line would descend more vertically than would a net. Shakespeare produces an astonishingly rapid plunge *en abîme:* on the edge of an abyss for which *Hell* seems a good enough word, Edgar imagines Tom imagining Frateretto seeing (hearing about?) Nero casting into we know not what.

If Shakespeare created his angler by combining Rabelais's Nero and Trajan and perhaps throwing in the *Monk's Tale,* he might have been encouraged to do so by Harsnett's taste for Lucian. That the *Declaration* is Lucianic has not gone unnoticed, yet the point needs stressing, particularly as the author explicitly associates fake exorcism with *Menippos.*[74] *Menippos* has no Nero or Trajan; here, though, is the locus classicus of the world-as-a-stage metaphor that Shakespeare adopts. Like Lear, Menippos discovers the equality of the dead after they lose the same "lendings" and "proud array" that Lear strips off without waiting to die. Lucian even describes infernal trials as bizarre, if less terrible than the one Lear conducts in this same scene. Recollecting Epistemon's trip, then, makes more audible a Lucianic humor that adds to the play's agony. Yet Frateretto's image is also memorable because it is, in all this pain and storm, so quiet: a fragment from a Stygian piscatory eclogue. However one reads *Lear* — as redemptive or as blasted heathendom, as supporting the authorities' detestation of staged demonic possession or as forgoing Christian consolation — the nonexistent demon's fantasy news haunts the mind, unexorcized. Compelling a belief that defies both reason and revelation, it supports readings that refuse to simplify the play's tonality by finding either comfort or despair.[75] To paraphrase Pascal, this play's "nothing" is not the nothing of the philosophers, and one inhabitant of that nothingness has gone fishing. Nero deserves a worse fate, but *Lear* is not about getting what one deserves.

Around the time that Shakespeare wrote *Lear,* Thomas Tomkis was finishing *Lingua* (1607), the spirited if sexist play I discussed earlier in connection with Rabelais's frozen words. As the plot unfolds, Tomkis plays for laughs a similar interest in possession, subversion, and the netherworld, indicating more clearly than Shakespeare the texts through which he has thought. Lingua's page is Mendacio, who was brought up in Crete — so famous for liars — and who says (Is he lying?) that he "held old Homers pen when hee wr[o]te his Illiads, and his Odisses," helped Herodotus "pen some part of his muses, lent Pliny inke to write his history, rounded [whispered to] Rabalais in the eare when he historified Pantagruell, as for Lucian I was his Genius, O those two Bookes De Vera historia howsoever they go under his name, Ile be sworne I writ them every title." He "would faine have jogged Stow and great Hollingshead on their elbowes," but he has had better luck with "the mirror of Knighthood, Bevis of Southampton, Palmerin of England, Amadis of Gaule, Huon de

Burdeaux, Sir Guy of Warwick[,] Martin marprellate, Robin-hood, Garragan-tua [in this company he sounds like the chapbook giant], Gerilion and a thousand such exquisite monuments as these" (sig. D1).

Among the discourses that interest Tomkis is the language of novelty-seeking invention. He reworks a scene from the *Quart livre* (61–62), in which Gaster, the innovative stomach with an M.A., invents resourceful defenses against cannon balls launched by the "horrible poudre" that makes Nature confess herself outdone by art. (Othello's good-bye to his profession — "And O you mortal engines, whose rude throats / Th'immortal Jove's dread clamors counterfeit, / Farewell!" [III.3.355–57] — gains further resonance set next to Rabelais's troubling image of artful guns outperforming natural thunder.) King James might have been amused by Tomkis's scene, or perhaps a little irritated, for the satire of "belly-sprung" cleverness applies also to the "projectors" about whom his subjects were complaining. That the "projection" includes anti-ballistic technology may be relevant to the play's other concerns, for gunpowder, so recently in the news, was then often associated, sometimes scatologically, with Hell and modern ingenuity.[76] But if the play mocks fatuous confidence in improvement, it also laughs at newfangled historiography: Memory rejects what he sees as a recent fashion for depths and margins, saying that nowadays most "Schollers" bring "such paltry things to lay up for them, that I can hardly finde them againe," because "now every trifle must be wrapped up in the volume of eternitie" and a "dog cannot pisse in a Noble-mans shoe, but it must be sprinkled into the Chronicles" (sig. D4). *Lingua* does not wish to rethink traditional hierarchies.

For Tomkis, Rabelais's Hades encloses this same social disorder. When Appetite remarks that even while purporting to "profit the people with translations" Lingua has "vilye prostituted the hard mysteries of unknowne Languages to the prophane eares of the vulgar," Phantastes replies: "This is as much as to make a new hell in the upper world, for in Hell they say Alexander is no better then a Cobler, and nowe by these translations every Cobler is as familiar with Alexander as he that wrote his life" (sig. F2v).[77] The complaint is an old one, once directed at biblical translation. Why is Phantastes bothered? His jocular tone does not conceal unease at direct access to learning and royal *arcana*. Many rulers (and allegorists) would have agreed, fearing lest the mysteries of statecraft be profaned, the interiority of magnates turned outward. In this regard, Tomkis chose his infernal worker well, for in Hades the conquering ruler attends to the feet, while here on earth, in a newly upside-down society, experts on shoes can observe the head. "He that wrote his life" seems to escape criticism, but Plutarch was neither king nor cobbler, and Phantastes may think him outside the system.[78]

It may also be significant, in a play printed soon after James's accession and Harsnett's *Declaration*, that Lingua is next called a witch who "exerciseth her tongue in exorcismes" and has impersonated Truth. Rabelais's comic Hades, in other words, brings thoughts of subversion, intrusion, disguise, and falsely claimed power over the underworld. And Lingua belongs to the dangerous sex: she rails against "men in authority," jests at their honors, and gives wives "weapons to fight against their husbands." A pun sums her up: "She is a common whore and lets every one lie with her." This whorish vaginal mingling of men's seed parallels both the confused mixture of rulers and laborers in Epistemon's Hell and the jostling babble of jargons and styles in this play. In nearly every way it can, *Lingua* rejects the heterogeneous for the layered and hierarchical, even if it is evident that Rabelais "rounded" Tomkis in the ear a good deal of what Mendacio had once whispered to him. It is not clear what Tomkis himself thinks of Lingua's house arrest — lasting until she is eighty — behind Gustus' guards. As a playwright he needs lies as much as anyone, and his very puns affirm duplicity and impersonation.

A few years after Tomkis wrote *Lingua*, although just when is unclear, John Webster finished *The White Devil*, a play that likewise comments on theatricality, subversion, and spurious deviltry. There is a hallucinatory demon in this play too (if it is hallucinatory), for as the villain Bracciano dies, he thinks he sees a devil. The scene makes a good transition to Webster's revision of Epistemon's report: during what another villain, Flamineo, calls these "unfortunate revels," the once "famous Pollititian" Bracciano hears that in Hell "A slave condemn'd, and given up to the gallowes / Is thy great Lord and Master," an inversion played less for restorative laughs than for the pleasure of imagining revenge.[79] Shortly after this, Flamineo stage-manages a false death for himself (dying in earnest a few lines later). With atheist and satirical nonchalance, he asks: "Whither shall I go now? O Lucian thy ridiculous Purgatory — to find Alexander the great cobling shooes, Pompey tagging points, and Julius Caesar making haire buttons, Haniball selling blacking, and Augustus crying garlike, Charlemaigne selling lists [strips of cloth] by the dozen, and King Pippin crying Apples" (V.6.108–13).[80]

Flamineo has already played with images of demotion, pretending that as an under-rewarded retainer he would "rather go weede garlicke . . . be mine own ostler; weare sheepe-skin lininges; or shoes that stinke of blacking; bee entred into the list of the fourtie thousand pedlars in Poland." Now his mind still runs on social debasement: the garlic, blacking, and peddling have been sent to Hell and attached not to disgruntled parasites but to the formerly powerful. He foresees no job for himself; his role as cynical observer will continue — if there really is a Hades he can play Menippos or Epistemon. More puzzlingly, he names the notorious Lucian, but his celebrities are all found in the 1532 *Pantagruel*. Like Rabelais's shameless wordplay, Flamineo's awful jokes (Pipin sells pippins, the African Hannibal sells blacking, bald Caesar works with hair) imply a sometimes self-reflexive and sometimes reversed underworld with a taste for the ironically appropriate as well as the humorously indecorous. Because the names hint laughingly at onomastic or geographical determinism, moreover, anyone called Flamineo should think twice before evoking such a "Purgatory."

Rabelais's Hades is modified, but it helps Webster to indicate matters that his tragedy plays with elsewhere. "What difference is," asks Francisco, "betweene the Duke and I? no more than betweene two brickes: all made of one clay. Onely 't may bee one is plac't on the top of a turret; the other in the bottom of a well by meere chance" (V.1.106–09). A Lucianic perspective on flesh, roles, and hierarchy that Rabelais's satire sustains. Like *Lear,* moreover, *Devil* hints at a world under the stage while remaining undecided about that world's reality: Is it to be welcomed, to be feared, or is the rest silence? Young Giovanni asks: "What do the dead do, uncle? do they eate / Heare musicke, goe a-hunting, and been merrie, / As wee that live?" Francisco answers, "No, cose; they sleepe" (III.2.331–34). But Bracciano's shade appears to walk, while Flamineo believes he is going out like a candle. Webster's characters talk or dream of digging and descending, straining "above law and above scandall," or bending thoughts to the "cursed dungeon" of Hell: vertical elongations that help explain why Webster remembered Epistemon's trip.

His is also a play with an unsettled view of identity, of what makes one brick differ from another. Is it language? Perhaps, for Webster, too, makes comedy of jargon: Rabelais would recognize the lawyer who with "learn'd verbosity" calls on "literated Judges" to "connive" their judgments (III.2.29–53). Flamineo's version of Epistemon's Hades well serves such questions of identity: Is a Pipin who sells pippins more himself, or does he collapse into his name if we recall what his unspecified "apples" might be? The scene mocks power, but if authority suffers in Webster's Flamineo's Lucian's purgatory, authorship both suffers and triumphs in this play that so often incorporates other writers' fragments. By ascribing Rabelais's fantasy to Lucian, Webster excises the name of his immediate model yet restores the topos's original paternity, while for once, in this brief comedy of names, naming an author. Again, though, Rabelais's humor intensifies not festive gaiety but comic horror.

Around the time of *The White Devil*, John Selden also remembered Epistemon's visit. In notes he wrote for Michael Drayton's *Poly-Olbion* (1612), when the verse mentions King Arthur's annual feast at Pentecost, Selden recalls how Epistemon reports that members of the Round Table now hold jobs.

Some heralds, he says, imagine Arthurian coats of arms "with as good warrant as Rabelais can justifie, that Sir Lancelot du Lac fleys horses in hell, and that The Knights of the Round Table use to ferry [devils on holiday] over Styx, Acheron, and other rivers, and for their fare have a fillip on the nose and a peece of mouldy bread." You may read about these knights in Caxton (that is, Malory), he adds, but "From such I abstaine."[81] But he does not abstain, for he quotes a carnival version of that same fantasy. Rather than using Epistemon's vision to help him imagine subversive deceit, though, he relates it to thoughts on fiction and history and to a desire (not concealed by his humor) to go in fancy down to where the dead and much of their material history lie buried. Epistemon's trip is a comic version of one that any antiquary would gladly take. Rabelais's irreverence would not displease the scholar whose studies were to show no tenderness toward British myth or Stuart claims. If he quotes Rabelais to laugh at feigned legend, he also enjoys a fiction in which devils share his impudence and heroes are discomfited.

A topologically related passage in *Pantagruel* tells of a trip not into Earth's hollows to see kings but into a king's intestines. The visits are psychologically akin. Not everyone would agree that "the body [is] a Hell, in respect of the mind, . . . compast with Stygian waves," yet to see innards as an underworld and Hell as a devouring womb/tomb/stomach is emotionally plausible.[82] Shortly after Epistemon's stay in Hades, and just after Alcofribas has emerged from Pantagruel, the giant becomes constipated. (Scrutiny by an author may be bad for the colon.) So he swallows a medical team that is traveling in bathyspheres; digging hard, his doctors clean him out and the patient then vomits them up like, we hear, the Trojan horse ejecting the Greeks (*P* 33). A simile to ponder: a crucial moment in the translation of empire is figured as regurgitation of the little by the big, and a good giant is laughingly associated with an episode of betrayal, religious hypocrisy, and hostile penetration.

James I remembered the passage, and no wonder, for Pantagruel's swallowing of his doctors, although playfully described, hints at cannibalism and at the body's unimaginable depths and labyrinths.[83] Like Epistemon, the giant's doctors are ingested into a strange gulf but then expelled in a collective resurrection that parallels Panurge's "miracle," analogues of Lucian's sailors caught in the whale that Rabelais borrowed and Pantagruel killed (*QL* 33–34). There is no question that Pantagruel wants his inner filth located and removed, but James takes the story *in malo;* his (mis)reading parallels Tomkis's distaste for cobblers who know too much about Alexander.

In 1612 the king published *His Majesties Declaration Concerning Conradus Vorstius,* hoping to persuade Leiden University to expel for heresy a recently hired Arminian theologian; the university authorities wished first to hear from Vorstius himself. James's diatribe makes a stunning appendix to Jonathan Goldberg's study of the king's contradictory desire for a public display that would still keep statecraft a close secret.[84] Angrily collapsing genders (James is a "Nursing Father of the Church" [sig. A3]) and figuring religious discourse as bodily function (Vorstius disgorges poison; therefore Leiden should "purge" itself of him), James warns that heresy turns states "upside down" (sig. E3v) by invading God's *arcana*. Starting in the Netherlands, its fire has crept "into the bowels of Our own Kingdome" (sig. C2v). Heretics like this "Monster" (sig. D2v) fly "aloft" to see what is *non scrutanda;* but they also go *down*. God is "the sercher of the heart and reines" who knows James's sincerity despite "ill" interpretations by those "whose corrupted stomacke turnes all good nourishment into bad and pernitious humors" (sig. A3v). Reluctantly, he says, James will make public his argument with the university (thereby displaying those sincere reins that he says God has an eye on). Leiden should realize that we risk "destruction" if we dare "to enter not onely into the secret Cabinet of God, but to intrude our selves into his Essence, to prie into his most inward parts, and like the Physicians of *Pantagruel,* to visit with torch-light all the most hidden places in the Essence of God" (sig. G4v). James now moves from *arcana* that seem as much close stool as cabinet, as much privy as privy council, to Moses' sight of God's "hinder parts" and then, still in the same paragraph, to the poet Du Bartas's wise silence on the sin that destroyed Sodom.

Does James know what his language is doing? Vorstius believed that God contains "multiplicitie" (sig. G2v), but James's own analogy hints that God is full of shit. And to slide from a prince's blocked *arcana* to what we would call homosexuality has poignance coming from one who condemned sodomy yet called the duke of Buckingham his wife.[85] According to James, this intruder who lets "his pen run at random" and "disgorge" the heresies with which his book is "farced" (sig. D2v) — as though the upturner of commonwealths were a fat carnival rioter — is a moral featherweight. Vorstius treats serious matter lightly, "as if it were but about the tale of Tobyes dogge" (sig. H3); filled with "fancie," he is "a forger of new opinions, by which hee would faine make himselfe singular" (sigs. I2–I2v). When writing about heresy, then, James thinks of secrecy, fantasy, innovation, individualism, and the body with apprehensive excitement. And, nestled in the complex, is a reference if not to Epistemon's vision then to its topological cousin, the descent into the giant prince, Pantagruel.

Rabelais's comic spelunking disproves the Sybil's warning that going to Avernus is easy but returning is hard ("hic labor, hoc opus"): in *Pantagruel,* the work is infernal/internal and the return effortless. James's arguments sweat with irritation. Pantagruel *welcomes* subjects inside, joking with his own author about the latter's defecating in his host's throat and unembarrassed by the doctors who locate interior dirt. James had, or thought he had (and thought God had), something to hide. Whatever Rabelais's loyalties, he could treat with easy humor the penetration and scrutiny of a prince's body. There is no sign that this disturbed François I. I doubt the English were very disturbed either, but they did not let the humor pass unchanged, and their king rejected lax openness in favor of absolutist enclosure. The grotesque body is classicized —and classified.

I close this chapter with another text that shows the ambiguities of reversal: Thomas Randolph's *Hey for Honesty,* written in about 1626, updated by "F.J" around 1648, and printed in 1651 (I have already noted its allusion to Gargantua). Aristophanes, on whose *Plutus* the play is based, chats with the translator and the upstart Cleon. Once powerful enough to "breathe out taxes," the demagogue had "outed" the "wicked Cavalier" Aristophanes for speaking against him, so the translator had better not laugh, or the dead despot will "make the Furies sequester thy noddle, / And Radamanth my clerk shall have a warrant / To plunder all delinquents dare look wan, / In scorn of Cleon the committee-man." Aristophanes scoffs: "Foh, now I smell a tanner! Why, sir, who scrapes your hides in hell, while you are on this side Acheron? If you make not speedy return, the devil will want leather to make Œacus a pair of boots."[86]

This looks like the infernal work topos: an ex-tyrant tans hides in Hades, perhaps alongside Lancelot flaying horses. Yet Cleon had in fact started out as a hide-scraper. " 'Tis true, I was a tanner," he says hotly; "what of that?" The scene offers no exact parallel with Epistemon's vision, and instead of Alexander mending shoes, we have as an author a "poor cobbler of another's wit." Cleon's tumble back to his origins, however, may suggest Hell's carnival justice (and Cromwell's possible fate). Lucian and Rabelais have no Cleon in their underworlds, but it would suit "F.J."'s anti-"Puritan" tone to recall authors so dubious in godly eyes. *Hey for Honesty* often refers to Hell (one character offers to pay Charon for a friend's ferry trip), and there is something Lucianic in Mercury's image of what might happen now that the once-blind Plutus can see and men, thanks to the resulting income redistribution, neglect the gods: "Let cuckold Vulcan / Go earn his meat by making spits and dripping-pans, . . . Let Phoebus turn Welsh harper, go a-begging, / And sing St. Taffie for a barley-crust. / Let Cupid go to Grub Street, and turn archer: . . . Juno turn oyster-quean, and scold at Billingsgate; / Bacchus may make a drawer at a tavern" (p. 475). To see gods "turning" to base trades would not displease Menippos (or Rabelais).

"F.J." reverses no worlds. Demoting Alexander may put down the mighty from their seats, but humbling an ambitious tanner represses the revolution. In the 1640s, however, those who were recasting the kingdom were themselves no lovers of carnival — as so often, the war of political sausage and political herring has few clear lines. What can be said is that "F.J.," too, uses Epistemon's vision or related images for purposes other than festivity. Revising infernal reversal can be hard cultural work, even if it also offers comic relief.

5

The Fantasies of "Mad Rablais"
Exploiting the Unreal

In a culture that is ambivalent about the mental powers that can set lovers' eyes rolling or lead a nervous nocturnal traveler to suppose a bush a bear, Rabelais's fantasy seemed variously repellent or engaging. Either way, it was rhetorically useful. Michael Drayton jokingly calls Rabelais himself mad. *Nimphidia, The Court of Fayrie* (1627), a mock epic about the tiny fairy knight Pigwiggen, names earlier triflers:

> Olde Chaucer doth of Topas tell
> Mad Rablais of Pantagruell,
> A latter third of Dowsabell,
>   With such poore trifles playing.[1]

Drayton plays deftly with perspective: Sir Topas encounters the giant Olyphant, and the maker of tiny Pigwiggen remembers Pantagruel. And because his speedy tetrameters describe small beings who suffer an insanity worse than Orlando's, undergo more adventures than Don Quixote, fight in fishscale armor, descend to the underworld, and practice magic, he clearly shares Rabelais's interest in fanciful disproportion.

Others thought Rabelais not so much mad as the maker of concoctions that figured madness in the real world.

Pantagruel's Dreams and the Stuart Masque

James I enjoyed coarse foolery, and for political (and perhaps sentimental) reasons he encouraged rustic festivity and sport. When watching court entertainments, though, he liked to see monstrosity curbed.[2] In Stuart masques, when form and light triumph over confused obscurity, the resolution finds a largely neoclassical expression, one sustained by the Italian (or French) sources for Inigo Jones's sets and costumes.[3] Yet ambiguities remain. Like carnival, reformation lives off enormity — a Justice Overdo needs a Bartholomew Fair, just as Jones's perspective lines speed more effectively toward their vanishing point thanks to the clouds or shrubbery against and through which they move. The more urgent the classicizing imperatives of the masque's aesthetics, the more urgent the need for gaps, bulges, mixtures, and fantasy. The value to Jones and his colleagues of earlier tastes in foolishness should not be underestimated.

It is thus agreeable to find that in addition to the modish Italian and French artists a more old-fashioned draftsman helped costume the Stuart masque, one whose printer credited his work to Rabelais. In 1565 Richard Breton, a Huguenot printer with London ties, published in Paris a collection of grotesques, stating on the title page that they are "de l'invention de maistre François Rabelais: et derniere oeuvre d'iceluy, pour la recreation des bons esprits" (Invented by Master François Rabelais, his last work, for the recreation of good and happy spirits). Whatever *invention* means here, *Les songes drolatiques de Pantagruel* is not by Rabelais. The artist was almost certainly François Desprez, who had affixed his anagrammatized name to the preface of a similar collection, the *Recueil de la diversité des habits,* also published by Breton. The pictures owe something to Hieronymous Cock's prints of Bruegel, although they appear in isolation, one to a page, with no defining context.[4]

These are dreams, says Breton's brief preface, of the excellent and marvelous Pantagruel, once celebrated for his heroic deeds, of whom some more-than-truthful histories admirably tell. Nor did Panurge ever see more admirable things on his last travels (perhaps an allusion to the *Navigations de Panurge*).[5] We are invited to study these marvels closely, for Breton says teasingly that he will leave to others the "sens mistique." Some of the figures' codpieces would stun Panurge, yet the images are not obscene, and only a few imply an upside-down world — Pantagruel imagines nothing so clear as reversal but rather dreams up incongruities and monsters. Breton knows the dreams will not please everyone, for many people are themselves "lunatiques"; others will be amused, and maybe "bons esprits" will use them for "mascarades." In fact, some clever English wits did just that.

There are hints that *Songes* was known in England before the Stuart masques began. The earliest may be a remark by "E.D." [Daunce?] in his *Prayse of Nothing* (1585) that although some might condemn a fuss over nothing, those "delighted in the study hereof" should also see "the macheronicall phantasies of Merlinus Cocaius, and slaepie Phantasmata of Francois Rabilois, men greatly traveled in this business" (sig. H1v). This could refer to Panurge's dream in *TL* 14, or even to Habert's *Songe de Pantagruel* (1542), yet the context, the word *slaepie,* the plural *Phantasmata,* and contemporary connotations of *phantasm* suit *Songes.* Not that "E.D." relishes fantasy; despite impertinent logic and a few jokes, his largely semantic paradoxes serve straightforward claims. Uppitiness of the imagination worries him, as do subjects who "floate over the landmarke of due obedience, for no other cause . . . then for nothing" and "woulde drawe the governments of Princes to the ordinary rule of themselves" and "undermine their naturall dwellings, and countrye walles."

There is also evidence that English playwrights knew *Songes.* Barnabe Barnes's *Divils Charter* (1607) is a drama of treachery, attempted sodomy, and corruption that, as one might expect in a play put on at court soon after the Gunpowder Plot, shows "the Strumpet of proud Babylon, / Her Cup with fornication foaming full." As the ruffian Frescobaldi, thinking he is alone, makes wild thrusts and passadoes, a fellow villain exclaims:

> What Mandragon or salvage Ascapart,
> what Pantaconger or Pantagruell
> Art thou that fightest with thy fathers soul
> Or with some subtill apparitions
> Which no man can behould with mortall eyes.
> Or art thou ravished with bedlamy
> Fighting with figments and vaine fantazies
> Chimeraes or blacke spirrits of the night. (III.v)[6]

This Pantagruel, hallucinator and not hallucination, is no noble Utopian prince, although the hint that Frescobaldi is both giant and father-fighter touches briefly on a submerged generational conflict, which gives depth to Gargantua's concerned paternity and his son's loyalty.[7] The whiff of false diabolism—the play has a real devil as well, as if to hedge Barnes's pneumatological bets—is strengthened by Frescobaldi's claim to be the ghost of the king of Calcutta; his companion pretends to conjure him by "Mulli-sacke" (sherry) and "purple Aligant the bloudy gyant" (*alicant* is a Spanish wine). Barnes's Pantagruel seems to combine Rabelais's giant, here read as an im-

Figure 3 *Songes drolatiques* 60
(Courtesy the Columbia University
Libraries)

pious rebel, with the stagy phantasms that Breton claimed Rabelais dreamed up, in a context in which wine begets demonic giants — or names of giants.

It is in such an air of dementia, I have argued above, that Webster's Bracciano goes to his death in *The White Devil* (1612), dying a few moments before Flamineo's impudent invocation of Lucian/Rabelais. Poisoned and "fall'n into a strange distraction," Bracciano thinks he sees someone "In a blew bonnet, and a paire of breeches / With a great codpeece. Ha, ha, ha, / Looke you his codpeece is stucke full of pinnes / With pearles o'th head of them" (V.iii.99–102). Editors usually explain that such codpieces were a "fashion of the time," although the scanty evidence comes from the sixteenth century.[8] But the context of "brain-sicke language," together with the codpiece's size and the pins' pearl heads, recalls *SD* 60 (fig. 3): the creature wears a bonnet, if no breeches, and a sardonic smile. According to Bracciano, his devil is "a rare linguist," and he hopes to "dispute with him."[9] I cannot prove that Webster (or the costumer, if the figure was visible) had seen Desprez's oversexed smiler, but it seems likely, and the vision certainly recalls the atmosphere surrounding some evocations of Rabelais or his inventions: tensely ludic, tricky, lunatic, deceptively diabolic.

The first trace of *Songes* I detect in the masques comes in Ben Jonson's *Vision of Delight,* performed on Twelfth Night 1617. Early in the masque, Delight summons Night, who will "all awake with phantoms keep, / And those to make delight more deep." Night then calls on Fant'sy: "Now all thy figures are allowed, / And various shapes of things." Fant'sy emerges from a cloud to give a long speech that Stephen Orgel calls a "verbal antimasque" and Night calls a "waking dream."[10] "Songes drolatiques" are exactly what Fant'sy produces — not high vatic dreams but drolleries. Admitting, like Breton, that no one dream pleases everybody, she makes a crowd of them, a tumble of absurdity and metamorphosis. After Fant'sy's speech an antimasque of phantoms comes forth, and one can assume that some would correspond roughly to figures from the preceding evocation. I quote from Fant'sy's speech, identifying some drolleries in *Songes* that the dreams recall. They may have analogues elsewhere, but I cannot locate any beyond a few in Cock's Bruegel. Nowhere outside *Songes*, it seems important to stress, is there such a *concentration* of parallels:

> And Fant'sy, I tell you, has dreams that have wings
> And dreams that have honey, and dreams that have stings;[11] [Fig. 4]
> Dreams of the maker and dreams of the teller,
> Dreams of the kitchen and dreams of the cellar.[12]
> . . . .
> Your ostrich, believe it, 's no faithful translator
> Of perfect Utopian; and then it were an odd piece
> To see the conclusion peep forth at a codpiece.[13] [Fig. 5]
> The politic pudding hath still his two ends, [Fig. 6]
> Though the bellows and bagpipe were nev'r so good friends.[14] [Figs. 7–8]
> . . . .
> If a dream should come in now to make you afeard,
> With a windmill on his head and bells at his beard,[15]
> Would you straight wear your spectacles here at your toes,
> And your boots o' your brows, and your spurs o' your nose?[16] [Figs. 9–10]
> . . . .
> If the bell have any sides, the clapper will find 'em. [Fig. 11]
> There's twice so much music in beating the tabor [Fig. 12]
> As i'th stockfish, and somewhat less labor.
> . . . .
> For grant the most barbers can play o' the cittern,
> Is it requisite a lawyer should plead to a gittern?[17] [Fig. 13]
> . . . .
> The haunches of a drum with the feet of a pot [Figs. 14, 7]
> And the tail of a Kentishman to it — why not? (Ll. 53–102)[18]

Eventually dawn brings light, order, and royalty.

Jonson's procedure is quite unlike that of Davenant and Jones's later *Luminalia* (1638). There, too, dream yields to "brightness" and Night gives pleasure: she will

Figure 4 *Songes drolatiques* 116
(Courtesy the Columbia University Libraries)

Figure 5 *Songes drolatiques* 10
(Courtesy the Columbia University Libraries)

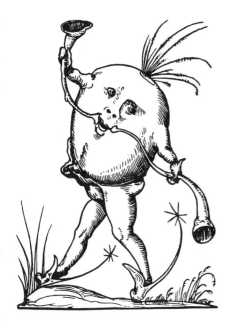

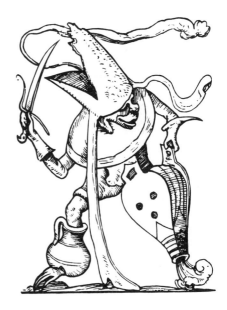

Figure 6 *Songes drolatiques* 85
(Courtesy the Columbia University Libraries)

Figure 7 *Songes drolatiques* 82
(Courtesy the Columbia University Libraries)

Figure 8 *Songes drolatiques* 74
(Courtesy the Columbia University Libraries)

Figure 9 *Songes drolatiques* 5
(Courtesy the Columbia University Libraries)

Figure 10 *Songes drolatiques* 8
(Courtesy the Columbia University Libraries)

Figure 11 *Songes drolatiques* 32
(Courtesy the Columbia University Libraries)

Figure 12 *Songes drolatiques* 34
(Courtesy the Columbia University Libraries)

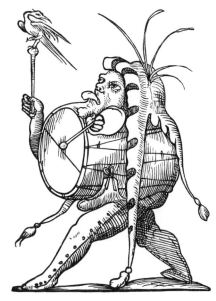

Figure 13 *Songes drolatiques* 96
(Courtesy the Columbia University Libraries)

Figure 14 *Songes drolatiques* 65
(Courtesy the Columbia University Libraries)

Produce fantastic creatures of the night,
Though not t'advance, yet vary their delight;
. . . .
All that our striving mystery presents
Will be but foils to nobler ornaments.[19]

Jonson's own phantasmata have a more important task: they "vary" but "deepen" delight. Davenant's City of Sleep is less ridiculous than mysterious: the masque has given up the carnivalesque for strange trees, golden mountains, falling towers, windmills, and a rainbow city. There is, however, an allusion to Rabelais: one antimasquer (played by the queen's dwarf) is Piecrocal, a captain who serves Oberon. He must be named for Utopia's bilious enemy, Picrochole. It is right that this lovely escapist spectacle should have a braggart whose global ambitions first satirized Charles V but who is now prettified for Henri IV's daughter into a diminutive servant of the Fairy King.

Jonson's phantasms serve more than "delight," for his antimasque is dramatically integrated into the night's revels. Jonson and Jones must have found *Songes* useful in this regard precisely because its silliness creates a realm not so much opposed to courtly harmony as anterior to it, sustaining it. This construction of a suspect but vital irrationality matters whether we read the masques in their political context or, more generally, as representing the mind. The derangements that *Songes* illustrates come from a part of the soul — fancy — that for all its dangers relates intimately to freedom and creativity. Pantagruel's drolleries are cousins of figures like Opinion, Fantasy, Mania, and Capriccio; requiring reform or banishment, they are not in themselves evil.[20] The implications for the Stuart court's political culture are serious. No government welcomes lunacy or subversion, yet the rigidity of the Stuarts' attempted absolutism seems tied to a reluctance to permit fertile disorder into the upper reaches of mind and state as readily as Le Strange said James let his own excrement climb collarwards. Although Jonson upheld the king's theories, his imagination, like the king's body, said something more complicated.

On Twelfth Night 1618, the court saw *Pleasure Reconciled to Virtue*. We have seen that Jonson's "bouncing belly," Comus, is cousin to Rabelais's Gaster, but the masque may also have a trace of *Songes*. Apparently a tun and some flasks danced an antimasque, and among Desprez's grotesques are two walking barrels (*SD* 42 and 120); the second leaks into little creatures drinking the liquor.[21] Whatever his source, Jonson's possibly Pantagruelian barrel as well as his genuinely Rabelaisian belly indicate those pleasures that unshape and "extinguish man" (l. 98), as Hercules says when rejecting them, yet that remain as basic as dreams. The masque failed to please, and when Jonson reworked it as *For the Honor of Wales,* performed a few weeks later, he apologized. One character in the new antimasque of Welshmen explains: "There was neither poetries nor architectures nor designs in that belly-god, nor a note of musics abut him"; another praises the new goat dance as "a properly natural device . . . no tuns, nor no bottles."[22] The Rabelaisian or *Songes* style is unnatural and irrational, but goats, one could argue, are half-way to being ancient satyrs.

For the next few years Jonson's antimasques, although figuring the rude or ridiculous, avoided the phantasmagoric. Then, in *Neptune's Triumph* (written for Twelfth Night 1624 but unperformed), Jonson once more turned not only to Rabelais — a reference to his oracle of the bottle almost defiantly recuperating the offending vessels of *Pleasure* — but also, I think, to *Songes.* Celebrating the safe return of Prince Charles, wifeless, from Spain, the masque opens with a dialogue between two artists, a poet and a cook. The poet, who prefers the cellar to the kitchen, expresses such scorn for antimasques ("heterogene . . . outlandish nothings," ll. 157–60) that some readers have been misled into thinking Jonson himself disdained them.[23] Undeterred, probably because he too speaks for Jonson, the cook summons out of his stewpot an antimasque led by "Amphibion" Archy, the king's dwarf. This production number is a satirical hodgepodge, an ironically (because Hispanically) named "olla podrida" of state rumor and gossip. The cook pours out enormity and unreason and thus also *prima materia* for the shaping imagination; without it, there would be nothing to harmonize. Jones's designs are hard to interpret, even assuming that they have been accurately identified.[24] No sources have been found. One fishy creature is structured like *Songes* 18, although his snout is that of a Renaissance dolphin and he has acquired a hat. There are fish-men in Bruegel and Bosch, but Jones's image resembles that of Desprez in having arms and an upright posture. In any case, Jones's costumes are closer in style to *Songes* than to his usual sources. As in *Delight,* alien elements enlarge the stylistic range.

One other piece of evidence comes in the multi-authored *Faire Maide of the Inn* (1625), a sort of antimasque that includes faked conjuring and a frog dance. Forobosco, "a cheating mountebank," talks his gulls into such get-rich-quick schemes as starting a new religion in Germany or investigating fashions on the moon. In one plan, an Englishman in the monster-exhibiting trade will go to meat-poor Madrid and astound the locals by roasting an English ox: "That would be the eight[h] wonder of the world in those parts," going "beyond all their garlike Olla Podrithoes, though you sod one in Gargantuas cauldron — bring in more mony, then all the monsters of Affrick."[25] This is the only cauldron of Gargantua that I know of, and it has an "olla podrida," just like the pot in *Neptune's Triumph,* printed shortly before this play was published. It too cooks up monsters and anti-Spanish humor. Maybe this is a reference to the chapbook giant, yet the coincidence remains; the writer (Webster is a strong possibility) could have read or heard of Jonson's pot and its fantastic creatures, seen a connection with Desprez and Rabelais, and made a mental slide to the other giant.

Once more, though, Jonson came to be — or was made to be — uncomfortable with this style of fantasy. So he revised, turning his failed *Triumph* into *The Fortunate Isles* and exchanging his stew for more reasonable fantasies. Skelton, Scoggin, and others in the new antimasque are unpolished but more "natural" than the ambulatory artichoke, fish-man, and other monsters Jonson had planned the year before. For the second time Desprez's manner had been only fleetingly useful, as though the play of styles Jonson manages so well in *Delight* had become harder to sustain or more difficult for audiences to enjoy. Pantagruel's dreams would be used again, but as objects of satire only.

Rabelais's name — and perhaps Desprez's designs — appear briefly in James Shirley's *Triumph of Peace* (1634). *Peace* was designed in part to criticize country gentry with fancy court notions, as well as monopolistic "projectors" who were hoping to get rich. One antimasque satirizes the inventiveness that irked those worried by greed-serving "novelty." After Fancy ("prince of th' air" and "bird of night") makes his way past the court guard, not by violence but "With jests / Which they are less able to resist," the scene changes to a tavern, a world of bottle-fed fantasy if not of the oracle of the bottle. Socially there is a demotion as well: the imagination flies up on alcoholic vapor but comes from further down the mental and economic scale. Now Fancy, hermaphrodite child of Mercury and Venus, presents a set of "projections," such as a refrigerated bridle, an automatic thresher, a double-boiler, and diving equipment.[26] When Novelty's husband, Opinion, sees this last figure he asks, "But what thing's this? A chimera out of Rabelais?" Fancy calls it a "new project":

> A case to walk you all day under water,
> So vast for the necessity of air,
> Which, with an artificial bellows cool'd
> Under each arm, is kept still from corruption.
> With those glass eyes he sees, and can fetch up
> Gold, or whatever jewels ha' been lost,
> In any river o' the world. (Ll. 369–78)

Figure 15 *Songes drolatiques* 14
(Courtesy the Columbia University
Libraries)

Since *Gargantua et Pantagruel* has nothing like this "chimera," and since *Chimera* had strong links with "phantasm" and "dream" (see the *Oxford English Dictionary*) as well as with monstrous heterogeneity, it is likely that Opinion is thinking of *Songes*. No one drollery fits these lines, but many have its ingenuity, and *SD* 14 (fig. 15) contains a case, what could be a glass observation panel, and some fish.

These "projections" seem less clearly derived from some deeper world than do the dreams of Jonson's *Delight*. Significantly, Shirley's feathered and bat-winged Fancy exits "fearfully" when Peace appears, whereas Jonson's Fant'sy presents and identifies the king. For all its uncertainties, its allegiance that hovers between the discontented lawyers for whom Shirley wrote and the king whom the Inns of Court wished to please, *Peace* shows a more absolute rejection of dreams. In the meantime, "Rabelais" is evoked in a tavern and linked not to the grotesque — for the fantasy here is too mechanical to suit a book margin or doorway — but to individual whimsy masquerading as socially productive invention. It is as though Quaresmeprenant had loved Rube Goldberg and laid their misbegotten baby at the patent office door. Shirley means us to laugh, and we do: this puffing pseudogrotesque scuba diver is liminal after all, making his way out of the tavern on the wave of the future.

Peace ends with dawn — an illusory dawn for Charles I. In William Davenant's *Salmacida Spolia* (performed January 21, 1640) some have seen signs of growing strain. The masque's editor T. J. B. Spencer calls it "a kind of exorcism aimed at the subversive forces abroad in England."[27] The villain is Discord, a "malicious Fury" who appears in a storm (1). In Renaissance iconology, storms often allegorize Fortune, beating in vain against Fortitude and Charity. There may be something of that meaning here too: the title claims a sweatless and bloodless conquest by reason and love, "sine sanguine sine sudore," of misfortune due to external tumult and not to Charles's own actions.[28] Discord unleashes antic figures that demonstrate how hard it is to "cure / The People's folly" (178–79), but they are halted by the king under the name "Philogenes or Lover of his People" (12). Among them are "Four grotesques or drollities, in the most fantastical shapes that could be devised" (242–43).

Fittingly, in a work citing the Rosicrucians and with a "Wolfgangus Vandergoose" among the characters, this antimasque has a northern, Bruegelesque flavor. The four "drollities" (figs. 16–17), as one might guess from their name, are taken straight from *Songes* (figs. 18–21). The top figure in Orgel and Strong's figure 427 of *Inigo Jones* is copied closely from *SD* 31, although Jones has shrunk his codpiece; the lower figure reverses and simplifies *SD* 106. The other drollities, Orgel and Strong's figure 428, are based on *SD* 77 and 64. The former is now less grotesque about the face and has no cutlery, but his shoes and attitude are the same, and his codpiece outdoes that of his model; the latter has changed his arm position and his direction, but the heavy features remain, as does the hat. Pantagruel's dreams, although not among his most fantastic, provide the style of a past age, as though English rebels were old-fashioned as well as crazy. Also significant is a further shift in how the dreams illustrate unreason. Fantasy is here further diminished: no longer a fruitful if limited mode of seeing, it is not even (as it had been for Shirley) a source of early capitalist dementia. Figures like those of Desprez or "Rabelais" now indicate a specific political menace to a kingdom in early revolution, fully embodying the psychological and political inversion that threatens parallel hierarchies of apprehension, reason, and opinion and king, court, and commons. The integration of masque and antimasque that deepens Jonson's best work has come further undone, as witness the harshness with which these "dreams" are not so much superseded as exiled—bad news, in fact, for Charles, who should have listened harder to his drollities.

Allusions to Rabelais or Pantagruel by "E.D.," Barnes, and Shirley that link him to Desprez's manner would reinforce his reputation as a fabulating namer of idle nothings; if some enjoyed such nothings, others used his name to conjure up thoughts of feigning or lies. In either case, English reaction shows ambivalence toward poesis, the power of words to make monsters ex nihilo and then allow the nihil to spread in a negative ontological contagion. Those who took the printer Breton's word that his "songes" were the "invention" of

Figure 16 From figure 427 in Orgel and Strong, *Inigo Jones* (Devonshire Collection, Chatsworth. Reproduced by permission of the Chatsworth Settlement Trustees.)

Figure 17 From figure 428 in Orgel and Strong, *Inigo Jones* (Devonshire Collection, Chatsworth. Reproduced by permission of the Chatsworth Settlement Trustees.)

Figure 18 *Songes drolatiques* 31 (Courtesy the Columbia University Libraries)

Figure 19 *Songes drolatiques* 106
(Courtesy the Columbia University Libraries)

Figure 20 *Songes drolatiques* 77
(Courtesy the Columbia University Libraries)

Figure 21 *Songes drolatiques* 64
(Courtesy the Columbia University Libraries)

Rabelais could assume that the author of *Gargantua, Pantagruel,* and parodic prognostications (possibly including *Admirables* and the *Navigations*) had once more played Phantastes. Written reaction to Rabelais's creation of forms such as never were in nature inscribed significant issues: the mental and cultural role of the imaginative faculty, the legitimacy of fiction and the marvelous, the reality and nature of nothing and negation, the nightmares of religious or theological illusion, and the social and spiritual risk of "projections," whether inventions like those Jones staged or the insubstantial pageants generated by fear and desire.

The Fabulations of Impiety

Physically, marvels and monsters were concentrated at the margins of the medieval and early modern world, but culturally they were central to the European imagination. Some writers found in Rabelais (or para-Rabelais) a monstrosity producing less pleasure than dismay—negative wonder. That they personally feared the imagination may be doubted but not the cultural fact of that fear and its usefulness in polemic. The rhetoric of negative wonder deflates an enemy by refusing to take him seriously, while simultaneously using images of enlargement and monstrosity to show the threat he poses to others. Caesar is a mortal who puffs himself up, says Shakespeare's Cassius, but he is also a Colossus who bestrides the earth and endangers the republic. He is little, so we can kill him; he is too big, so we ought to. Exploiting both an ancient suspicion of fantasy and an equally ancient taste for marvels and astonishment, negative wonder is an analogue of the giant-pygmy pairing— that anamorphic monster one might call "Gargatom."

At times, then, English writers appropriate or cite Rabelaisian fantasy to indicate what has gone horribly yet risibly wrong in the minds of others. The issues raised are not trivial; they include worries concerning illusion, consumption, and the Mass. Not all references to Rabelais and (para-)Rabelaisian giants are hostile, and one fantasy of engulfment is literally entertaining: William Lithgow's *Most Delectable, and True, Discourse . . . of a Peregrination in Europe, Asia and Affricke* (1623 ed.) praises the Pratolino gardens for trees, ponds, "artificial fountaines," and "exquisite banqueting roome, contrived among sounding unseene waters, in forme of Gargantus body" (sig. Bb2v). This must be the colossal *Apennines,* carved from living rock by Giovanni Bologna in the 1580s.[29] The statue contained a dining room and also had a dovecot in its head, as though it were as flutter-brained as the fanciful sculptor who made it. To eat inside a giant, giving new depth to the phrase "mise en abîme," might put the symbolically sensitive off their feed: fantasy, like a giant, can take us in.

Protestants thought that among Christendom's worst fantasies was the belief that bread can be transubstantiated into Christ's body by the mere hocus pocus of a "Hoc est corpus." That is why giants' open-mouthed size and comic fictionality made them good symbols of "papist" lunacy, of negative wonder. Do Catholics say they eat God? The cannibals![30] Giants eat people, too, for although they have too much flesh already, they want more. They are the letter made ever more fleshly by a misreading of Christ's words at the Last Supper. And because giants are also rebels (like recusants), tyrants (like the pope), mocking boasters (like Catholic polemicists), and sexually perverse (like monks), Protestants found them valuable for attacking the Mass and other "popish" illusions. That such name-calling was satiric did not make it more genial, as witness Alexander Cooke's growling remark in *More Worke for a Masse-Priest* (1621) that "according to Poperie, A man may eate his god with his teeth, as a Cyclops ate Ulysses companions" (sig. A2). On the other hand, since giants are for the most part imaginary, Cooke can also underline his belief that Catholics fool themselves. The problem is that they fool others, too, engulfing them in an abyss of illusion.

Thomas Scott was adept at projecting negative wonder, a mixture of snorting contempt and justified fear. His *Digitus Dei* (1623), written to advance his widely noted if imprudent campaign against James's foreign policy, is a sermon on the warning in Luke 13 to repent or perish. It has much to say about Catholic "Poeticall fictions," the Gunpowder Plot (fed by poisoned "Romish Milke" from Rome's "Adulterate Teates"), and God's terrible swift sword. Although condemning them, Scott opened his imagination to giants and wonders: Cardinal Robert Bellarmine is a "Romish Goliah," he says, whose arguments could not "wrest the Staffe and Sling" out of James's hand, while atheism is a "Monster" accompanying the "Dwarfe Ignorance." Scott is interested chiefly in the destruction that God's punitive digit can cause — hence his title. Why does God finger certain buildings? Why burn a house in which papists had been saying Mass but spare the nearby Fortune Theater? Because theaters, like brothels, do not pretend to be other than what they are, whereas Catholics call their false shows true. When the Fortune later caught fire, he explains, this was punishment not for staging plays but for doing so on the Sabbath.

After the Catholic house's fire, says Scott, had anyone — even "equivocating" recusants — witnessed communion "Cakes" rise again "from under the ruines," Scott might have believed in the Mass. As it is, he will go on thinking of papists as themselves transubstantiated by Circe's "Cup of Abhominations" into such "Don Quixshots or Gorgantuahs as would eat up their God Almightie at a mouthfull" or, rather, "imagine themselves to be such Monsters as could doe it" (sig. D4v). The body, including Christ's, and how to relate it to the Word and words is the issue, as is fantasy. Catholics have "rob'd our Saviour of Head, Heart, Hands, Feet, of a true Body, of his Humanitie." In this fancied theft, the Gorgonized "Gorgantuah" is pure monster — a Polyphemus, a folklore cannibal, a Gogmagog-cum-Saturn. He is thus imaginatively real, although of course Scott's point is that Catholics merely *think* they are cannibals. By summoning a giant associated with "Legendarie stuffe" (sig. B1), Scott can have his polemical cake and eat it: the Mass is terrible in its dark rites, its blood and raw flesh, and yet at the same time laughable — not *trans-* but *in*substantial. Whether Scott's mockery has actually exorcised illusion is another matter, for "Gorgantuah" the theophage is a powerful figure.

Rabelais himself, as a name and author, could be useful to Protestant argument in part because his fantasies are, like the Mass, deliberately created fictions. Not only do his giants take in a pilgrim here, an author there: their creator was interested in the nature of bodies, words, and space. So although (or even because) Rabelais was neither clearly Protestant nor clearly Catholic, his name could be evoked in scoffs at papist illusion.

De missa papistica . . . adversus Robertum Bellarminum (1603), by Matthew Sutcliffe, dean of Exeter, is an angry book: angry at transubstantiation, at fantasy, at impiety. A fierce debater, in 1609 Sutcliffe founded a short-lived college in Chelsea dedicated to fighting recusancy with study and polemics; James I laid the cornerstone. Here, Sutcliffe tackles Bellarmine with gusto. The cardinal's deceptions, he asserts, rely on a misunderstanding of Christ's "This is my body." Yes, communion bread "mysticè, et symbolicè, et sacramentaliter verè est corpus Christi" (is truly Christ's body in a mysterious, symbolic, and sacramental fashion). To take it as literal flesh, though, is to deal insanely with "Chimeras" and to take Christ's words "carnally." This is not just a matter of reading with the flesh rather than with the spirit, of sticking to signifiers and missing the signified. The mistake is literal: one imagines that one is eating flesh in a literally bloody carnality. This is profoundly unnatural, says Sutcliffe, for normal people flee inhuman "anthropophagi."

Bellarmine, then, argues "ridiculè." Indeed, says Sutcliffe, the cardinal's reasons are such "quod vix in fabulis *pantagruelinis* fingere ausus est impius ille fabulator Rabelaisius" (that the impious fabulator Rabelais would hardly have dared feign in his fictions about Pantagruel, sigs. Ff1–Ff1v). The sarcasm is neither arbitrary nor comfortable. Debates on the Eucharist necessarily involved assumptions about signs. Can bread be a sign if its substance collapses into the signified flesh? Signs require difference, not identity. Because Catholics concede that the bread continues (accidentally, as it were) to look and taste like bread, the question of what happens to its substance is tied to the reality of a world in which the sacrament's actuality, whatever that might be, is taking place. One Christian's invisible realm may be another's Cloud-cuckoo-land, yet no Protestant could discount all invisibilia and remain Christian. Rabelais and Bellarmine fabulate impiously — but Sutcliffe, too, believes in things that nobody can see.

Patrick Forbes, future bishop of Aberdeen, was likewise impatient with figments. He wrote *A Defence of the Lawful Calling of the Ministers of Reformed Churches* (1614) to vindicate the right of Protestant clergymen to claim an Apostolic succession: despite the rupture with the pope, they have an unbroken tie to Saint Peter through the successive laying-on of hands at ordination. This topic, too, invites serious thought on the relation of ancient words and gestures to the present and on the difficulty of historically tracing something real but invisible — and hence subject to the charge that it is fantasized. Forbes, whom the *DNB* calls "good, godly, and kind," was understandably annoyed at being termed a "glorying Goliath" by a recusant reader, and his title page asserts sharply that the "impertinent and rediculously deceitfull" questions answered in this tract were written in his adversary's "dottage." A major topic is the misused imagination, a sensitive issue precisely because Forbes defends a Church that he not only concedes but insists is "invisible": ancient, Apostolically descended, and, unlike the pope's all-too-material church, perceived only by the faithful. The true church's age and invisibility was vital to Reformation claims, for without some such theory Protestants would have been even more vulnerable to the charge that they dealt in mere novelties fabricated by Opinion.

His church, Forbes thinks, has been there right along, unseen, hidden within the false and visible one. Catholics are the feigners. They pretend that the Antichrist is yet to come, whereas the Gospel's "waxing light" shows that he is here, in Rome. This makes them "paint out . . . Chimeraes, wherby they may stupifie and detaine foolish hearts in expectation of such an Antichrist, as shall come, I warrant you, *ad grecas Calendas*." The papists' Antichrist must be some "dumb Devil" begotten "betwix some feind or fairie, and a devised Daniel, who hath I warrant you, two thousand yeares agoe, lost all the writings of his genealogie." Catholics try to "delude the Worlde, with such foolishe fantasies"; and indeed some people are deluded. Why? By "perversenes of mindes and guiltines of conscience," they "runne to such doting dreames, and ridiculous raveries, as, albeit they were not refelled [confuted] by cleare Scripture, yet, were fitter to bee an addition to Rables, or to make up the last booke of *Amades de Gaule*, then to bee reputed profound pointes of Christian wisedome" (sigs. D1, I3v–I4). Rabelais, then, is a fantasy-monger. The affiliation with romance is intriguing, for Rabelais's work had begun as an "addition" to the chapbooks, just as other writers did indeed make "additions" to his works, and just as (said reformers) Catholics had added to God's word and laws. *Amadis,* especially, in a fine demonstration of romance's antipathy to closure, received addition upon addition. To the making of fictions there is no end, and Forbes's train of thought implies that fictional theology will stop only when the equally fictional Greek kalends finally arrive.

Secular fantasy may have distressed some people because it is a reminder that things invisible to mortal sight may be so because they are, quite simply, not there. The common phrase "you're just seeing things" may apply to the "Pantagruel" in *The Divils Charter* who fences with air, but faith itself rests on the evidence of things unseen. If Chimeras are hard to see, so, nowadays, are virgin mothers and talking snakes. "Wisdome is Queene," says the anonymous *Apollo Christian, or Helicon Reformed* (1617), when objecting to fictions like Saint George's fight with the dragon, and Wisdom "fareth not with Faëries" (Sig. C2v).[31] But what if Wisdom is just a fairy? In turning around to laugh at his own fictions, Rabelais plays with a truth both uncomfortable and exhilarating: much in Scripture would not be out of place in works that many condemned as fantastic. Hence the disgust or delight some have found in thinking that his genealogies, for example, mock their biblical counterparts. When Rabelais claims that nothing in his account of Gargantua's nonvaginal birth violates Christian faith (an earlier edition quotes Paul on how "Charity believeth all things"), it is easy to see how some concluded that he found the Gospel as improbable as tales about giants.

It is more likely that Rabelais agreed with Erasmus's comment on the adage *Sileni Alcibiadis:* like Sileni, some passages in the Gospels seem foolish but are wise within. Thomas Browne had something like this in mind when remarking in *Religio medici* that he has read without harm such skeptics as Lucian even though "there are in Scripture Stories that do exceed the Fables of Poets, and to a captious Reader sound like Garagantua or Bevis." (The spelling suggests the chapbook giant, although a few lines later Browne mentions Rabelais). Browne is not a captious reader; for him charity does indeed entail believing if not all things then a great many. But he has flirted with calling Scripture fantasy, evoking in order to exorcise a Lucianic "Rhetorick of Satan" that may "pervert a loose or pre-judicate belief."[32] Nor is it the Bible alone that makes Browne remember Rabelais or almost-Rabelais. His *Pseudoxia epidemica* (1646) recounts with genial skepticism (for there was also much in which he did not believe) the tale of Milo, the Greek athlete "who by daylie lifting a Calfe, attained an ability to carry it being a Bull." This, says Brown dryly, "is a witty conceit, and handsomely sets forth the efficacy of Assuefaction [habituation]." They say that in the Olympics "for the space of a furlong, he carried an Oxe of foure yeares upon his shoulders; and the same day hee carried it in his belly; for as it is there delivered he eate it up himselfe: Surely he had beene a proper guest at Grandgousiers feast, and might have matcht his throat that eate sixe pilgrims for a salad." The margin says "In Rabelais."[33] Browne recalls the somatic energy of *Gargantua,* its pleasure in the thought of sheer intake; but he does so in the context of what the wise may believe and what they will take as fantasy.

Theaters, as Scott says, work openly in the figment trade; unlike churches, they may lawfully peddle falsehood. I close this section with the Rabelais of Jasper Mayne — playwright, translator of Lucian, and royalist divine — who entangles theatrical fantasy and religion in his worldly *Citie Match,* performed at Whitehall and published at Oxford in 1639. This comedy, filled with in-jokes and topical allusions, has moments of irreverence that might drive the theater's enemies to further censure, for Mayne flirts with impiety when he arranges for a fake religious rite (he had, says the *DNB,* a taste for "unseasonable practical jokes"). To make the fakery funnier, he attaches the name Rabelais to it. In Act IV the aptly named Plotwell tells Aurelia, who must marry so as to save their mutual fortune, that "The scene is laid already; / I have transformed an English Poet [one Salewit] into / A fine French Teacher, who shall joyne your hands / With a most learned legend out of Rabelais." Later, Salewit reports that the counterfeit ceremony went off as planned in a French church (which served Huguenot refugees and required no marriage license): "I've read a Fiction out of Rabelais to 'em, / In a religious tone, which he [the deluded bridegroom] believes / For good French Liturgie. When I had done / There came a Christening." Plotwell asks: "And didst thou baptize / Out of thy Rabelais too?" Drawing the line at counterfeiting a genuine sacrament (which marriage, for Protestants, is not), Mayne has his poet say: "No faith, I left 'em / In expectation of their Pastor." If that pastor was anything like Calvin, he would have been aghast at what had been going on in his church. At last all is revealed, and Plotwell tells the bridegroom, the rich Mr. Warehouse, "Wonder not, Sir, you / Were married but in jest. Twas no church forme, / But a fine Legend out of Rabelais" (sigs. L2v, O2v, R2v).[34]

Mayne assumes an audience that can identify Rabelais (that the "fiction" is also a "legend" adds medieval overtones). It matters for the play's stratified social world that only the better-educated would know what to make of the name.[35] The allusion has a double function: it gives witty characters higher polish — more gloss, more glossolalia — while differentiating their multi-tongued and print-aware selves from the single-languaged, ignorant, and gullible. Some of the literate, though, might find Mayne's casual way with ritual disturbing, even while recognizing that the recitation of a merely literary text protected genuine rites from serious sacrilege. The risqué quality, the defiance of the Puritans whom the play derides, lies in the juxtaposition of the marriage ceremony and, of all things, "fictions" by the French Lucian. Satire spatters acid on innocent bystanders: the report of a bride and groom being joined by readings out of *Gargantua et Pantagruel* permits the mind to allow a libertine wit near a real church. This is why Rabelais and others who ridiculed what they saw as superstition could disturb those who might agree on the fact of falsity but feared parody's contamination: laughter at false belief can resound in a true one's churches.

Mayne's own take on fantasy's relation to faith was complex. Here Rabelaisian legend sits in a nested set of comic fictions. A decade later the human tendency to make things up looked more dangerous, now that revolutionary lunatics were claiming to perceive truths that were invisible to royalists. In a 1647 *Sermon Against False Prophets*, preached in Oxford "after the Surrender of that Garrison," Mayne dismisses those prophesying against the king. Such seers "see" "visions, perhaps; But such as Aeneas in Virgil saw among the shades" (sig. A3v); in other words, "fictions." We cannot eradicate images from language, or language from society, continues Mayne, but we can strive for clarity and not, like squids, blacken with ink the water in which we swim (sig. A4). Like many who detested flummery, Mayne cites Lucian (sig. C4v). Indeed, about the time he wrote *The Citie Match* he was translating Lucian's works, eventually publishing a lovely edition (1664) with a preface defending his author as a "sharpe" satirist "who reform'd the Times." Lucian would know what to do with "Seditious, Rump Grammarians" and false preachers with "bubbles of Expression": he "would doubtless send such Garagantua, tumid Orators to the Doctor who cured Lexiphanes of his Fustian disease" (sig. A3v–A4). Rabelais himself had prescribed a sort of Lexiphanic purge for his Limousin scholar. This adjectival Garagantua, though, with his tell-tale chapbook "a," represents loudmouth rebels who need an emetic to help them vomit out their idle bombinations. Rebellious sectaries speak in Garagantuan bubbles; loyal royalists read Rabelais and Lucian.

Nonbooks

Mayne's false clergyman reads from a genuine book — as a prayerbook it is a fantasy, but as a real volume it has bulk and dimension. Inside *Pantagruel et Gargantua*, however, are texts that exist only as titles and promises of books, holes in Rabelais's fiction that open onto nothingness or — depending on one's temperament — alternative realities.[36] Some sound attractive. Panurge's monograph on long codpieces would be the definitive study, and inhabitants of Pantagruel's inner world would have read with interest, had they been able to get hold of a copy, Alcofribas's *Histoire des Gorgias,* on his adventures in the giant's "gorge" (a pun on "gorgeously dressed" that may also glance at the sophist Gorgias, author of a lost treatise denying that anything is real, or if real knowable, or if known communicable). Oscillating between being and nonbeing, they are in some ways the librarian's equivalent of negative wonder.

Pantagruel's seventh chapter lists scores of such titles, some by real men, said to be in the famed (imaginary) library of Saint-Victor, in Paris.[37] Collectively, they exact a humanist and evangelical revenge on enemies of the new learning, making often scatological or indecent fun of obscurantist theologians, logic-chopping scholastics, outdated doctors, myopic glossators. Some "authors," not least the Sorbonne's Noël Béda, had threatened the careers and lives of such men as Rabelais (and of his future patron, Marguerite de Navarre, whose *Miroir de l'âme pécheresse* Béda tried to have censored in 1533). In rhetorical effect, the library's titles are not unlike the satirically fantasized *Letters of Obscure Men,* by Ulrich von Hutten and others out to satirize scholastic obscurantism. Rabelais credits to the paunchy Béda, for example, a *De optimitate triparum* and to "Magister Ortuinum" — Ortwin, von Hutten's chief butt — an *Ars honeste petandi in societate* (The art of farting politely in society). One book might be useful to logicians: *Quaestio subtilissima, utrum Chimera, in vacuo bombinans, possit comedere secundas intentiones, et fuit debatuta per decem hebdomadas in concilio Constantiensi* (A highly subtle question: Whether the Chimera, bombinating [buzzing, vibrating] in a vacuum, can eat second intentions, particularly as it was batted around for ten weeks at the Council of Constance). Not a bad conundrum.[38] A few other titles are given real authors; *De patria diabolorum,* for instance, is by "Merlinus Coccaius" (Folengo). Most, however, are unascribed.

Although this is Europe's first imaginary library, the notion of a book extant only in some future or parallel world was not new. The end of Lucian's *True History* announces more adventures to come, a pledge one early scribe called "the biggest lie of all."[39] Nor are Rabelais's bookless titles the only way to generate subsidiary fictions. Where are those lines the loving Astrophil writes his Stella? They cannot be, to judge from how he describes them, the same ones printed under Philip Sidney's name. Other works gain unreality from an apparatus such as that given John Taylor's *Nonsence upon Sence* (1653), which identifies itself as the third part, fourth impression, fifth edition, and sixth addition, written on white paper in a brown study in the year "Millimo, Quillimo, Trillimo, Daffadillimo" (similarly, his preface to *Jacke a Lent* [?1617], cites page 30,000 of a work on "the Antiquitie of Ginger-bread" by one "Nymshag an ancient Utopian Philosopher").[40]

Occasionally, English writers show signs of knowing Rabelais's nonbooks, adopting or imitating them for purposes ranging from deriding individuals to the more ambiguous pleasure of inscribing nonentity or considering its pertinence to invention, referentiality, and belief. Nature may abhor a vacuum, but language — like the Chimera — can bombinate in it, if at the price of being batted around by philosophers and theologians.

The first written allusion to the library of Saint-Victor I can find is in *Pierces Supererogation* (1593), a diatribe Gabriel Harvey fired at Thomas Nashe in the pair's pamphlet war. Nashe's Latinisms are "junkets" and "fritters," scoffs Harvey, that might suit the man who "compiled" the commentary *De optimitate triparum* (sig. Z3v).[41] Harvey does not mention Rabelais, probably because elsewhere he jeers at Nashe for imitating him, but the sally works better for a reader of *Pantagruel,* especially one who remembers that the imagined "compiler" is fat Noël Béda — so well acquainted with tripe, so impressively swelling with his own.[42] Happier to name Rabelais, James I recalls Rabelais's nonbooks in a letter he sent his "little beagle," Robert Cecil, in October 1605. Yes, says the king, expenses are worrisome. And yes, ambassadors are demanding: the French (Christopher de Harlay, comte de Beaumont) "is such an insatiable epitome of avarice as I doubt not but he hath found out a new art of begging whereupon he may add a book to the bibliothèque of his countryman Rabelais." James had a point: some weeks later John Chamberlain detailed for Dudley Carleton the envoy's successful demands for horses, plate, pictures, jewels, and sixty tuns of the Lord Treasurer's wine, which he then sold.[43] Nor did James shrink from citing *Pantagruel;* Sir Anthony Weldon, who hated the Stuarts, admitted that James had "as many ready witty jests as any man living."[44] True, the king's two written notices of Rabelais — here and in his tirade on the "heretic" Vorstius — do come in passages voicing pique, not delight.

Quick with a jest, James could also be maladroit (his mind-boggling reading of Juno as himself, Aeneas as Bothwell, and "the rest of the gods" as Elizabeth was meant to soothe an English queen nettled by his quoting Virgil's "If I cannot prevail upon the gods, I will stir up Hell").[45] In the letter to Cecil, the pleasantry does not work quite as well as it might. James catches one rhythm in Rabelais's library, for a number of titles begin with "On the art of" or "On the method of," and it is true that some humiliating titles are credited to actual, dignified men. But the point of most of them is their parodic unreality. Harlay's fancied *De arte mendicationis* would be — as witness his own productive mooching — useful if déclassé nonfiction, even closer to the literal truth than Béda's book on tripe. James's joke is not bad, though, and it helps him graciously/defensively say to Cecil, in effect, "We both know we have money trouble; we also have read the same witty books and view with some detachment the irritating folly of others, especially foreigners."

The year 1605 also saw Joseph Hall's *Mundus alter et idem*. As I have noted, its voyages to not-so-alien nations of swillers, gluttons, viragos, fools, and thieves have less of Rabelais's spirit than one might expect. Moreover, although Hall enjoys self-reference and punning names, provides such Lucianic touches as eroded monuments to give his parodic societies a specious antiquity, and places his narrator on a ship called *Phantasia,* Hall distrusts the imagination. Citizens of Solitaria, in the land of Fooliana, spend time "framing fictions to themselves of things never done, nor never likely to bee done: in beleeving these their fictions, and in following these beleefes: This is the reason why they abhorre company, and hate to bee interrupted in their ayrie castle-buildings."[46] "Look who's talking," one might object: "Your own inner Solitarians have jumped the wall and are halfway into the keep." Yet Hall's ambivalence is typical of anti-Utopians, who fear what corrupt human desire can devise, and Utopians — like More's Hythloday — who fear the ruptures subjectivity makes in a rational social order. Nor does Hall betray Lucian in this regard, for both debunk philosophers' fantasies.

It was the translator, John Healey, whose *Discovery of a New World* (ca. 1609) more thoroughly enjoys a Rabelaisian breeziness, roughing up the original's Latin elegance and intensifying its interest in nonentity. That interest was hardly negligible. Hall, who had a good ear for political flatulence (he quotes an elected official as promising to "preserve us as wee were now, and make us as wee would bee"), tells how on the official's "belt of State," gems spell out a motto that Healey translates as: "NOTHING, IF NOT BEYOND." These are resonantly ironic words in a nowhere world, with or without an echo of the Hapsburg "Plus Ultra." Healey, though, can push much further "beyond" Hall's "nothing": when the latter calls his Lent-bird, RUC, huge, Healey reports that its beak is "almost" as big as "halfe the Equinoctiall circle" and in the margin explains *almost* by conceding that the beak's arc "wants some 359. degrees, 59. min. 60. seconds."[47] By my calculation, and assuming that the marginal note has its figures right, this is -180 degrees. The RUC has a nonbeak, if a big one.

Unlike *Mundus, Discovery* alludes to Rabelais, commending him in the preface (although not by name) as a wise doctor, and inventing or revising some Rabelaisian nonbooks, a satirical technique in which Hall was less interested. Healey shelves these in his margins, creating fantasy texts on the borders of a known text just as Hall's Antipodal lands sit at the borders of the known world. His titles help Healey invent fresh fantasies that both sustain the comic fiction that all this is real and let nonbeing flourish If *Chimera* and *vacuum* are valuably empty words, imaginary book titles are empty wordstrings, chimerical meta-vacuity making whole Potemkin villages of illusory discourse behind which stretch wastes of blank pages.[48] To the making of nonbook titles there need be no end, a plenitude as disconcerting as the null sets to which infinity is paradoxically akin.

Healey's fictive titles, like Rabelais's, can be indecent. Two are sexual. One comes next to a paragraph on Pye-nople, capital of Letcheritania, a region of Tenterbelly. The city is now a "poore ruined pile," similar to Britain's Verulam, but a note remarks that Oysterpy-nople and Potato-py-nople "flourish untill this day: beeing founded by Hercules, upon his copulation with 50. women upon one night. *Georg. Cap. curant. de punct. Aretinens. lib. 27*" (p. 25). Whoever "Georg. Cap." was, Hercules' nocturnal labors are mentioned by Diodorus Siculus and Pausinas. Aretino is likewise real, and whatever else *punct.* stands for, it must pun on the "punks" about whom he wrote so infamously. A punk joke would have point, needling the myth of Hercules' prowess and Letcheritania's reality (at least as a male hope). After all, Hercules' feat would be just another night's work for a busy punk, even if in the hero's case the results, they say, were fifty male babies who grew up to found cities in Sardinia. The implications are disturbing: Hercules founds Letcheritanian cities by spreading his seed around, but what sort of founding mothers are these? Punk(t)s? To ask why Hercules is not also a punk(t) would be feminist anachronism, but the pun does emit dissonance. The patriarch has fifty women, but under more Aretino-like circumstances one *punctum* — one "nothing" — could accommodate fifty Herculeses. The joke sits cheekily atop a citation of Spenser's *Ruines of Time,* another work on foundation and loss. Had Spenser's ruined Verulam enjoyed as much sexual vigor as Hercules, it might have survived. It may be no accident that several lines later we find the reference to the wall that has been artfully constructed of bones that is (I think) Gluttony's version of Panurge's genital bulwark against Paris's enemies. Hall exchanges obscenity for recycled leftovers, but Healey has also thought about how sex relates to urban decay.

In "Shee-landt" sex determines power, for women rule men. Dolled up and leaving the housework to the menfolk, they go dancing in taverns and playhouses. Healey writes: "Dauncing is here taken in the largest sence, including both the moderne, as galiard, pavan, Jig Etc. and the ancient, called the beginning of the world. vide Rab. Apodemat. 7. chap. 3" (p. 70). This is another nonbook, although the notion is old, most suavely expressed in John Davies' *Orchestra:* dancing began the world when the elements (or, if one prefers, atoms) leapt into orderly motion at Love's command. But "dancing" is also that other activity, the "olde daunce" of which Chaucer's Wife of Bath says she

172 Fantasies of "Mad Rablais"

knows the art. I cannot guess what "Apodemat." is an abbreviation of; the hint of "footless" (a [without] pod [foot]) might be relevant. Does the mention of "Rab." add sexual innuendo?

Some of Healey's nonbooks laugh at gourmandise. Tenterbellian politicians prosper according to their girth, some having rounded out from thin origins in "shoppikins" at the city's edge. A note explains: "You shall find the word in *Antony Mundaies discourse of the reformation of Redfaces*" (p. 27). You will have to look a long time, however, although Munday was a real man who wrote many real books. Tenterbellians are not themselves great readers, their scholars studying only "Apicius his Institutions of the Arte of Muncherie" (p. 30), a real work that Healey treats with curious hesitation; perhaps he thought it was lost.[49] Their library houses ranks of "potts and kannes," in which freshmen have "lesser measures, the sophisters [sophomores] larger, and so up to the Graduates." An acid note adds: "We have some Universitie men that are too well read in these authors, yes verily, some study them so sore that they bring themselves of on their legs by it, saith Panurg, in his *Le Tric-trac clericorum*" (p. 30). Healey revises an anonymous work at Saint-Victor's, *Le trictrac des Freres Frapars* (The backgammon of the Belly-Bumping Brothers; Cotgrave glosses "Frere Frappart" as "a lustie, strong, tough Frier; a good boxer, a sound knocker; a notable striker, a bellie-bumper"). Healey knows that *frères* are clerics, but he either missed or rejected the sexual sense of *Frapars*.

His Rabelais can be scatological, however. One note further identifies a city in Tenterbelly: "Lickingoa is a colony, sent from Goa in the East Indies, saith Pantagruel in his *Merda Geographica*. lib. 7 chap. 39. Sect. 594." Pantagruel, celebrated traveler, is evidently an authority on the Antipodes, the upside-down world, and on population shifts. But his "geography" is really "shit" — lots of it, too, if the work's seventh book alone has thirty-nine chapters and the thirty-ninth has at least 594 subsections. Nor do "Merde" and "Licking" make a happy coupling for gourmands. Healey's Rabelais is recognizably "dirty," then — and the maker of a giant who pens nonbooks on nowheres. (Hall introduces a giant, the great All-Paunch, who ousted the indigenous population of Thrivingois, a foundational act that reverses the usual pattern; it also recalls, perhaps, how the thriving Papefigues had been conquered by the Papimanes [*QL* 45, the chapter with the lickers of asses' rears].)

Also scatological (if not explicitly Rabelaisian) is a book Healey invents when he tells about a choleric province of Fooliana. Every man there goes armed, even "if he goe but to my neighbour Johns." The *Oxford English Dictionary* does not find *john* in the sense of water closet before the eighteenth century, but Healey's explanatory note must be a John [Harington]/Jakes/

Ajax joke: "*John Fifticankoes, Ajax* his sonne and heyre, according to the pedigree drawne by *Peter de qui,* in his *Catalogus Dunsor. Joannens. lib. 2. Cap. 17*" (p. 95). This is the tone of Rabelais's library, not least in its glance at [John] Duns Scotus, the scholastic whose name unfairly gave rise to the word *dunce.* John has fifty "cankoes," whatever they are. A *cancro* was a sore or cancer, so he may be in trouble, perhaps something like the trouble Frère Jean got into when he wiped himself with a papal decretal (*QL* 52). Who "Peter de qui" is, I have no idea; as a genealogist and cataloguer he resembles Rabelais.

Healey saves his deftest marginal allusion for late in the book. Stopping for a while in Theevingen, the narrator goes into the astrology business, "spying marvells in the heavens urinall as methodically as any Star-gazer" and writing "an infallible prognostication of these present times." "Right," says a note, "for this is but a discovery of *Mundus alter et idem*" (p. 131). Adroit exhibitors of nonbooks know when to hold up the real thing.[50]

About the same time Healey was translating *Mundus,* John Donne was making a *Catalogus librorum aulicorum incomparabilium et non vendibilium* (The courtier's library of rare books that are not for sale), probably finished by 1611 but not printed until 1650.[51] Evelyn Simpson calls its thirty-four Latin titles "an elaborate jest in the manner of Rabelais," although there were by now other French imaginary libraries with such satirical titles as "*The Grand Chronicle of Cuckolds,* Dedicated to the King of Navarre, with the Observations of the Sieur de Champvalon" (a lover of Navarre's wife, Marguerite de Valois).[52] Rabelais is Donne's most likely model, however. Both aim at powerful men: in Donne's case these include Robert Cecil, Francis Bacon (enemy of the earl of Essex, with whom Donne sympathized), Richard Topcliffe (an inquisitor of Catholics who kept a rack at home for his convenience), and Bishop William Barlow (preacher of a sermon against Essex that, Donne thought, slavishly said what Robert Cecil told him to say). By now Donne had probably abandoned his Catholicism but not his detestation of informers, torturers, and toadies.

Donne was drawn to nullity as such. For him, Love's "art did expresse / A quintessence even from nothingnesse"; it is "re-begot / Of absence, darknesse, death; things which are not," aware that by pasting maps on a blank sphere cartographers can make its "nothing, All."[53] A note, probably written in July 1604, appended to the Burley manuscript's copy of a verse letter "To Sir H[enry] W[otton] going to Venice," adds (I have brought the superscript letters down to the line): "Sr though pchance it were nevr tryed except in Rabelais his land of tapistry it may bee true yt a pygmey upon a Giant may see further then ye giant so after a long letter this postscript may see further into yo then that if yo will answer to 2 questions whether yo have yr last despatches at court or whether yo make many dayes stay there or at London. such a one as I may yett kisse yr hand."[54] The pygmy peering from atop a giant descends from a comment by Bernard of Chartres, but Donne relocates him to the nowhere country of Satin or Tapestry (*CL* 29–30).

Satinland literally embroiders the (non)facts of nature, its vegetation and animals becoming artifacts. The happy result is that fourteen phoenixes are found here, as are manticores, thirty-two unicorns, the golden fleece, the skin of Apuleius's golden ass, elephants, werewolves, Aristotle, Mid-Lent on horse-back, Triton, and a buttock-shaking beast with two backs. The price of textile living is high: the birds, we read, do not sing. Donne's pygmy-cum-giant is not perfectly suited to Satinland, being more grotesque than never-never, and the experimental note ("tryed") might suit Quintessence's projectors more than this flat world of wonders that the narrator and crew observe but that itself seems not to do or see much of anything. Yet Donne's pleasure in the made-up is evident. "Rabelais his land of tapistry" is not unlike the Library of Saint-Victor, being a collocation of words with few referents in what we call reality. Even the narrator and Pantagruel, *within the text* (itself a fiction) are more real than manticores or an equestrian Mid-Lent. Maybe.

Both Rabelais's and Donne's libraries, then, record bombinations in the void. Indeed Donne has his own Chimera: *Chimaeram praedicari de Antichristo autore Sorbonistâ anonymo* (That Chimera is a prophecy of Antichrist, by a nameless Sorbonnist). He, too, mocks absurd subtleties, inventing for Nicholas Hill, who believed in atoms, a *De sexu et Hermaphroditate dignoscendâ in Atomis* (On determining sex and hermaphroditism in atoms — a topic that seems less foolish in our age of charmed quarks and left-handed molecules). Some titles suggest skepticism, like John Dee's *De navigatibitate aquarum supercoelestium, et utrum ibi an apud nos navis in firmamento in judicio sit appulsura* (On the navigability of the waters above the heavens, and whether on Doomsday a ship in the firmament would dock up there or down here with us). Others, like many at Saint-Victor, are scatological: Cardanus, says Donne, has written *De nullibietate crepitûs* (On a fart's nowhereness), while John Harington has turned his expertise to a biblical question: *Hercules, sive de modo quo evacuabatur à faecibus Arca Noae* (Hercules, or How Noah's Ark was cleansed of its fecal matter). And distaste for occult triviality inspires Pico's *Pythagoras Judaeo-Christianus, Numerum 99 et 66 verso folio esse eundem* (The Judeo-Christian Pythagoras, or How the numbers 99 and 66 are the same if the page is reversed).

Donne is more impatient with Renaissance occultism and Platonic airiness than with late scholasticism — his philosophical butts are Europe's Picos and Dees, not its Bédas. Other differences, too, demonstrate how ironic angles of vision on emptiness and the chimerical can start from different subjectivities and cultural positions. Rabelais was not a courtier when he wrote *Pantagruel,* his context being more professional (and monastic) than the court world that Donne, whatever his distaste and denials, sought. Later, when he had Cardinal Du Bellay and the queen of Navarre as patrons, Rabelais was still more likely to be anti-academic, anti-papal, or antimonastic, than anti-court.

Those who navigate the straits near kings can, of course, laugh at courts, but on the whole Rabelais avoids this particular genre of satire (although Panurge can look like a scruffy courtier and Picrochole has some detestable counselors). Donne addresses elite fops and layabouts: "The mentally lazy think they know enough if they can show credibly that other people's knowledge is imperfect," he says in the preface, but this approach may make you unpopular. At court you will have little leisure for literature, granted how late you get up and how long it takes to arrange your dress, face, gestures. Citing titles that others have not heard of, though, will give the impression that you have read much. "I have therefore jotted down for your use the following catalogue that, with these books at your elbow, you may in almost every branch of knowledge suddenly emerge as an authority, if not with deeper learning than the rest, at least with a learning differing from theirs" (pp. 39–43). Indeed so, for this "difference" ("aliter doctus") derives precisely from naming bits of nothing, gaining authority from access to an infinite universe of possible titles. And if it is true that Donne distrusted print, then his imagining a little library of pageless books that exist only in the zodiac of his own wit is yet more significant. What is the material history of books with names but no bodies?

Yet unlike Rabelais, Donne attaches real authors to all but one of his titles. Citing these books will lend a courtier authority and the books are themselves by authorities. This difference between the two catalogues may register a shift toward authorship's increased emotional, economic, and cultural importance. *Pantagruel*'s seventh chapter, written at first by an anagram, focuses most of its attention on the titles of trivial or foolish texts even while laughing at some flesh-and-blood people. Donne's catalogue, although not printed in his lifetime, assumes a much tighter connection between the silly texts and the silly men who write them. Rabelais mocks a few actual men, like Ortwin, but in prosecuting folly Donne is more apt than Alcofribas to name names.

Francis Bacon, one of Donne's butts, had likewise been reading Rabelais in the early seventeenth century. I have noted how his *Advancement of Learning* (1605) appropriates passages from *Gargantua* on deceptive appearances and allegory. Jocular citations of Rabelais were doubtless common at a court in which the king himself, along with Jonson, Hall, Jones, Carew, Donne, and others knew his work (as did Bacon's friend John Selden, who mentions Saint-

Victor's library in his notes to Drayton's *Poly-Olbion*). It was not until the mid-1620s, though, that the former Lord Chancellor named Rabelais, several times, in printed books. Perhaps he had earlier found "Rabelais" beneath the dignity of his gravely eloquent periods and unsuited to the great work of reforming European thought. Now he felt differently, quoting Rabelais in his collection of apothegms and twice mentioning his collection of nonbooks. These latter citations show traces of self-conscious hesitation. Both simplify Rabelais's irony. Neither shows interest in nonbeing.

Bacon's *De dignitate et augmentis scientarum* (1623) is a Latin expansion of *Advancement*. Book VI, on language, addresses King James (I quote from Gilbert Wats's 1640 translation):

> Certainly any man may assume the liberty (Excellent King) if he be so hu-
> mourd, to jest and laugh himselfe, or his owne Projects. Who then knowes
> whether this worke of ours be not perchance a Transcript out of an Ancient
> Booke found amongst the Books of that famous Library of S. Victor, a Cata-
> logue whereof M[aster] Fra. Rabelais hath collected? For there a Book is
> found entitled Formicarium Artium [The anthill of the arts]; wee have indeed
> accumulated a litle heape of small Dust; and laid up many Graines of Arts and
> Sciences therein, whereto Ants may creepe, and there repose a while, and so
> betake themselves to new labours. (Sigs. Kk1–Kk1v)

In the 1640 edition, but not the 1623, the margin reads "Liv.2. c.7. des faicts et dicts du bon Pantagr."

Like a number of allusions to Rabelais, Bacon's smiling self-deprecation is a bonding gesture: he and James have read the same difficult not-very-respectable book, and although Bacon has fallen from power and been (briefly) impris-oned, he shares a discursive world with his king. The playfulness produces an odd sprezzatura. Presenting *De augmentis* as a hillock of dust is deliciously inappropriate, for this once singularly powerful ant and his hill of philosophy are in truth Gargantuan. Real ants are tiny, collectively organized, and unre-lentingly laborious. Exactly who is doing what in Bacon's pleasantry is unclear. Bacon has made this heap by gathering grains to build a structure in a formic version of the inductive method.[55] Other ants, though, may use it as a rest stop before getting back to work. Expanding human knowledge is toil; creeping into Bacon's great Latin anthill of a book (a suggestive metaphor for the reading process) is repose.

Rabelais's point has meanwhile shifted. His anthill had connoted what is wrong with the *old* methods: busy, not joyful; heaped, not carpentered with number, weight, and measure; petty like Sorbonne theologians, not expansive like Pantagruel; and tunneling down, not looking up — a shrunken parody of the mount of learning on which the seven liberal arts are traditionally posed. Bacon's ants are small enough to serve his self-mockery but still admirable: the next sentence recollects how Solomon (to whom James was sometimes flatteringly compared) enjoined sluggards to learn from them. Rabelais's title is in fact disorienting: Barbara Bowen wonders whether its ants are students or professors and whether the analogy means that they scurry around aimlessly or "heap up and use their store."[56] She does not expect an answer. Bacon's wit is disciplined and disciplinary, urging us to read and then resume labor. Especially in the early 1530s, Rabelais would have shared some of Bacon's hopes for the future of humanity, yet his greatness lies partly in his sympathy for the mind's grasshoppers as well as its ants. In any case, Bacon has signaled to a king he must have hoped would again favor him that he understands the royal wit and, while retired and aging, has stayed valuably busy.

Two years later, in the 1625 version of his essay "Of Unity in Religion," Bacon again mentions the Library of Saint-Victor.[57] What concerns him is how Christians' self-indulgent quarreling encourages scoffing atheists: "It doth avert them from the Church, and maketh them, *To sit downe in the chaire of the Scorners.*" Imagining religious difference as grotesque gesture and movement, Bacon hesitantly cites Rabelais: "It is but a light Thing, to be Vouched in so Serious a Matter, but yet it expresseth well the Deformity. There is a Master of Scoffing; that in his Catalogue of Books, of a faigned Library, sets Downe this Title of a Booke; *The morris daunce of Heretikes.* For indeed, every Sect of them, hath a Divers Posture, or Cringe by themselves, which cannot but Move Derision, in Worldlings, and Depraved Politickes, who are apt to contemne Holy Things."[58] Bizarre stance (literally outlandish — *Morris* means "Moorish") represents mental eccentricity. Doubtless Rabelais was likewise troubled by the vain particularity and multiple imaginings that rend Christ's seamless garment. His "Morisque des Hereticques," though, is darker than Bacon suggests, for his heretics almost certainly dance at the end of a rope, perhaps over a fire (or this is how many Rabelais scholars take the title). Has Bacon missed the ugly point? Perhaps. Rabelais scoffs, if he does scoff, at the spectacle of what power does to dissenters, not just at religious whimsy as such. If he did write the closing chapters of the *Cinquième livre*, after all, he gave the priestess Bacbuc wine that tastes different to different Christian palates. As so often, Rabelais is hard to pin down tonally: a Morris dance is festive, if faintly heathen, but painful for the heretics footing their way to eternity. Bacon's point is simpler: Christians should cease hopping about, doff their estranging mental costumes, and agree on the basics.

Thomas Browne would have liked Bacbuc's wine, for more than Bacon he wanted to live and let live in matters of belief. In *Religio medici* (1635), right after the remark that the fables of "Garagantua" are no more incredible than certain parts of Scripture, he lists religious puzzles that he insists do not test his own faith (but that he is evidently willing to publish). Fussing with them is not worth our time: there are a "bundle" of topics inviting oversubtle prying into mystery, "not only in Philosophy, but in Divinity" that although "proposed and discussed by men of most supposed abilities" are "not worthy our vacant hours, much less our serious Studies. Pieces only fit to be placed in Pantagru-ell's Library, or bound up with Tartaretus *De modo Cacandi* [How to shit]" (p. 30). The margin says "In Rabelais, a french author." Browne sends "curiosity" and logical niceties to languish in comic nonbeing.

Like Rabelais, he somatizes that nonbeing: scholastic pickiness is both irrel-evant and excremental, for "Tartaretus" suggests Tateret, a real theologian and commentator on Aristotle with a name all too like *tarter*, slang for visiting the privy. The book's title implies what academics and philosophers really pro-duce — the printing house is the outhouse. Even imaginary shit is ambiguous, though, because scatology brings abstractions down to earth (compare Swift's more-than-Rabelaisian *Gulliver's Travels*). As the "curious" scribble away they extrude mere excrement, yet in fact they should keep such fundamental matter in mind, rectifying their sense of the embodied human condition. Poor Tartaretus/Tateret/Tartarus is not content to do what comes naturally. Nei-ther can those who are too proud to trust Scripture, whatever its occasional Gargantuan absurdities. In a happy pun the ambiguity extends to Browne's phrasing, for the problems he "places" in Rabelais's library are "bound up" with a book on defecation: such texts are both dung and constipation.[59]

At some point Browne made his own fantasy library, lodging it in his imag-ined *Musaeum Clausum* near such curiosa as extract of cuttlefish-ink (a cure for hysteria) and a picture of Oedipus hearing what he had done to his par-ents.[60] *Musaeum* is less satirical than Rabelais's library, more nostalgic, a fancied balm for scholarly pain at what time and chance have done to history's record. It houses, for example, "A punctual relation of Hannibal's march out of Spain into Italy, and far more particular than that of Livy, where about he passed the River Rhodanus . . . what Vinegar he used, and where he obtained such quantity to break and calcine the Rocks made hot with fire"; a commen-tary on Hanno the Carthaginian's account of his trip along the African coast; Seneca's letters to Saint Paul; and "A Commentary of Galen upon the Plague of Athens described by Thucydides." The titles are lost or fictitious but they were or might have been real, and Browne's deeper fantasy is that what should have been, or once was, in fact is or might be. Rabelais finds many ways to package absurdity and nothingness; Browne imagines repairing absence and loss, pulling buzzing Chimera back to safety from her vacuum. Logocentric metaphysicians and Petrarchan lovers are not alone in aching for presence. Graphocentric bibliophiles want it too.

Marginal Fantasies: John Selden's Rabelais

As an antiquary, John Selden longed to turn absence to presence: to restore, through research and logic, data buried by Time or mislaid by ignorance.[61] I have already explored his allusions to Rabelais on excremental glosses, Bridoye-like style, and the word for penis, evidence that he read *Gargantua et Pantagruel* attentively, doubtless welcoming its exasperated and amused skepticism toward legend masquerading as history. Yet the uses to which he put that skepticism show an ambivalence concerning the fancy, an ambivalence the two writers also shared. Both found medieval legend risible; both enjoyed perpetuating it. Rabelais wrote books with preposterous fictions; Selden cited some of those and other fictions when annotating the first eighteen books of his friend Drayton's *Poly-Olbion,* published — together with these annotations — in 1612.

Whatever the sense of history developed in the Middle Ages, it seems likely that intellectuals in the Renaissance put increased distance between historical narrative and invented tale.[62] In this development Selden played a role, training himself and others (such as Bacon) to examine sources, compare authorities, calculate chronology, sniff out anachronism, and study coins, inscriptions, statuary — anything that might, as William Camden said, "renew ancientrie, enlighten obscurity, clear doubts, and recall home Verity by way of recovery."[63] When Drayton asked the young Selden to "illustrate" his poem, he must have known that his friend would treat skeptically the legends in this epic "Chorographicall" work.

The preface by Selden, for example, supports yet undermines his friend's enterprise. Drayton's own preface complains that nowadays verse is "deduc't to Chambers" and that the "Idle Humerous world" rejects whatever "savors of Antiquity." Women may find his poem difficult, he adds irritatingly, and others would rather read foreign "fantasies" than the "Historie of their owne Country delivered by a true native Muse." Those indifferent to "ancient and noble things" prefer foggy ignorance to the "Feelds of the Muses" where harmonious birds lead you up "an easy hill" from which you may then make "a soule-pleasing Descent" to see nymphs bathing "in their simple naked bewties" and hear "harmlesse Shepheards" piping. Selden's chatty preface undercuts these claims. Drayton imagines his nymphs unclad, but Selden knows that even a chorographical poem dresses truth in figures. His own landscape has no hills; indeed, with what may be a pun he says, "my worke here [is] to adde plaine song after Muses descanting" (p. xi). Yet he knows that the Muses are themselves a fancy and he can employ metaphor: "My thirst compeld me alwayes seeke the Fountaines" (referring to evidence).[64]

In his "illustrations," Selden provides a study in civilized ambivalence: carefully separating fact from fable, he welcomes both, adding new fictions for recreation and insight. His method includes an ironic indulgence that accepts a poet's licensed fancy while keeping it in its place. Although there can be no tolerance for "grosse absurdities in our Chronologies" (p. 93), Drayton and the reader may fantasize because, after all, this is poetry. Meanwhile, Selden shows how to write good history: the key is chronology, for in Selden's annotations we see emerging from the chaos of chronicle what can be called a time-line. Although Selden was not the first to hang nice, clean facts out to dry on such a line, stringing up the one we still use was the work of the later Renaissance.[65] "Synchronisme," says Selden, is "the best Touch-stone" (p. viii), and chronology "the most excellent note to examine truth of historie by" (p. 166).

Selden's suspicion of the "Chaos of Mythique inventions" (p. 16) does not lead him to expel fictions from his commentary, for even as he helps us through Drayton's fable-voicing landscape he relays tales — often inviting us to laugh at them — and quotes poems like "that Fiction of the Muses best pupil, the noble Spenser" (p. 210). Sometimes he cites Rabelais, for it is the down-to-earth antiquary, not Drayton's flying muse, who most enjoys such fictions. There is, moreover, a coherent subtext just beneath Selden's references, for most concern fantasy, and several of these in turn suggest that the fictions in question touched his feelings about the past and the netherworld — that realm where much of the past now lies.

Selden laughs at the "deduction of our British Monarchy" from Brute and the legend that Caesar built Arthur's Seat in Edinburgh, such fancies by "wanton Poets" being as "warrantable" as "Ariosto's . . . *Rowlands*, Spensers Elfin Story, or Rablais his strange discoveries" (p. ix). This is dismissive, but Selden also gives these tales from British dreamtime company that he admires. "As warrantable," after all, means just that. The danger is in mixing categories, in thinking that Brute belongs in history as well as in *The Faerie Queene*. Yet here, at the start of his effort to comb out Drayton's "winding" fictions (as he calls them in his preface), Selden evokes other winding stories, separating them from his own beliefs but including them in his field of vision. A little later (p. xiii) his target is changed but his effect the same: the purblind ignorant, he says, have their "best learning" "purchast from such Volumes as Rablais reckons in S. Victors Library" and are "furnisht in our old story" only by "Compilers" like Higden, Caxton, Stowe, Grafton, or Holinshed. A heap of un-methodical chronicle is juxtaposed to nonbooks, scholastic nonsense of the sort Selden and Rabelais both found ridiculous. Bad scholarship is pedantic and unreal—but also the object of inventive and proliferating laughter. Sharing Rabelais's humor, Selden knows the utility of a nonlibrary to which he can return books he rejects and from which he can check them out again when he has a mind.

More resonant is a comment on lines concerning what Selden calls "Fabulous Jupiters ill dealing with his Father Saturne, . . . deposing him, and his privities cut off" (p. 16). The story that Saturn, castrator of his father Sky, underwent an orchidectomy himself is seldom found in classical art or Renaissance mythography, perhaps because, allegorically speaking, to unsex Father Time suggests a temporal closure that is obviously yet to come.[66] Making Jupiter's usurpation more exactly parallel to Saturn's is fine political irony, though, especially if one is interested in the constitutional relevance of past conquests to the political claims of Britain's latest dynasty. Selden denies that Saturn's island prison may be located in "Thuly," north of Scotland: "Neyther Geography (for I ghesse not where or what this Isle should be, unlesse that *des Macraeons* which Pantagruell discovered [see *QL* 25]) nor the matter-self permits it lesse Poeticall . . . then the Elysian fields, which, with this, are alwayes laide by Homer about the [utmost ends of the earth]; a place whereof too large liberty was given to faine, because of the difficult possibility in finding the truth." Why remember the Macréons? Selden means us to smile skeptically, of course, but he also teasingly pretends to think that Pantagruel, not Rabelais (whose name he cites in the margin), discovered them; he thus resituates author and story. "Macraeons" then invites mention of Elysium, fabled land of desire where the illustrious meet in tranquil greenery, free (if we may trust Virgil) from distinctions of fact and fiction and free also from anachronism and the ruins of time. This is what history is *not,* yet Selden makes sure our minds rest for a moment in those deep fields.

Any reader who took up the implied invitation to look at Rabelais would find that the Macréons (the name means long-lived) inhabit an island where Pantagruel and his companions find repose after a tempest that Renaissance readers probably associated with the winds of Fortune and the troubles of the Counter-Reformation: with history, in other words. Nearby, in a dark forest, the travelers are told, are ruined temples, obelisks, and pyramids with inscriptions and epitaphs in hieroglyphs and other ancient languages. The news inspires Panurge to some disgraceful connections between *Macréon* and *maquerelle* [bawd], but Pantagruel learns that this island is home to shades of dead heroes. This in turn generates talk about the deaths of the great and then a story of Pan's death that makes the giant, reading allegorically and poetically, cry tears as big as ostrich eggs when he remembers the dying Christ. No wonder the episode struck Selden: the physical disappearance but imaginary persistence of heroes and the cessation of oracles (on which the legend of Pan's death touches) are good food for antiquarian thought; and, he might have thought wryly, Macréon antiquities would keep him busy for years. So he sends us to a fictional version of his own undertaking, a place of ancient epitaphs, monuments, and learned dialogue, where the shades still walk, perhaps available for conversation, amid inscriptions that are at least partially decipherable by the learned. Macréon Island, as unreal but also as real as the island of wounded and deposed Father Time, is Selden's own paradise, ideal analogue of his own enterprise; it is where good antiquarianism goes when it dies, where history and Time might even be cured and story verified through decoding strange letters and interviewing the famous.

Under- and otherworldly thoughts continued to haunt him. Drayton writes of Gaulish customs like round tables or the separation of the genders at Pentecost, a practice his singing nymphs claim derives from Trojan ritual. Selden will have none of this (p. 89). Some texts list Arthur's knights, he says, in a passage I have quoted in another context. But they do so with as much justification as Rabelais's description of Lancelot in Hell. He then quotes, in French, Epistemon's report on what he had seen while dead: Arthurian knights playing infernal ferrymen for the devils' recreation, earning for each crossing only "a fillip on the nose and a peece of mouldy bread" (*P* 30; Selden's margin summarizes the passage in English). Find out about these knights in Caxton (that is, Malory), he adds, for "From such I abstaine." Rabelais has been summoned to help subvert Camelot, yet the subversion is set in those same Elysian Fields recently associated with Saturn and the Macréons, a postmortem world where one can glimpse those whom Time has taken — again, a semi-parodic version of the antiquarian undertaking that both sends up Drayton's stories and, poignantly, suggests Epistemon's good fortune in going all the way down, below tombs and inscriptions, below buried coins and statuary, to where the dead great live on, if only in caricature.

Selden's next citation of Rabelais comes in an entertaining account I have likewise mentioned earlier: a husband feeds his wife a magic ram's shoulder to trick her into revealing any infidelities she may have committed. After duly noting the tale's implausibility, Selden suggests that because this method also helps predict the future, its use might have calmed Panurge's fears (109). It would also, of course, enable an antiquary to test the faithfulness of historians and chroniclers.[67] Later, in his notes to Drayton's ninth song and its mention of "The fearles British Priests under an aged Oake," Selden again remembers

Rabelais, if briefly, saying that in France "the yonger country fellowes, about New-yeares tide in every Village give the wish of good fortune at the Inhabitants dores, with this acclamation, *Au guy l'an neuf;* which, as I remember, in Rablais is read all one word, for the same purpose." This means, as the margin says, "To the Mistle, this new yeare" (p. 195).[68] Selden works this into a discussion of the Celtic god Belenos's similarity to Apollo. But he also mentions that some say mistletoe was the golden bough that "Sibyll counsell'd Aeneas to carrie with him to Proserpine" (p. 195). Once more Rabelais appears, this time with Virgil, in the context of a descent to knowledge of the past and future. What Aeneas learns thanks to his mistletoe includes bitter news; but he emerges better informed about history, even if he leaves by the gate of false dreams. Selden might have reflected that such a golden passport would serve the turn of antiquaries as well.

Selden has only one more reference to Rabelais in the "illustrations," perhaps because the British material he found so deliciously silly soon diminishes. A note on Song XI scoffs at late medieval monks' "dissembled bestiall sensualities" (when not "Sodomites," they were fathering bastards) and ignorance: "for Hebrew or Greeke . . . they understood not, and had at least (as many of our now professing Formalists [Puritans?] Latine enough to make such a speech as Rablais hath to Gargantua for Paris Bels" (p. 240; see *G* 19, the parody of university jargon). Rabelais takes a final turn as an anti-scholastic fiction maker on the margins of history. There remains, however, one less friendly citation. In the index under "Clarence" (Richard III's murdered brother), Selden cites a rumor that the duke freely chose to be drowned in a butt of malmsey wine. This, he says, is "shamefully laid on" him by Francis Matenesi, "a Divine, and professor of Story and Greeke in Cologne," and "is also slanderously reported among Rablais his tales [*QL* 33]. But it worst of all becomes a profest Historian as Matenesi is" (p. 583). Imagining the Macréons is a fantasy one can half pretend to join, but telling tales about a real English duke is slander, and telling tales when one professes to be a historian is intolerable.

The slanderous report is Panurge's, not Rabelais's. Whether the latter believed it or simply changed the story to suit his trickster, the context of what Selden remembers once more extends the subtext to which I have referred. Panurge's envious invocation of Clarence and his end comes as he sees the terrible, water-spouting whale that he takes to be Leviathan coming to swallow him into its "Hellish jaws"—a fall *in* and *down,* not to the Elysian Fields, not even to Macréon Island or Saturn's Thule, but into their negation, an engulfing and presumably illegible darkness. The whale's ancestor in Lucian's *True History* carried inside him enough men and creatures to give any historian plenty of material, but this monster is an antiquary's nightmare.

Pantagruel, more at ease with other worlds (he contains one) and with time (*he* shows no fear of the marriage process) has no trouble making the whale go belly up, spouting its last, one assumes, into the salty depth that so terrified Panurge. A thought-provoking moment in Rabelais's tales, and one that Selden may have remembered for more than the annoying laughter that further subverted the dignity of an English duke.

Selden's notes are thus ambiguously related to the growing rift between fiction and history. Bent on distinguishing fact from legend, he entangles us in story and poetry because he finds them amusing and because they express what "history" cannot: longings and hesitations about his own project that are difficult to articulate directly. He might have noticed, too, that Drayton's assemblage of topomachic rivalries paralleled his own research as he tried to make constitutional history out of the transitions from British to Roman to Saxon to Norman rule. His equivalent for Drayton's babbling brooks and rumbling mountains is the multiplication of sources, arguments, citations, doubts, and the importation of other voices into his personal and even egocentric discourse. His "illustrations" bring resonance and ambiguity along with clarification.

This is praise, for it is no longer evident that a single timeline is the one true way to arrange events, just as vanishing-point perspective now seems less a step forward to accurate representation than one valuable way to indicate perception. Selden's sense of the slipperiness of data and his multiplication of conflicting versions of events make his illustrations too fat and unkempt to squeeze into a linear system, no matter what his methods elsewhere. It is easy to understand why he enjoyed the polyvocal and elusive Rabelais. As he must have sensed, *Poly-Olbion*'s refusal to stick to one story or one point of view allows him to buy into history on margin while working out his version of how Britain developed a polyolbioned set of traditions and practices too complex and multi-rooted for one king's will to reshape. Selden was fortunate in his liminality: on the edges of Drayton's poem it is *he* who has liberty.

Family Trees in the Wood of Error

One way fathers can evade earthly mortality, Gargantua advises his son in the eighth chapter of *Pantagruel,* is to beget offspring who extend the paternal name and being (the giant's deceased wife, Badebec, must presumably make do with her reward in giant Heaven).[69] Until recently, patrilinear descent was more a matter of faith than knowledge, and thus of nervous laughter. Yet the possibility of self-delusion in male self-perpetuation can be only one reason for Renaissance England's interest in genealogy. Aside from the resonant fact of lineage itself—the string of progenitors stretching into what one father, Prospero, calls "the dark backward and abysm of time"—genealogy has a practical meaning for the transfer of property and power and a cultural meaning that is not exhausted by concern for identity, wealth, honor, or influence. Such meaning is elusive, although it must involve sources and origins, whether of genres, sin, titles of nobility, the true church, dynasties, or words, and identity's relation to the deforming and unforming difference—indeed, *différance*—that time makes.[70] Time will of course consume the father as it eats its way along the generations. It has even been argued that when Rabelais's Grandgousier says to his newborn, "que grand tu as!" (How big you have!] he is gazing, not without consternation, on genital evidence of genealogy's dark side: generational supplantation.[71]

No matter what the increased mobility of early modern society, social ascent was enabled by claims to noble descent; if one's ancestors were in sober fact titled and important, so much the better. Boasting of such forebears could, however, be greeted by others with irony, irritation, or amused disbelief. And what better symbol of inflated family pride than a giant, especially if the genealogical claims lack substance? Processional giants were notorious for being empty or merely stuffed. As fathers' fathers are traced further back into the past they, too, grow into something huge yet suspect. Because giants are large like parents but also infantile, liminal indixes of both the archaic and the new, they are appealing (if threatening) as ancient yet novel forefathers. Their antiquity makes them hard to disprove even as one may guess that they are also, like many genealogies, pure fantasy. Gargantua makes a good pseudo-ancestor, and his son Pantagruel had the further advantage—as far as most readers probably knew—of being a deliberate and recent invention.

It can be hard to tell if mentions of Gargantua recall Rabelais's genealogical comedy or the chapbook orphan; in either case, the pride and folly of glancing arrogantly back along a human timeline would be similar. Two allusions to Gargantua also complicate gender and tangle the temporal lines. One is in Thomas Randolph's *The Jealous Lovers* (printed 1632), in a comment on the "Gargantuan" style the author elsewhere found funny or grating. A young woman asks Asotus, a wastrel whose name is Greek for "dissolute" and almost English for "a sot," how he would answer insults to his beloved. His reply imagines the offence being given not by some crude male but by the lady to whom he speaks:

> Madam, were you made
> From bones of Hercules and brawn of Atlas,
> And daughter were unto Gargantua great,

> And wrong my mistress, you should hear my rage
> Provoke my blade, and cry *Blade, canst thou sleep*
> *In peaceful scabbard? Out, thou beast of terror!*
> *And, lion-like, roar this disdainful wight*
> *to Pluto's shades and ghosts of Erebus!*[72]

In this odd exchange, *she* is Gargantua's brawny daughter and *he* talks giantese. Whichever giant Asotus envisions, one cannot imagine any history in which Gargantua's daughter could be made of Hercules and Atlas, dead long before Gar[a]gantua's parents were forged of whalebone and before Rabelais's Grandgousier — himself descended from Hercules and Atlas — conceived his son.

It was widely believed that family pride particularly characterized the Spanish and that such pride was largely bluster. The Spanish had come down in the world since the previous century, which may be why giant and pygmy combine with such strange synchrony in William Habington's comedy *The Queene of Arragon* (1640). Here we meet Brumsilldora, a dwarf with the nickname Gargantua. Asked about his family, he replies,

> My Ancestors were Giants, Madam. Giants
> Pure Spanish, who disdain'd to mingle with
> The blood of Goth or Moore. Their mighty actions
> In a small letter Nature Printed on
> Your little Servant. (I.i)

Because Spain, home of the giant Geryon, had likewise been "tumid and swelling" in the days of that great Armada (which was often compared to a giant), and because its people shared the Flemish taste for huge processional figures, it is not surprising to find a Spanish giant, although it is startling to find one who is so short. Why so small? "By the decay of Time," he says, and the effect of the "barren hills / Of Biskay." His name preserves his forebears' memory: "They shall live / In me contracted." Tiny Gargantua is his own *concordia discors*, reconciling dwarf and giant through *descent* in every sense and, furthermore, expressing this condition in terms that recall the age's images and techniques of contraction (he is a living box where ancestors lie compacted, a miniature book of the sort popular with curiosity collectors, a text written in nature's equivalent of the shorthand invented not many decades earlier).[73] His words also evoke the sometimes obscure connections between giants and the abyss of time that take us back to Gargantua's possible folklore origins.

Family trees receive another blow in John Ford's *The Ladies Trial* (1639), a play that mocks the feudal pride of one rival to England's power(Spain) and the fat smugness of another (Holland). In English stereotypes, the feudal Spaniards glory absurdly in their noble ancestors, and the bourgeois Dutch have no ancestors worth boasting about. Pretty young Amoretta, lisping and "fantastick" heroine of Ford's subplot, will marry only a nobleman. With her father's permission, two young lords scheme to jest her back down to earth. They persuade a "Bragadotio Spaniard" to court her "under pretence of being / Grandee of Spain, and cousin to twelve princes"; and, as his rival, a "rich coxcombe" will present himself as a hero of "the late Flemish wars." The latter will say

> He is descended from Pantagruel,
> Of famous memory by his fathers side,
> And by the mother from Dame Fusti-Bunga,
> Who troubled long time with a strangury,
> Vented at last salt-water so abundantly,
> As drownd the land twixt Sirixia and Vere,
> Where steeples tops are onely seen: hee casts
> Beyond the Moone, and will be greater yet
> In spight of Don [that is, the Spaniard].[74]

Each pseudowooer has fancy forebears. The don, with blood as "rich and haughty, / As any the twelve Caesars," has a ducal "discent" that will "crowne" him as his rival's "superior," while the fake Flemish hero derives his "pedigree" from King Oberon, "courageious Mounti-banco," and Harlequin. His grandfather was Count "Hans van Herne," he says, "the son / Of Hogen Mogen" [pig-Dutch for "high and mighty"], who cut the throats "Of veirteen hundred Spaniards in one neict." When the Spaniard exclaims "Oh Diabolo" he replies,

> Ten thousand Divels, nor Diabolos
> Shall fright me from my pedigree, my uncle
> Yacob van Flagon drought, with Abraham Snorten fert
> And yongster Brogen foh with fourscore hargubush,
> Manag'd by well-lin'd Butter-boxes, tooke
> A thousand Spanish Jobber-nowles by surprise. (II.845–46; IV.1967–2012)

This is the company Pantagruel keeps on the Dutchman's side. The abashed Amoretta eventually submits to her father and is congratulated on her prudent humility, but meanwhile pedigrees themselves have come to look frayed. Some are fictional at best, and as one character remarks, many children inherit lands owned by fathers "who peradventure never begot them: my mothers husband was a very old man at my birth, but no man is too old to father his wife's childe" (III.1615–18). Exactly—which renders problematic Gargantua's moving hopes for earthly immortality.

The impulse to locate ancestors was not just a social or political matter in early modern England; it had significance for tracing true doctrine's lineage.

This may be why Sir Edward Hoby thinks of Pantagruel when he is defining religious arrogance. Hoby was a gentleman, one whose contempt for the sale of ancestors may derive as much from armigerous snobbery as from distaste for pride, although he touches upon problems more complex than mere greed for undeserved gentility. His *Curry-Comb for a Coxe-Combe: Or, Purgatories Knell* (1615), as the title page indicates, answers *Purgatories Triumph over Hell, Maugre the Barking of Cerberus in Syr. E. Hobyes Counter-Snarle* (St. Omer, 1613). In fact written by the prolific Catholic polemicist John Floyd, this work is signed "I.R.," which Hoby pretends stands for "Jabel Rachil": *rachil* is Hebrew for spy or slanderer, while Jabal is the "father of suche as dwel in the tentes, and of suche as have cattel" (Gen. 4:20). Pantagruel appears in a liminary poem by Anthony Tonstall: this Jabal must be "kin to Nabal or Pantagruel. / Nabal and Jabal differ but a letter, / Nabal a foole, this Jabal little better." Nabal's name does mean "fool," but he was also a mocker (1 Sam. 25). A "mighty" man (it may be relevant that "mighty man" is an alternative to "giant" in some translations), "churlish," and given to drink, Nabal rails at David's men when they ask for help. He typifies, says the Geneva Bible's margin, "covetous wretches" who "in stede of releving the necessitie of Gods children, use to revile their personnes and condemne their cause."

Pairing Pantagruel with such a man is a sad way to read Rabelais, but Hoby's own allusion is more genial. Assuming a tone of easy humor toward Floyd's "Hob[b]yhorse" puns, he makes his own horse jokes. He invents a groom, Nick, a "merrie grigge" who learned his Latin from Oxford students. When a minister warns that heretics sometimes try to give their beliefs a specious ancient authority, talk turns to antiquity and ancestors (sig. D2). Some, says one "Major," try to be older than the moon lest they appear no gentlemen; if Christ himself had established monasticism they would reject it as the work of someone from "an upstart family." Nick replies ironically: "Were I a rich man it should cost me an hundred pound twice told, but I would have Saturne or Priamus to stand on the top of my line. I would not sticke to alter two or three letters of my name, to make my selfe of kinne to Pantagruel."[75]

The mention of Pantagruel, even more than that of Saturn (considered a historical personnage by euhemerists), ties the fantasies propelling heresy to those behind the Jacobean sale of ancestors. Social climbing and religious novelty each issue from a risky part of the brain. To make his genealogical fiction believable, moreover, Nick would need to modify his name, rupturing the patrilinear descent of name and body that genealogy was intended to sustain. Hoby distrusts modern social fantasy; like Donne in Satire III, he prefers beliefs that trace back through real fathers to a Son who is one with the

Father. As he laughs at the sale of forebears, Nick's allusion to Pantagruel also undercuts the Trojan mythology that political fiction still maintained. Unlike Tonstall's association of Pantagruel with Nabal, though, the reference is benign: Rabelais, too, had preferred authentically ancient faith and found more recent legends funny.

One J. Ap-Robert's *The Younger Brother His Apology* (Oxford, 1624) summons Rabelais's giants when denouncing primogeniture and asserting a father's right to divide his estate as he pleases. This seems a straightforward effort to transfer more legal power over sons to the male head of a household. The cultural dynamics are complex, though, for while the English eldest-take-all rule could impoverish younger sons, it also preserved the integrity of a family's wealth. But what if the eldest is a riotous scoundrel? Do not equity and reason justify disinheriting him? Not even "anthropophages" eat their relatives, yet such a son consumes his parents while supporting "by Force or Fraud, a damned Crew of Roring Divels in the shapes of Men":

> Tali Bacchus erat, tali Gargantua vultu;
> > Tale triplex mentum Pantagruelis erat.
> So did old Bacchus, or Gargantua swell;
> And such a Bull-chin was Pantagruell.
> And of the whole Mad-cap-Fraternity (for such they will needs be Sworne Brothers)
> Pestis, quâ gelidum Boreae violentius Axem
> > Nulla vel infecit, nulla vel inficiet:
> A greater Plague to this our Northerne Clime
> Never yet came; nor can, in After-Time. (Sig. H4v)

The margin identifies Pantagruel as "of the Family of the Treble-chins" and the madcap fraternity as "Fratres in male: or fraterrimi (as was said of Friers)."[76] Ap-Robert cites neither giant as an ancestor. Each, rather, represents a swelling superfluity that diminishes a family. The image is not that of a father and son but of brothers ("fratres in male," monkish "fraterrimi") ingesting a friend's patrimony, threatening patrilinear continuity through a disorder instigated by the very sons who should perpetuate that continuity.

Ap-Robert is a shadowy figure, but because his book was first published in St. Omer (1618; this edition had no allusion to Rabelais), it seems likely that he was Catholic. His interest in paternal authority, patrimony, and the relative position of sons is not detachable from other questions: Must we believe that, as Donne put it, "Truth a little elder is"? Recalling how Jacob assumed the rights of his brother, Esau, Calvinists liked to claim those of firstborn sons to an authentic but narrow Israelite lineage, relegating papists and others to illegitimacy and disinheritance.[77] Yet "papists" could argue for post-biblical revelation and the legitimacy of an unfolding religious heritage. And if a political heir is less suitable than some claimant from a younger line? England's recent political history raised a host of questions about royal birthrights. At the start of Spenser's *Mutabilitie Cantos,* Mutabilitie recalls how Titan was overthrown by his younger brother Saturn, and then saw rule pass to his nephew Jove. Even heavenly inheritance can move slantwise. Ap-Robert need not have had these precise thoughts for his claims to emit such religious or political overtones — and Rabelais's giants often appear at just such moments of cultural disharmony.

Might Rabelais's texts, as texts, serve a genealogical metaphor? William Crashaw, a Protestant divine who did not live to see his son Richard become a Catholic poet, was as eager to sort out genuine from bastard books as others were to tell true family trees from woods of error. Attacking "Romish Forgeries," his *Falsificationum Romanorum* (1606) argues that greed and ambition have led the pope to appropriate books belonging to the true, invisible Church and to falsify others. Catholics say reformers have sabotaged texts, but it is popes who impede truth's temporal descent by trying "to corrupt the writings, and raze the records of the world." Nor will papists let people read good books, "but you must first have them ripped and ransacked, cut up and carved, tossed and translated, maymed and mangled as shall please the humors of two or three Jesuits or dominicke Friars." Catholics will take your fathers' books, left to you as his heir or executor, and give them to friars, who thus "use your owne goods." Yes, some books deserve rough treatment: had Catholics "forbidden or purged Machiavel, Rabelesse, Peter Aretine, and such like and no more, I should have given them the hand of fellowship, but when they prohibite holy and auncient Writers . . . I must needs draw backe the hand of fellowship, and cast them the gantlet of defiance" (sigs. ¶1, B1v, H1–H1v). Some Catholic authorities had indeed tried to "purge" out Rabelais. Does Crashaw know this? Perhaps he remembers Calvin on how Rabelais was protected by Cardinal Du Bellay, or perhaps he knows that many Catholics enjoyed *Gargantua et Pantagruel.* He certainly assumes that his readers know what there is in the work that halts his fancied handshake with fellow censors and purgers.

William Vaughan and the Limb of Leviathan

Precisely because lineage stretches back through a mist of years, its politics intersect with lies and delusion. Lies were much on the mind of one Welsh gentleman, William Vaughan, after his wife was struck down by lightning and the neighbors, concluding that she must have been up to no good, wagged their tongues. A report even circulated that the devil had made off with part of her body. The widower responded with a long tract on slander: *The Spirit of Detraction Conjured* (1611).[78] Helping this "spirit" is pride, not least pride of family. A section on magistrates (sigs. Vv2–Vv2v) declares that true gentlemen will defend their country in wartime, not try to link themselves genealogically to Lancelot. Boasters claim descent from "Demigorgons, I would say Demigods," but "When Adam delv'd and Eve span, / Who was then the Gentleman?" False gentlemen are the "swaggering Libertines" whom a "Braggadochian Cavaleere" of a demon prods to brag that "their lips are their own" to use as they please in wounding others (from Psalm 12, commonly read as condemning slanderous braggarts at Saul's court). Courtiers or would-be courtiers, says Vaughan, glory in their "greazie Gentry" when carousing "amidst their Tobachanales," calling themselves "true Trojanes, true Gentlemen, lineally descended without disparagement from great Garagantua, whose olde Auncestour (as that Lucian of France scoffing Rabelais reported) was the first that ever plaied at Dice with spectacles on his nose."

"Garagantua" recalls the chapbook, but Vaughan names Rabelais and remembers *Pantagruel*. This "Auncestour" is "Morguan," adopted for Pangatruel's lineage from Pulci's *Morgante maggiore* (1483); as Vaughan says, he was the first to play dice while wearing "bezicles" (*P* 1). Even readers unacquainted with him would see the relevance to courtiers of his taste for dice and would reflect that no ancestor with eyeglasses could be *very* ancient. Vaughan found him funny, but does the mention of Lucian and scoffing make Rabelais another atheist detractor? Perhaps Vaughan shared the hunch of some later critics that the chapter satirizes biblical genealogies, yet he seems to hear in it more mockery than blasphemy.[79]

No writer who invents the word *tobachanales* lacks wit. Vaughan's thoughts on fantasy, though, were mixed. Born in 1577 to a prominent family (his brother became earl of Carbery and he himself was knighted), he attended Oxford, traveled, and developed opinions on nearly everything. He soon began writing poetry, publishing Latin verses when he was twenty. Later, in praising the Newfoundland colony he started in 1617, he named himself Orpheus Junior, after the poet who sang Jason's fleece-seeking Argonauts across the Black Sea to Colchis. He called his settlement Cambriol in honor of Wales and put his impress on the land with such names as Vaughan's Cove and Golden Grove (for his family's Welsh estate). Although the venture failed, he retained his hopes for Newfoundland, publishing most of his propaganda on its behalf after the colony was reorganized in 1619.

For Orpheus Junior, one of Newfoundland's attractions is its materiality. It shimmers with distance, wealth, and novelty, but unlike papist fables, Utopia, gossip, Pantagruel, and tobacco smoke, it is real. As early as his *Golden Grove* (1600, a set of essays on this and that), Vaughan had shown this not uncommon bias against the fantastic: he is careful when citing Thomas More to refer to the "faigned Utopians," in one case adding, "But I leave the Utopians to their nullibies [nowheres]" (sigs. P1, X7).[80] And, of course, he assumes that "stageplaies are nothing els, but pompes and showes" (sig. K1). In *The Golden Fleece*, the last part of which is devoted to Newfoundland, the author's distrust of fantasy persists. Newfoundland is material: "This no Eutopia is, nor Common-wealth / Which Plato faign'd," he writes to the king, adding in Latin that he offers the king nothing beyond the material (sig. a2v–a3). This is not merely reassurance to potential colonizers. Solidity mattered to Vaughan, which is why Orpheus Junior sings a paradoxical myth of Canadian substantiality. New Colchis, even if the gold from its fish and woods is still unrealized, is realer than fancy-plagued Britain.

No wonder, then, that *Detraction* fears the wit's capacity to dream, invent, babble, lie, and desire the unreal. Amused by *Pantagruel* and happy, as I have shown, to quote Rabelais approvingly on Bennett's Boot and greedy doctors, Vaughan seems also to have found cause for alarm. His Pantagruel is another of impiety's fabulations — feigned, feigning, and Satanic. *Detraction*'s peroration therefore both uses and parodies the language of exorcism against a creature sprung from Leviathan (devil and sea-monster) in what may be an inadvertent recollection of the giant's family connection with whales and his double role as swallower and monster-queller:

> Ascend then yee spirits of ever-darkning night, advance your selves on high, yee spightfull spirits of Contradiction, extend your stings, intend your Circles, and convict your fellow spirits, if yee can. . . . At the least, presume not to take in hand this important taske, to confound this powerfull Pantagruell, the limme of that mighty Leviathan, least your winged members (as Sathans subjects) doe contrarie one another, and so divided through civill discord they occasion the finall subversion of your whole dominion. One graine of Faith prevailes more then a masse of Masses, then millions of Ceremonies, of mens Inventions, for the convicting of Spirituall Monsters.
>
> Goe thy way then O detracting spirit, notwithstanding all these stings, tuskes, clawes, contradictions, carpings, calumniations, and cavillations of savage people, of Aristarches, of Catoes, of Momistes, of Monsters, and Usurpers; goe thy way, (I say) convicted, I adjure and conjure thee in the name of the Father, of the Sonne, and of the Holy Ghost. (Sig. Zz1v)[81]

Like Zeus, Vaughan hurls giants and monsters to Tartarus.

He does so because he associates Rabelais with the evil gossipers who afflict him. For hundreds of pages he has denounced the "Giant-like" detractors who "reare up mounts against the Heavens, re edifying proud Babels Towre" (preface), the "pratling Momes, and tatling Niobes" who indulge in "carousing, and Tobacconizing" while the spirit of detraction sneaks into them and overthrows "mans little world." Why are Brute's descendants so brutish? When in their cups, they vent opinions on God's secret judgments. Then, their "store of discourse" exhausted, they get "drunken" on smoke and "after long houghing, halking and hacking" recount "tales of Robin-hood" (sigs. A1–A3). A related danger is a "curiosity" pressing beyond God's "non ultra" and into his "unrevealed essence" (sigs. C4v–D1). Another is belief in "phantasticall spirits," for no devil can truly "appeare in outward formes of illusion" (sigs. H4–I2v). The printing press has given the devil a new modus operandi as he teaches youth to "detract, to lash out fearful othes at ever other word, to reade baudy ballads, books of his own Apostles, even of Aretine, of Machiavell, of Rabelais, and of our English cast-awayes. . . . The best of us sometimes hee possesseth, with Chymerizing ploddings, like ayrie castles, and nibbles (as a Mouse) on our malignant hearts" (sig. I3v). Rabelais once more keeps the bad company he often found in England: Machiavelli and Aretino. And, by proximity, he is linked to imaginative fabrication. Why does Chimera-making suggest a rodent nipping the heart? Because the airy castles are the objects of impotent desire? Vaughan evokes the pain of longing even as he affirms the unreality of its object.

Satan also stimulates the prying to which the "busie-headed French" are given. When in France the amazed Vaughan heard them "scot-free revile and raile at their chiefe Magistrates, with talkative Curiosity, scanning their honest deedes. From whom, even as we borrow new-fangled dresses, and courtly complements, so doe we (like curious Apes) receive their poysonous Adder of Detraction" (sigs. M2–N1). Even in England, detractors spread political news, as though Britain were a "petulent Democracie" (sig. Q1); others explode "the gun-powder of their blasphemies" like Titans (sigs. R2, R4, V3); they are spiritual Goliaths who discharge against Vaughan "Iambicke volumes, or rather vollees" (sig. A3).[82] Some demons encourage superstition, so Vaughan tells of Catholic idolatry and conjuring. False spirituality subverts princes' sovereignty: "Laugh on yee King-killars," he tells Jesuits; you will weep in the next world. We should not question "Princes sceptems"; and "utopian Chymerizing Schollers" should stop prying into politics (sigs. Ss3–Ss4v).

Vaughan's long tract thus deals with issues that weigh on many: sins of the tongue, papist subversion, slander, fiction, fake lineage, gunpowder, and superstition. His anguished contempt for empty fantasy had good cause in the "vaine rumours" from "bruitish [brilliant pun!] mouthes" concerning his family (sig. ¶4v). And yet, having undergone what he believed to be providential rescues from shipwreck and thunder, he wished to deplore religious fraud without denying the miraculous. On the one hand he sarcastically "conjures" the demonic Pantagruel and refuses to read natural disaster as divine punishment. On the other, by ironically exorcizing the devils who possess slanderers, Vaughan complicates his point: his "demons" are mere personifications, but badmouthing really is diabolical. Like *Lear* and *The White Devil,* his text is undecided on how the supernatural relates to the natural, and the very brimstone on the breath of his "curious" slanderers makes more plausible an outlook he rejects.

One might think that an author who calls Pantagruel a limb of Leviathan would lack gaiety, yet Vaughan learned from the "Lucian of France." His *Golden Fleece,* which never names Rabelais, may echo the *Tiers livre*'s prologue (if not Lucian, or Robynson's preface to *Utopia,* or Eliot's introduction to *Ortho-epia Gallica*). A prefatory epistle reports seeing men of deep insight who "find themselves puzled, gravelled, and almost at their wits end" over how to "reforme Errours" and "restore Trading." But "when I had called to mind that Action of Diogenes, how he tumbled up and downe his Tub very laboriously at such time, when all his Neighbours prepared themselves for Armes, I resolved likewise to do somewhat, and by tossing too and from the barrell of my Conceits, albeit barren and inferiour unto many thousands in this Kingdome, to encourage others to lend their hands unto the Publicke prop." A poem that Vaughan imagines Sidney reciting on cuckoldry somewhat resembles Hippothadée's humane advice to Panurge on marriage (sig. Hh4; *TL* 30). And Vaughan makes if not a nonbook then a nonrepository, saying of some verses he fancies sung "in the Amphitheater at Parnassus" by the patron saints of Charles I's united kingdom that a "true copy" is "registered in the Library of [Apollo's] Court" (sig. Lll2).

Vaughan, then, has Rabelaisian touches. True, he also knew Nashe. *The Newlanders Cure* (1630) tells, not without relish, how the "scurrilous Pamphleter" would work himself up by drinking aqua vitae with gunpowder, which "wrought so eagerly uppon his Braine, that hee would often beate himselfe about the noddle, and scratch the Walls round about him, untill hee met with some extravagant furious Termes" (sig. B2v). Vaughan has his own extravagant terms, and passages in *Detraction* suggest he read of "Garagantua" and "powerfull Pantagruell" with an ear for style. His critics are "Archilochian Cynickes with their Satyres, Iambickes, and Libels, with their So and So, with their vies and revies, with their phi fie upon it, fie upon it, to dash and blurre it over, to taunt, to teare it, to fling their caps at it, to make Tennisballes, and to bandy it away if they can" (sig. P4v). And not far from the mention of Pantagruel he urges:

Temper the manifold malapertnesse of thy tongue, of thy tempting tongue, of thy tickling tongue, of thy tatling tongue, thy taunting tongue, thy vaunting tongue, thy jesting tongue, thy gibing tongue, thy jarring tongue, thy warring tongue, thy checking tongue, thy chiding tongue, thy clattering tongue, thy clacking tongue, thy carping tongue, thy babling tongue, thy boasting tongue, thy blazing tongue, thy blaspheming tongue, thy railing tongue, thy reviling tongue, thy scoffing tongue, thy scolding tongue, thy nicking tongue, thy nipping tongue, thy quipping tongue, thy tripping tongue, thy defaming tongue, thy detracting tongue; temper the phreneticall furie of this little Tyrant . . . and whet it not against thy neighbour, whom Baptisme hath regenerated and adopted to the self same heritage, as well as thy selfe. (Sig. Yy1)

The paragraph closes with a quatrain on verbal restraint: Lenten antacid after a spread of verbal fat food. In his own way, Vaughan was not a bad Menippean — perhaps he found solace in his semi-Rabelaisian feast of language for his wife's loss and his neighbors' slimy-lipped cruelty.

Coda

Gabriel Harvey's Double Vision

Gabriel Harvey knew the *Croniques admirables,* either in French or as *The History of Gar[a]gantua.* He also owned some of Rabelais's work. In his copy of Guicciardini's 1571 *Detti e fatti,* now at the Folger Library, he includes the "dicta factaque heroica Gargantua" in a 1590 list of books he owned, translating a phrase ("la vie, faicts & dicts heroiques de Gargantua") that is found on title pages of the *Oeuvres* but not on those of the chapbooks or *Gargantua.*[1] When he first read Rabelais is unclear. His friends included the diplomat and poet Daniel Rogers, who had lived in Paris and known Ronsard, and when he was working for Leicester in the 1570s Harvey would have met others familiar with French writings. Another friend was the printer John Wolfe, chief purveyor of pamphlets on French affairs, who on April 6, 1592, entered a "Gargantua his Prophesie" (which was probably never published) in the Stationers' Register. Conceivably this was a translation of Rabelais's 1532 *Pantagrueline Prognostication;* it certainly sounds like a satire or mock almanac.[2]

Harvey — the darkly handsome, gauche, vain, irritable, ambitious scholar who longed (with real but minimal success) to advise the great and approach the *arcana* of power and policy — is an unlikely admirer of so expansive a writer as Rabelais. Yet Harvey was no prig, whatever his scorn toward the social rot he saw, or claimed to see, around him. He enjoyed Lucian, had a weakness for Aretino, and read jestbooks. In Rabelais he perceived a fanciful ironic canniness that was invisible both to the writer's simpler detractors and to those who admired his earthiness, but pleasing to a scholar impressed — overimpressed — by secrecy, stratagem, charm, irony, magic, the convolutions of narrative, and whatever is indirect, coiled, astute, foxy, panurgic. Harvey, I think, wanted to play fox to Elizabeth's lion (no wonder Spenser's skeptical animal fable, *Mother Hubberds Tale,* vexed him), to be a more reputable Panurge to some royal Pantagruel. In other words, in part of his mind Harvey valued in Rabelais elements of the very guile and imagination that many were to fear as "projection," plot, and "policy." But this subtle writer is only one of Harvey's two Rabelais, the other being a monster-witted railer.

Harvey's chameleon Rabelais changes with his rhetorical and material surroundings, becoming more admirable the less Harvey's opinions are vulnerable to scrutiny. When Harvey attacks Nashe, his Rabelais (whose work may include the chapbook *Gar[a]gantua*) is scurrilous and fantastic. In marginalia, whether self-expression or notations for later use, his Rabelais writes cleverly for the cosmopolitan likes of Harvey. Harvey's Rabelais thus resembles his Aretino: condemned in print, respected in the privacy of manuscript — or "semi-privacy," if Anthony Grafton and Lisa Jardine are correct in thinking that Harvey's jottings sometimes served as notes for reports to political figures.[3] His creation of such personae as Eutrapelus ("Mr. Witty"), moreover, hints at some drama staged for an applauding audience visible to the ego's inward eye. The culturally shifting lines between public and private spaces in a society vary likewise within the self.[4]

In print, Harvey is less interested in giving a sober estimate of Rabelais than in using his name to degrade Nashe. Perhaps this was an error. The crowd Harvey hoped to please — if not the queen, whose views on Rabelais are unrecorded, then young men with a future (James VI among them) — was beginning to notice *Gargantua et Pantagruel* with amusement, and Rabelais's name was soon famous in court and legal circles. Although pseudomoralizing exhibitionists like Hall and Guilpin adopted the scoffing drunken Rabelais of legend, on the whole, Harvey's stiffly upright if rhetorically promiscuous attitude toward "Nashery" aligns him too straitly with grumpy clerics and shocked moralists, as though the Cambridge scholar and rope-maker's son in him had got the better of the would-be courtier and politico. In any case, Harvey's public Rabelais and Gargantua are railers, the author more intellectual and the giant more a traditional bigmouth. Rabelais is also a feigner of monsters.

Harvey's campaign against railing begins with *Foure Letters and Certeine Sonnets, Especially Touching Robert Greene and Other Parties by Him Abused* (1592), a set of prose epistles to various recipients that may at times aim at the Horatian or even Menippean but that in their gnarled rhythms, logorrhea, moralism, and defensive self-display awkwardly anticipate the verse satire of five or six years later. The book's most original feature is a concluding sequence of twenty-two quasi-accusatory, quasi-repentant "Funerall Sonnets" that memorialize the recently deceased Greene, whom the main text attacks. Little noticed in studies of the sonnet, these lines make odd reading: exhortations to charity and expostulations against "cancred peevishnes" (no. 8) mingle with such barbs as telling Greene that "over-lowd hast rung the bawdy bell" and "Vermine to Vermine must repaire at last" (no. 18).[5]

The Rabelais of *Letters* typifies the railing that the verminous Greene had deployed and that Harvey deplores and perpetrates. Even Spenser is guilty: "Invectives by favour have bene too bolde: and Satyres by usurpation toopresumptuous: . . . and I must needs say, [Spenser's] Mother Hubbard, in heat of choller, forgetting the pure sanguine of her sweete Feary Queene, wilfully over-shott her malcontented selfe" (p. 15). Some pages later Harvey circles back to make the same point, this time naming Rabelais. The state suffers from buffoonish wit and "surmounting Rhetorique" in this "Martinish and Counter-martinish age" wherein "everie one super-aboundeth in his owne humor, even to the annihilating of any other." Such "Satyricall Spirits" are

> gowty Divels, and buckram Giants: Midasses, and golden Asses: Cormorants, and Drones, Dunces, and hypocritical hoat spurres, Earthwormes, and Pinchfart Penny-fathers: that feede not their hungry purses and eager stomackes: they have termes, quoth a marvellous doer, steeped in *Aqua Fortis,* and Gunnepouder, that shal rattle through the skies, and make Earthquakes in such pesauntes eares, as shall dare to sende them awaie with a flea in their eare: (howe might a man purchase the sight of those puissant, and hideous termes?) they can lash poore slaves, and spurgall Asses mightily, they can tell parlous Tales of Beares and Foxes, as shrewdlye as mother hubbard, for her life: they will dominiere in Tavernes, and Stationers shops, to die for't: they will be as egregiously famous, as ever was Herostratus, or Pausanias, or Kett, or Scoggin: Agrippa, and Rabelays but Ciphers to them: they have it only in them. Would Christ, they had more discretion in them, and less rancour. (Pp. 54–55)[6]

Agrippa may be here because he belittled human wisdom; the others are temple-destroying, rebellious, tricky, or scoffing. Such men, says this friend of John Wolfe's, haunt taverns and printing presses, being presumably both drunks and multipliers of words (visible words, too — like Rabelais's *paroles gelées* — if one might indeed purchase the sight of them).[7] Harvey also draws on his age's ambivalence toward the invention of gunpowder and the dark resourcefulness it represents, for his imagined railer impresses the vulgar by expelling words with explosives, being a "mightie Bombader of termes." Rabelais's crowd, then, is subversive, inventive, angry, inflated, noisy, and in its cups.

Gargantua figures more often than Rabelais in *Pierces Supererogation* (1593), a word-tumbling tantrum of a reply to Nashe (who had taken Pierce as a sobriquet) and other polemicists. He seems a mélange of the chapbook and Rabelaisian giants, for Harvey was happy to treat any available Gargantua as an enlarged Nashe. That he appears when Rabelais goes unmentioned, though, may indicate some tonal discrimination: for the most part, the giant is a vulgar loudmouth, whereas his maker is guilty of more complex sins. Nashe, of course, is guilty of everything, an ape "that can but mowgh with his mouth, gnash [!] with his teeth, quaver with his ten bones, and brandish his goose-quill . . . as if it were possessed with the sprite of *Orlando Furioso,* or would teach the clubb of Gargantua to speake English" (sig. S4v; true, Gargantua's club [CA 14] could already by now speak English if it could speak at all). Harvey feigns fear: "Pore I must needes be plagued; plagued? nay, brayed & squised to nothing, that am matched with such a Gargantuist, as can devoure me quicke in a sallat; and thundreth more direfull threatnings against me, that onely touched him; then huge Polyphemus rored against Ulysses, that blinded him." Nashe gives himself mere airs, not true thunder, for the giant who eats men with his salad (G 38) is more comic than terrifying, even if his cannibalism may also represent real fears of engulfment.

Only if Harvey writes forcefully can Nashe be made to confess that "all the shreddes, and ragges of his flashingest termes, are worne to the stumpes." Nashe "brayeth open warre against him, that can bray the Asse-drumme in a morter; & stampe his Jewes-trumpe to Pindust. Tom Drumme, reconcile thiselfe with a Counter-supplication [Nashe had just written *Supplication to the Divel*]: or suerly, it is fatally done; and thy S[t]. Fame utterly undone world without end. As savory a Sainct . . . as the cleanely disbursing of the dirtpurse of Sir Gargantua, that made king Charlemaine, and his worthy Chivalry, laugh so mightily, that their heads aked eight days after" (sig. V1v–V2). Harvey puns, as had Nashe, on *Pierce* and its homonym, *purse.* Gargantua did own an imposing purse, but this one is the bag tucked in the body at the end of the colon — another instance of how writers can read each other as excreting not words but feces. Words have heft and materiality, but the stuff stinks. Harvey remembers how English ale disagreed with the chapbook Gargantua: to the hilarity of Arthur's courtiers, who laugh so hard they have a week-long headache, the distressed giant empties himself against London's city walls.[8]

Either Harvey's memory has let him down or he has wittingly knighted Gargantua and transported him to a Carolingian court. Did he think the giant so French that he must be returned across the Channel? That Arthur, hero of

Harvey's friend Spenser's epic, should not be given a servant with so little bowel control? More to my point here, Harvey borrows (para-)Rabelaisian scatology to comment on language: Nashe's carnival vulgarity reverses orifices.[9] This does not make him more engaging, for Harvey's language implies that Charlemagne's knights laughed *at* Gargantua. In *Admirables* the laughter is friendly, and after Arthur remarks merrily that Gargantua might serve as "artillery" against his enemies, the giant is restored to health with a big salad.

"Gargantua," then, is a club-wielding and cannibal thunderer with a grotesque body, an undercivilized object of laughter. As a man-mountain of verbiage he well represents Tom Nashe, "the huge Gargantua of prose, and more then the heaven-surmounting Babell of Ryme" (sig. Z2). He is also a trickster: "Legendaries may recorde woonderments: but examine the suttellest Counsels, or the wilyest practises of Gargantua himselfe, and even Gargantua himselfe, albeit his gowne were furred with two thousand, & five hundred Foxskinnes, moght have bene his Pupill" (sig. Bb3v). The furred gown is from *CA* 15, where "deux mil cinq cens peaulx de regnardz saulvaiges" line Gargantua's "robbe de chambre"; Harvey, no mean classicist, must recall that *fur* is also Latin for "thief" and that foxiness means trickery, *panourgia*. When Nashe was a student, Harvey reports, he kept a fox cub whose "Actes and Monuments are notorious" (a John Foxe joke). Maybe so, but Gargantua's own wiles are harder to identify. Is Harvey thinking of such escapades as the chapbook giant's making his penis a bridge or his popping enemies into his purse? In any case, Gargantua and Nashe are tricksters who "practice," a word carrying a pejorative flavor in early modern English.

Nashe the Gargantua also plays at harmful "phantasticalitie" (*Supererogation,* sig. D2v, one instance of many). Generating phantasms, he eclipses reason by encouraging one of the mind's most problematic capacities, the same one that others located behind projections, plots, rebellion, slander, even tobacco smoke. In England's social drama, Nashe is a one-man antimasque. Harvey's rhetorical problem, of course, is that his reply reads like simply another, opposed, antimasque.

Over and over, *Foure Letters* notes the dangers of "monstrous newfanglednesse" (p. 41), of "new new writers, the Loadstones of the Presse" (p. 82). The good writer uses "heavenly Eloquence" as "noble Sir Philip Sidney and gentle Maister Spencer have done, with immortall fame." For "Right artificiality, (whereat I once aimed to the uttermost power of my slender capacity,) is not mad-brained, or ridiculous, or absurd, or blasphemous, or monstrous: but deepe-conceited, but pleasurable, but delicate, but exquisite, but gratious, but admirable: not according to the fantastical mould of Aretine, or Rabelays, but according to the fine modell of Orpheus, Homer, Pindarus, & the excellentest wittes of Greece, and of the Lande, that flowed with milke, and hony" (p. 67, referring to David and Solomon). Whatever Aretino's obscenity and prince-scourging or Rabelais's dirt and drink, here the pair is guilty of a crazy humor too bizarre for finesse or craft.

Supererogation repeatedly indicts Nashe and others for indulging a novelty-obsessed, publicity-seeking fancy. Rabelais is a fellow offender, found among romancers and jesters. The object of Harvey's contempt (here John Lyly) is a "mad lad," once the "fiddle-stick of Oxford, now the very bable of London" (sig. R4, punning on *babble, Babel,* and *fool's bauble*). His "bawdie Inventions" show that he will

> alledge any impudent, prophane, or blasphemous fiction to serve his turne. So he may soone make-up the authenticall Legendary of his Hundred merrie Tales: as true peradventure, as Lucians true narrations; or the heroicall histo-ryes of Rabelais; or the brave Legendes of Errant Knights; or the egregious prankes of Howleglasse, Frier Rush, Frier Tuck, and such like, or the re-nowned Bugiale [that is, the court in Rome] of Poggius, Racellus, Luscus, Cincius, and that whole Italian crew of merry Secretaryes in the time of Pope Martin the fift; of whom our worshipfull Clarkes of the whetstone, Doctour Clare, Doctour Bourne, M. Scoggin, M. Skelton, M. Wakefield, divers late historiologers, and haply this new Tale-sounder himselfe, learned their most-wonder-full facultie. (Sig. S1)[10]

One would not know from this that Harvey owned and annotated jests, and Italian ones at that. Later in 1593 he extracted Rabelais the fantastic jester from this crowd and again paired him with Aretino: "When the sweet Youth [Nashe] haunted Aretine, and Rabelays, the two monstrous wittes of their languages, who so shaken with the furious feavers of the One: or so attainted with the French Pockes of the other?" (*A New Letter of Notable Contents,* sig. B3). Monstrosity of wit is sick and pocky, as though even while fancies flitter from the head or hand, in the rest of the body sexual diseases work their way out through the skin.

Nowhere in these three printed books (the only ones by Harvey, I believe, that name Rabelais or Gargantua), is the author of *Gargantua et Pantagruel* mentioned with respect or liking, being treated more scornfully than Lucian himself. He is present in *Supererogation,* however, unacknowledged yet iden-tifiable by those keeping up with French writers. Harvey is stung, for instance, by Nashe's mockery of his inkhornisms. After all, Nashe is an offender him-self: "In a phantasticall emulation [he] presumeth to forge a mishapen rable-ment of absurde, and ridiculous wordes, the proper bodges of his newfangled figure [of rhetoric], called Foolerism." Harvey lists examples, including "ink-hornisme" itself and the bruising epithet "Pistlepragmos," applied to him by

Nashe for writing *Foure Letters*. So he consigns such nonwords to the nonlibrary of Saint-Victor: "How many sundry dishes of such dainty fritters? rare junkets, and a delicate service for him, that compiled the most delitious Commentaries, *De optimitate triparum*" (sig. Z3v). Harvey means the scholar Noël Béda, for whom Rabelais had invented a book on tripe, although gross Sorbonnical obscurity seems scarcely relevant to the mercurial Nashe. Again, Nashe's words are material: tripe disguised as gourmet fare.[11]

In Harvey's published works, "Gargantua" and "Rabelais" mean railing monstrosity, novelty, strategic ingenuity, verbal inflation, the pox, and a tendency to hang around taverns and print shops. In his marginalia, the names still mean trickiness and are, on at least one occasion, still associated with the pox; but Rabelais and giant become more sympathetic.

In truth, Harvey was among Rabelais's most appreciative readers — "Meus Rabelaesius," he calls him in the margin of Ludovico Domenichi's 1571 *Facetie, motti, et burle,* claiming that he has him at his fingertips, and elsewhere in the same volume reporting that Rabelais is among the "singulares auctores" he reads daily.[12] Harvey simply never says so in print. Hypocrisy? Yes, by later standards and perhaps even by his own. Or one could call his approach not the poetics but the tactics of allusion: what he says when denouncing Greene or Nashe is not opinion but fusillade. Nor is it the case, I think, that as Harvey aged he became more conservative and more likely to disapprove of a comic writer he had once enjoyed. The young can be less tolerant than the old; despite Rabelais's contempt for professional and religious obscurantism, he was not radical in any way that would unnerve Harvey; and the tone of the marginalia has no smooth trajectory over time. We seem to have, rather, a clear case of an early modern reader posing himself in different attitudes to fit different rhetorical circumstances: one public, polemical, and meant for the many, the other semiprivate and if not self-expressive (a problematic concept in any age) then meant for the few — friends, colleagues, office-holders, or Harvey's own interior personae.

A fine example of Harvey's double vision — one eye on vice to be condemned in print and another at work in a would-be statesman's private study — is the contrast between his scornful reference in *A New Letter* to Rabelais's "French Pockes" and a jest he scribbles in a copy of William Thomas's *Historie of Italie* (1561). Next to a discussion of the "Morbus Gallicus," Harvey writes that some Neapolitans and Spaniards came back from the West Indies with syphilis and then passed it on to "Courtesans" who in turn infected Charles VIII's French soldiers at the siege of Naples. "Therefore Dr. Rablais was found before the statue of Car[olus] 8[,] as a monk thought praying to him by mistake for a s[ain]t. But as the Dr. told him he was not so much a Monk or

Blockhead[;] he was there praying for his [Charles's] soul [cropped and illegible] the facultys Benefactor as having spread the Pox" (Sig. Mm4, at Harvard).[13] The "faculty" is Montpellier's medical school, and Rabelais's prayer springs from gratitude for the increased business. The story, for all its implausibility, shows the mentality Harvey could ascribe to Rabelais, even if in jest. This Dr. Rabelais is the medical man of the prologues, the summoner of pocky drinkers marked by signs of past sexual adventure. But he is also, I imagine, a satirist who extends verbal irony into bodily gesture, a witty performer commenting on the world's spreading corruption and his own profession's greed. It need not matter whether Harvey believed the tale. Like other presumably apocryphal stories about Rabelais, it shows not simple cynicism but self-conscious and ambivalent mockery.

It is in fact Rabelais's subtlety that most pleases Harvey. Relishing (in his marginalia) stratagems, ruses, "policy," he thinks that as a satirist Rabelais was in some admirable sense devious. His allusion in *Pierces Supererogation* to Gargantua's "wilyest practises" radiates censure and resentment, yet in the margin of his Domenichi he notes in what seems a friendly manner that Rabelais is an outstanding "panurgus" and, in an informed comment on genre, compares him to Henri Estienne's Menippean *Apologie pour Hérodote*: "Rabelaesius etiam altera Apologia Herodoti. Egregius panurgus, Rabelaesius" (p. 428). This is, for Harvey, a compliment.[14] On other pages he notes the "gran intelligenza del Panurgo" and includes Rabelais among the authors of "stratagems" (pp. 431, 460). He does not mean, I take it, that Rabelais lies like Nashe; the notes show, rather, an appreciation, tinged with envy, I suspect, of tactical foxiness and narrative twist.

Harvey's Rabelais is "wily," but wily like Ulysses, a royal hero who fascinated this political observer and politic would-be. In *Pierces Supererogation* he admits, half-heartedly, that he is "neither Ulysses, nor Outis ["Nobody," the pseudonym Ulysses takes when the blinded Polyphemus asks his name], yet perhaps I can tell, how No-boddy may doe. . . . Polyphemus was a mightie fellow, and conjured Ulysses companions into excrements (fewe Giants ever so hideous, as Polyphemus): but poore Outis was even with him, and Noboddy conjured his goggle eye, as well" (sig. R3v). Outis is smaller than the Polyphemus who ate Greek sailors (Harvey was no social giant), but he is smarter (like a professor). "Nobody" the tricky and satirical northern European "Niemand," moreover, has a pictorial and generic connection with the chapbook Garagantua — he of the subtle "practices" — and with Howleglass. Is Rabelais the giant-maker also an Outis-maker? Perhaps. A note in Harvey's Guicciardini, next to the story of how Cincinnatus only reluctantly abandoned his plow to rule Rome, explains, "Panurgus: vel Outis" (p. 215).[15] It is a little cynical, this revision of a noble-minded farmer and statesman into a wily panurgus, but Harvey's epithets are probably more admiring than derogatory.

Rabelais's foxiness operates by irony and indirection. In the margin of his Guicciardini, Harvey includes him among those who write with "vivide ironia," paradox, and hyperbole, although, if I understand him, he also thinks that the Italian historian whose work he is annotating is a "cunning pragmatician" who outdoes Tiberius, Rabelais, and Aretino (p. 89). More subtly, in his copy of Erasmus's 1507 commentary on Euripides' *Hecuba,* Harvey adds: "Those comedies please best that are not comedies, and tragedies that are not tragedies." Hence, in other genres, Homer and Virgil stand out in writing epic, Frontinus for his stratagems (Harvey owned and annotated the 1539 *Strategemes* of Sextus Julius Frontinus), Henri Estienne for his *Apologia Herodoti,* "Rabelaesium in Heroicis Gargantuae," Sidney for *The New Arcadia,* and Domenichi for jests. "Give me," he says, "fables that are not fables, apologies that are not apologies, and . . . adages that are not adages" (sig. *8).[16] Whether Harvey refers to generic mixtures or to texts that treat genre like a reversible coat—elegy that is epithalamion, romance disguised in shepherds' weeds, or romantic pastoral that strains toward epic—is uncertain. More obvious is a taste for generic obliquity and wiliness that parallels his admiration of political savvy.

Harvey considers Rabelais funny, not monstrous. On a leaf of *Facetie* he says that even Rabelais can feign frigidly ("Etiam Rabelaesius fingit frigide"), but feigning is not Nashery. Only once in the marginalia I have seen does he hint at anything coarse in Rabelais, and even here he could be recalling the chapbook. Annotating Joshua Sylvester's 1592 translation of Du Bartas's lines on Jonah, he exclaims: "Bionis epitaphium [that is, Bion's lament for Adonis]: but sublimed. Henrici Epinicon [Du Bartas's poem on Henri IV's victory at Ivry]: But quintessenced. Ilias Iliados: but multiplied. Gargantuisme: but refined. Aretinisme: but disciplined. Singularitie: but civilis'd."[17] Perhaps Harvey means that Du Bartas's energy contains and improves upon Bion's grief, *Yvry*'s sweep, Homer's vivid but briefer tempest, the crude hyperboles in *Gargantua* (unless Harvey remembers the storm in the *Quart livre,* from which Gargantua is absent), Aretino's powerful but licentious imagination, and an artistic originality with anything eccentric or grotesque polished away.

This Rabelais has finesse. In the margins of his 1542 Quintilian, Harvey writes that charming things please, serious ones have strength, and what is wittily ingenious and magnificent flourishes. As examples he cites Quintilian himself, Valla, Luther, Ramus, Agrippa, More, Paracelsus (Harvey had a taste for the occult), Aretino, "Rabelaesius," and Machiavelli.[18] It may be Rabelais's subtlety, not his irony as such, that led Harvey to place him higher than

Aretino in his (private) estimation. Rabelais alone, he says, "will putt downe all the Italian, or Spanish poets, in words or in deeds" (*Facetie,* p. 426; "deeds" may mean narrative, not actions by the man himself). "I prefer," he writes elsewhere in the same volume, "Chaucer to Petrarch and Boccaccio or Ariosto and Rabelais to Aretino." And, in his Guicciardini, he calls Aretino "nothing" compared to Rabelais (p. 321).[19]

Harvey's semi-private Rabelais, "my Rabelais," is shrewd, funny, clever. And secular. If there is no trace in the marginalia I have seen of the scoffing atheist known to many, neither is there any trace of the evangelical Christian. Harvey is precise on the matter. Like his contemporaries, he was comfortable with well-framed pigeon holes for different genres and styles, a literary dovecot in which to nestle sorted and tagged authors. Or, to shift metaphors, he enjoyed locating what Hans Robert Jauss calls a "horizon of expectation" against which to position a given text. Rabelais goes in the "wittily ingenious and satirically worldly" box, some distance from the "great religious epic-writer" box in which Harvey puts Du Bartas. So he praises as worthy the ancient classical writers "Bartasium, ob divinum furorem [that is, his heavenly inspiration]: Rabelaesium ob humanum [his 'humanity,' his learning and secular abilities]," and — because like other critics Harvey also has a box for the composite — "Chaucerum ob mixtum" (*Facetie,* p. 321). More pithily: "In jest, Rabelais: in earnest, Bartas singular" (p. 428). With both of them, a man has a full world, which must be why Harvey says he likes to read "Bartasium, cum Rabelaesio" (p. 326), as though *Gargantua et Pantagruel* were a usefully earthy counterweight to the starry levitations of Du Bartas's Uranian muse. A statesman, even a professor, can devote only part of his time to divine poetry, and it is well to keep some secular irony handy.

Harvey's remarks also illuminate a note in his Guicciardini saying that one is a pedant and no philosopher if one is not first an Aristippus (the ancient hedonist) or a Rabelais.[20] It is Harvey's persona (or self-inspiring fancied model) Eutrapelus who reads thus, and although he is "always earnest and absolutely steel-like in his most worthy studies," his name connotes suave wit, not solemnity.[21] Reading Rabelais keeps the *eutrapelia* in Eutrapelus, distinguishing this knowledgeable and worldly scholar/statesman from the rustic Cambridge pedants who had failed to appreciate Dr. Harvey.

Perhaps Harvey enjoyed Rabelais because he found in him something he missed in himself, something he needed and cultivated but never quite integrated. Harvey had the elements: a love of language, a flair for wordplay, an impatience with scholasticism (he was, after all, a Ramist), and learning. But he remains Salieri, not Mozart. What Harvey lacks is not eutrapelia or humor. He lacks Pantagruelism. In his writings, whatever he was like in real life when bending his elbow with Spenser or cracking jokes he found in Domenichi, he has little sense of joy, not least the joy of freedom from concern over life's fortuities — "les choses gratuites" — among which one could well reckon the failure to win academic fellowships or political place.

In this regard Harvey significantly misread his Rabelais. Eutrapelus, he says, reads instrumentally, gathering only what leads to his present goal.[22] But that is probably no way to read Rabelais and certainly not how to ballast one's ship with Pantagruelion. In the very long run the deepest error of this irritating, intelligent, erudite, sensitive, angry, and frustrated man was to focus so narrowly on Rabelais's irony and "humanum." (He did so in part, I think, because he found irony not merely a weapon or device but a comfort; a note on page 168 of his Guicciardini reads: "Ironia, a present restorative at all oppositions, or afflictions.") Harvey's secular, jesting Rabelais is a fine Rabelais for many purposes: learning to smile at the instability or emptiness of words, working up liberating belly laughs, finding a more refined consolation in the ridicule of academic pretension, stretching the mind with paradox and monsters. But to the extent that there is more to Rabelais than this, to the extent that he writes *also* with a passion and a faith that allow Pantagruelion its full power — the power to make sails, paper, and a hangman's rope, certainly, but also the power to survive fire, including (be it whispered) heresy-hunters' persecutory fire — to that extent, by reading him only as ironic, hyperbolic, comic, foxy, or fantastic, Harvey misses the point. This is true, I think, even if he grasped that much of Rabelais's satire is directed at church authority and that he is thus in a sense "divinum" as well as "humanum," or, like Chaucer, "mixtum."

For Rabelais does not scorn or ironize from mere anger, ebullience, eutrapelia, or fantasticality. His irony and wordplay may float over the abyss that some perceive under his language, but the abyss is not quite empty, and more than Chimeras thrive in it. Had Harvey not so distinguished the "human" Rabelais from the "divine" Du Bartas he might have spared himself his breathless overestimation of the latter and found even deeper pleasure in *Gargantua et Pantagruel*. And yet one may be pardoned for hoping that in truth he had "his" Rabelais at his fingertips because his heart told him about something in this writer beyond what could be expressed in the printed war with Tom Nashe or in the marginally more irenic safety of his own library. There may even be a moral here for modern academics whose theories (and antitheories), like Harvey's, are more punitive than heuristic, more judgmental and categorizing than liberating, more learnedly ironic than open to pleasure and joy. Drink.

Notes

Translations are my own unless otherwise identified; I have consulted versions by Thomas Urquhart (now once more in print, with a fine introduction by Terence Cave), Donald Frame, and Burton Raffel. I have regularized i and j, u and v, retained italics only when they seem significant, and occasionally added accents to avoid ambiguity. In quoting Rabelais I ordinarily use the edition by Pierre Jourda (Paris: Garnier, 1962). Early modern pagination being so inaccurate, I cite Renaissance books by the signature letter; I omit the place of publication unless the city is other than Paris for French books or London for English ones.

Introduction

1. In "What Is an Author?" trans. Josué V. Harari, in *The Foucault Reader,* ed. Paul Rabinow (New York: Pantheon, 1984), 101–20, Michel Foucault remarks that "if we proved that Shakespeare did not write those sonnets which pass for his, that would constitute a significant change and affect the manner in which the author's name functions" (106). Yes, but I suspect that such a discovery would matter more to us than to many in earlier centuries. Even I do not quite know what to call the author(s) of the *Cinquième livre*. Rabelais? "Rabelais"? Rabelais et al.? Mireille Huchon, *Rabelais grammairien* (Geneva: Droz, 1981), argues that the fifth book is a compilation by later hands making use of pages that Rabelais wrote but did not use. In any case, some Renaissance "authorship" is so multiple, layered, entangled with the words of others that even armed with all the facts, one might be hard pressed to name the "author(s)." In certain areas of

our own culture (most spectacularly the performing arts) this can still be the case. True, as Jack Stillinger says in *Multiple Authorship and the Myth of Solitary Genius* (Oxford: Oxford University Press, 1991), 187, whatever our own ease with collaborative writing, few of us cherish anonymity, and even postmodern critics guard their status as "authors" with ferocity.

2. "They plow the shore and commit seed to sand."

3. Early modern rhetorical training, which despite humanist stress on context often encouraged the fragmentation of texts and subsequent redeployment of the fragments, together with the period's keen sense of personality as performance, can limit the applicability of current theories of allusion and intertextuality. Thus the fascinating taxonomy offered by Udo J. Hebel, "Towards a Descriptive Poetics of *Allusion*," in *Intertextuality*, ed. Heinrich E. Plett (Berlin and New York: Walter de Gruyter, 1991), 135–64, tends to assume more often than might a Renaissance teacher or poet that alluding to a name or passage invites a conscious memory of the prior text containing that name or passage.

4. See, e.g., Katharine Eisaman Maus, "Proof and Consequences: Inwardness and Its Exposure in the English Renaissance," *Representations* 34 (1991), 29–52, and Joshua Scodel, "The Medium Is the Message: Donne's 'Satire 3,' 'To Sir Henry Wotton' (Sir, more than kisses), and the Ideologies of the Mean," *MP* 90 (1993), 479–511.

5. Stanley Stewart's "A Critique of Pure 'Situating,'" *New Literary History* 25 (1994), 1–19, debates the matter in an amusingly skeptical dialogue.

6. Terence Cave, "Reading Rabelais: Variations on the Rock of Virtue," in *Literary Theory/Renaissance Texts,* ed. Patricia Parker and David Quint (Baltimore: Johns Hopkins University Press, 1986), 78–95 (89).

7. As François Rigolot says in "Interpréter Rabelais aujourd'hui," *Poétique* 103 (September 1995), 269–83, whatever the chasms dividing us from the past, the "disposition mentale" of Rabelais's age accords in some regards (notably its keen awareness of words' proliferation and instability) with postmodern thinking.

8. Huntington Brown, *Rabelais in English Literature* (Cambridge: Harvard University Press, 1933; repr., New York: Octagon Books, 1967); Marcel de Grève, *L'Interprétation de Rabelais au XVIe siècle (ER* 3, 1961), chap. 4.

Chapter 1: Para-Rabelaisian Complications

1. I borrow "Para-Rabelaisian" to mean texts associated with but not in fact by Rabelais from John Lewis's introduction to François Habert's *Songe de Pantagruel, ER* 18 (1985), 103–62.

2. *NRB* 130; Plan, no. 45: "Panurge, disciple of Pantagruel. With the deeds of the mighty giant Bringuenarilles, etc." and "The voyage and navigation made by Panurge the disciple of Pantagruel to unknown and foreign Islands with many marvelous things hard to credit that he said he had seen and that he describes in this present volume. And many other delights that will incite the hearers to laugh." The author was possibly one "Jean d'Abundance," if that is not a pseudonym; see the fine introduction to *Le Disciple de Pantagruel,* ed. Guy Demerson and Christiane Lauvergnat-Gagnière (Paris: Nizet, 1982). John Lewis, "Rabelais and the *Disciple de Pantagruel,*" *ER* 22 (1988), 101–22, describes mutual borrowing. I ignore, despite their possible relevance to later seventeenth-century

readers, masques at the Bourbon court with characters from Rabelais. See H.-E. Clousot, "Ballets tirés de Rabelais au XVIIe siècle," *RER* 5 (1907), 90–97, which describes such compositions as a 1626 Shrove Tuesday masque based on the birth of Pantagruel, and Lazare Sainéan, *L'Influence et la réputation de Rabelais* (Paris: Gamber, 1930); Catherine Campbell is making a study of them.

3. Lewis's notes to Habert in *ER* 18 identify Rabelais's borrowings.

4. Ruth Calder, ed., *Louenge des femmes* (New York: Johnson Reprint, 1967). Rabelais was the first to use Plato's androgyne in French, says Jerome Schwartz, in "Scatology and Eschatology in Gargantua's Androgyne Device," *ER* 14 (1977), 265–75. I have not seen the *Catalogue des malheureux* ascribed by its author, Laurent Desmoulins, to "le Disciple de Pantagruel" (Paris, 1549) or a spurious 1549 *CL* (*NRB* 11).

5. A vagina.

6. That is, the student in the "nourishing, famed, and celebrated school one calls [the University of] Paris writes to "his good friend living in the celebrated and famous city of Lyons." I quote Rabelais, *Oeuvres* (Paris: Dalibon, 1823) VIII, 321–33.

7. The 1823 edition of the *Oeuvres* has "degubler," which must be a typo.

8. In *Oeuvres*, 1823 ed., VIII, 334–38: "The Philosophical Cream (or Chrism) of Pantagruel's encyclopedic questions, to be disputed Sorbonistically in a decretal school near St. Denis in Paris."

9. "*Whether,* a Platonic idea, fluttering dexterously under the opening to Chaos, could chase off the squadrons of Democritus' atoms" and "*Whether,* just for the long hair given to the metamorphosed bear [Ursa Minor?], having the backside shaved à la buggery to make a beard for Triton, [the bear] could be the guardian of the arctic pole." Some editions omit the second item.

10. Jacques Boulenger, "Le 'Nouveau Panurge,'" *RER* 3 (1905), 408–31, gives a description and excerpts. I quote from the 1617 Toulouse edition: *Nouvelles recreatives . . . d'un renommé vieil-homme nommé Panurge.*

11. Because of a youthful poem, Beza was accused of bisexual indecency; see my "English Writers and Beza's Latin Epigrams: The Uses and Abuses of Poetry," *Studies in the Renaissance* 21 (1974), 83–117.

12. This section is an abbreviated form of an essay that appeared in Barbara Bowen ed., *Rabelais in Context: Proceedings of the 1991 Vanderbilt Conference* (Birmingham, Ala.: Summa, 1993). The title is an allusion to Stanley Fish's *Is There a Text in This Class? The Authority of Interpretive Communities* (Cambridge: Harvard University Press, 1980). Reader response theory, reception studies, and the sociology of reading have produced a growing literature. My aim is less to advance it theoretically than to recover a dissonant and often individually conflicted set of responses to one group of texts and names. I have profited from, e.g., Susan R. Suleiman and Inge Crosman, eds., *The Reader in the Text: Essays on Audience and Interpretation* (Princeton: Princeton University Press, 1980), and David Bleich, *Subjective Criticism* (Baltimore, Md.: Johns Hopkins University Press, 1978). On Renaissance readers, see Heidi A. Brayman, "Impressions from a 'Scribbling Age': Recovering the Reading Practices of Renaissance England" (Ph.D. diss., Columbia University, 1995); Robert Darnton, "History of Reading," in Peter Burke, ed. *New Perspectives on Historical Writing* (University Park: Pennsylvania State University Press, 1992), 140–67; Anthony Grafton and Lisa Jardine, *From Humanism to the Humanities:*

Education and the Liberal Arts in Fifteenth- and Sixteenth-Century Europe (London: Duckworth, 1986), chap. 4; Eugene R. Kintgen, "Reconstructing Elizabethan Reading," *SEL* 30 (1990), 1–18, and Kintgen, *Reading Tudor England* (Pittsburgh: University of Pittsburgh Press, 1996); and William H. Sherman, *John Dee: The Politics of Reading and Writing in the English Renaissance* (Amherst: University of Massachusetts Press, 1995).

13. Hans Robert Jauss, *Toward an Aesthetic of Reception*, trans. Timothy Bahti (Minneapolis: University of Minnesota Press, 1982), chap. 1.

14. Susan Noakes, *Timely Reading: Between Exegesis and Interpretation* (Ithaca: Cornell University Press 1988), ix, notes that reading can vary hourly within one person's mind.

15. Mary Thomas Crane, *Framing Authority: Sayings, Self, and Society in Sixteenth-Century England* (Princeton: Princeton University Press, 1993), explores the implications of this.

16. In *The View from Minerva's Tower: Learning and Imagination in* The Anatomy of Melancholy (Toronto: University of Toronto Press, 1989), E. Patricia Vicari claims that "Burton's favorite among the modern satirists is 'that French Lucian,' Rabelais" (176–77, alluding to a passage in "Democritus to the Reader"). I doubt, however, that Burton read Rabelais; cf. J. B. Bamborough, "Burton and Cardan," in *English Renaissance Studies Presented to Dame Helen Gardner,* ed. John Carey (Oxford: Clarendon, 1980), 180–93.

17. The edition of Burton's *Anatomy of Melancholy* by Thomas C. Faulkner, Nicolas K. Kiessling, and Rhonda L. Blair, with an introduction by J. B. Bamborough (Oxford: Clarendon, 1989–1994), uses the 1632 text as copytext.

18. In his "Consolatio ad uxorem" and "Consolatio ad Apollonium," Plutarch tells how when Zeus apportioned honors to the gods he gave Mourning hers with the proviso that she reward worshipers by moving in with them.

19. There are virtually no French books listed in *The Library of Robert Burton,* ed. Nicolas K. Kiessling (Oxford: Oxford Bibliographical Society, 1988).

20. The margin cites "lib.3. Anthol. cap 20"; see *The Greek Anthology,* ed. W. R. Paton (Cambridge: Harvard University Press, 1917), II, Book VII, no. 353. The wording implies that Maron is a poet, but the epitaph is by Antipater of Sidon on one Maron who grieves that the cup carved on her tombstone is empty.

21. G 41: "May a hundred devils take me if there aren't more old drunks than old doctors."

22. Euphormio could be John Barclay, a Catholic who mocked Jesuits and Puritans and who for a time had James I's patronage; a better candidate is the "Euphormio" whose *Coronia Regia* (1611), sometimes attributed to Gaspar Schoppe, attacks James (and his sexuality) with some scurrility. Boccalini wrote the popular *Ragguagli di Parnaso.* The demagogue Demades in fact supported Philip of Macedon.

23. See, e.g., the final arguments of "Democritus Junior."

24. Burton, *Anatomy of Melancholy,* ed. Faulkner et al., 8, 11.

Chapter 2: Reshaping Gargantua

1. See Brown's edition of *The Tale of Gargantua and King Arthur by François Girault c. 1534* (Cambridge: Harvard University Press, 1932); cf. Marcel de Grève, "La Legende

de Gargantua en Angleterre au XVIe siècle," *Revue belge de philologie et d'histoire* 38 (1960), 765–94. A shorter version of this chapter appeared as "Reshaping Gargantua," in *L'Europe de la Renaissance: Mélanges offerts à Marie-Thérèse Jones-Davies, Cultures et civilisations*, ed. Jean-Claude Margolin and Marie-Madeleine Martinet (Paris: Touzot, 1989), 477–91.

2. For editions of this chapbook, see Plan; John Lewis, "Towards a Chronology of the 'Chroniques gargantuines,' " *ER* 18 (1985), 83–101; and *NRB* 117–29. Mireille Huchon, *Rabelais grammairien* (Geneva: Droz, 1981), 390–405, argues for Rabelais's editorship of *Grands et inestimables*, the 1533 version, and *Le Vroy gargantua. Les Chroniques Gargantuines*, ed. Christiane Lauvergnat-Gagnière and Guy Demerson, with Robert Antonioli, C. Bonilauri, Mireille Huchon, John Lewis, and B. Teyssot (Paris: Nizet, 1988), includes *Admirables* and a very informative introduction.

3. See Raymond C. La Charité, "Au temps que les bestes parloient," *Recreation, Reflection and Re-Creation* (Lexington, Ky.: French Forum, 1980). Salved by love, not foxfur and moss, Gallemelle's wound makes a baby.

4. Giants like rocks; see Francis Vian, *La Guerre des géants: Le Mythe avant l'époque hellénistique* (Paris: Klincksieck, 1952), 259–64. In Thomas Middleton's *A Fair Quarrel*, II.ii, a character suggests that Corineus, victor over the giant Gogmagog, had carried Michael's Mount under his arm to its present position off the Cornish coast.

5. On Gallimasue, see François Cornillat, "L'Autre géant: Les 'Chroniques gargantuines' et leur intertexte," *Littérature* 55 (1984), 85–97.

6. "Popular" literature is a problematic concept. Peter Burke, *Popular Culture in Early Modern Europe* (New York: Harper, 1978), argues that Europe was split less between elite and popular than between the few with a range of discourses and the many inhabiting narrower worlds. Cf. Natalie Z. Davis, "Printing and the People," in her *Society and Culture in Early Modern France* (Stanford: Stanford University Press, 1975), and Jean-Paul Berlioz, "Aspects populaires des Chroniques Gargantuines," *RHR* 11 (1980), 63–74.

7. Paul Sébillot, *Gargantua dans les traditions populaires* (Paris, 1883, repr. Paris: Maisonneuve, 1967), and G.-E. Pillard, *Le Vrai Gargantua* (Paris: Editions Imago, 1987).

8. Sébillot, *Gargantua*, 3.

9. See (*cum grano salis*) Henri Dontenville, *La France mythologique* (Paris: Tchou, 1966) and *Histoire et géographie mythiques de la France* (Paris: Maisonneuve, 1973); Pillard, *Le Vrai Gargantua*; and Jean Larmat, *Le Moyen âge dans le Gargantua de Rabelais* (Paris: Les Belles Lettres, 1973), 141–81. Dontenville, *Histoire*, 299–300, locates a twelfth century "géant Garganeüs." He thinks Gargantua is a son/aspect of Belenos related to the Gallic Mercury and Mars.

10. Walter Stephens, *Giants in Those Days: Folklore, Ancient History, and Nationalism* (Lincoln: University of Nebraska Press, 1989), explores the politics of some Renaissance giantology. He considers Rabelais impatient with protonationalist nonsense like that of Jean Lemaire de Belges. Stephens is sobering, but one may still imagine an older giant, noun, or energy. For a respectful dissent from his views on Rabelais, giants, and folk culture, see Guy Demerson, "Géant de chroniques et géants de chronique. Rabelais entre Jean Bouchet et Erasme," *RHR* 37 (1993), 25–50. Demerson points out that some folklore giants are "good." I would add that even evil creatures can be "popular," like

Norwich's dragon, Snap (Robert Withington, *English Pageantry: An Historical Outline* [Cambridge: Harvard University Press, 1918], 23 ff.), or Antwerp's Antigonus (René Meurant, *Géants processionnels et de cortège en Europe, en Belgique, en Wallonie* [Tielt: Veys, 1979]). The latter was an "espouventable Geant," says the 1550 *Triumphe d'Anvers* (sig. L1v) of his effigy, "horrible, et tirrannicque," but he remains a sort of city mascot. Cf. René Darré, *Géants d'hier et d'aujourd'hui* (Arras: Imprimerie de la Nouvelle Société Anonyme du Pas-de-Calais, 1944).

11. Saint Michael's Mount, off the Cornish coast, once had a giant.

12. *The Tryall of Chevalry,* IV.i, in *A Collection of Old English Plays*, ed. A. H. Bullen (repr. New York: Blom, 1964), III; A.-M. Lecoq, "La Grande conjonction de 1524 démythifiée pour Louise de Savoie," *BHR* 44 (1982), 52, notes that Jean Thénaud's giant, Gargalasua, had fifty "chartees de foin" (loads of hay) in each button.

13. Sig. R3; *CA* 15: "boteaulx de foing."

14. *CA* 15; Taylor, in a sonnet of ca. 1611 (Spenser Society; repr. New York: Burt Franklin, 1967, I, 222).

15. *The Second Report of Doctor John Faustus,* Short Title Catalogue 10715.3, Oxford, sig. H2v; STC 10715, sig. H1, has Gargantua's *son.*

16. Sig. X2–X2v. Allusions to a "popular" Gargantua can appear near those to Rabelais or in texts by writers (Browne, Tomkis, and Mayne) who read him.

17. The Stationers' Register, ed. Edward Arber (London, 1875), II.

18. H. R. Plomer, "Some Elizabethan Book Sales," *The Library* 7, ser. 3 (1916), 318–29.

19. Wilson, *Arte of Rhetorique,* ed. Thomas J. Derrick (New York: Garland, 1982), 391, notes that if Saint Christoper is as big as he is pictured he might be "kynne to Garganteo." Page 36 has the goose.

20. E. S. Leedham-Green, *Books in Cambridge Inventories* (Cambridge: Cambridge University Press, 1986) I, Greenwood, no. 94.

21. H. S. Bennett, *English Books and Readers 1558–1603* (Cambridge: Cambridge University Press, 1965), 265.

22. F. P. Wilson, "The English Jestbooks of the Sixteenth and Early Seventeenth Centuries," *HLQ* 2 (1939), 121–58, notes the transactions.

23. On giants, in addition to Stephens, see Susan Stewart, "The Gigantic," in her *On Longing* (Baltimore, Md.: Johns Hopkins University Press, 1984), which is helpful on liminality if muddled on Gogmagog (82).

24. See a letter to Joseph Mead, Dec. 3, 1626, in Thomas Birch, *The Court and Times of Charles the First* (London, 1848) I, 179–80; quoted by Stephen Orgel and Roy Strong, *Inigo Jones: The Theatre of the Stuart Court* (Berkeley: University of California Press, 1973), I, 43–44. The letter mentions "Gargamella," as in Rabelais, but calls Gargantua Pantagruel's son.

25. On the issues (Are we shrinking? Is the world dying?) see Jean Céard, "La Querelle des géants et la jeunesse du monde," *JMRS* 8 (1978), 37–76.

26. George Hakewill, *An Apologie . . . of the Power and Providence of God,* sig. Bb3v. Hakewill cites Jean de Chassanion, *De gigantibus* (Basle, 1580), who defended giants against the *Gigantomachia* of John Goropius Becanus.

27. Grève, "Gargantua," 773, notes how often England's Gargantua is linked with "romans de chevalerie" and "facéties populaires."

28. In "Oratio praevaricatoria" (1632), Thomas Randolph tells various figures that they are now outclassed: Quixote is "idiota," Orlando less "furioso," and "Garagantua" smaller (Randolph, *Works*, ed. W. C. Hazlitt [London, 1875], II, 679–70).

29. Cf. Robert P. Adams, "Bold Bawdry and Open Manslaughter: The English New Humanist Attack on Medieval Romance," *HLQ* 23 (1959), 33–48. David McPherson, "Roman Comedy in Renaissance Education: The Moral Question," *SCJ* 12 (1981), 19–30, disagrees with Russell Fraser, *The War Against Poetry* (Princeton: Princeton University Press, 1970), that philosophical or political agendas underlie sexual worry. (As Freud almost said, sometimes a penis is just a penis.) Cf. Marc Fumaroli, "Jacques Amyot and the Clerical Polemic Against the Chivalric Novel," *RenQ* 38 (1985), 22–40, and Jean-Philippe Beaulieu, "*Perceforest* et *Amadis de Gaule*: Le roman chevaleresque de la Renaissance," *R&R* 15 (1991), 187–97. Disquiet concerning interiority and the longings lurking there is further evidence that early modern Europe did indeed have a strong awareness of subjectivity, however conceived and structured. As Katherine Eisaman Maus remarks in "Proof and Consequences: Inwardness and Its Exposure in the English Renaissance," *Representations* 34 (1991), 29–52, "The 'problem of other minds' as it engages English Renaissance thinkers and writers" is often "not so much whether those minds exist as of how to know what they are thinking," a "problem" contributing to the age's "pervasive suspicion of other people's motives and the conviction that conspiracy was everywhere" (37, 36).

30. *Restraint* was entered 1567/8 with a preface dated April 1568; except for allusions by Wilson and Marcourt this is the first printed English reference to Gargantua I can find.

31. My thanks to Steven May for alerting me to an earlier version in Baxter's 1578 translation of Calvin. In a prefatory "Baxters complaint, with an admonition to the Reader" some bumpy fourteeners lament that "We doo delight in matchevile his cruel pollecie, / And reade the booke of Arthurs knights being full of Papistrye. / And Guy of Warwicke, Scoggins gests, and Gargantua, / The court of Venus, Howleglasse, Legenda Aurea . . ." (sig. B3).

32. Robert Holland's verse life of Christ (1594) compares Catholic legends to "the monstrous fables of Garragantua" (sig. A5).

33. Cf. La Noue, *Discours politiques et militaires* (Geneva, 1587 ed.), Book VI, sig. R3v; there is no Gargantua here or in E. Aggas's 1588 translation.

34. I quote Roger Kuin's edition of Robert Langham's *Letter* (Leiden: Brill, 1983). Here and in "Langham's *Letter*: Facts and Problems," *The Library* 7 (1983), 115–25, Kuin persuades me of Langham's authorship; but see David Scott, "William Patten and the Authorship of 'Robert Laneham's *Letter*,'" *ELR* 7 (1977), 297–306.

35. This is said by, e.g., Grève, "Gargantua." Cf. J. C. Furnivall, ed., *Robert Laneham's Letter* (London: Kegan Paul, 1890); Kuin provides further identifications. On the event's politics, see Philippa Berry, *Of Chastity and Power: Elizabethan Literature and the Unmarried Queen* (New York: Routledge, 1989), 95–100.

36. *Dobsons Drie Bobbes*, ed. E. A. Horsman (Oxford: Oxford University Press, 1955), 1; see Avril S. O'Brien, "*Dobsons Drie Bobbes*: A Significant Contribution to the Development of Prose Fiction," *SEL* 12 (1972), 55–70.

37. See Laura Stevenson, *Praise and Paradox: Merchants and Craftsmen in Elizabethan Popular Literature* (Cambridge: Cambridge University Press, 1984): she may

underplay Beaumont's ambivalence. I quote from John Doebler's edition (Lincoln: University of Nebraska Press, 1967). In her edition (Paris, 1958), M.-T. Jones-Davies thinks that the reference to Gargantua (III.iv.31) recalls Rabelais.

38. Henry Glapthorne, *Wit in a Constable,* in *Plays and Poems* (London, 1874) I, 185, 182.

39. John Taylor, *The Sculler* (1612) in *Works* III, 499; among the other indignities Gargantua suffered in England was his occasional demotion from noun to adjective — "Gargantua" here means "big."

40. Bernard Capp, *The World of John Taylor the Water-Poet, 1578–1653* (Oxford: Clarendon, 1994), 190.

41. On Taylor's languages see, e.g., "A thiefe" in *Works* II, 282; for "Rablaies" see *A Dogge of Warre* (1628?), *Works* II, 364, listing writers about trifles.

42. Taylor, *Sir Gregory Nonsence His Newes from Noplace,* 1622, in *Works* II. See also *A Bawd* (1635), in *Works,* third collection (Spenser Society Reprint 19, 1876), 269. *Jacke a Lent* (1617? and 1620) is in *Works* I; like *QL*'s Quaresmeprenant, Jack lacks "affinitie or propinquitie with flesh and blood." *Odcombs Complaint* (1613; *Works* I, 221–22) has samples of Utopian and Bermudian.

43. Taylor, *Sir Gregory Nonsence,* in *Works* I, 160.

44. Taylor, *Taylors goose* (1621), in *Works* I, 120.

45. Taylor, *To the Honour of O Toole* (first pub. 1622), in *Works* I, 177. The preface cites Amadis in France, Gogmagog in England, Quixote in Spain, and Gargantua "almost no where" (176) — a Utopia joke?

46. Taylor, "Certaine Sonnets"; see *Works* I, 222. Polyphemus, Gogmagog, and Tom Thumb also appear.

47. Taylor, *Sir Gregory Nonsence,* in *Works* I, 160, 162.

48. Taylor, *Sence upon Nonsence,* sig. A2v, in *Works,* Fourth Collection.

49. Quoted in John B. Friedman, *The Monstrous Races in Medieval Art and Thought* (Cambridge: Harvard University Press, 1981), 163–64. On giants' grotesquerie and romance aspect, see Mary B. Campbell, *The Witness and the Other World: Exotic European Travel Writing, 400–1600* (Ithaca: Cornell University Press, 1988), chap. 2. A version of my discussion here of Gargantua's association with Tom Thumb — thus creating an anamorphic figure I call Gargatom — appears in *Monster Theory: Reading Culture,* ed. Jeffrey Jerome Cohen (Minneapolis: University of Minnesota Press, 1996), 75–91.

50. From Caxton's translation of a later prose version: the *Mirrour of the World,* ed. Oliver H. Prior (London: Early English Text Society, 1913), 97.

51. See Paula Findlen, "Jokes of Nature and Jokes of Knowledge: The Playfulness of Scientific Discourse in Early Modern Europe," *RenQ* 43 (1990), 292–331, and Jean Céard, "Tératologie et tératomancie au XVIe siècle," in *Monstres et prodiges au temps de la Renaissance,* ed. Marie-Thérèse Jones-Davies (Paris: Touzot, 1980), 5–15.

52. "A.B.," *Merie Tales of the Mad Men of Gotam,* ed. Stanley J. Kahrl, and Richard Johnson, *The History of Tom Thumbe,* ed. Curt F. Bühler (Evanston, Ill.: Northwestern University Press, 1965).

53. Tom's bold claim to negation is further evidence for Jeffrey Knapp's argument in *An Empire Nowhere: England, America, and Literature from* Utopia *to* The Tempest (Berkeley: University of California Press, 1992) that the English could imagine England as a

marginal trifle, a Nowhere/Fairyland, as a way of inscribing but evading the tension of wanting and not wanting empire.

54. I cannot identify the perhaps fictional White. Parker's "When the King Enjoys His Own Again" was long a favorite with Stuart loyalists.

55. This last is a reference to the famous statue of Erasmus reading a book; legend says he turns a page each midnight.

56. John Hare, *St. Edmund's Ghost, or, Anti-Normanism* (1647), repr. in *Harleian Miscellany* VIII (London, 1811), 94–106.

57. "F.J.," *Hey for Honesty* (1651); for the dates, see G. E. Bentley, *The Jacobean and Caroline Stage* (Oxford: Oxford University Press, 1967), under "Randolph."

58. Thomas Randolph, *Hey for Honesty,* in *Works,* ed. Hazlitt, II, 422–23; cf. *Plutus* ll. 557–61. Randolph's Gargantua recalls the chapbook, but see below for a possible echo of *P* 30.

59. "Erastophil"'s *Apologie for lovers* (1651, sig. D12v) asks: "What a Monster had [Alexander] been, if his body had been but of the same tumid and swelling bulk with his mind? Certainly Garagantua had been a meer Pigmie to him."

60. The doublet may be from *G* 8.

61. Leonard Barkan, *Transuming Passion: Ganymede and the Erotics of Humanism* (Stanford: Stanford University Press, 1991), explores his myth.

62. Henry Glapthorne, *The Hollander,* in *Plays and Poems* (London, 1874) I, 84, 111, 135.

63. Glapthorne, *The Hollander,* in *Plays* I, 154. Stephen Greenblatt, "Fiction and Friction," in *Shakespearean Negotiations: The Circulation of Social Energy in Renaissance England* (Berkeley: University of California Press, 1988), 77, links early modern interest in sex changes to a taste for prodigies. Katharine Eisaman Maus finds a similar scene in Ben Jonson's *Epicoene* hinting that "all heterosexual interaction" has "the potential for trickery (*Inwardness and Theater in the English Renaissance* [Chicago: University of Chicago Press, 1995], 151).

64. Compare Mother Bunch in *Pasquils Jests, Mixed with Mother Bunches Merriments* (1604), by William Fennor? She is 20,000.5 inches less a finger's breadth tall and 11,002 plus a nail's breadth wide; her laugh rings "from Algate to the Monuments at Westminster" and makes the Tower lions roar in terror; her fart "blew downe Charing-Crosse, with Pauls aspiring steeple" (an anti-phallic touch); and her daily diet includes 3 oxen, 23 1/4 sheep, 180 capons, 1,188 larks, and tuns of ale (*Shakespeare Jest-Books,* ed. W. C. Hazlitt [1864; New York: Burt Franklin, n.d.], III, 7–11).

65. John W. Shroeder, "Spenser's Erotic Drama: The Orgoglio Episode," *ELH* 29 (1962), 140–59.

66. Roland Antonioli, "Le Motif de l'avalage dans les chroniques gargantuines," *Etudes seiziémistes offertes à V.-L. Saulnier* (Geneva: Droz, 1980), 77–85. Cf. Tediousness in the anonymous *The Mariage of Witte and Science* (1569/70), who says "Hoh hoh hoh," brains Science's wooers, and eats them.

67. Thomas Nashe, *Have with You to Saffron-Walden,* in Nashe, *Works,* ed. R. B. McKerrow (Oxford: Blackwell, 1966), III, 34–35.

68. Nashe, *Works,* I, 59; I, 176; I, 242; III, 186; I, 320; I, 367; III, 157–58 (the last from *Lenten Stuffe* [1599]).

69. On pigs, dogs, and carnival, see Peter Stallybrass and Allon White, *The Politics and Poetics of Transgression* (Ithaca: Cornell University Press, 1986), chap. 1.

70. James Shirley, *Love Tricks*, licensed in 1625 and printed in 1631 as *The School of Complement;* in Shirley, *Dramatic Works and Poems*, ed. William Gifford and Alexander Dyce (1833; New York: Russell and Russell, 1966) I, 45 and 40. Giant-talk connotes political or social tumescence. Shirley's prologue to *The Brothers* (licensed 1626; *Works* I) states: "Treason may be wrapt in giant prose," and a boaster in Tommaso Garzoni's *Hospitall of Incurable Fooles* (1600, sig. B4) "stands upon puntoes with his drawen sword, like another Gargantua."

71. Shirley, *Dramatic Works,* I, lxxix and lxxiii; Randolph's lines are in his *Poems,* ed. G. Thorn-Drury (London, 1929), 143. The grammarian Lycophron was notoriously hard to understand.

72. In *CA* 16 Gargantua requests deerskins from the Ardennes for his purse. I thank my student Benedict Robinson for thoughts on genre.

73. Mark Bracher, "Contrary Notions of Identity in *As You Like It*," *SEL* 24 (1984), 225–40, calls the match a defeat of "exclusiveness and envy." I would add the notion of giants' link with primogeniture; cf. Louis A. Montrose, "'The Place of a Brother' in *As You Like It*: Social Process and Comic Form," *Shakespeare Quarterly* 32 (1981), 28–54.

74. From Virgil, *Aeneid,* Book III, line 658, referring to Polyphemus as "a hair-raising, shapeless, huge monster."

75. Carnival roughness peeps through the jovial evasions explored by David Kastan, "Workshop and/as Playhouse: Comedy and Commerce in *The Shoemaker's Holiday*," *SP* 84 (1987), 324–37.

76. "A Whetstone for Liars," in *The Pepys Ballads,* ed. Hyder E. Rollins (Cambridge: Harvard University Press, 1929) II, 185–90.

77. See Roger O. Iredale, "Giants and Tyrants in Book Five of *The Faerie Queene*," *RES* 17 (1966), 373–81. More generally, see Françoise Joukovsky-Micha, "La Guerre des dieux et des géants chez les poètes français du XVIe siècle (1500–1585)," *BHR* 29 (1967), 55–92, and Jean Céard, "La Révolte des géants, figure de la pensée de Ronsard," *Ronsard en son IVe centenaire* (Geneva: Droz, 1989), 221–32.

78. Brice, *A Briefe Register in Meter* (1599 ed.), sig. A7; Hanmer, *The Great Bragge and Challenge of M. Champion a Jesuite,* sig. G1; Samuel Garey, *Great Brittans Little Calendar* (1618), sig. L1.

79. Hanmer, *The Jesuites Banner* (1581), sig. E4; W. S[eres], *A Dialogue Agaynst the Tyrannye of the Papists* (1562), sig. B3v, on Cacus; Alexander Ross, *Tonsor ad cutem rasus* (1627), sigs. D3, D5.

80. The claim that two bodies can share space had some classical support, notes Richard Sorabji, in *Matter, Space, and Motion: Theories in Antiquity and Their Sequel* (Ithaca: Cornell University Press, 1988).

81. Sig. C4v; my other quotations are from John Vicars's 1624 translation, *Babels balm* (sig. N8 cites the Gunpowder Plot).

82. John Taylor derides rebels who dream they can hurl "mountaines at the head of Jove" like "Gargantua or Polipheme, / Or Gogmagog" (*Superbiae Flagellum* [1621], in Taylor, *Works* I, 46).

83. On the snobbery, cf. Sharon Achinstein, "Audiences and Authors: Ballads and the Making of English Renaissance Literary Culture," *JMRS* 22 (1992), 311–26.

Chapter 3: Copia Verborum *and the Seat of the Scorner*

1. David H. Thomas, "Rabelais in England: John Eliot's *Ortho-epia Gallica* (1593)," *ER* 9 (1971), 97–126. Gabriel Harvey had a copy. Shakespeare read him: see J. W. Lever, "Shakespeare's French Fruits," *Shakespeare Survey* 6 (1953), 79–90, and Joseph A. Porter, "More Echoes from Eliot's *Ortho-epia Gallica* in *King Lear* and *Henry V*," *Shakespeare Quarterly* 37 (1986), 486–88. Frances Yates, "The Importance of John Eliot's *Ortho-epia Gallica*," *RES* 7 (1931), 419–30, thinks Eliot satirizes Juan-Luis Vives and Claudius Holyband. Juliet Fleming, "*The French Garden:* An Introduction to Women's French," *ELH* 56 (1989), 19–51, scolds Eliot for having only two women in his text; in fact, the French shows that he has more.

2. Alice Berry, " 'L'Isle Medamothi': Rabelais's Itineraries of Anxiety (*Quart livre* 2–4)," *PMLA* 106 (1991), 1040–53 (p. 1049).

3. Ralph Robynson's epistle to William Cecil in his 1551 translation of *Utopia* evokes the siege, the bustle, and Diogenes; Robynson calls his text his own tumbled tub. Andrew Weiner, "Raphael's Eutopia and More's Utopia," *HLQ* 39 (1975), 26, believes that Robynson adapts Rabelais. Perhaps; or he could follow Rabelais's model, Lucian's "How to Write History," or Guillaume Budé's paraphrase. Robynson's version has little "to dizzy the reader, to tumble his consciousness," as Florence Weinberg describes Rabelais's effect in "*A Mon Tonneau Je Retourne:* Rabelais's Prologue to the *Tiers Livre*," *SCJ* 23 (1992), 548–63 (p. 555). It was in turn redone as a dedicatory epistle in "W.B."'s translation of Achilles Statius's *History of Clitiphon and Leucippe* (1597). Ben Jonson and William Vaughan perhaps appropriated this or some other tun (see below), and George North's translation of Philibert de Vienne's *The Philosopher of the Court* (1575) remarks that if Diogenes were to bring his tun to court, "would not the Pages roll him up and downe; But if he were a Menippus, or Fryer John of Saincte Anthonies order [i.e., Frère Jean], they woulde prayse him better" (sig. E1v).

4. In one exception, Eliot adopts for friendship(?) vocabulary that Rabelais applies to heterosexual sex: "Valerian my deare friend, my neere cousin. Come, cullion let me crush thy callibisters [genitals] with accoling [hugging] thy buttockes" (sig. q3). Thomas cites G 39, which has hugging but no crushed privates.

5. Eliot can put on modesty, translating "tresbien chier" as "go to the &c. lustily" (sig. l4).

6. On what might be in the barrel see Weinberg, "*Tonneau*"; for Terence Cave, *The Cornucopian Text: Problems of Writing in the French Renaissance* (Oxford: Clarendon, 1979), the text's "very celebration of fertility, plenitude, presence, reveals an inverse movement towards emptiness or absence" (187).

7. See Lazare Sainéan, *La Langue de Rabelais* (Paris: Boccard, 1922–23), II, and Mireille Huchon, *Rabelais grammairien* (Geneva: Droz, 1981).

8. "Do you wish," says Her Trippa, "to know the truth more fully by fire-divination, by sky-divination (made famous by Aristophanes in his *Clouds*), by water-divination,

by bowl-of-water-divination (so celebrated among the Assyrians and recently used by Ermolao Barbaro)? In a basin of water I will show you your future wife tumbling about with two knaves." "When," says Panurge, "you put your nose in my ass remember to remove your glasses."

9. I.e., no more than readers can understand Aleman's thieves' cant by turning the leaves of John Minsheu's *Ductor in linguas* (1617 et seq.); the punctuation is confusing.

10. Thomas Browne, *Miscellaneous Tracts,* in Browne, *Works,* ed. Geoffrey Keynes (London: Faber, 1928–1931), V, 95–96. Browne adds a nonsense epistle in French; Olivier Leroy, *Le Chevalier Thomas Browne* (Paris: Gamber, 1931), 79–82, identifies its Rabelaisian phrases.

11. Kathleen Lambley, *The Teaching and Cultivation of the French Language in Tudor and Stuart Times* (Manchester: Manchester University Press, 1920), and Douglas A. Kibbee, *For to Speke Frenche Trewely: The French Language in England, 1000–1600: Its Status, Description and Instruction,* Amsterdam Studies in the Theory and History of Linguistic Science 60 (Amsterdam: John Benjamins, 1991).

12. Lucy Ferrer, *Un devancier de Cotgrave: La Vie et les oeuvres de Claude de Sainliens* (1908; Geneva: Slatkine, 1971). Marcel de Grève's too skeptical "Limites de l'influence linguistique de Rabelais en Angleterre au XVIe siècle," *CLS* 1 (1964), 15–30, misses Holyband's citations of Rabelais. See also Mark Eccles, "Claudius Hollyband and the Earliest French-English Dictionaries," *SP* 83 (1986), 51–61.

13. See, e.g., Michael A. Screech, *Rabelais* (Ithaca: Cornell University Press, 1979), 401–10. Under *trespassé,* Randle Cotgrave's *Dictionarie of the French and English Tongues* (1611) has "*Il pisse pour les trespassez.* An equivocation; for it may either signifie the dead (upon whose graves the Papists use to sprinkle holie water) or have relation unto *Traicts passez;* draughts of drinke alreadie swallowed downe." In William S. Wood's facsimile edition (Columbia: University of South Carolina Press, 1950).

14. Lawrence D. Kritzman, *The Rhetoric of Sexuality and the Literature of the French Renaissance* (Cambridge: Cambridge University Press, 1991), 201–13, says they "deprive the biblical [text] of the epistemological delusion of its transcendental status," making "biblical utterance" seem "ridiculous" (203). Rabelais undermines Scripture only if a reader makes him do so, but Kritzman's response shows why some found that writer dangerous.

15. Badebec died giving birth; Holyband forgot which book has the scene.

16. See Lazare Sainéan, "Les Interprètes de Rabelais en Angleterre et en Allemagne," *RER* 7 (1909), 137–258; Vera E. Smalley, *The Sources of "A Dictionarie of the French and English Tongues" by Randle Cotgrave (London, 1611)* (Baltimore: Johns Hopkins University Press, 1948); and Peter Rickard, "Le 'Dictionarie' franco-anglais de Cotgrave (1611)," *Cahiers de l'Association Internationale des Etudes Françaises* 35 (1983), 7–21. Cotgrave is also intrigued by legal and political terminology as well as by proverbs and provincial dialects.

17. The precision in this case may be illusory, for in fact the passage reads: " 'Voilà,' dist Frere Jan, 'un *comme* mal à propous.' " Perhaps the printer misread "comme mal" as "commenial." Jean puns on the sound "con" nestled in "comment"; on this and other puns see Guy Demerson, "Les Calembours de Rabelais," in *Le Comique verbal en France au XVIe siècle* (Warsaw: University of Warsaw Press, 1981), 73–93.

18. Rabelais would have recalled how Publius Claudius, taking the auspices before a battle in the First Punic War, was angered by the chickens' refusal to eat; telling them to drink instead, he had them thrown into the ocean — and lost the battle (Cicero, *De natura deorum*, II.7).

19. E.g., *cremasteres*: "two sinewes, or muskles, wherby the cods do hang," and *emonctoire*: "an Emunctorie; a kernallie place of the bodie, that serves for the voyding of such humors as be superfluous in, or offensive unto, a principall, or noble part; such be under th'eares for the braines, th'armpits for the heart, and the groine or share for the liver; also, a snuffer."

20. On Rabelais's sexual lexicon, see Raymond C. La Charité, "An Aspect of Obscenity in Rabelais," in *Renaissance and Other Studies in Honor of William Leon Wiley*, ed. George B. Daniel, Jr. (Chapel Hill: University of North Carolina Press, 1968), 167–89.

21. The generosity is purely verbal and yet not quite, in Renaissance terms, thereby immaterial. On the ways food, feast, and language related to each other in humanist discourse, see Michel Jeanneret, *A Feast of Words: Banquets and Table Talk in the Renaissance* (Chicago: University of Chicago Press, 1991). For all its workaday utility, Cotgrave's dictionary also has ties to the Menippea, holiday, and festive talk.

22. That fate is also in the *Dictionarie: croque-quenouille* is "he whose wife beats him with a distaffe: ¶Rab." The *Dodechedron of Fortune*, a prognostication system fathered on Jean de Meung and translated by "Sir W.B." (1613), claims, in "The French Author to the Reader," that methods of prognostication have been "most curiously sought and published by the [sic] Rabelays in his Pantagouelisme. And although that jestingly, as mockes, hee puts them out, yet neverthelesse hee speaketh not without a purpose and meaning" (sig. ¶2v). The meaning is unspecified, perhaps because the French had said only that the "facetie" masks "erudition." Donald Stone guided me to Harvard's copy of the 1556 edition of the French; the 1560 French edition drops the allusion.

23. Bodleian (80 R40 Art), noted in *NRB* 80; the glosses I quote are on leaves 14–16 in what seems to be an early seventeenth-century hand. I thank Jane Anthony, an Oxford graduate student, for checking the hand and transcriptions. This could be the 1599 *Oeuvres* in Thomas James's *Catalogus librorum Bibliothecae publicae quam T. Bodleius in academia Oxoniensi nuper instituit* (Oxford, 1620). The 1605 catalogue lacks Rabelais.

24. A version of the following discussion appears in my "Jonson's Rabelais" in *New Perspectives on Ben Jonson*, ed. James Hirsh (Madison, N.J.: Fairleigh Dickinson University Press, 1997), 35–54. I have not been able to identify Skynner. *NRB* spells it "Skynnir," but the "e" (like that "Beniamin") resembles "e" in "the," the top merging with the next letter. This edition has the "Epistre du Limousin," "Chresme philosophale," and "Deux epistres à deux vieilles." William Drummond, Jonson's Scottish host, included Rabelais in a list of "Books red be me" in 1609; see Robert MacDonald, *The Library of Drummond of Hawthornden* (Edinburgh: Edinburgh University Press, 1971).

25. I thank Robert C. Evans and H. R. Woudhuysen for confirming that the glosses are Jonson's; the latter is "90 percent" sure. The volume is mentioned by Richard Proudfoot in "Richard Johnson's *Tom a Lincoln* Dramatized: A Jacobean Play in British Library MS Add. 61745," in *New Ways of Looking at Old Texts: Papers of the Renaissance English Text Society 1985–1991*, ed. W. Speed Hill (Binghamton, N.Y.: MRTS 107, 1993).

26. Bruce Thomas Boehrer, "The Poet of Labor: Authorship and Property in the Work of Ben Jonson," *PQ* 72 (1993), 289–312, ties Jonsonian linguistics to claims of authorship and a unique self (indicated by his dropping the "h" from his name; this inscription reinserts it).

27. See Marcel Tetel, "La Valeur comique des accumulations verbales chez Rabelais," *Romanic Review* 53 (1962), 96–104. On lists as "escrime gratuit" exorcizing thought through style, see François Rigolot, *Les Langages de Rabelais* (ER 10; Geneva: Droz, 1972), 162–72.

28. Thomas Nashe, *Strange Newes* (1592), in Nashe, *Works,* ed. Ronald B. McKerrow (Oxford: Blackwell, 1958) I, 282.

29. Jewell's request that Harding not "dismembre my sayinges, and culle out my woordes, and take choise of my sentences, without regarde what goeth before, or what cometh after" (sig. ¶3) might modify the belief(which I share) that Renaissance writers and readers tend to ignore context. There are splendid lists in Hendrick Niclaes's allegorical *Terra pacis* (trans. 1575). T. W. Hayes, "The Peaceful Apocalypse: Familism and Literacy in Sixteenth-Century England," *SCJ* 17 (1986), 131–43, calls them Rabelaisian; to me they indicate a material world through which pilgrims pass, whereas Rabelais's lists suspend that world as words go forth and multiply.

30. Thomas Wilson, *Arte of Rhetorique,* ed. Thomas J. Derrick (New York: Garland, 1982), 327–28, 391, 36.

31. *Miscellaneous Prose of Sir Philip Sidney,* ed. Katherine Duncan-Jones and Jan van Dorsten (Oxford: Clarendon, 1973), 21–32. Duncan-Jones calls Rabelais a probable source, citing the final Latin tags (16, 181).

32. Alan Hager, "Rhomboid Logic: Anti-Idealism and a Cure for Recusancy in Sidney's *Lady of May,*" *ELH* 57 (1990), 485–502, cites Wilson and the pedants of Italian comedy. I agree that Sidney cannot parody the anti-Aristotelian scholar Peter Ramus, and not just because of friendship: Rombus is scholastic and Ramus modern.

33. See A.-F. Bourgeois, "Rabelais en Angleterre," *RER* 3 (1905), 80–83. But Holofernes's sounding of the "b" in "debt" and "doubt" is humanist pedantry. B. J. Sokol, "Holofernes in Rabelais and Shakespeare and Some Manuscript Verses of Thomas Harriot," *ER* 25 (1991), 131–35, considers him a parody of Harriot.

34. *Tom A Lincoln* (ca. 1611–1616), ed. John Pitcher (Oxford: Oxford University Press, for the Malone Society, 1992), xxxi, quotes Rabelais and Jonson's gloss. Edmond Huguet's *Dictionnaire de la langue française du seizième siècle* (Paris, 1925) cites Rabelais and Philips van Marnix (read in England). In his *Defence of the Articles of the Protestant Religion,* William Barlow notes the "rude gloses of Bardocuculion Monkish Friers," recalling *CL* 3 or Marnix, whom Huguet also cites.

35. The 1595 translation (sigs. Bb1–Bb1v), republished in 1602 as *Englandes Bright Honour; Satyre ménippée: De la vertue du catholicon d'Espagne et de la tenue des estatz de Paris* (1594), ed. Charles Marcilly (Paris: Garnier, 1889), 331 (the allusion to Rabelais reads: "le bon Rabelais, qui a passé tous les autres en rencontres et belles robineries, si on veut en retrancher les quodlibets de taverne et las saletez des cabarets"). On authorship, see Eugene Kirk, *Menippean Satire: An Annotated Catalogue of Texts and Criticism* (New York: Garland Press, 1980), and on this passage, W. Scott Blanchard, *Scholars' Bedlam: Menippean Satire in the Renaissance* (Lewisburg, Pa.: Bucknell University Press,

1995), 33–35 (91–107 are on Rabelais). *Satyre,* parts of which first circulated in 1593, supports Henri IV against the Ligue; on its context and methods, see *Etudes sur la "Satyre Ménippée,"* ed. Frank Lestringant and Daniel Ménager (Geneva: Droz, 1987).

36. *The Letters of John Chamberlain,* ed. Norman E. McClure (1939; Westport: Greenwood, 1979) I, 45.

37. That is, "they seem like a robe made of cloth of gold, glorious and utterly precious, that was embroidered with dung," for "there are no volumes in the world so beautiful, embellished, and elegant as the texts of the Pandects [large collections of legal texts]; but the hem, that is the glossing by Accursius [a thirteenth-century authority], is so disgraceful and stinking that it is mere nastiness and filth."

38. "First, to preserve the form, the omission of which renders what one has done valueless, as is proven very well by [legal citations follow]; added to which, you know too well that often in judicial procedures forms destroy materialities and substances; for form being changed the substance is changed [more citations]." Bridoye seems to say that by examining the evidence he observes the formalities, and that this then changes and even abolishes what is material — it's time to get out the dice.

39. On Selden's threat to royal politics and clerical funding, see Daniel R. Woolf, *The Idea of History in Early Stuart England* (Toronto: University of Toronto Press, 1990), chap. 7 (p. 207 mentions Selden's stylistic limitations and 214 and 237 his development into a "philological historian"). Cf. Paul Christianson, "Young John Selden and the Ancient Constitution, 1610–1618," *Proceedings of the American Philosophical Society* 128 (1984), 271–315.

40. John Selden, *De Diis Syris,* in Selden, *Opera,* ed. David Wilkins (London, 1726) II, 373–74: "But to squander credence on this sort of conjecture is not my habit. This demigod, if memory does not fail me, is given as 'Nephleseth' for 'Miphlezeth' in François Rabelais's most witty satires and very learned jests." The word is defined as a penis in *QL*'s "Brievfe Declaration" and by Cotgrave (with a "¶Rab"); it is the name of the Sausage Queen in *QL.*

41. I do not know what "bread-band" means.

42. Monks "eat the shit of the world, that is, its sins, and as mache-merdes [dung-eaters and, says Cotgrave, nasty fish] people confine them [literally, toss them back] to their retreats." Urquhart translates *retraictz* as "privies and secessive places." If a machemerde is a *saupe,* then "on les rejecte" means that monasteries are both privies and the depths into which one throws back worthless fish.

43. Francis Bacon, *The Advancement of Learning* I.3, ed. Arthur Johnston (Oxford: Clarendon, 1974), 22–23. Johnston cites Rabelais.

44. "Sileni were, in the old days, little boxes like those we now see in apothecary shops, painted outside with such entertaining and frivolous figures as harpies, satyrs, bridle-geese, horned hares, saddled ducks, flying goats, harnessed harts, and other images fantasized at pleasure to make people laugh (as did Silenus, mentor of the good Bacchus); but inside one stored fine drugs, like balm, ambergreese, amomon, musk, civet, with jewels and other precious things. Such they called Socrates, for seeing him from the outside and judging him by his appearance, you would not have given an onion's root-end for him, he was so ugly in body and ridiculous in his demeanor, with a pointed nose, the look of a bull, the face of a fool, simple in his habits, rustic in dress, poor in fortune, unlucky with

222 Notes to Pages 68–72

women, unfit for any political office, always laughing, always drinking toasts to every-body, always joshing, always hiding his divine knowledge. But opening this box you would have found inside it a heavenly and priceless drug: a superhuman understanding, marvelous virtue, invincible courage, unparalleled sobriety, settled contentment, perfect assurance, and an astonishing disregard of everything for which humanity so much watches, runs, works, sails, and fights."

45. "Do you believe, upon your word, that when Homer wrote the *Iliad* and *Odyssey* he thought of those allegories that Plutarch, Heraclides Ponticus, Eustatius, or Cornutus squeezed from him and that Politian in turn stole?"

46. Bacon, *Advancement,* Book II, section 4 (p. 82); the note cites *Gargantua.* Bacon's shift shows the interest in originality examined by Achsah Guibbory, "Imitation and Originality: Cowley and Bacon's Vision of Progress," *SEL* 29 (1989), 99–120.

47. Plutarch, "How a Man May Become Aware of His Progress in Virtue," in his *Moralia,* trans. P. H. de Lacy and Benedict Einarson (Cambridge: Harvard University Press, 1959), I, 421, sec. 79. Jean Guiton, "Le Mythe des paroles gelées," *Romanic Review* 31 (1940), 3–15, gives the chief sources, including Caelius Calcagninus. Screech, *Rabelais,* 377–439, outlines theories known to Rabelais that reconcile Plato and Aris-totle on signs and signifieds. In "A propos de paroles gelées et degelées (*Quart Livre* 55–56): 'Plus hault sens' ou 'lectures plurielles'?" in *Rabelais's Incomparable Book,* ed. Raymond La Charité (Lexington, Ky.: French Forum, 1986), Gérard Defaux argues that Rabelais shows the hermeneutic primacy of the literal and material, not the impossibility of interpretation.

48. Guiton notes the scene's "exotisme nordique et macabre." See also A. P. Stabler, "Rabelais, Thevet, L'Ile des Démons, et les Paroles Gelées," *ER* 11 (Geneva: Droz, 1974), 57–62, and Kim Campbell, "Of Horse Fish and Frozen Words," *R&R* 14 (1990), 183–92, who notes how discovery narratives raised issues of authority and eye-witnessing.

49. V.-L. Saulnier, "Le Silence de Rabelais et le mythe des paroles gelées," in *François Rabelais: Ouvrage publié pour le quatrième centenaire de sa mort, 1553–1953* (Geneva: Droz, 1953), 233–47.

50. Jerome Schwartz, *Irony and Ideology in Rabelais: Structures of Subversion* (Cam-bridge: Cambridge University Press, 1990), 189–94, notes the pilot's practicality.

51. Evelyn M. Simpson, *A Study of the Prose Works of John Donne* (Oxford: Claren-don, 1948), no. 6, p. 310. The unsigned letter is among those in a manuscript collection of disparate materials, found near a copy of Donne's "To Sir H.W. at his going Ambassador to Venice" with a postscript mentioning Rabelais. Donne would have been intrigued by the legal and scriptural implications of *seeing* words.

52. I quote from the anonymous facsimile: Thomas Coryat, *Coryates Crudities* (Glas-gow: James MacLehose, 1905). "Crudities" are youth's raw produce.

53. For the Popehawk, see *CL* 1–8, which is also the first half of 1562's *L'Isle sonante,* nucleus of 1564's *CL;* Dones's plural is incorrect, for Pantagruel's companions meet only one "Papegault," the normal complement at a given time. As for the sausage wars, Florence Weinberg, "Layers of Emblematic Prose: Rabelais' Andouilles," *SCJ* 26 (1995), 367–77, explains the episode's satire of German and Swiss Protestants. If this is right, Dones has missed the point: at some distance from the events of the 1540s, he hears laughter only at conservative Catholics, not at intransigent Reformers. On the anger

behind the episodes that Dones singles out, see Gérard Defaux, "Rabelais contre les Eglises: Pour une 'lecture cosmographique' du *Quart Livre*," *ER* 30 (1995), 137–202. Defaux's Rabelais is harsher, at least in the later books, than the more irenic evangelical some see.

54. "Song composed in fool's rhyme, suited to the style of the book's author, made in praise of this heroic Odcombian giant, named not Pantagruel but Pantagrue—not Goose or Gosling but 'Alldimcran(e)ium' [*grue* can mean crane or nitwit]—here costumed as a hodgepodge, hash, or mincemeat [a "cabirotade," says Cotgrave, is "stewed meat, compounded of Veale, Capon, Chicken, or Partridge, minced, spiced, and layed upon severall beds of Cheese"], so as to find a place in the library of the Abbey of St. Victor at Paris between Marmotretus' *De baboinis et Cingis* and [Béda's] *De optimitate triparum,* and to bear the title *Coryate's Cabirotade: Concerning the Apodemistichopezologie of Odcombe in Somerset.*" After some foolery Whitaker turns to Rabelais: "Silence, Rabelais: and humbled be the pride / Of thy great Sausages, which gave such warm reception / To thy Giant in the Ferocious Isle: / To this Odcombian Giant stone and stump / Have spoken, explained themselves, entertained him / Courted him, indeed kept him sane / In this work: but knowest thou why? / His crested head [as in coxcomb?] gave unto him this law: / That since of local men he did not know the tongue / 'Mid trees and stones he'd pass his frenzy's rage." My thanks to Roger and Marie-José Kuin for help in translating Whitaker. I cannot identify him; Was he related to William Whitaker (1548–1595), master of St. John's, Cambridge?

55. Patricia Parker, "On the Tongue: Cross Gendering, Effeminacy, and the Art of Words," *Style* 23 (1989), 445–65, shows how Erasmus and Tomkis allow that men misuse speech and then call the misuse womanish. She dates the play before ca. 1602, but see F. S. Boas, "'Macbeth' and 'Lingua,'" *MLR* 4 (1909), 517–20. Cf. Douglas Bruster, "'In a Woman's Key': Women's Speech and Women's Language in Renaissance Drama," *Exemplaria* 4:2 (1992), 235–66. The solemnity with which the play is being read distorts its tone and hence its cultural significance, whatever the value of exposing a misogyny Tomkis does not conceal.

56. See *P* 9; Joseph Hall calls Antipodean common in the 1590s (*Virgidemiae* VI.i).

57. Tomkis adopts passages on ingenuity and projection from *QL* on Gaster the stomach-lord that come shortly after the frozen words episode.

58. Thomas Nashe, *An Almond for a Parrat*, in *Works*, ed. R. B. McKerrow (Oxford: Blackwell, 1966), III, 341–42; Leland H. Carlson, *Martin Marprelate, Gentleman: Master Job Throkmorton Laid Open in His Colors* (San Marino, Calif: Huntington Library Press, 1981), 70.

59. "Esprit abstraict, ravy, et ecstatic, / Qui frequentant les cieulx, ton origine, / A delaissé ton hoste et domestic, / Ton corps. . . . / Vouldrois ty poinct faire quelque sortie / De ton manoir divin, perpetuel? / Et ça bas veoir une tierce partie / Des faictz joyeux du bon Pantagruel?" Rabelais mentions a "third part," but at least two copies of his works place the poem early (see *NRB* 48); Nashe was not alone in finding the poem introductory to most of the work.

60. D. J. McGinn, "Nashe's Share in the Marprelate Controversy," *PMLA* 59 (1944), 952–84, argues that Nashe wrote *Almond,* and Von Werner v. Koppenfels, "Thomas Nashe und Rabelais," *Archiv für das Studium der Neueren Sprachen u. Literaturen* 207

(1970), 277–91, thinks that Nashe knew Rabelais well. For McKerrow, Rabelais "thought for himself," whereas Nashe was "purely conventional" (V, 128–31). But Nashe's subversiveness lies in his words' flight from moral significance into turmoil, game, and nonsense. Cf. Jonathan Crewe, *Unredeemed Rhetoric: Thomas Nashe and the Scandal of Authorship* (Baltimore: Johns Hopkins University Press, 1982), 33: "The Puritan world Nashe displays in *Almond* threatens to become one of utopian indifference, festive vitality, and animal well-being. . . . Nashe's consciousness both of Rabelaisian excess and Erasmian folly heightens the ambivalence of his representation." On what Nashe and Rabelais share, see Neil Rhodes, *Elizabethan Grotesque* (London: Routledge, 1980), and Rhodes, *The Power of Eloquence and English Renaissance Literature* (New York: St. Martin's Press, 1992). Lorna Hutson, *Thomas Nashe in Context* (Oxford: Clarendon, 1989), argues that "while Rabelais conceives of bodies as renewable organisms in a grotesquely growing and changing world, Nashe conceives of them as bodily material, part of society's expendable resources" (15).

61. Arthur Saul's *The Famous Game of Chesse-Play,* republished in 1618 with additions by "Jo. Barbier," may owe terminology to the chess ballet in CL 23–24. Chess rules had changed, letting the queen move any distance in a line of empty squares (Henry J. R. Murray, *A History of Chess* [Oxford: Clarendon, 1913]), and Barbier wonders whether, going "abroad" with "unlimited commaund," she should be called a "duke" (sigs. C3v–C4). Saul says: "If in her march shee prove severe, / and taketh all she may, / Tis for the safegard of the King, / that shee makes cleare the way. / For this she may not blamed be, / that seekes her King to save, / It is her glory for to strive[,] / her King in peace to have (sig. A8v).

Saul's rules resemble those in *CL;* in both, for instance, a knight "leapes" (*sault*). Barbier says the French call bishops "archers" and derive *roc* (rook) from "custode de la roche," as in *CL.* Thomas Middleton's *A Game at Chess* (1624), a theatrical *succès de scandale* in which Catholic powers try to checkmate England, may owe something to *CL* — or to the 1618 *Famous Game.* Paul Yachnin, "*A Game at Chess* and Chess Allegory," *SEL* 22 (1982), 317–30, sees a debt to *CL,* but N. W. Bawcutt, "New Light on Middleton's Knowledge of Chess," *NQ* 232 (1987), 301–02, traces the terminology and the rook's replacement by a "duke" to Barbier. For other material and references, see my "Housing Chessmen and Bagging Bishops: Space and Desire in Colonna, 'Rabelais,' and Middleton's *Game at Chess,*" in *Soundings of Things Done: Essays in Early Modern Literature in Honor of S.K. Heninger Jr.,* ed. Peter E. Medine and Joseph Wittreich (Newark: University of Delaware Press, 1997), 215–33. A link remains with *CL* if Saul and Barbier had read about the erotically charged dance that Panurge watches on his way to his own endgame: a decision to be mated.

62. The following paragraphs adapt my "Nipping Taunts and Angry Porcupines: Humour and Satire in the Renaissance," in the forthcoming Renaissance volume of *The Cambridge History of Literary Criticism.* See also Raymond A. Anselment, *"Betwixt Jest and Earnest": Marprelate, Milton, Marvell, Swift and the Decorum of Religious Ridicule* (Toronto: University of Toronto Press, 1979), chap. 2.

63. Marvin T. Herrick, *Comic Theory in the Sixteenth Century* (Urbana: University of Illinois Press, 1964), chap. 3, and (for the cardiac theory) Laurent Joubert, *Traité du ris* (1579), ed. and trans. as *Treatise on Laughter* by Gregory de Rocher (University: University of Alabama Press, 1990). De Rocher's *Rabelais' Laughers* and Joubert's *"Traité du*

Ris (University: University of Alabama Press, 1979) shows how Renaissance humor — relying on pain and humiliation yet in some ways charitable — differs from our own.

64. Nashe the Younger tells of a man with a blocked gut who prays for salvation: when his fool says God will hardly grant him Heaven after denying him "so small a matter as a fart" he laughs his obstruction loose (*Miscelanea*, 1639 ed., sig. Nn3). Joubert, *Traité du ris*, 127–28, tells — like others before him — of men cured by laughing at monkeys.

65. See Joanna B. Lipking, "Traditions of the *Facetiae* and Their Influence in Tudor England," Ph.D. diss., Columbia University, 1970, and George Luck, "Vir Facetus: A Renaissance Ideal," *SP* 55 (1958), 107–21.

66. Charles Estienne's *Dictionarium*, e.g., describes Lucian as "primum Christianus, demum fidei desertor: sed tandem suae improbitatis luit poenas gravissimas, nam à canibus devoratus misere interiit" (1596 ed.).

67. Francis Bacon, *The Essayes or Counsels, Civill and Morall,* ed. Michael Kiernan (Cambridge: Harvard University Press, 1985), 12, 53.

68. Francis Bacon, *Apothegms New and Old,* in Bacon, *Works,* ed. James Spedding, R. L. Ellis, and D. D. Heath (1857–74; New York: Garrett Press, 1968), VII, 131, item 46. Another "apothegm," appealing to the lawyer in Bacon, appears in the posthumous 1661 *Resuscitatio:* "Rabelais tells a tale of one [Bridoye] that was very fortunate in compounding differences. His son undertook the same course, but could never compound any. Whereupon he came to his father and asked him, *what art he had to reconcile differences?* He answered, *he had no other but this: to watch when the two parties were much wearied, and their hearts were too great to seek reconcilement at one another's hands; then to be a means betwixt them, and upon no other terms.* After which the son went home, and prospered in the same undertakings" (*Works,* VII, 170, item 44; cf. *TL* 41).

69. "I am going to seek a great Perhaps" and "Draw the (bed)curtain, the farce is played out." For such anecdotes see Lazare Sainéan, *L'Influence et la réputation de Rabelais* (Paris: Gamber, 1930); Marcel de Grève, *L'Interprétation de Rabelais au XVIe siècle* (*ER* 3, 1961), chap. 4, and "François Rabelais et les libertins du XVIIe siècle," *ER* 1 (1956), 120–50; Pierre Villey, *Marot et Rabelais* (Paris: Champion, 1923), chap. 14; and Lucien Febvre, *The Problem of Unbelief in the Sixteenth Century,* trans. Beatrice Gottlieb (Cambridge: Harvard University Press, 1982). Wills were also ascribed to Rabelais, such as "Je dois beaucoup, je n'ay rien vaillant, je donne le reste aux pauvres" (I owe much; I possess nothing of value; I give what remins to the poor: Sainéan, *Influence,* 94). Guillaume Colletet's mid-seventeenth-century *Notice sur François Rabelais* rebuts such stories and, less plausibly, insists on Rabelais's orthodoxy; although the manuscript burned in 1871, extracts had been published in 1867 (repr. Geneva: Slatkine, 1970). But then, the French are born scoffers, says an English version of Giovanni Botero's *Travellers breviat* (1611 ed., sigs Q1–Q1v), citing a dying man who says of the priest bearing the Host, "I know it is our Saviour, he comes to me as he went to Jerusalem . . . carried by an Asse." Another declines communion: "I eate no flesh on Friday."

70. Morris bought the Lyons 1596 *Oeuvres* (*NRB* 78) for two shillings, sixpence. In 1608, he was about twenty-eight. See T. A. Birrell, *The Library of John Morris: The Reconstruction of a Seventeenth-Century Collection* (London: British Library, 1976), no. 1153; he also had Lucian, Poggio, *Satyre ménippée,* and Aretino.

71. Grève, "François Rabelais et les libertins du XVIIe siècle."

72. As Dorothy Gabe Coleman says in *Rabelais: A Critical Study in Prose Fiction* (Cambridge: Cambridge University Press, 1971), 2, each side "became increasingly sensitive to irreverence and gaulois obscenity." True, some polemicists quoted Rabelais urbanely. In *The Jesuites Catechisme* (1602), a translation (by W. Watson?) of Estienne Pasquier's Catholic but anti-Jesuit *Catechisme des jesuites* (Paris, 1602), a speaker recalls the dispute between Ramus and Pierre Galland: "This enmity, Rablays the Lucian of our age, in the preface of his 3. booke, and after him Joachim Bellay, a gallant Poet, in one of his chiefe Poems, scoffed at, with expresse inventions, which are the best passages in all theyr bookes" (sig. F3, citing *QL* prol.). Someone copied this on the inside front cover of a copy of the 1605 Antwerp *Oeuvres* (*NRB* 82, at Harvard); an inscription reads: "Johannes Giles Ex dono Roberti Stephani." Pasquier also says Jesuits have "more tricks of legier du maine, then Maister Peter Patelin, or Frances de Villon, or Panurde de Rabelais: for all that these three worshipfull Doctors did, was but in matters of trifles" (sig. Ff3v). And Jesuit victories are "imaginarie," like those of Picrochole as described by the "wise foole Rablais" (sig. Hh1; the French has "sage-fol").

73. I.e., "wicked and impious . . . and utterly atheist," from *In Evangelium secundum Matthaeum, Marcum et Lucam, commentarii* (1553); in Febvre, *Problem,* 140.

74. "François Rabelais ayant humé de ce poison, s'est voulu moquer de toute religion, comme un vilain et profane qu'il estoit. Dieu lui osta tellement le sens, qu'ayant mené une vie de pourceau, il mourut aussi brutalement et tout yvre, se moquant de ceux qui lui parloyent de Dieu et de sa misericorde."

75. "Not an anabaptist, not a papist is Rabelais, / Nor yet one of the Reformed religion: / Hence, if you should ask what sect he seeks: / Either he's of no sect, or he was an atheist."

76. I translate "Dei metus inest, neque hominum reverentia," "omnia, divina, humanaque proculcat, et ludibrio habet," "venenum" and "maledicentias."

77. Cf. Henri Busson, "Les Eglises contre Rabelais," *ER* 7 (1967), 62; *QL* 32 mentions "Demoniacles Calvins" and "enraigez Putherbes" as "monstres."

78. Thomas James, *Appendix ad catalogum* (1635).

79. Prescott, "Beza," and Alain Dufour, "Le mythe de Genève aux temps de Calvin," in Dufour, *Histoire politique et psychologie historique* (Geneva: Droz, 1966).

80. I have not seen puns on *Rabshakeh,* but in 1536 Jean Visagier denied "Rabelais" has *rabie* (rabies) and *laesus* (wound; in Grève, *Interpretation,* 30).

81. Benvenuto Italiano's *Il passagiere* (1612), dialogues on travel translated as *The Passenger* by a Mr. King, fears mockery by those with "the Gall of Rabilius" (sig. A3); Is this Rabelais? Cf. Constantia Munda, *The Worming of a Mad Dogge* (1617) sig. B3v, on Joseph Swetnam.

82. Thomas Carew, *Coelum Britannicum,* in *The Poems of Thomas Carew,* ed. Rhodes Dunlap (Oxford: Clarendon, 1949), 156–57. Carew's Momus, like Lucian's, is *creatively* negative. Victor Turner calls liminality "the Nay to all positive structural assertions, but as in some sense the source of them all, . . . whence novel configurations of ideas and relations may arise" (quoted by Barbara Babcock-Abrahams, "'A Tolerated Margin of Mess': The Trickster and His Tales Reconsidered," *Journal of the Folklore Institute* 11 [1975], 185).

Quicksilver Interlude

1. There is no connection with the god Pan beyond a shared Greek word for "all" and, perhaps, a similarly skittish sexual swagger. On the name see also Jerome Schwartz, "Panurge's Impact on Pantagruel (*Pantagruel*, Chapter IX)," *Romanic Review* 67 (1976), 1–8, and Ludwig Schrader, *Panurge und Hermes: Zum Ursprung eines Charakters bei Rabelais* (Bonn: University of Bonn, 1958). On tricksters see especially Paul Radin, *The Trickster* (1956; New York: Schocken, 1972); Barbara Babcock, " 'A Tolerated Margin of Mess': The Trickster and His Tales Reconsidered," *Journal of the Folklore Institute* 11 (1975), 147–86; and Wayne A. Rebhorn, " 'The Emperour of Mens Minds': The Renaissance Trickster as *Homo Rhetoricus*," in *Creative Imitation: New Essays on Renaissance Literature in Honor of Thomas M. Greene*, ed. David Quint, Margaret W. Ferguson, G. W. Pigman III, and Wayne A. Rebhorn (Binghamton, N.Y.: MRTS 95, 1992).

2. Robert Griffin, "The Devil and Panurge," *Studi Francesi* 47–48 (1972), 329–36; Raymond La Charité, *Recreation, Reflection and Re-Creation: Perspectives on Rabelais's Pantagruel* (Lexington, Ky.: French Forum, 1980), chap. 4, notes his roving, seediness, lies, sophistry, glossolalia, hunger, and lawsuits.

3. Galen, *Opera*, ed. Carolus G. Kühn (Leipzig, 1827) 5.251, 6.269, 14.27, 14.54, 15.105; Kühn translates with such terms as *subdola* and *fraudulenter*. Cf. Vivian Nutton, "Rabelais's copy of Galen," *ER* 22 (1988), 181–87.

4. Schrader, *Panurge und Hermes*, 123, 126. Gérard Defaux, *Le Curieux, le glorieux et la sagesse du monde dans la première moitié du XVIe siècle* (Lexington, Ky.: French Forum Monographs 34, 1982), calls Panurge a "boule de mercure" (12).

5. Plautus in fact seems not to have used *panurgia*, although Ambrosius Calepinus' dictionary (Venice, 1571 ed.) also cites him: "Panurgia te in pistrinum dabit." Maybe he remembers Terence's *Andria*, ll. 198–200, when the slave Davy is told not to be *callidus* or "I'll send you to the mill."

6. Aristophanes, *The Knights (Hippeis)*, ed. and trans. Benjamin B. Rogers (London: Bell, 1910), ll. 44–45.

7. Cicero, *Pro Quinto Roscio*, secs. 27–32, trans. John Henry Freese (Cambridge: Harvard University Press, 1967). Schrader and Screech, who mention him in passing, call Panurge a surname; I suspect it is a nickname suitable for an actor or slave.

8. Norman O. Brown, *Hermes the Thief: The Evolution of a Myth* (Madison: University of Wisconsin Press, 1947). William R. Dynes, "The Trickster-Figure in Jacobean City Comedy," *SEL* 33 (1993), 365–84, thinks that dramatists gave the Trickster "unrelenting distrust" of society's "economic imperatives," but an ambiguous economic role is one of his persistent traits. Panurge is linked to demonic subtlety in Antoine Marcourt's Reformist *Livre des marchans* (1533). See also Joseph Porter, *Shakespeare's Mercutio: His History and Drama* (Chapel Hill: University of North Carolina Press, 1988). Richard Hillman, *Shakespearean Subversions: The Trickster and the Play-Text* (London: Routledge, 1992), notes that Falstaff looks back to Folly, Pantagruel, and Montaigne (117); I find him more panurgic: a vocal thieving coward beloved by a prince who sees through him.

9. Trans. "E.A.," sig. U6, in "Of the Philosophers Stone," loosely combining *P* 17 and *TL* 2. Later, La Noue says dryly that although modern monks study hatred, Rabelais

"doth paint us them out more moderate and tractable: for so farre were they from sclaundering and hurting, that contrariwise they sought to bee merie and make good cheere with all men. Among the rest he speaketh of Frier Bernard Lardon, restant in the good towne of Amiens, whose like was not to be found againe in 36. Monasteries. *His superiour contemplations,* saith he, *remained in the autenticall raunges of the same towne, and his inferiour in the deepest sellers in Laon in Laonoise,* which were best furnished with good wines. Moreover, this good Frier was alwaies merie and lively as a pretie untamed Asse, and as learned as his [breviary] could extend" (sig. Z4; cf. *QL* 11).

10. Sidney's *Defense of Poesy* cites defenders of debt and plague, recalling Francesco Berni, who defended both.

11. Turner died in 1599. Jonson: "No man has his servant more obsequious and pliant, then gentlemen their creditors"; Erasmus: "Servos nemo magis habet obnoxios, quam debitor suos creditores"; Panurge: creditors are "tant humble, serviable et copieux en reverences"; Turner: "tam humiles, tam obsequentes, tam reverenter usque ad genua supplices." On Turner, see Camilla Nilles, "The Economy of Owing: Rabelais' Praise of Debts," *Etudes de lettres* 2 (1984), 73–88, and Annette H. Tomarken, *The Smile of Truth: The French Satirical Eulogy and Its Antecedents* (Princeton: Princeton University Press, 1990), 57–58, who calls Turner more serious than Rabelais.

12. Thomas Tomkis, *Albumazar,* in Dodsley's *Select Collection of Old English Plays,* ed. W. C. Hazlitt (repr. New York: Benjamin Blom, 1964) V. Like Panurge, Pandolfo rejects signs of his fate. The jargon ("Necro-puro-geo-hydro-cheiro-coscinomancy") epitomizes that in *TL.* Like many texts with Rabelaisian touches, the play satirizes projects: one "Gorgonian" headpiece has amplifiers shaped like donkey ears.

13. Daniel Russell, "Panurge and His New Clothes," *ER* 14 (1977), 89– 104, notes that although Panurge wishes to be a married burgher, Pantagruel says he looks like a heretic; Dindenault, in *QL,* calls him a cuckold.

14. Ben Jonson, *The Case Is Altered,* in Jonson, *Works,* ed. C. H. Herford and Percy Simpson (Oxford: Clarendon, 1954) V.v.20–21, V.xii.88– 91. Although he does not mention Jaques, Dennis Quinn, in "Polypragmosyne in the Renaissance," *Ben Jonson Journal* 2 (1995), 157–69, is helpful on Jonson's interest in panurgic "curiosity."

15. Gregory de Rocher, *Rabelais's Laughers and Joubert's "Traité du Ris"* (University: University of Alabama Press, 1979), 59–68, uses the scene to contrast modern and Renaissance humor. See also Marcel Tetel, "Rabelais and Folengo," *Comparative Literature* 15 (1963), 357–64; Bernadette Rey-Flaud, "Quand Rabelais interroge la farce: Les Moutons de Panurge et l'épilogue du *Pathelin,*" *Littératures* 15 (1986), 7–17, argues that Panurge's taciturnity reverses the farce's verbal contest and shows words, like the sheep, self-destructing.

16. As Alice Berry argued in a talk at the 1993 meeting of the Modern Language Association.

17. I.e., that Rouzeus found in Rabelais and applied to commentators. Day cites problem 17 of *Problem[atum] miscellan[eorum Antaristotelicorum centuria]* (Liège, 1616); I have not seen it.

18. In a 1993 paper presented at the annual meeting of the Modern Langauge Association, Karen Cunningham described some bizarre cases mooted at the Inns. I thank her for advice.

19. For Michael Downes, "Panurge, Ulysse et les 'gens curieux,' " *ER* 13 (1976), 139–45, "curiosity," opacity, and debt make Panurge the traditional bad courtier. In the same volume, Gérard Defaux cites Panurge's need to dominate ("De *Pantagruel* au *Tiers livre:* Panurge et le pouvoir," 171).

20. Edwin Duval, "Panurge, Perplexity, and the Ironic Design of Rabelais's *Tiers Livre,*" *RenQ* 35 (1982), 381–400.

21. "Chose bien commune et vulguaire entre les humains est le malheur d'aultruy entendre, prævoir, congnoistre et prædire. Mais ô que chose rare est son malheur propre prædire, congnoistre, prævoir et entendre! Et que prudentement le figura Æsope en ses *Apologes,* disant chascun homme en ce monde naissant une bezache au coul porter, on sachet de laquelle devant pendent sont les faultes et malheurs d'aultruy tousjours exposées à nostre veue et congnoissance, on sachet darriere pendent sont les faultes et malheurs propres; et jamais ne sont veues ne entendues, fors de ceulx qui des cieulx ont le benevole aspect."

22. "N'estez vous asceuré de vostre vouloir? Le poinct principal y gist: tout le reste est fortuit, et dependent des fatales dispositions du ciel. . . . Il se y convient mettre à l'adventure, les oeilz bandez, baissant la teste, baisant la terre et se recommand à Dieu au demourant, puys qu'une foys l'on se y veult mettre. Aultre asceurance ne vous en sçauroys te donner."

23. John Donne, *Satires, Epigrams and Verse Letters,* ed. W. Milgate (Oxford: Clarendon, 1967). Back home, the narrator has "a trance / Like his, who dreamt he saw hell" (ll. 155–57). Most hear an allusion to Dante, who has no "trance"; Donne may mean *Pasquine in a Traunce* by Caelius Curio, a report on postmortem worlds that was translated by William Phiston (1566, 1584). *Pasquine* warns "that in the night none can worke, that is to say in death" (sig. aa2); cf. Satire III: "Yet strive so, that before age, deaths twilight, / Thy Soule rest, for none can worke in that night" (ll. 83–84).

24. Hence the allusion to Babel, says Nancy Mason Bradbury, in "Speaker and Structure in Donne's *Satyre IV,*" *SEL* 25 (1985), 87–107. Cf. James S. Baumlin, *John Donne and the Rhetorics of Renaissance Discourse* (Columbia: University of Missouri Press, 1991).

25. Jerome Schwartz, *Irony and Ideology in Rabelais: Structures of Subversion* (Cambridge: Cambridge University Press, 1990), 34, notes the "complicity" of Panurge and Pantagruel.

26. For Terence Cave, in "Panurge, Pathelin and Other Polyglots," in *Lapidary Inscriptions: Renaissance Essays for Donald A. Stone, Jr.,* ed. Barbara C. Bowen and Jerry C. Nash (Lexington, Ky.: French Forum, 1991), Panurge's Babel-like impudence undercuts Gargantua's univocal paternal advice. Edwin M. Duval, *The Design of Rabelais's Pantagruel* (New Haven: Yale University Press, 1991) and Schwartz, *Irony and Ideology in Rabelais,* note how talk postpones charitable action.

27. Schwartz, *Irony and Ideology in Rabelais,* 33; so too Duval, *Design of Rabelais's Pantagruel,* 66.

28. In Joshua Scodel, "The Medium Is the Message: Donne's 'Satire 3,' 'To Sir Henry Wotton' (Sir, more than kisses), and the Ideologies of the Mean," *MP* 90 (1993), 479–511 (p. 498). Scodel, too, notes the association of Phrygius with Cybele's eunuchs.

29. Thomas Hester, *Kind Pitty and Brave Scorn: John Donne's "Satyres"* (Durham:

Duke University Press, 1982), 119–27, calls Phrygius a "purist," not atheist. Like Panurge he does not *dare* commit himself.

30. Baumlin, *John Donne and the Rhetorics of Renaissance Discourse*, 127.

31. Donne puns on *will* as erotic desire and *do* as sexual intercourse. Emory Elliott, "The Narrative and Allusive Unity of Donne's *Satyres*," *JEGP* 75 (1976), 105–16, notes allusions to adultery.

32. Robert Griffin, "The Devil and Panurge," *Studi Francesi* 47–48 (1972), 329–36; cf. Catharine Randall, "Le Cocuage hypothétique de Panurge: Le Monde à l'envers dans *Le Tiers Livre*," *Constructions* 1 (1986), 77–86. Douglas Bruster, "The Horn of Plenty: Cuckoldry and Capital in the Drama of the Age of Shakespeare," *SEL* 30 (1990), 195–215, likewise sees a link to "cornucopia and horned animal ritual" (197).

33. G. C. Moore Smith, *Gabriel Harvey's Marginalia* (Stratford-upon-Avon: Shakespeare Head Press, 1913), 139; see below on Harvey's panurgic Rabelais and above on Nashe the Younger's version of what the bells told Panurge.

34. Bruster, "Horn of Plenty"; Katharine Eisaman Maus, "Horns of Dilemma: Jealousy, Gender, and Spectatorship in English Renaissance Drama," *ELH* 54 (1987), 561–83 (p. 563).

35. Ben Jonson, George Chapman, and John Marston, *Eastward Ho!* ed. C. G. Petter (London: Ernest Benn, 1973), V.v.175–84. Jean says: "Si tu est coqu, *ergo* ta femme sera belle, *ergo* tu seras bien traicté d'elle; *ergo* tu auras des amis beaucoup; *ergo* tu sera saulvé" (*TL* 28): "If you're a cuckold, therefore [i.e., one can infer] your wife will be beautiful, therefore you'll be well treated by her, therefore you'll have many friends, therefore you'll be saved." Cf. Nicholas Breton, *Cornu-copia, Pasquils Night-cap: or, Antidot for the Head-ache* (1612): cuckoldry helps with debt, and "Patience such a noble vertue is, / As will in fine promote him unto blisse" (sigs. P3, M2v). For other encomia see Tomarken, *Smile of Truth,* 192–97.

36. Margaret Jones-Davies, "Paroles intertextuelles: Lecture intertextuelle de Parolles," in *Collection Astrea* 1 (Actes du colloque *All's Well That Ends Well* [Montpellier: Publications de l'Université de Paul Valéry, 1985]), 65–80. Alexander Welsh, "The Loss of Men and Getting of Children: 'All's Well That Ends Well' and 'Measure for Measure,' " *MLR* 73 (1978), 17–28, compares the plays to *TL;* my comments here elaborate on their insights. Patricia Parker's study of words and begetting, *"All's Well That Ends Well:* Increase and Multiply," in *Creative Imagination,* ed. Quint et al., 355–90, mentions Panurge (but not Welsh or Jones-Davies).

37. "Equivocal" and "drum": V.iii.250–53 (Parolles is also a drum in III.vi; cf. Panurge's dream of being a beaten drum); "fox": III.vi.102; "linguist": IV.iii.236; "businesses": I.ii.206; "eating": V.ii.53–54; "knave": V.iii.249.

38. G. K. Hunter's edition of *Eastward Ho!* (London: Routledge, 1966) quotes Rabelais.

39. Michael Drayton, *Poly-Olbion,* in Drayton, *Works,* ed. John W. Hebel (Oxford: Blackwell, 1961) IV, 109.

Chapter 4: Body Matters

1. Everard Guilpin, *Skialetheia; or A Shadowe of Truth, in Certaine Epigrams and Satyres,* ed. D. A. Carroll (Chapel Hill: University of North Carolina Press, 1974), 60–61. Guilpin means Aretino's *Puttana Errante;* the poetess Elephantis wrote erotica.

2. Gail Kern Paster, *The Body Embarrassed: Drama and the Disciplines of Shame in Early Modern England* (Ithaca: Cornell University Press, 1993), chap. 3, notes that laxatives and purges reinforced early modern scatology.

3. My heartfelt thanks to Ian Moulton for sending me a transcription of these poems in MS Rawlinson Poet. 120, at the Bodlein Library (a slim manuscript that may have been transcribed by one "H.S."). If "ex pag: 572" and "de pag. 710" cite Rabelais pages, the translator must have seen the whole *Oeuvres*. Professor Moulton, who adds that this is the only reference to Rabelais he has seen while examining nearly two hundred poetic miscellanies, notes that the hand is very difficult. I indicate what he cannot even conjecturally decipher with periphrases. The French reads: "Grand Tibault, se voulent coucher / Avecques sa femme nouvelle, / S'en vint tout bellement cacher / Un gros maillet en la ruelle. / 'O! mon doux amy (ce dict elle), / Quel maillet vous voy je empoingner? / — C'est (dict-il) pout mieulx vous coingner. / — Maillet (dict elle) il n'y faut nul: / Quand gros Jan me vient besoingner, / Il ne me coingne que du cul.' " and "Jenin, tastant un soir ses vins nouveaulx, / Troubles encor et bouillans en leur lie, / Pria Quelot apprester des naveaulx, / A leur soupper, pour faire chere lie. / Cela feut faict. Puys, sans melancholie, / Se vont coucher, belutent, prennent somme. / Mais ne pouvant Jenin dormir en somme, / Tant fort vesnoit Quelot, et tant souvent, / La compissa. Puys: 'Voylà, dist il, comme / Petite pluie abat bien un grand vent.' " The earthy vulgarity of the verses is notable, but the point is primarily the clever talk and peasant wit.

4. Relevant literature is vast. Jean Larmat, *Le moyen âge dans le Gargantua de Rabelais* (Paris: Les Belles Lettres, 1973), sets Rabelais's grossness and misogyny in a time before indecency "met des gants ou se voile" (66). For Stephen Greenblatt, "Filthy Rites," *Daedalus* 111 (1982), 1–16, Rabelaisian scatology has an ideological edge: not "naive self-expression of an unregenerate popular spirit," it opposes efforts to smooth the body.

5. John Harington, *A New Discourse of a Stale Subject, called The Metamorphosis of Ajax: Written by Misacmos, to His Friend and Cosin Philostilpnos*, ed. Elizabeth S. Donno (New York: Columbia University Press, 1962). *Misacmos* is "filth-hater"; *Philostilpnos* is "lover of the squeaky-clean."

6. Joseph Loewenstein, "The Public Toilet: Harington and Intellectual Property," a paper presented at the 1996 meeting of the Renaissance Society of America in Bloomington, Indiana; I thank Professor Loewenstein for sharing a copy of this witty investigation of Harington's "Cambridge and Inns of Court imagination" and of how he, like so many writers mentioned in this book, associates excrement with words. The range of issues raised, as Loewenstein notes, takes in how the public/published and private/privy relate to each other.

7. William Engel, "Was Sir John Harington the English Rabelais?" in *Rabelais in Context: Proceedings of the 1991 Vanderbilt Conference*, ed. Barbara C. Bowen (Birmingham, Ala.: Summa, 1993). Nor does Harington, says Engel, share Rabelais's heteroglossia, preferring his own quirky voice. Yes, yet Harington parcels out his text among two pseudonyms and a set of initials (his servant T[homas] C[ombe]). He wrote at a time when English townships were better regulating waste; see Walter King, "How High Is Too High? Disposing of Dung in Seventeenth-Century Prescot," *SCJ* 23 (1992), 443–57. T. G. A. Nelson, "Death, Dung, the Devil and Worldly Delights: A Metaphysical Conceit in Harington, Donne, and Herbert," *SP* 76 (1979), 272–87, notes *Ajax*'s equation of dirt and sin.

8. Cf. Ruth Hughey, "The Harington MS at Arundel Castle and Related Documents," *Library* 15 (1935), 388–444.

9. Not that Harington avoids sexual innuendo. Misacmos asks a servant to look up *confornicari:* "Looke it sirra there in the dictionarie. Con, con. Tush what dost thou looke in the French? [*Con* is "cunt."] thou wilt make a sweete peece of looking, to looke for *confornicar* in the French: looke in the Latin for *fornicor.* F, fa, fe, fi, fo, for, foramen, forfex, forica, forma, fornicator (now I think I am neare it) *fornix, fornicor, aris, are . . .*" (p. 135). Donno calls this a remarkable imitation of "the process of word hunting"; it imitates another process, too.

10. Joseph Hall, *Virgidemiae,* III.6, in Hall, *Collected Poems,* ed. A. Davenport (Liverpool: Liverpool University Press, 1949).

11. Raymond La Charité, *Recreation, Reflection and Re-Creation: Perspectives on Rabelais's* Pantagruel (Lexington, Ky.: French Forum Monographs 19, 1980), notes Pantagruel's destructive but regenerative mix of fire and water.

12. Ronsard, *Oeuvres complètes,* ed. Gustave Cohen (Paris: Gallimard, 1950) II, 784–85, from the 1554 Bocage, withdrawn in 1578: "Du bon Rabelais, qui boivoit / Toujours ce-pendant qu'il vivoit, . . . / Il chantoit la grande massuë, / Et la jument de Gargantuë, / Le grand Panurge, et le païs / Des Papimanes ébaïs, / Leurs loix, leurs façons et demeures, / Et frere Jean des Antoumeures, / Et d'Episteme les combas; / Mais la Mort, qui ne boivoit pas, / Tira le beuveur de ce monde, / Et ores le fait boire en l'onde / Qui fuit trouble dans le giron / Du large fleuve d'Acheron." Compare four lines in a manuscript of epitaphs that is now at Yale University (Osborn fb.143, compiled in 1694, but with some older material). They ask, "Pluto Prince of shades Infernall / Where sad souls ne'er Laugh but burne all / Bee kind to Rablais and they'll all / Fall a Laughing great and small" (p. 2).

13. Hall may believe that Rabelais was a drunk or he may be recalling, e.g., *G* 5.

14. See Davenport's notes indexed under "Rabelais." John Minsheu, *Ductor in linguas* (1626 ed.), says *Pantagrueliste* is "one altogether for throat and belly," from *pan* (all) and *gru* (crane). Lost is Pantagruelism's joyful scorn of fortune and the spiritual symbolism described by Florence Weinberg, *The Wine and the Will: Rabelais's Bacchic Christianity* (Detroit: Wayne State University Press, 1972).

15. Joseph Hall, *Another World and Yet the Same: Bishop Joseph Hall's* Mundus Alter et Idem, ed. John Millar Wands (New Haven: Yale University Press, 1981). On genre, sources, style, and orthodoxy, see Richard A. McCabe, *Joseph Hall: A Study in Satire and Meditation* (Oxford: Clarendon, 1982).

16. Sanford M. Salyer, "Renaissance Influences in Hall's *Mundus Alter et Idem,*" *PQ* 6 (1927), 320–34. Wands finds the parallels "unconvincing" (xxvi). Frank Livingstone Huntley, *Bishop Joseph Hall and Protestant Meditation in Seventeenth-Century England* (Binghamton, N.Y.: MRTS 1, 1981), which includes Hall's meditations, thinks "He whose provision for every day was thirty measures of fine flour, and threescore measures of meal, thirty oxen" (167) is "probably Gargantua," but Hall means Solomon (2 Kings 4:22–23).

17. Ronald J. Corthell, "Joseph Hall and Seventeenth-Century Literature," *John Donne Journal* 3 (1984), 249–68 (p. 257).

18. Hall, *Mundus,* trans. Wands, 26; compare *P* 15.

19. Edwin Duval, *The Design of Rabelais's Pantagruel* (New Haven: Yale University Press, 1991), 74–75, sees pride humbled. For François Rigolot, the lady recalls Jesus,

likewise, if metaphorically, beset by dogs; see "Rabelais, Misogyny, and Christian Charity: Biblical Intertextuality and the Renaissance Crisis of Exemplarity," *PMLA* 109 (1994), 225–37.

20. *Report on the Manuscripts of the Marquess of Downshire,* 2 vols. (London: Historical Manuscripts Commission, vol. 75, 1924, 1936), II, 73–75, from the papers of William Trumbull the elder, ed. E. K. Purnell and A. B. Hinds.

21. Thomas Lodge, *Wits Miserie, and the Worlds Madnesse,* in Lodge, *Complete Works,* ed. Sir Edmund Gosse, 4 vols. (London, 1883; New York: Russell and Russell, 1963), IV 13, 29.

22. "Aretine in his mother Nana" refers to dialogues between a prostitute and her daughter; Des Périers wrote indecent stories.

23. Brown, *Rabelais,* 93. Material in this section appears in my "Jonson's Rabelais" in *New Perspectives on Ben Jonson,* ed. James Hirsh (Madison, N.J.: Fairleigh Dickinson University Press, 1997), 35–54.

24. John Lemly, "Masks and Self-Portraits in Jonson's Late Poetry," *ELH* 44 (1977), 251. Cf. Frank Whigham, "Reading Social Conflict in the Alimentary Tract: More on the Body in Renaissance Drama," *ELH* 55 (1988), 333–50. Bruce Thomas Boehrer, "Renaissance Overeating: The Sad Case of Ben Jonson," *PMLA* 105 (1990), notes that "a famous fat man and legendary drunkard construct[s] a cult of personality around his own excessive girth while excoriating his contemporaries for eating and drinking too much" (1072).

25. See, e.g., Don K. Hedrick, "Cooking for the Anthropophagi: Jonson and His Audience," *SEL* 17 (1977), 233–45, and Joseph Loewenstein, "The Jonsonian Corpulence, or The Poet as Mouthpiece," *ELH* 53 (1986), 491–518.

26. Katharine Maus, "Satiric and Ideal Economies in the Jonsonian Imagination," *ELR* 19 (1989), 44.

27. Loewenstein, "Corpulence," 508–11. On Jonson's Christianized Menippeanism, see Douglas Duncan, *Ben Jonson and the Lucianic Tradition* (Cambridge: Cambridge University Press, 1979).

28. Jonathan Haynes sees a move from festive modes in "Festivity and the Dramatic Economy of Jonson's *Bartholomew Fair,*" *ELH* 51 (1984), 645–68; Richard M. Berrong, *Rabelais and Bakhtin: Popular Culture in* Gargantua and Pantagruel (Lincoln: University of Nebraska Press, 1986), finds the same in Rabelais.

29. Ben Jonson, *Every Man in His Humor,* in Jonson, *Works,* ed. C. H. Herford and Percy Simpson (Oxford: Clarendon, 1954), I.iv.123–30.

30. On excrement, words, and evangelical thinking, see Jeffrey C. Persels, " 'Straitened in the bowels,' or Concerning the Rabelaisian Trope of Defecation," *ER* 31 (1996), 101–12.

31. Terrance Dunford, "Consumption of the World: Reading, Eating and Imitation in *Every Man Out of His Humour,*" *ELR* 14 (1984), 131–47 (p. 142). Paster, *Body,* links *Fair*'s urinating women to "verbal fluency" (25). On words and inflation see Wayne A. Rebhorn, "Jonson's 'Jovy Boy': Lovewit and the Dupes in *The Alchemist,*" *JEGP* 79 (1980), 355–75.

32. On mountebank language, see Carol Clark's engaging *Vulgar Rabelais* (Glasgow: Pressgang, 1983).

33. David Riggs, *Ben Jonson: A Life* (Cambridge: Harvard University Press, 1989), 176.

QL 45, satirizing persecution, plays on *fig* as anal growth, fruit, obscene gesture, denunciation to authorities, and female genitalia; see Frank-Rutger Hausmann, "Comment doit-on lire l'épisode de 'L'isle des papefigues' [*QL* 45–47]," in *Rabelais en son demi-millénaire,* ed. Jean Céard and Jean-Claude Margolin (Geneva: Droz, 1988; *ER* 21).

34. Some jobs are proverbial, but only Rabelais collects so many; the note in Peter Happé's edition (Manchester: University of Manchester Press, 1994) finds no "close parallel" for the fleas, but they are in *CL* 21. Robert C. Evans, *Jonson and the Contexts of His Time* (Lewisburg: Bucknell University Press, 1994), chap. 4, sets *Devil* against disputes over "projection." See also Joan Thirsk, *Economic Policy and Projects: The Development of a Consumer Society in Early Modern England* (Oxford: Clarendon, 1978).

35. Evelyn B. Tribble's chapter "Genius on the Rack" in her *Margins and Marginality: The Printed Page in Early Modern England* (Charlottesville: University Press of Virginia, 1993), 130–57, sees tension between Jonson's claims as an author and glosses that cite other authority. Rabelais is among these authorities.

36. Peter Hyland, " 'The Wild Anarchie of Drinke': Ben Jonson and Alcohol," *Mosaic* 19.3 (1986), 25–33, contrasts the "gargantuan drinker" (26) to the moralist, suggesting that Jonson flirted with notions of Bacchic inspiration; Hyland's use of "Apollonian" and "Dionysian" values is anachronistic, though, for as god of prophecy Apollo can likewise inspire rapture.

37. I follow David Quint, *Origin and Originality: Versions of the Source* (New Haven: Yale University Press, 1983), 192–204.

38. On *Staple* and Shrovetide see, e.g., Anthony Parr's edition of the play (Manchester: Manchester University Press, 1988), which notes parallels in Rabelais to Carnival "wars," farts from dead bodies (cf. III.ii.98), and Hearsay's college (cf. *CL* 30). I would add Diogenes rolling his barrel (*TL* prol.): the Induction describes Jonson in the tiring house "rolling himself up and down like a tun i'the midst of 'em": he *is* the barrel.

39. Guillaume Ranchin's Gallican *Review of the Councell of Trent* (Oxford, 1638, trans. G. L[angbaine]) quotes this chapter: "Mr. Francis Rabelais said not without cause in his merry Pantagruell by way of a common proverbe: Since the Decree away did flie / And souldiers knapsackes wore. / Since Monkes would need on horsebacke ride, / The world's worse than before" (sig. Vv3: Depuis que Decretz eurent ales, / Et gens d'armes porterent males, / Moines allerent à cheval, / En ce monde abonda tout mal).

40. E.g., George Hakewill, *Apologie* (1627), sig. Bb3v.

41. Ben Jonson, "Over the Door at the Entrance into the Apollo," in *Works,* VIII, 657. The editors' note cites *CL,* as does Richard S. Peterson's evocative discussion of vessels in *Imitation and Praise in the Poems of Ben Jonson* (New Haven: Yale University Press, 1981), chap. 3. Had Jonson read Petronius? The *Satyricon*'s Sybil lives in a bottle (but wishes only to die).

42. The poem before *Gargantua* concludes: "Mieux est de ris que de larmes escripre, / Pour ce que rire est le propre de l'homme." Barbara C. Bowen, "Rire est le propre de l'homme," *Rabelais en son demi-millénaire,* 185–90, shows how for Rabelais joy will replace laughter as our "propre." Roland Antonioli, *Rabelais et la médecine* (Geneva: Droz, 1976; *ER* 12), examines Rabelais's medical career and his novels' medical theories and interests. See also James P. Gilroy, "Rabelais, The Good Doctor: Health and Sanity in the *Quart livre,*" *European Studies Journal* 2 (1985), 27–34. On Rabelais's growing

unwillingness to base anatomy on analogy, see Marie Madeleine Fontaine, "Quaresme-prenant: L'Image littéraire et la contestation de l'analogie médicale," in *Rabelais in Glasgow,* ed. James A. Coleman and Christine M. Scollen-Jimack (Glasgow: James A. Coleman and Christine M. Scollen-Jimack, 1984), 87–112.

43. *NRB* mentions some early modern British owners of Rabelais's works, not always giving even a rough date for inscriptions and manuscript marginalia. Thomas Lorkyn, Regius professor of medicine, had a copy of Hippocrates' aphorisms (1543; *NRB* 106); he got it from Dr. Perne, Dean of Ely, and left it to Cambridge University Library in 1591. *NRB* argues that the "wide diffusion of [*Hippocratis ac Galeni libri aliquot, ex recognitione Francisci Rabelaesi* (Lyons: Sebastian Gryphius, 1532)], together with the frequent presence of copious and scholarly manuscript notes, show[s] the esteem in which Rabelais was held as a humanist doctor" (p. 528). But outside the academic world even those who recognized Rabelais as an expert usually gestured toward the "other" Rabelais.

44. See below. Compare the career of Rabelais's English contemporary, Dr. Andrew Borde, probable editor of jestbooks starring Scoggin and Gotham's nitwits who wrote in a style that many people in later generations found unseemly or baffling in learned men. Like Rabelais, Borde had been a monk, studied at Montpellier, and written medical texts; he too was intrigued by prognostication, played on his name (once calling himself Andreas Perforatus), and acquired a reputation as a drunk and womanizer that may owe more to racy prose than racy deeds.

45. Quoted by Marcel de Grève, "François Rabelais et les libertins du XVIIe siècle," *ER* 1 (1956) 135 and 142; he does not mention Milles.

46. John Healey, *The Discovery of a New World (Mundus Alter et Idem) [c. 1609],* ed. Huntington Brown (Cambridge: Harvard University Press, 1937), 145–49.

47. Milton's contemptuous comments on Hall are quoted and discussed by Wands in his introduction to Hall, *World,* 14–15.

48. James Howell, *Familiar Letters* (1650) II, no. 29. Anne Killigrew (a "minion of the Muses") gets his verse, Sir Lewis Dives and Endimion Porter get his Spanish so they can read *La picara Justina;* his Italian goes to the "Turky and Levantine" merchant company, and his Latin to his "mother Oxford." Howell is unusual in linking Rabelais to a female reader.

49. There may also be a whimsical notice of Rabelais in Myles Jennynges's translation of Etienne de Maisonneuve's *Gerileon of England* (1583). Here are giants with names like Percival, Ferclaste (an "unreasonably bigge Giante"), and Mitrocarde. Ergoferant (a scholastic?) and Androfort (manly!) have stolen the clappers from a bell tower to twirl, which sounds like Gargantua's sort of trick. The giants are tended by a Dr. "Rabalon" (sig. D4). Years later Charles Bertie saw relics of Rabelais's medical days: The Historical Manuscripts Commission report on the Lindsey papers (vol. 79, ed. C. G. O. Bridgeman and J. C. Walker, 1942) quotes an entry in his journal on a visit (Feb. 11, 1661) to a monastery room in Brissac "where the famous François Rabelais the physician some time dwelled." On June 10, at Montpellier, he saw a picture of Rabelais "as also his robe and capuchon conserved in great veneration" (pp. 319, 346).

50. Bad doctors are a problem in R.E[den?]'s 1577 translation of Prudent le Choyselat's *Discourse of Housebandrie* (1567), which warns chicken farmers to avoid "suche Phisitions, which have naught els to doe then to walke their Mules [slippers, not animals], as

thei were whiche were observed by Maister Francis Rables Pentagruell, to departe out of their lodgyng at sixte of the clocke in the mornyng, and to returne at Noone without strikyng a stroke" (sig. C3). Choyselat may mean the Isle of Sabots, where men arise at dawn, don boots and spurs, and then fall back into bed until noon (*CL* 26).

51. Robert Dallington, *View of France,* Shakespeare Association Facsimiles 13, ed. W. P. Barrett (Oxford, Oxford University Press, 1936).

52. François de la Noue has a similar allusion — with a hungry Frère Jean, Neapolitan teeth-picking, and a context of architectural criticism — in the third of his *Discours politiques et littéraires* (Bâle, 1587).

53. For *doriphages,* see *TL* prol., and on Lucifer's colic after eating fricasseed sergeant-at-law, see *P* 4; cf. *QL* 46, in which the devil is said to be tired of feeding on Hell's endless supply of lawyers.

54. On Hayman, see Gillian T. Cell's entry in *Dictionary of Canadian Biography* I (Toronto: University of Toronto Press, 1966). Articles by M. H. M. MacKinnon, Allan Pritchard, and Robin Endres cited by David Galloway in the *Dictionary of Literary Biography* 99 ("Canadian Writers Before 1890," ed. W. H. New; Detroit: Gale Research, 1990) note in passing the translations from Rabelais. An earlier version of this section, entitled "Rabelaisian Apocrypha and Satire in early Canada: The Case of Robert Hayman," appears in *Editer et traduire Rabelais à travers les âges,* ed. Paul J. Smith (Amsterdam: Rodopi, 1997), 101–16.

55. See Plan, no. 109, on the poem's authorship. I quote the Lyons 1620 edition, backdated to 1558, sigs. Ooo2v–4v (my copy once belonged to a Jesuit college).

56. Habert: "Vieille, qui n'as aultre dieu que Bacchus, / Qui de putains renverse les bas culs"; *CL* 45 rhymes "Bacchus" and "bas culz."

57. The Renaissance saw a surge of cruel poems on old women. For the French, see Jacques Bailbé, "Le thème de la vieille femme dans la poésie du seizième et duoodébut du dix-septième siècles," *BHR* 26 (1964), 98–119, which notes *TL* 17 and Habert's diptych, and my *"Translatio Lupae:* Du Bellay's Roman Whore Goes North," *RenQ* 42 (1989), 397–419.

58. Although I read the Bower of Bliss (*Faerie Queene* II.xii) differently, my argument owes much to Stephen Greenblatt's chapter on Spenser in *Renaissance Self-Fashioning: From More to Shakespeare* (Chicago: University of Chicago Press, 1980), as well as to Peter Stallybrass, "Patriarchal Territories: The Body Enclosed," in *Rewriting the Renaissance: The Discourses of Sexual Difference in Early Modern Europe,* ed. Margaret W. Ferguson, Maureen Quilligan, and Nancy J. Vickers (Chicago: University of Chicago Press, 1986), 123–42.

59. Walter Ralegh, *Discovery of Guiana* (1596), in Ralegh, *Selected Prose and Poetry,* ed. Agnes M. C. Latham (London: Athlone, 1965), 165. Louis A. Montrose, "The Work of Gender in the Discourse of Discovery," *Representations* 33 (1991), 12, cites his "proleptically elegiac sympathy for this unspoiled world." Soon after publishing *Quodlibets* Hayman left for Guiana, where he died in 1629.

60. Hayman's verse is likewise unjustling: "I doe not, nor I dare not squib the State: / Such oultrequidant sawcines I hate" (II.1).

61. For an earlier version of this section, see my "Intertextual Topology: English Writers and Pantagruel's Hell," *ELR* 23 (1993), 244–66.

62. Samuel Kinser's informative and humane *Rabelais's Carnival: Text, Context, Metatext* (Berkeley: University of California Press, 1990) focuses on *QL*, not rejecting Bakhtin's great, flawed book but avoiding its nostalgia. He shows how Rabelais acts to confuse identities and issues in Lent's war on Carnival, not to champion an anachronistic "materialism."

63. This is chap. 20 in the 1532 edition of *Pantagruel*, ed. V.-L. Saulnier (Geneva: Droz, 1946). Most now find the scene a parody of such texts as *Le Calendrier des bergers* and *Les Quatre fils Aymon*. See, e.g., Lucien Febvre, *The Problem of Unbelief in the Sixteenth Century*, trans. Beatrice Gottlieb (Cambridge: Harvard University Press, 1982), 212–39; Manfred Bambeck, "Epistemons Unterweltsbericht im 30. Kapital des *Pantagruel*," *ER* 2 (1956), 29–47; Michael Screech, *Rabelais* (Ithaca: Cornell University Press, 1979), 96–97; and Jerome Schwartz, *Irony and Ideology in Rabelais: Structures of Subversion* (Cambridge: Cambridge University Press, 1990), 40–41.

64. Thomas More put *Menippos* into Latin (*Complete Works* III.1, ed. Craig Thompson [New Haven: Yale University Press, 1974], 169–79); a ca. 1530 edition has an English translation. See also Benjamin Boyce, "News from Hell: Satiric Communication with the Nether World in English Writing of the Seventeenth and Eighteenth Centuries," *PMLA* 57 (1943), 402–29. Edward B. Williams, "The Observations of Epistemon and Condign Punishment," *Esprit Créateur* 3 (1963), 63–67, notes that Rabelais imagines reversals on the model of Lazarus trading places with Dives. In Eileen Gardiner's *Visions of Heaven and Hell Before Dante* (New York: Italica, 1989), most souls just suffer, but in Charles de Bourdigné's *Faifeu* (1532?), poets sport while big shots labor; see Janis Pallister, "Three Renaissance Sojourns in 'Hell': *Faifeu, Pantagruel, Le Moyen de Parvenir*," *Romance Notes* 17 (1976), 199–203.

65. *Le grant kalendrier et compost des Bergiers* (Paris: Payot, n.d.), I.lxix; D.C. Peck, "'News from Heaven and Hell': A Defamatory Narrative of the Earl of Leicester," *ELR* 8 (1978), 141–58. The chafed earl would pity Balaam, who has boiling semen poured over him for helping Moabite women seduce Israelites: see Martha Himmelfarb, *Tours of Hell: An Apocalyptic Form in Jewish and Christian Literature* (Philadelphia: University of Pennsylvania Press, 1983), 78. In *Tarltons Newes out of Purgatorie* (1590), Ronsard must recite clichéd verse. Such activity is caricature, not reversal.

66. Some shades are busier: monks teach abortion and uxoricide, Saint Francis angles for souls in Purgatory, and Saint Dominic makes beads. On such texts, see Eugene Korkowski, "Donne's *Ignatius* and Menippean Satire," *SP* 72 (1975), 419–38.

67. Cf. Thomas Dekker, *Newes from Hell; Brought by the Divells Carrier* (1606), revised as *A Knights Conjuring* (1607) and recycled for *Dekker His Dreame* (1620). I quote from Dekker's *Nondramatic Works*, ed. A. B. Grosart, 1885, II. Near the "Stigian Lake" (142), "Will Summers [Henry VIII's fool] gives not Richard the Third the cushions, the Duke of Guize and the Duke of Shoreditch have not the bredth of a bench between them," and Lucke (another fool) "shall have as much mat, as Sir Lancelot of the Lake" [whom Epistemon sees flaying dead horses]. "It was a Comedy, to see what a crowding (as if it had beene at a new Play) there was upon the Acherontique Strond." Charon seats them on a bench made of "skulls of the great, the least of them once belonging to an emperor like Charlemagne" [who is there in Hades in the 1532 *Pantagruel*].

68. William Shakespeare, *King Lear*, in Shakespeare, *Complete Works*, ed. Stanley

Wells and Gary Taylor (Oxford: Clarendon, 1986), Quarto, 13.1822; elsewhere I use the Riverside edition by G. Blakemore Evans (Boston: Houghton Mifflin, 1974). *Lear* was first performed between 1605 and 1608; the wording shows that Nero is on the cold sluggish Styx.

69. See Gérard Walter, *Nero,* trans. Emma Craufurd (London: Allen and Unwin, 1957), chaps. 3–4.

70. William Elton, *King Lear and the Gods* (San Marino, Calif.: Huntington Library, 1966), 310–17, cites *CL* 21, where Entelechie's officers plow the shore, put carts before horses, break eels across the knee, and skin them from the tail; cf. *Lear* II.4.121–25. The same officers "de neant faisoient choses grandes, et grandes choses faisoient à neant retourner," not sharing Lear's belief that "nothing will come of nothing" (I.1.90).

71. Walter, *Nero,* 264–65.

72. Plutarch, *Moralia,* trans. P. H. de Lacy and Benedict Einarson (Cambridge: Harvard University Press, 1959), VII, 297–99.

73. F. E. Budd, "Shakespeare, Chaucer, and Harsnett," *RES* 11 (1935), 421–29. Like many, Budd does not distinguish methods of fishing, saying Nero angled; classical texts are clear on the gold nets. See also, on faked possession and Harsnett, Stephen Greenblatt, "Shakespeare and the Exorcists," in his *Shakespearean Negotiations: The Circulation of Social Energy in Renaissance England* (Berkeley: University of California Press, 1988), 94–128; I doubt, though, that "acknowledging theatricality kills the credibility of the supernatural" (109); minds vary.

74. John L. Murphy, *Darkness and Devils: Exorcism and* King Lear (Athens: Ohio University Press, 1984), 72, notes Harsnett's taste for Lucian. The fake exorcists, e.g., "had surely met with Menippus" returning from Hell (sig. G3v). Frank Brownlow, Harsnett's astute editor, tells me he doubts Harsnett read Rabelais. Yet names in this "stygian comedy" (sig. K3) include Caesar and popes Sixtus and Alexander, also in *P* 30. The style can be Rabelaisian (or Nashean), and his exorcist could be Quaresmeprenant's cousin (*QL* 30–33): "His body a piller of burning brasse, his hands flames of fire, his gloves, his girdle, his hose, his shirt, lumps of sea-coales of hell: his amice, his maniple, and his stole, streamers of scorching smoke, . . . spouting out holy-water with his mouth, breathing out fire, and brimstone at his nostrils, evaporating frankinsence at his eyes, the picture of an asse burning brimly at his eares, his head crawling with dead-mens bones: the picture of our Lady flashing at his breast: nicknames of fire, and blood running upon his backe, *ave-maries,* and *salve Reginaes* sparkling downe to his heeles" (sig. N4).

75. Judith Anderson, "The Conspiracy of Realism: Impasse and Vision in *King Lear,*" *SP* 84 (1987), 1–23, wittily says, "Nothing at the end tells us exactly what and in what sense Lear 'sees,' and nothing will." E. W. Tayler, "King Lear and Negation," *ELR* 20 (1990), 17–39, is likewise helpful on nothing.

76. Dekker's *Artillery Garden* (1616), perhaps remembering Rabelais, praises guns as source of further invention and compares powder to inspiration; see J. R. Hale, *Renaissance War Studies* (London: Hambledon, 1983), 406, 410. Cf. Ullrich Langer, "Gunpowder as Transgressive Invention in Ronsard," in *Literary Theory/Renaissance Texts,* ed. Patricia Parker and David Quint (Baltimore: Johns Hopkins University Press, 1986), 96–114. Richard Hardin notes puns on Fawkes's name ("fox" and Guy/[dis]Guise may be relevant too) in "The Early Poetry of the Gunpowder Plot: Myth in the Making," *ELR* 22 (1992), 62–79.

77. That Alexander, not Philip, is a cobbler signals Rabelais. In Tomkis and Webster (see below) he cobbles, but in *P* he fixes bodyhose (*chausses*), not shoes (*chaussures*). A.-F. Bourgeois, "Rabelais en Angleterre," *RER* 3 (1905), 80–83, hears an echo of *P* in Falstaff's remark (1 *Henry IV* IV.2.116–17) that "Ere I lead this life long, I'll sew netherstocks, and mend them"; if so, Shakespeare understood *chausses*.

78. Cf. Ernst Kantorowicz, "Mysteries of State: An Absolutist Concept and Its Late Medieval Origins," *Harvard Law Review* 48 (1955), 65–91.

79. John Webster, *The White Devil*, ed. F. L. Lucas (New York: Macmillan, 1959), V.3.152–55.

80. The wordplay parallels Rabelais's: Nicolas "pape tiers," e.g., works as a "papetier."

81. Drayton, *Works*, ed. J. William Hebel (Oxford, 1961) IV, 89. Selden quotes the French, providing a translation in the margin.

82. Abraham Fraunce, *The Third Part of the Countesse of Pembrokes Yvychurche*, sig. H2. Jean Starobinski, "The Inside and the Outside," *Hudson Review* 28 (Autumn, 1975), 333–51, who calls Hades "consummately retentive," argues that "in the eyes of suspicion, the hidden inside is a metaphor of the realm of the dead" (338).

83. Marcel Tetel, *Rabelais* (New York: Twayne, 1967), 29, stresses Rabelais's playfulness. M.-T. Jones-Davies explores giantism's inner "anti-monde" in "Le Monstre, expression de l'insécurité dans la littérature et les spectacles de la renaissance anglaise," in M.-T. Jones-Davies, ed., *Monstres et prodiges au temps de la Renaissance* (Paris: Touzot, 1980), 26–41. On reworking the Jonah myth as a "medical fable" see Alice Berry, " 'Les Mithologies Pantagruelicques': Introduction to a Study of Rabelais's *Quart livre*," *PMLA* 92 (1977), 471–80.

84. Jonathan Goldberg, *James I and the Politics of Literature: Jonson, Shakespeare, Donne, and Their Contemporaries* (Baltimore: Johns Hopkins University Press, 1983), chap. 2. Although he ignores this tract, Goldberg's study helps place its concerns. Frederick Shriver, "Orthodoxy and Diplomacy: James I and the Vorstius Affair," *English Historical Review* 85 (1970), 449–74, explains James's aims.

85. Goldberg, *James I*, 84. James needed Pantagruel's doctors. Nicholas Le Strange tells how the king, out hunting, "shitte in his Breeches (according to his usuall manner) and so followed the chace, squeesing and charning so long, that it wrought out at the toppe of his collar; the Lord Holdernesse . . . smelling the businesse, your Highnesse is much polluted, sayes he; sure thou has stood on thy Head, Man, and shitt thy selfe, how comes it out at thy Cragge else? my Lerds, see our Salaman, is this the Salaman yea talke on?" ("*Merry Passages and Jeasts*": *A MS Jestbook of Sir Nicholas le Strange (1603–1655)*, ed. James Hogg [Salzburg: Institut für Englische Sprache und Literatur, 1974], 92–93). Whatever the story's truth, James was not squeamish.

86. Thomas Randolph, *Hey for Honesty*, in Randolph, *Works*, ed. W. C. Hazlitt (London, 1875), II, 380–81. Zeus made Oeacus (or Aeacus) judge of Europeans in Hades (see Plutarch, "Consolatio ad Apollonium," secs. 120–121, in *Moralia*), requiring him and the defendants to be nude. Plutarch does not say whether Zeus allowed boots.

Chapter 5: The Fantasies of "Mad Rablais"

1. Michael Drayton, *Nimphidia, The Court of Fayrie*, in Drayton, *Works*, ed. J. William Hebel, Kathleen Tillotson, and B. H. Newdigate (Oxford: Shakespeare Head

Press, 1961) III, 125; Drayton writes of "Dowsabell" in his fourth eclogue. On rhyparography, see Rosalie Colie, *Paradoxia Epidemica: The Renaissance Tradition of Paradox* (Princeton: Princeton University Press, 1966); her chapter on Rabelais quotes *CL* prol. on the author as a "petit riparographe."

2. Leah Marcus, *The Politics of Mirth: Jonson, Herrick, Milton, Marvell, and the Defense of Old Holiday Pastimes* (Chicago: University of Chicago Press, 1989), explores James's support of festivity under attack by strict-minded moralists. Jonson, she argues, had a mixed reaction to James's "delight in the carnival grotesquerie of traditional pastimes" (12). Peter Platt, *Reason Diminished: Shakespeare and the Marvelous* (Lincoln: University of Nebraska Press, 1997), likewise thinks that the Jonsonian masque shows ambivalence toward the wonderful. For a longer version of this section see my "The Stuart Masque and Pantagruel's Dreams," *ELH* 51 (1984), 407–30.

3. On sources, see Stephen Orgel and Roy Strong, *Inigo Jones: The Theatre of the Stuart Court* (Berkeley: University of California Press, 1973), I, 43–44.

4. On authorship and sources, see the edition by Jean Porcher of the *Songes drolatique* (Paris: E. Losfeld, 1959). *Songes* was imitated in a 1598 book published at Augsberg (Jurgis Baltrusaitis, *Réveils et prodigues: Le Gothique fantastique* [Paris: A. Colin, 1960], 304). I reprint here illustrations from the facsimile by Edwin Tross (Paris: 1870). Michel Jeanneret's facsimile edition of *Songes* (La Chaux-de-fonds: Editions [vwa], 1989) notes the images' ties to decoration and teratology.

5. "Tresexcellent, mirificque Pantagruel: homme jadis tres-renommé à cause de ses faicts heroiques, comme les histoires tresplusque veritables en font des discours admirables . . . et ne croy point que Panurge en ait jamais veu ne cogneu de plus admirables en pays où il a faict n'agueres ses dernieres navigations."

6. In his edition of *Divils Charter* (Louvain: A. Uystpruyst, 1904), R. B. McKerrow does not mention the *Songes*. I cannot identify Pantaconger or Mandragon.

7. In act III, scene ii, Frescobaldi boasts of his lineage, and Barnes's devil equivocates Jesuitically. Jaqueline E. M. Latham, "Machiavelli, Policy, and *The Devil's Charter*," *Medieval and Renaissance Drama in England* 1 (1984), 97–108, claims that Barnes lacks *Macbeth*'s sense of "metaphysical or spiritual reality"; yet he raises similar issues.

8. John Webster, *The White Devil*, ed. F. L. Lucas (New York: Macmillan, 1959), 196. See also *Songes* (*SD*) 99. A.-F. Bourgeois, "Rabelais en Angleterre," *RER* 3 (1905), 80–83 notes the connection.

9. Lucas takes "linguist" as "master of language," not "polyglot," for "the Tempter" has "a persuasive tongue." But Satan, running a multinational business, must be multilingual.

10. Orgel, in Ben Jonson, *The Complete Masques*, ed. Stephen Orgel (New Haven: Yale University Press, 1969), 486; see ll. 33–34, 39–40, 49–106.

11. *SD* 29 has wings; for more honey see *SD* 7 and 84. Bruegel's *Superbia* has a similar sting figure and a vaguely similar beehive; Desprez unites them in one figure, Jonson in one line. See Louis Lebeer, *Catalogue raisonné des estampes de Bruegel l'ancien* (Brussels: Bibliothèque Royale Albert Ier, 1969).

12. *SD* 44: a creature tasting the contents of his steaming body/pot; *SD* 42: a barrel-bodied funnel-headed creature with what looks like a kitchen knife; and *SD* 128: a barrel-creature with cup, pitcher, and flaccid breasts, surrounded by small, frogoid animals. *SD* 22 and 97 are likewise culinary.

13. Utopian is Pantagruel's tongue. I read *piece* as "artillery" (*Oxford English Dictionary*) and *conclusion* as punning on "tail." Cf. John Taylor's *To the Honour of O Toole* (1622): "And all men know that never such an od piece / Of fighting mettle, sprung from Mars his Codpiece" (1630; Taylor, *Works* [Spenser Society 1869; repr. New York: Burt Franklin, 1967], 177).

14. I read *pudding* as intestines and not, like Orgel, as the phallus.

15. Orgel links the windmill to gluttony's grinding of food, noting a windmill-head in Bruegel's *Gula*. *Windmill* also meant a pinwheel, sometimes indicating "a fanciful notion, a crochet" (*Oxford English Dictionary*). *SD* 95 wears one on his head.

16. Desprez's boot, but not the figure, is from Bruegel's *Invidia*.

17. *SD* 105 also has a bell. I include *SD* 96, although it is not clearly a barber or lawyer. In *P* 3 a woman has "visage de rebec," which Huntington Brown (*Rabelais in English Literature* [Cambridge: Harvard University Press, 1933; repr. New York: Octagon Books, 1967], 210) thinks is echoed by Shakespeare (*Love's Labor's Lost,* V.ii) when Boyet calls Holofernes "A cittern-head." True, the *Oxford English Dictionary* notes that citherns often had a grotesquely carved heads, citing several such comparisons.

18. *Songes* has no Kentishmen (long rumored, if only as a joke, to have tails), but *SD* 39 is a cheerful simian fisherman with an impressive tail.

19. Davenant and Jones, *Luminalia,* in Orgel and Strong, *Inigo Jones,* II, 706ff.

20. On such figures, see D. J. Gordon, *The Renaissance Imagination,* ed. Stephen Orgel (Berkeley: University of California Press, 1980), 179–84.

21. Orgel and Strong give the account by a Venetian diplomat (*Inigo Jones,* I, 279–84).

22. Ben Jonson, *For the Honor of Wales,* in *Complete Masques,* ed. Orgel, ll. 182–83, 295–98.

23. On *Neptune's* opening, see Stephen Orgel, *The Jonsonian Masque* (Cambridge: Harvard University Press, 1965), 91–97.

24. Orgel and Strong, *Inigo Jones,* II, 380–81.

25. *Faire Maide of the Inn,* in John Webster, *Complete Works,* ed. F. L. Lucas (London: Chatto & Windus, 1927), IV; see IV.ii.172–79 (*SD* 67 and 87 show grotesque frogs). Nor are Webster's and Jonson's olla podridas that year's only Spanish stews. William Crosse's *Belgiaes Troubles and Triumphs* (1625) claims that Spaniards are "Bigge lookers in their high Castillian ruffes, / But meere Quixotes, Rodomantading braves"; "full of emptinesse," they are a mere "Hotch-Potch" of Spanish, Portuguese, "salvage" and Moor (sig. I4).

26. James Shirley, *The Triumph of Peace,* ed. Clifford Leech, in *A Book of Masques* (Cambridge: Harvard University Press, 1967, repr. 1970), 275–313, ll. 188–89. A.-F. Bourgeois, *RER* 9 (1911), 171–72, first noted a connection with *SD*.

27. T. J. B. Spencer, introduction to William Davenant's *Salmacida Spolia,* in *A Book of Masques,* p. 339. I cite line numbers.

28. See Edgar Wind, *Giorgione's Tempestà* (Oxford: Clarendon, 1969), on tempests; for Davenant on his title, see *A Book of Masques,* 348–49.

29. Virginia Bush, *The Colossal Sculpture of the Cinquecento* (New York: Garland, 1976), p. 293 and fig. 321.

30. On this "herméneutique cannibale," see Frank Lestringant, "Catholiques et cannibales: Le Thème du cannibalisme dans le discours protestant au temps des guerres de religion," in J.-C. Margolin and Robert Sauzet, eds., *Pratiques et discours alimentaires à*

la Renaissance (Paris: Maisonneuve et Larose, 1982), 233–35. Although he ignores giants, Lestringant notes a fear of primitive rawness (a "retour au cru").

31. Such writers presuppose the old distinction between eikastic images that feed the active intelligence and phantastic images that delude it. Distrust of fantasy persists. In a provocative essay using Bakhtin on carnival and Tsetvan Todorov on fantasy, Deborah N. Losse calls the two modes incompatible, for fantasy assumes a supernatural and medieval "vertical and hierarchical . . . time-space." It "divert[s] our attention from the focus of Rabelais's fictional universe — man himself, the proper domain of the carnival" ("Rabelaisian Paradox: Where the Fantastic and the Carnivalesque Intersect," *Romanic Review* 77 [1986], 322–29). This seems Puritanical. In practice and in Rabelais, carnival and fantasy are less readily distinguishable.

32. Thomas Browne, *Religio medici,* in Browne, *Works,* ed. Geoffrey Keynes (London: Faber, 1928–31) I, 28–29, using the 1682 edition. Browne wrote in 1635; there was an unauthorized edition in 1642.

33. Thomas Browne, *Pseudoxia epidemica,* ed. Robin Robbins (Oxford: Clarendon, 1981), I, 601; cf. *G* 4–5, 38.

34. The people who dominated English court life would not have found Genevan culture likeable.

35. Gale H. Carrithers, Jr., "City-Comedy's Sardonic Hierarchy of Literacy," *SEL* 29 (1989), 337–55, shows how such plays drew class lines by dramatizing degrees of literacy; what "distinguishes the big winners from the big losers is superior facility with texts" (350). Plotwell, a good panurge, quotes a text that his apparently monolingual hearers cannot recognize.

36. See Fred J. Nichols's beguiling "Generating the Unwritten Text: The Case of Rabelais," *L'Esprit créateur* 28 (1988), 7–17.

37. François Moreau, "La Bibliothèque de l'Abbaye de Saint-Victor," *Littératures* 19 (1988), 37–42, notes the lack of Bibles in this list.

38. Barbara C. Bowen, "Rabelais and the Library of Saint-Victor," in *Lapidary Inscriptions: Renaissance Essays for Donald A. Stone, Jr.,* ed. Barbara C. Bowen and Jerry C. Nash (Lexington, Ky.: French Forum, 1991), 159–70, examines this title; she notes that Ortwin in fact had humanist credentials, angering von Hutten and his collaborators more by his bias against Jewish books than by his ignorance as such.

39. Lionel Casson, *Selected Satires of Lucian* (New York: Norton, 1968), 57.

40. John Taylor, *Jacke a Lent,* in Taylor, *Works,* fourth collection (Spenser Society 21, 1877), sig. A1. Nicholas Breton's *Strange Newes out of Divers Countries* (1622) reports titles (*Presidents of Imperfections, Newes of No Importance,* and *Labour in Vaine*) and gives précis. One concerns the city of Nullibi, where a student "labour[s] much to bring all to nothing"; cf *CL* 21.

41. A liminary poem in French by Lawrence Whitaker for Thomas Coryat's *Coryats Crudities* (1611) mentions the same volume in a kindlier spirit, saying *Crudities* might fit, retitled in new giant words, between the tripe commentary — here ascribed to "Tirepetanus" (Fart-Drawer) — and Marmoretus on monkeys.

42. Barbara C. Bowen notes that the title suggests both the tripe that people (especially peasants) eat and the tripe inside Béda; see "Les Géants et la nature des tripes," *ER* 31 (1996), 65–73.

43. *Letters of King James VI and I,* ed. G. P. V. Akrigg (Berkeley: University of Califor-

nia Press, 1984), 269–70 (a note cites Chamberlain); *The Letters of John Chamberlain,* ed. Norman E. McClure (Westport, Conn.: Greenwood, 1979), I, 213–15.

44. Quoted in *James I by His Contemporaries,* ed. Robert Ashton (London: Hutchinson, 1969), 14; Weldon died in 1648. James read jestbooks, alluding to Scoggin in a 1591 letter to James Maitland (*Letters of King James VI and I,* 113). He names a speaker in his *Daemonologie* (1597) Epistemon, perhaps thinking of Pantagruel's friend.

45. *Letters of King James VI and I,* 130 (April 13, 1594), 132–33 (June 5, 1594).

46. Joseph Hall, *Mundus alter et idem,* trans. John Healey as *Another World and Yet the Same (Mundus Alter et Idem),* ed. Huntington Brown (Cambridge: Harvard University Press, 1937), 91. Hall directs his satire more at phantasm-generating melancholy.

47. Hall, *Mundus alter et idem,* trans. Healey, 42, 41, 37.

48. On *chimera* and *vacuum* as "empty names" that are useful in logic, see Desmond Paul Henry, *That Most Subtle Question (Quaestio Subtilissima): The Metaphysical Bearing of Medieval and Contemporary Linguistic Disciplines* (Manchester: Manchester University Press, 1984), 1–3.

49. *De re coquinaria,* misattributed to the Augustan Apicius, contains recipes for dormice and other delicacies. Healey's note: "For some such bookes he wrote, witness Suidas."

50. Page 134 mentions a "*History of Mercury* (a booke unknowne to us)" that the locals consider "as holy as the Turkes do their Alcoran."

51. John Donne, *Catalogus librorum aulicorum incomparabilium et non vendibilium,* ed. Evelyn Simpson, trans. Percy Simpson (London: Nonesuch, 1930). I use Simpson's translation throughout. The books are not for sale for obvious reasons, but "non vendibilium" may also connect to Donne's ambivalence toward print. Annabel Patterson, *Reading Between the Lines* (Madison: University of Wisconsin Press, 1993), 185–86, 191–92, sees *Catalogus* as evidence that Donne still distrusted courts and power.

52. In the *Library of Madame de Montpensier;* on which book, see J. H. M. Salmon, "French Satire in the Late Sixteenth Century," *SCJ* 3 (1975), 57–88.

53. John Donne, "A Nocturnall" (recalling *CL's* Quintessence, whose servants manipulate nothing) and "A Valediction of Weeping."

54. Printed with other notes and letter in Evelyn M. Simpson, *A Study of the Prose Works of John Donne* (Oxford: Clarendon Press, 1948), 319–20.

55. A nice point that was once made to me by Annabel Patterson.

56. Bowen, "Library," 169, quoting Bacon's *Novum organum,* I, 95.

57. Francis Bacon, "Of Unity in Religion," in Bacon, *The Essayes or Counsels, Civill and Morall,* ed. Michael Kiernan (Cambridge: Harvard University Press, 1985), 12. Kenneth A. Hovey, "'*Mountaigny* Saith Prettily': Bacon's French and the Essay," *PMLA* 106 (1991), 71–82, shows the increased presence of France, and its supposed flaws, in the 1612 and 1625 editions. For Bacon, he says (80), "Rabelais is in the end only 'a Master of Scoffing.'" This is the *impression* Bacon gives when discussing high matters; his borrowings from *Gargantua* betray a deeper engagement.

58. "Master of Scoffing" has an academic flavor: Rabelais is a *magister*. The 1638 Latin translation misses this point, "Insignis quidam Jocandi Artifex" (sig. O8v) demotes him from magister to craftsman; the title is now *Saltationes florales, et gesticulationes haereticorum*.

59. Imaginary libraries stayed popular. Paul Lacroix, *Catalogue de la Bibliothèque de l'Abbaye de Saint-Victoir* (Paris: Techener, 1862), lists many French ones. See also *The Fanatick Library: Being a Catalogue of Such Books as Have Been Lately Made, and, by the Authors, Presented to the College of Bedlam* (1660), a sneer at the defunct Commonwealth. It includes: *The Rump's Seminary: or, The Way to Find out the Ablest Utopian Commonwealth's Men; Lucri bonus est odor ex re quâlibet*, "a Treatise written in defence of the seizing on the boy's Close-stool Pan, and reserving the contents for his own profit, because the lad was so profane as to carry it on a Sunday. By Alderman Atkins, Shit-breeches," and *The Defect of a Virtue Is Worse Than the Excess*, "a Treatise showing how much better it is to be hung like a stallion with Henry Martin, than with the lord Mounson to want a bauble" (*Harleian Miscellany* VIII, 71–73).

60. *Musaeum Clausum,* in Browne, *Works,* V, 131–42.

61. This section condenses my "Marginal Discourse: Drayton's Muse and Selden's 'Story,'" *SP* 88 (1991), 307–28.

62. Bernard Guenée, *Histoire et culture historique dans l'occident médiéval* (Paris: Aubier-Montaigne, 1980), objects to historians who populate the Middle Ages with naive storytellers (367). Lee Patterson, "On the Margin: Postmodernism, Ironic History, and Medieval Studies," *Speculum* 65 (1990), 87–108, thinks the history of historiography is too often the story the Renaissance told about itself. See also F. Smith Fussner, *The Historical Revolution: English Historical Writing and Thought, 1580–1640* (New York: Columbia University Press, 1962).

63. Quoted by Stan Mendyk, "Early British Chorography," *SCJ* 17 (1986), 459–81. See also Daniel R. Woolf, "John Selden, John Borough and Francis Bacon's *History of Henry VII, 1621*," *HLQ* 47 (1984), 47–53, and Woolf, *The Idea of History in Early Stuart England* (Toronto: University of Toronto Press, 1990). On Selden's evolving view of history, see Paul Christianson, "Young John Selden and the Ancient Constitution, c. 1610–18," *Proceedings of the American Philosophical Society* 128 (1984), 271–315. *Chorography* merges topography, fact, and local legend; see Stan Mendyk, *"Speculum Britanniae": Regional Study, Antiquarianism, and Science in Britain to 1700* (Toronto: University of Toronto Press, 1989), introduction. There is little on Selden's "illustrations," as he called them, in David S. Berkowitz, *John Selden's Formative Years: Politics and Society in Early Seventeenth-Century England* (Washington, D.C.: Folger Books, 1988). Joseph M. Levine, *Humanism and History: Origins of Modern English Historiography* (Ithaca: Cornell University Press, 1987), 52–53, says Brutus and Arthur "fell before [Selden's] critical pen"; but Selden also *adds* to what Drayton tells.

64. Drayton, *Poly-Olbion,* in *Works,* IV, xii. Many rivers have origins "remote from conceit of most piercing wits" (212); so do dynasties. Richard Helgerson, *Forms of Nationhood: The Elizabethan Writing of England* (Chicago: University of Chicago Press, 1992), 108–24, argues that the title page's Albion governs a cartographical scene that was once dominated by royal arms—a nice parallel with Selden's research.

65. Donald J. Wilcox, *The Measure of Times Past: Pre-Newtonian Chronologies and the Rhetoric of Relative Time* (Chicago: University of Chicago Press, 1987).

66. Cf. Boccaccio, *Genealogia,* VIII, 1, and pl. 25 of Erwin Panofsky's *Studies in Iconology* (New York: Harper, 1972). Selden shares the old uncertainty toward Saturn: devouring Time is also the golden patron of Saturnalia, now resting on his ocean isle. See

Samuel L. Macey, *Patriarchs of Time: Dualism in Saturn-Cronus, Father Time, the Watchmaker God, and Father Christmas* (Athens: University of Georgia Press, 1987).

67. Fussner, *Historical Revolution*, 293, quotes Selden's *Table Talk* on bad history as cuckoldry: "The Clergy would have us believe them [on tradition] against our own Reason, as the Woman would have had her Husband Against his own Eyes: What will you believe your own Eyes before your own sweet Wife?"

68. See *P* 11, where Baisecul uses *aguillanneuf* in his mishmash of an oration before Pantagruel.

69. Among the Creator's gifts to humanity, says the giant, is the power to gain earthly immortality by perpetuating name and seed through legitimate marriage: "Entre les dons, graces et prerogatives desquelles souverain plasmateur Dieu tout puissant a endouayré et acorné l'humaine nature à son commencement, celle me semble singuliere et excellente par laquelle elle peut, en estat moretel, acquerir une espece de immortalité, et, en decours de vie transitoire, perpetuer son nom et sa semence. Ce que est faict par lignée yssue de nous en mariage legitime." Rabelais himself fathered children, and although forbidden "mariage legitime" had them legitimized.

70. The sixteenth century was "distinguished by its sustained preoccupation with genealogies," writes Richard M. Berrong in "Genealogies and the Search for an Origin in the 'Oeuvres' of Rabelais," *South Atlantic Bulletin* 42.4 (1977), 75–83. So, in England, was the seventeenth century. Berrong links this obsession to issues of authority. On genealogy and fatherhood (although I distrust some of her arguments), see Carla Freccero, *Father Figures: Genealogy and Narrative Structure in Rabelais* (Ithaca: Cornell University Press, 1991), a study of how "the problematics of filiation haunt this text" (13).

71. Michael Seidel, *Satiric Inheritance: Rabelais to Sterne* (Princeton: Princeton University Press, 1979), 66. Seidel credits giants' link to genealogy in part to their earthy antiquity, seeing satire as rupturing continuity. Cf. Spenser's Geryoneo in *Faerie Queene* (V.x–xi), who feeds children to an idol shaped like his father.

72. Thomas Randolph, *The Jealous Lovers*, in Randolph, *Dramatic Works*, ed. W. C. Hazlitt, (London, 1875), I, 98.

73. On relating microcosm to macrocosm, see also Susan Stewart, *On Longing: Narratives of the Miniature, the Gigantic, the Souvenir, the Collection* (Baltimore: Johns Hopkins University Press, 1984), 37–44. Compare the anonymous *Lady Alimony* (printed 1659), also set in Spain, in which a "proud, peremptory, pragmatical" bully, once defied, melts into punctilious civility: "How this Gargantua's spirit begins to thaw! Sirrah, you punto of valour!" (I.ii–iii, in Dodsley's *Old English Plays*, ed. W. C. Hazlitt [repr. New York: Blom, 1964], XIV, 282–84).

74. John Ford, *The Ladies Trial*, in *John Ford's Dramatic Works*, ed. Henry de Vocht (Louvain: Librairie Universitaire, 1927), I.485–99. The land referred to is now North Beveland, a once much-flooded area between Zierikzee and Veere.

75. A marginal note adds: "A Jove tertius Ajax," quoting Ovid's *Metamorphoses*, XIII.28, in which Ajax boasts that he is the son of Telamon and thus grandson of Aeacus, son of Jupiter; I see no clear relevance to Pantagruel beyond a possible memory that some writers in the Renaissance (e.g., Jean Lemaire de Belges) imagined the gods as having originally been giant mortals.

76. I cannot tell what Ap-Robert remembers; *G* 7 says the baby giant has "almost eighteen chins."

77. Daniel Lord Smail, "Predestination and the Ethos of Disinheritance in Sixteenth-Century Calvinist Theater," *SCJ* 23 (1992), 303–23. Polemic invited genealogies. John Bale's *A Mysterye of Inyquyte Conteyned Within the Heretycall Genealogye of Ponce Pantolabus* (1545) traces heresy from Satan to his opponent's "stinkynge sodomitycall generation" (sig. B2v).

78. Sig. ¶4v notes the gossip about his wife. On Vaughan see Allan Pritchard, "From these Uncouth Shores: Seventeenth-Century Literature of Newfoundland," *Canadian Literature* 14 (1962), 68–78, and, on his role in settling Newfoundland (which he probably never saw), the introduction to *Newfoundland Discovered: English Attempts at Colonisation, 1610–1630*, ed. Gillian T. Cell (London: Hakluyt Society No. 160, 1982). A younger son, he says in his *Golden Grove* (1626) that Newfoundland offers space to those bent under primogeniture's Norman yoke (sig. Bbb3).

79. Vaughan's *Newlanders Cure* (1630) condemns maypoles, romances, Catholic legends, and the "upstart Dwarfe" who "Prates, how for Sires hee Giants had" (sig. H5v). Pantagruel's genealogy is one of those fancies that shift as times evolve: Franciscan humor in 1532 could later seem impiety. I agree with Edwin Duval, "Pantagruel's Genealogy and the Redemptive Design of Rabelais's *Pantagruel*," *PMLA* 99 (1984), 162–78; but by Vaughan's day such wit was risky.

80. Sig. T4v quotes *Utopia*'s less fantastic Book I with no added "faigned," whereas sig. Aa8 mentions "the (faigned) Syphograuntes." Vaughan considered it wise to keep reminding us that Utopians are unreal.

81. Aristarchus is the ancient critic; the censor Cato was a prig, perhaps, but not a Momus.

82. Archilochus's iambics supposedly drove victims to suicide.

Coda

1. P. 209, as repaginated in the Folger volume; editions after the first, which has "Panurge," add "et de son filz Pantagruel." Virginia Stern, *Gabriel Harvey: A Study of His Life, Marginalia, and Library* (Oxford: Clarendon Press, 1979), 232, thinks Harvey had a 1553 edition of the first four books or the Lyons 1588 edition.

2. On Harvey and Wolfe, see Clifford Chalmers Huffman's *Elizabethan Impressions: John Wolfe and His Press* (New York: AMS Press, 1988), chaps. 2 and 4. Huffman takes what Harvey says in print as opinion; I see stances inflected by context. F. P. Wilson, "Some English Mock-Prognostications," *Library* 19 (1938), 6–43, finds little of Rabelais in such texts; Huntington Brown, *Rabelais in English Literature* (Cambridge: Harvard University Press, 1933; repr. New York: Octagon Books, 1967), 37–41, thinks that "Adam Fouleweather, Student in Asse-tronomy" (Nashe?) read him for *A Wonderfull . . . Prognostication* (1592). In the late 1650s there was an anonymous royalist translation of *Pantagrueline* with prefatory verses jovially credited to Skelton (ed. F. P. Wilson [Oxford: Lutrell Reprints 3, 1947]). Bernard Capp, *English Almanacs, 1500–1800: Astrology and the Popular Press* (Ithaca: Cornell University Press, 1979), 233, reprints a page from a royalist mock almanac of 1665 assigning the date May 26 to "Garagantua."

3. Anthony Grafton and Lisa Jardine, " 'Studied for Action': How Gabriel Harvey Read his Livy," *Past and Present* 129 (1990), 30–78.

4. Because *eutrapelus* has an overtone of "tricky" as well as "urbanely jesting," Roger Kuin suggests to me that Nashe was a shady version of what Harvey wanted to be. For more personae, see Stern, *Gabriel Harvey,* and, on Harvey's private and public selves, James Nielson's elegant "Reading Between the Lines: Manuscript Personality and Gabriel Harvey's Drafts," *SEL* 33 (1993), 43–82.

5. Gabriel Harvey, *Foure Letters and Certeine Sonnets, Especially Touching Robert Greene and Other Parties by Him Abused,* ed. G. B. Harrison (London; repr. New York: Barnes and Noble, 1966).

6. *Pocky* recalls the readers in Rabelais's prologues. Giants made of buckram stretched over a frame are common in Harvey, symbolizing vanity and thirst for popularity: Nashe processes himself through the streets to the easy plaudits of the rough-palmed.

7. Harvey has earlier noted how a "printed diffamation" can fly on "wings of Mallice" (36). Living with the printer Danter, Nashe did haunt print shops; but Wolfe's friend Harvey was in no position to object. Again, Nashe is a frère enemie.

8. *CA* 25: "Ilz en eurent les passions plus de sept jours."

9. Among the poems concluding Nashe's *New Letter of Notable Contents* (1593) is a sonnet on the dead Marlowe as one of the "Magnifique Mindes, bred of Gargantuas race." "Jesu," Harvey asks, "Is that Gargantua minde / Conquerd, and left no Scanderbeg behinde?" (Scanderbeg led an Albanian anti-Turk resistance.)

10. This section is dated 1589; unless Harvey added touches before publication, his allusion is a fairly early sign of familiarity with Rabelais — or his title page.

11. Harvey can also make Rabelaisian lists; see above.

12. P. 394, as repaginated in the Folger volume, in a sentence saying that Harvey has his Rabelais, "meus Martialis," and "Domenicus meissimus" "ad unguem." The fullest study of Harvey's marginalia is Stern's *Harvey;* I thank her for alerting me to the second quotation, found on fol. 3v. Since I have not read all the marginalia I cannot say he never denigrates Rabelais. The fact remains that he praises him in his margins, not in print.

13. I thank Sarah Cusk and Heidi Brayman for helping me read the scrawl. J. E. G. Dixon, "The Treatment of *morbus Gallicus* in Rabelais," *ER* 25 (1991), 61–95, notes how little he medicalizes syphilis in his novels. Harvey's story makes a good addition to similar material in Winfried Schleiner, *Medical Ethics in the Renaissance* (Washington, D.C.: Georgetown University Press, 1995); chap. 6, "Renaissance Moralizing About Syphilis and Prevention," has several early modern references to the Charles VIII's syphilitic soldiers (164 also quotes the Dutch doctor Stephen Blankaart, 1650–1702, on how SPQR stands for "Spanische Pocken Quälen Rom": "Spanish Pocks Torture Rome").

14. In his Domenichi, Harvey lists such comic or satirical texts and writers as Martial, More, Boccaccio, Marguerite de Navarre's *Heptaméron,* Chaucer, and "Rabelaesii Heroica" (413). The next page adds Greene and Gascoigne.

15. True, "Panurgus" could be a generic trickster.

16. The volume is now at Harvard: "Placent etiam Comoediae, quae non sunt Comoediae; et Tragaediae, quae non sunt Tragaediae: ut utriusque generis multae egregiet apud Homerum, et Virgilium in Heroicis; Frontinum, et Polyaenum in Strategematis;

Stephanum in Apologia Herodoti: Rabelaesium in Heroicis Gargantuae: Sidneium in novissima Arcadia: Domenichum in Facetiis." Harvey cites the Greek who praised as great delicacies fish that are not fish and meat that is not meat. Give me, he adds, "Fabulas, non fabulas; Apologos non Apologos. Et sensi optima adagia, quae non adag."

17. Quoted by Eleanor Relle, "Some New Marginalia and Poems of Gabriel Harvey," *RES* 23 (1972), 401–16 (p. 412).

18. "Placent lepida; valent seria; florent animosa et magnifica ingenia," quoted in G. C. Moore Smith, *Gabriel Harvey's Marginalia* (Stratford-upon-Avon: Shakespeare Head Press, 1913). 119. Harvey signed this book in 1567 and again in 1579, although the note could be later.

19. "Malo Chaucerum quam Petrarcham; Boccacium, aut Ariostum Rabelaesium, quam Aretinum." I adopt Stern's translation in *Gabriel Harvey*, 175. As I hesitantly read the punctuation, though, while Harvey clearly prefers Rabelais to Aretino, the relation of Boccaccio and Ariosto to Chaucer, Rabelais, and each other is less certain. For the annotation to Guicciardini see p. 65: "Nihil Aretinus ad Rabelaesium."

20. P. 198: "Pedantius est, non philosophus, qui non est Aristippus, Rabelaesius, prius" (the last word is hard to read).

21. Quoted by Stern, *Gabriel Harvey*, 181: "Semper serius, et prorsus adamantinus in suis dignissimis studiis." Eutrapelus, reader of the classics and the Bible, also grasps chemistry, politics, polemics, stratagems, and nature's secrets. Stern thinks Harvey wrote many notes in his Domenichi while working for Leicester or hoping for a public career. He was still annotating the text in 1608.

22. Stern, *Gabriel Harvey*, 181: "sola decerpit suo scopo maxime conducentia." In his *Reading in Tudor England* (Pittsburgh: University of Pittsburgh Press, 1996), 58–76, Eugene R. Kintgen stresses the instrumental aims (and intertextual character) apparent in Harvey's marginalia, finding them typical of Tudor habits of reading; Kintgen also suggests that Harvey's selfconsciousness as a reader was encouraged by his awareness that those who borrowed books from his large library would see his notes.

Index